TOMMY GUN WINTER

Jewish Gangsters, a Preacher's Daughter, and the Trial That Shocked 1930s Boston

NATHAN GORENSTEIN

ForeEdge

ForeEdge
An imprint of
University Press of New England
www.upne.com
© 2015 Nathan Gorenstein
All rights reserved
Manufactured in the
United States of America
Designed by Mindy Basinger Hill
Typeset in Fanwood

For permission to reproduce any
of the material in this book, contact
Permissions, University Press
of New England, One Court Street,
Suite 250, Lebanon NH 03766;
or visit www.upne.com

Nothing in this book is invented.
All quotations are drawn from
trial transcripts, court documents,
contemporaneous newspaper
interviews, participants' written
accounts, and Massachusetts State
Police records. Where the author
speculates, it is so noted.

≡

≡

Library of Congress Cataloging-in-Publication Data
Gorenstein, Nathan.
Tommy gun winter : Jewish gangsters, a
preacher's daughter, and the trial that shocked
1930s Boston / Nathan Gorenstein.
    pages   cm
Includes bibliographical references and index.
ISBN 978-1-61168-426-1 (cloth : alk. paper) —
ISBN 978-1-61168-734-7 (ebook)
1. Organized crime — Massachusetts —
Boston — History — 20th century.
2. Gangsters — Massachusetts — Boston —
Case studies. 3. Jewish criminals —
Massachusetts — Boston — Case studies. I. Title.
HV6452.M4G67 2015
364.106'630974461 — dc23   2014045387

5   4   3   2   1

CONTENTS

PROLOGUE

≡

I Meet Murt

THE TRUTH ABOUT REPORTING is that nothing works like showing up. Climb into a car, spend an hour on the interstate or a day sprinting in and out of airports. Have a face-to-face conversation. Questions you never thought to ask will be answered.

When I began reporting this book, getting out of your chair was more a necessity than an option. Telephones were wired to a desk, documents were on paper, and paper was in a library or a government archive. Google was little more than a domain name. If I did my job well, I was out and about. It could be miserably inefficient. Add up the hours there and back, lunch and coffee, and you've blown the day.

A waste, except when it isn't.

I arrived in Needham, Massachusetts, in the last decade of the last century.

It was, and remains, an agreeable spot on the west side of I-95, nestled alongside tech companies and bifurcated by a commuter rail line to Boston. The combination has turned it into one of the richest Massachusetts towns no one has ever heard of.

Needham's history is notable for three events. The first was on April 19, 1775, when five local men died in the opening skirmishes of the Revolutionary War. The second took place in the 1880s, when broad stretches of the town were strip-mined for sand and gravel to fill in what is now Boston's Back Bay of townhouses and restaurants. The third occurred on a snowy February 2, 1934, when three young men arrived in a black Packard sedan. Two of them were brothers, Murton and Irving Millen, and the third was their friend, Abraham Faber. They were from the Boston neighborhoods of Roxbury and Dorchester. They remained in Needham for thirty minutes, and left behind two handfuls of empty submachine gun shells and a smattering of spent .22 caliber cartridges. Some were scattered inside the

Needham Trust Company; others were on an icy road. Also on the ground, and soon to die, were two town police officers, Forbes McLeod and Frank Haddock. Within a day the governor posted a reward of $20,000 — the equivalent today of $350,000 — for the capture of the three bandits. It was the largest reward in state history.

My day began at the town historical society. I was making my way through a stack of brittle newspaper clippings when a volunteer suggested I also speak with a police sergeant, Wayne Urquhart, known as *the* expert on the McLeod and Haddock murders, the subsequent investigation, and the record-breaking trial, famous for its length and a witness list of seventeen psychiatrists. So I drove across town to the police station, two stories of classic New England red brick, and asked for Urquhart at the front desk.

He appeared at the top of the stairs and bounced down into the lobby. A 101st Airborne pin was at the midpoint of his necktie, and he looked at me with unveiled annoyance.

On duty, Urquhart prosecuted local criminal cases in district court. Off duty, he played jazz drums and skippered a succession of sailboats. Urquhart was the department's unofficial historian, a job he was assigned by the chief but undertook with genuine curiosity and insight.

Usually that meant answering questions for high school students doing papers, but now and then a hopeful author appeared, believing there was a book to be written about the crime with its twists and turns and meanderings into psychiatry, sexual identity, interfaith marriage, dysfunctional families, disease, and mistaken identity. It was a tale of three young men who jettisoned their future. There was also a very beautiful girl, not much more than a child, who was a minister's daughter. Once, their story was the nation's gossip.

Now here I was, another hopeful writer, in midafternoon, yet with no appointment.

Then I told him my grandmother's maiden name. Urquhart motioned me upstairs, and we sat down opposite each other at a blond wood conference table.

The man who wielded the Thompson submachine gun in 1934 was Murton Millen. He stole the weapon from the state police. Had Murt lived, or at least stayed out of jail, we might have met. He grew up in a large two-story house near Blue Hill Avenue in what was then the Jewish neighborhood of Roxbury. His father, Joe Millen, was a Russian immigrant in business with a brother, William Millen, who was my great-grandfather. They started out as blacksmiths, banging together architectural metal from wrought iron, including the gates of the Norfolk County Courthouse in Dedham, where Sacco and Vanzetti were famously tried. William died young and afterward Joe stiffed his widow, Annie, out of her fair share of the business. That was her version, but it was likely true because a back hand to the family was very much in Joe's character. My mother grew up in Annie's household with her mother and three brothers following the death of their father.

I had heard stories of my mother's upbringing in the immigrant neighborhood, but never discussed, in my hearing, was the fantastical, disturbing tale of Murt and his brother Irv, which once dominated the lives of the extended Millen clan. Grand-uncles and -aunts who knew Murt and Irv as children were regular visitors when I grew up, but the brothers' names were never mentioned, nor was anything said about the tumultuous, desperate family that filled Joe's house. A whisper of the story first came from my sister. She shared a bedroom with Grandma, who one night revealed that there was a "bank robber" in the family. Some weeks later, when I was home on a college break, my sister pulled me aside to share the secret. Interesting, yes, but I gave it little thought, until one night three decades later when I saw my mother get angry.

It was at a party celebrating the career of a Millen cousin she had baby-sat as a teenager. My mother eschews conflict and values good humor and civility. But as my father and I stood holding drinks her face flushed with distress and disapproval. This was unusual. My mother walked over. A stranger had dared ask her about "the Millen brothers," she said. How tactless! It was simply impolite!

"Ah, don't worry," quipped my father, who was a bit of a tough guy. "I would have married you anyway."

Anyway?

That was interesting.

And there I was, a newspaper reporter.

My initial research, at the dawn of the Internet era, meant digging up bound volumes from a library shelf, scanning blurred microfilm, and flipping through pages of deed and mortgage records to trace unknown relatives.

It turned out there wasn't just a bank robbery. Murt and Irv were a veritable crime tsunami, knocking over what police speculated were dozens of movie theaters and shops. Sometimes they took hostages. As their ambitions grew their friend Abe became an accomplice. For more than eighteen months stories of their robberies and murders, the remarkable state police investigation, and finally their arrest and trial were blazoned across the front pages of Boston's newspapers. Murt led the gang and was faithfully followed by his younger brother, nicknamed "Brudgie" by family members and derided as "stupid" by his co-workers. Their partner in crime turned out to rank among the best-educated bank robbers in American history. Abe was a graduate of the Massachusetts Institute of Technology. He was an ROTC officer and an expert shot with a pistol, an aeronautical engineer who was part of the scientific elite. And at night he would climb onto the Millen porch roof and into Murt's bedroom window.

My time as a reporter taught me that the vast majority of stories fall into the category of commodity news, variations on the same set of facts, unique only in their ubiquity and predictability. Drug bust stories. White-collar fraud stories. Political scandals. Tales of philanthropic magnates, plucky children, and dread diseases. But on rare occasions a story materializes that is out of the ordinary. For a reporter it is a singular revelation. The best-known example must be Woodward and Bernstein and Watergate. Consider the moment they learned that a mere burglar's address book contained the initials "W.H." and a phone number for Nixon's White House.

Which is about how I was feeling even before I saw a photograph of Norma Brighton, Murt's brand-new wife. Or, rather, the hundreds of photos in dozens of newspapers. A glimpse of the minister's daughter explained why her image was splashed across the front pages of America.

And soon I realized it was only after Murt married Norma that the first person died.

So I told Urquhart that I, too, was planning a book.

His elbows rested on the table and his fingertips formed a steeple masking the lower half of his face. As I spoke he gave me a stolid, icy, police-interrogating-the-driver-on-the-side-of-the-road look. When I finished talking, his hands dropped and he smiled.

"You look like him," Urquhart said.

He meant Murt.

Then Urquhart walked out of the room. He returned with a thick, bound volume of documents. "Here," he said.

PART I

1

Murt Meets Norma

THE NEWS PHOTOGRAPHERS first spotted Norma Brighton Millen inside the NYPD headquarters in lower Manhattan, ten minutes by squad car from the midtown hotel where her husband had just tried to kill a cop.

She was sitting with her legs crossed, clasping her purse and wrapped in a Persian lamb coat with a thick fur collar. Her eyebrows were plucked into thin, curved lines that magnified the blue eyes gazing back at the crowd of reporters. Her lips were painted a rich, dark red, and she had brushed the hair back from her face in the latest style. She sat erect, her chin up, and a faint smile flickered across her face despite the collapse of her life a few hours earlier. It was a fact she had not yet grasped.

The photographers slid slim, square film negatives in and out of their boxy Speed Graphic cameras and juggled hot flashbulbs. They knew this photo was going out front. On page 1. Above the fold. But the rewrite men on the city desk needed details the black-and-white photos could not provide. What shade of blue were her eyes? Exactly how crimson were those lips? For that the desk relied on the beat reporters, and on this Sunday afternoon in February 1934, the reporters could not agree on the color of Norma's hair.

Later, some newspapers said it was blond, which was flat wrong. "Brown" was too bland for the striking young woman who nonchalantly nibbled on a chocolate bar as detectives grilled her husband, still bleeding from the truncheon that beat him to the hotel lobby floor. "Brunette" did not do justice to the luminescence that shimmered in the cigarette-fouled air. There was a tint of sunset in her hair. The tabloids could work with that. So the reporters decided they had themselves a redhead. A redheaded gun moll. Even better, she was a minister's daughter. They had hit the trifecta.[1]

When her father in Boston first tried to explain how his eighteen-year-old child had ended up with a hangdog-looking fellow wanted for murder—

actually, the murders of two Massachusetts police officers—the hair color question was already outstanding. "She is not red-haired as reports have announced," said Norman Brighton—the similarity of his first name to his daughter's always confused reporters new to the story—"but has brunette hair, which has a copper glint when the light strikes it."[2] The front-page account, one of a thousand newspaper stories soon to thud into Norma's life, did not say if the turn of phrase was the reporter's or the father's. But "brunette" was simply too ordinary and remained largely banished from the news pages. One reporter took to describing Norma as "titian-haired," which was far more romantic, even if it sent readers to the dictionary.

MURTON MILLEN NEVER SPECIFIED whether it was her hair or her cheekbones or maybe Norma's walk that caught his eye (an ordinary shade of brown) on the evening in 1933 when she whisked herself off the Palm Garden dance floor in Nantasket Beach to powder her nose and comb her hair and then return to sit by herself. It was the Saturday night of Labor Day weekend, the last holiday night of the summer, and both were alone.

They were among tens of thousands who filled the narrow, sandy peninsula, all eager to walk the broad beach along the Atlantic. The resort's first hotels were built in the nineteenth century and catered to America's burgeoning class of professionals, but Nantasket's short distance from Boston, just ten miles by water, soon turned it more egalitarian. In 1905 Boston investors opened Paragon Park, an ornate, idiosyncratic amusement park that later became famous for its 4,000-foot-long wooden roller coaster. It had an 88-foot drop that sent riders plummeting toward the ground at 53 mph. When the coaster opened in 1917, a Model T Ford topped out at a bracing 45 mph.

By the summer of 1933 Nantasket had dodged the worst effects of the Great Depression. Nearly one-quarter of the nation was unemployed, but on weekends tens of thousands still filled the seven-mile-long beach. At the end of July, when temperatures reached 98 degrees, authorities said that 300,000 people crammed onto the peninsula, and more than 50,000 automobiles, trucks, and busses created an impenetrable traffic jam.[3] Even an edict by Metropolitan District Police banning "brassiere bathing suits" did not dampen enthusiasm for beachgoing, though it prompted a run on swimsuits that covered a girl's midsection but exposed her back from shoulder to tailbone.[4]

Saturday was sunny and hot. It was Norma's second trip to the shore that season. The first had been in the spring, when she spent a week with her mother, Margaret, in Hampton Beach, New Hampshire. At the end of their stay Norma was offered a waitress job for $7 a week, plus tips, and a room above the restaurant. Her mother approved, and Norma, unexpectedly, had her first taste of independence. It did not last long. One explanation was that Norma proved incapable of calculating the nickels, dimes, and quarters of the customers' bills and was let go after one too many mistakes. Another was that Margaret had failed to consult with her ex-husband, the minister. That was the version Norma preferred. In her telling the job was "swell . . . until one day Dad sent a man from his office up to take me home."[5]

Nevertheless, Norman allowed Norma to accompany his ex-wife on the Nantasket excursion. Had he watched Norma enter the dance hall, however, the reverend would have ordered her back out the door. In the popular press, public dance halls were fonts of crime and debauchery, tenanted by "taxi dancers," women who made themselves available for hire, song by song. They spun fellows around the floor for 10 cents a dance, an enterprise some considered a close relative to prostitution.

Even Norma's mother objected, and she was no wallflower. Admission to the Palm Garden was 55 cents, more than the steamer fare. More important, her daughter had been voted the most beautiful girl in her high school class and Margaret saw that Norma's allure was no longer quite so unconscious. But her daughter insisted. Norma wanted to go dancing, and she had chosen the blue dress that showed off her eyes and the highlights in her hair. Now, in the second-floor dance hall, the reality of sitting alone, without a guy or a girlfriend, made her embarrassed and sad. The orchestra played a popular waltz, "Reflections on the Water," and couples whirled past.

"It was crowded and I was feeling more scared than ever, and I had just about decided to go back to the Boulevard Hotel when a boy came up," Norma wrote. He was tall, with long arms and legs and a narrow face and dark hair. He wore brown shoes, a brown suit, and a brown necktie. It was sometime after eight o'clock when he asked her to dance. He was Murt.

"He was nice looking, tall, with wavy black hair. I was excited, and just nodded, and stood up." They moved onto the dance floor as the band launched into "Learn to Croon," the Bing Crosby hit of the summer.

Murt admired her dress and the way she wore her hair. Norma saw that he was older than the boys back home, and when he asked for the next dance, she said no. Another man approached, and Norma rose to dance with him. Murt watched from the sidelines and returned to her side when the music stopped. They swept back onto the floor. During their first awkward dance they had exchanged little conversation, but now Murt introduced himself.

"My name is Murton Millen. What's yours?"

"Norma Brighton."

"That's a nice name."

"I like Murton Millen for a name, too."

"You can call me Murton."

It was a banal exchange, but he must have spoken with a charming grin acknowledging the awkwardness of their meeting, and Norma laughed. They danced and then bought orangeade and sipped it on the balcony that encircled the dance floor and overlooked the sea. Above them was a nearly full moon. Norma said that she and her mother faced a tiring return trip the next day, by boat to Boston and then an endless, noisy trolley ride to their separate homes. Murt listened closely. This was an opportunity. He had a car and was driving to Roxbury the next day. Why didn't he give Norma and her mother a lift? It was really no bother.

Murt also made a second offer—a nighttime drive along the beach. To that Norma said no. But she would like a ride home, if her mother agreed.

Mother and daughter were spending that summer getting to know one another after a five-year separation. Norma's parents had divorced in 1922, and while Margaret initially had custody of all three children, Thelma, Norma, and Clarence, when she remarried in 1927, Norma, twelve, went to live with her father. She did not see her mother again until 1932 but quickly understood that Margaret, an attention-demanding extrovert, was far more sympathetic to a girl's needs than the strict Norman Brighton, whose rules discouraged boys, dancing, and dates.

AS PROMISED, MURT SHOWED UP the next morning with his car. With him was his brother Irv. Margaret decided that Murt, twenty-four, was a well-bred, respectable young man. She was pleased when he said that a relative owned a local hotel, though it was more of a summertime boarding-house, and accepted his offer of transportation even after Murt explained she'd have to share the tight confines of the rumble seat with Irv. That young man seemed extraordinarily shy until Margaret realized, with a burst of sympathy, that he suffered from a seemingly intractable stutter. Irv tried to manage his speech by tapping his knee as he pronounced each word. That trick met with limited success. The impact of his impediment was compounded by a twitch. His head jerked to the side when he tried to utter a complete, unbroken sentence. He compensated with a nearly automatic smile, bright and dim all at once.

They settled in for the ride home. Murt turned to ask Margaret if she was comfortable. The Ford Roadster had two seats up front, where he and Norma sat, shielded by a fabric top. The rumble seat, stored beneath a flip-up metal lid where the trunk would ordinarily be located, exposed passengers to the wind and dust, and left them hoping it wouldn't rain. The Ford was a popular car, and Norma was impressed. A new model cost $495 at a time when the average family income was about $1,500.

It was a long drive north. The roads out of Nantasket were one lane in each direction. The travelers had to cover the twenty miles to Boston and then another twenty miles or so north to Margaret's apartment in Tewksbury, where she worked as a nursing assistant at a state hospital for the insane. Once there, Murt turned around and drove back to drop Irv at the family home in Roxbury and then finally headed west to Natick, another twenty-mile trek. "He talked all the way home," Norma said. "He told me he was an automobile mechanic now, but his brother and a couple of friends were going to open a radio store in Boston pretty soon."

It was a remarkable day. She had spent hours in a car with a virtual stranger, yet was comfortable chatting all the way to her father's house near Natick's Nonesuch Pond. They made another date, and another after that, and then Murt showed up in a different car, a Chevy. She wondered how he paid for it.

Oil stocks, Murt explained. He had made money in oil stocks.

2

The Box
Office Boys

THE HOLLYWOOD FILM rolling off the reel at the Oriental Theater in
Mattapan on March 10, 1933, was *Hot Pepper*. It would have been forget-
table except for its costar, Lupe Velez, who was sufficiently famous for her
nickname to have been used for the film's title. Sensuous and uninhibited,
a singer and a dancer, Velez was a favorite of the Hollywood scandal sheets,
given affairs with movie stars Gary Cooper and Charlie Chaplin and her
upcoming marriage to Tarzan himself, former Olympic-medalist-turned-ac-
tor Johnny Weissmuller.

Hot Pepper was about two buddies, former Marines, who were bootleggers and rum runners. Velez played a nightclub performer. The *New York
Times* described the movie as a "reprehensible comedy" but conceded
that audiences relished the wisecracks, Velez's screen charisma, and dance
numbers that showed her long legs to best advantage.

As the men in the Oriental's audience ogled, two figures approached the
ticket window that opened onto 1601 Blue Hill Avenue. A bored twenty-
two-year-old, Winifred Bailey, was sitting behind the cash drawer when
she looked up to see a gun pointing at her. "Turn over the dough!" barked
the robber, who was Murt, holding the weapon while his partner, Irv, stood
lookout on the sidewalk. Witnesses said he had attempted to disguise himself
as a blind man.[1] Despite the handgun aimed at her midsection, the doughty
Bailey wasn't buffaloed. "You'll get no dough here!" she barked back.[2]

It was a brave if not necessarily wise response, and it worked. Flummoxed
by the fearless cashier, the armed man stuck a "long barreled gun" through
the ticket window and fired twice, sending two .32 caliber bullets spinning
harmlessly past her. Bailey noted that the weapon's discharge was less a
"bang" than a "pfft." The two would-be robbers turned and fled.[3]

Bailey was rewarded with a burst of attention in the next day's papers.

Police had discerned a pattern of movie theater holdups. Robbing a cashier or sticking up a movie theater manager offered the chance of a decent score with little risk of bumping into an eager guard with a gun. As the robberies multiplied, police gave the gunmen a nickname, the "box office boys."[4] The oddly muffled shots Bailey heard, police later discovered, were deadened by Murt's homemade silencer, constructed with metal washers and compacted leather ovals to slow and quiet the expanding gases.

The siblings were not discouraged by their failure at the Oriental. Two weeks later the Shawmut Theatre on Blue Hill Avenue in Roxbury was hit by a single man who stuck up the box office, made off with $600, and escaped in a car driven by an accomplice. Buoyed by that success, Murt and Irv set out to revisit the Oriental Theater, this time with a far more daring plan. They would pillage the office safe, not merely the cashier's drawer. On the night of April 2, as the Oriental's manager pulled into his garage in suburban Newton, Murt and Irv emerged out of the darkness with guns in hand. They pushed the manager into a car, drove ten miles back to the Oriental, and forced him to open the office safe. The take was a disappointment, variously described as $150, $89, or less than $100.

The next box office robbery, on April 23, produced a better return. According to the papers, two men "dropped into the second floor office" of the Franklin Park Theater on Blue Hill Avenue in Dorchester and walked out with $700. Police believed the crimes were linked. Murt and Irv would continue to pull theater jobs. But in the meantime, they had scored enough money for a Ford Roadster or a Chevy.

Murt already had a brutal, self-interested worldview. It was the nearly inevitable result of his upbringing, combined with what that era called his "blood inheritance." When psychiatrists eventually tried to reconstruct his psychological history, one nationally known practitioner theorized that Murt lived his adolescence as a "solitary boy" often lost in books, before metamorphosing into an "egotistical, antisocial, defiant, even fearless" young man, governed by a "wild emotional expression, constantly devising easy means to do some act of violence irrespective of the consequences."

In part Murt was a familiar type, the young man as sullen teenager who believed that the life chosen for him by his parents and teachers was a scam for their own benefit. "That honesty stuff," Murt said, was "a bunch of baloney." It was just slick self-interest. "Everyone is trying to get it by hook or crook. They are all hypocrites," he said later. "I am not doing anything different from the big Wall Street crooks."[5]

Murt's height and physique, and his increasingly frequent sneer, were useful when he turned intimidating. His braggadocio, however, only masked a powerful streak of paranoia, combined with bouts of deep depression and mania. Nevertheless, Murt possessed a perverse charm, almost charisma, which worked best on personalities weaker than his own.

All in all, one psychiatrist said, he was the product of an "entirely criminal atmosphere" at home.

The psychiatrist was wrong. It wasn't the entire home. Just one man, Murt's father, "the old coot."[6]

JOE MILLEN WAS BORN IN 1877 into a family of blacksmiths, originally named Mordecai, near the village of Horodysche, a hundred miles south of Kiev in what was then Czarist Russia. The region had been racked by a series of pogroms, which by the 1880s had propelled the Jewish population into a mass migration. Two million, most peasants or little better, eventually fled Czar Alexander and his son, Nicholas II, and settled in America. The Mordecai family left in the 1890s, arrived in Boston, and Americanized their name to Millen.

Joe and two older brothers, Israel and William, put their skills to work making wrought iron fences, gates, and architectural ornaments. With three bosses, conflict was inevitable, and it erupted over how the brothers should take their wages. Israel and Joe wanted to pay themselves as profits came in, which meant their income could be high, low, or nonexistent. William argued for a steady weekly wage. The dispute became moot in 1904 when William died, apparently of a brain aneurism. His death further divided the family, what with his wife, Annie, complaining for decades that Joe had cheated her out of her widow's share of the business. That was just like Joe, at work and at home: rough, gruff, and oblivious to everyone but himself.

Even Joe's eldest brother, Israel, conceded that Joe was "a little cranky." Had Israel been blunter, or perhaps had a better command of the English language, he might have described Joe as narcissistic, self-absorbed, and fast to use his fists. Although he was settled in the New World, Joe embodied the worst of Russian nineteenth-century peasant culture. He wanted to be czar of his household and commander of his business empire, but neither fully cooperated.

For a time he was a successful entrepreneur. Helped by a booming economy in the 1920s, the wrought iron company flourished, and Joe purchased a sign company and then moved into contracting. He learned to play the angles in a Boston controlled by competing ethnic and political fiefdoms. Joe's style of doing business, however, left him short of goodwill. He became notorious for retaining a platoon of lawyers to sue clients and partners. By one estimate, he filed more than two hundred civil actions in Suffolk County Court in endless disputes with suppliers and subcontractors.[7]

His marriage to Carolyn Joseph in 1898 was difficult from the outset. They met when Joe hired her as the company bookkeeper, which set the tone for a relationship that fit Joe's view of himself as supreme leader of his household. But his vision of a domestic autocracy clashed with Carolyn's American upbringing in Cambridge. The strife worsened during fifteen years of childbearing marked by tragedy. Carolyn gave birth to eleven children, but only six lived to adulthood. Her firstborn died after eight days. Her second child, Frances, survived and as the years passed became leader of the household. Her first son to live to adulthood, Harry, was born in 1903. Then came six years of misfortune.

In 1904 twin girls arrived, Dorothy and Edith, but the first died at ten months, and Edith, who never learned to walk, died at six years. One day as Edith neared death, Joe brought home a bag of fresh cranberries, an inedible fruit until sweetened and cooked. That task was unimportant to the women busily tending the sick child. But Joe wanted dessert after his meal. "He started fighting with my mother because she hadn't cooked the cranberries," recalled Frances. An aunt eventually stepped in. "We'll cook them and keep him quiet," the older woman said in disgust.

The fifth child, Louis, succumbed at six months. The night he died Carolyn asked her husband to warm a bottle of milk for the baby while she sat by the bedside. "He said no, and started to swear and curse me." Carolyn rose to heat the milk on the coal-fired stove, fed the child, and fell asleep, exhausted. "When I woke up my baby was dead."

Childhood deaths were not uncommon in that era, nor were large families, and at the turn of the century immigrant Jews had a higher birthrate than the Boston Irish.[8] In 1909 Murt was born, followed in rapid intervals by Mary, Irving, and the youngest child, Idalyn, who arrived in 1920, but not before another newborn died. It was a stiff dose of trauma and, combined with the behavior of her husband, drove Carolyn to the city's mental hospital in 1922 for two days of observation.[9]

Carolyn was not a careful housekeeper, which added to Joe's increasing litany of complaints. Other Millen women who visited the home recalled stepping into the kitchen to see Carolyn—or Kitty, as they called her—sitting in a chair reading, dirty dishes strewn about and children racing underfoot.[10] At times Joe hired nurses and servants to handle the children, and as soon as they were able, Frances and Harry, the oldest, took charge of the household. Joe turned on them and their siblings, too. They ate too much, turned the gas heat up too high, and never cared to earn a week's pay, though by that he meant they refused to work in his businesses.

By the 1920s the family was living in an eleven-room house at 39 Lawrence Avenue. The neighborhood was already worn, though the house featured a broad, front porch with clusters of ornate Corinthian columns at each corner. Similar homes lined the street, many occupied by proprietors of shops and small businesses. Some years the family had a cook and a servant, and spent summers in a rented beachfront cottage. The luxuries did nothing to improve home life, and the family became a source of neighborhood amusement and dismay.

There were many stories. Once, Carolyn flung open a window and with a scream screeched for help. A neighbor raced over to find Joe in the kitchen with two of his daughters, Frances and Mary. "They were throwing things at each other," he saw in astonishment. And Joe, amid the cabinets and countertops, was running around "raving and swinging his hands.

"He was doing a lot of swearing . . . he kept saying he wanted poison and called them a bunch of lunatics."[11]

Joe believed his world was populated by reprobates scheming to cheat him and discerned similar threats at home. His treatment of Carolyn horrified his children, and as they grew older all rallied to her side. Joe became convinced his offspring were deliberately disloyal. "I ain't got no home," he told neighbors, and complained that behind his back, and sometimes to his face, his children ridiculed him as an "immigrant greenhorn." He returned the derision.

"They are not too bright, any of them. They are a lot of dumbbells, as I called them."

Shouts and blows erupted even over how Carolyn cooked the evening stew. The old coot increasingly became an outsider in his own house.

But none of the children punched Joe's ignition switch like Murt. As the years passed, Joe's blows made no dent in Murt's obstinance. He was growing into what a later era called a "problem child." The more uncontrollable and uncooperative Murt was, the more Joe disciplined with his hands. And the less it worked. "He had a grudge against Murt, always had a grudge. He seemed to hate him," said Carolyn. Once he concluded that Murt was eating too much and interrupted dinner to send his plate back to the pantry. Rarely did Murt react. "He would look at him kind of, his eyes would get mad and he would tighten his lips, that is all. Once in a while he would talk back to him. Once in a while, but usually never a word." Inside was fury. "His eyes would get terribly angry, and he would have that bitter look in his face," said his sister Frances.

In school he displayed bursts of temper, and at home he would lash out at a sibling and moments later lapse into sullenness.

"He felt that everyone was against him," said Frances, "especially so our family. I don't know why . . ." Frances tried to compensate for Joe's behavior, but her brother remained emotionally isolated. "I don't think I'd ever gotten into conversation with Murt all my life," she said.

Murt was close to Irv—they had a genuine loyalty to each other—and Irv idolized his older brother. Murt must have protected him from neighborhood ribbing. More often than not the two were inseparable. In time Irv became his "henchman."

"I used to have to force Irving to do what I wanted by beating him on the side of the head. Now I talk to him and he does it," Murt said. It was an exaggeration, but only in part.

By high school Murt understood that neither his home nor his own mind functioned like those of his neighbors and schoolmates. He began scouring the psychiatric section at the Boston Public Library, borrowing books by Freud, Jung, a popular Tufts University professor named Abraham Myerson, and a well-known New York psychiatrist, Smith Ely Jelliffe.

Much of what he compulsively read he did not comprehend. But he understood the symptoms, compared them with his own, and decided he was manic-depressive. In 1929 he sought out a psychiatrist.

At first he said he was seeking help for Irv, who had just turned seventeen. Despite his stutter, Irv refused to attend speech classes, as acknowledging his impediment was a greater blow to his self-esteem than his daily struggles. Irv papered over his unwieldy social interactions with his goofy smile. Joe leaned on business associates to give Irv a job, but nothing lasted for long. He pressured the new owner of the sign shop, which Joe had sold, into hiring Irv, who was soon nicknamed "stupid." He'd smile and shuffle and brush off the insults. It was just friendly kidding, Irv said.

The psychiatrist had little useful advice for Irv, though Murt had found one of the best—Myerson was a prolific author and nationally known psychiatrist and neurologist. His best-known book was *The Nervous Housewife*, in which he addressed what he saw as the central problem of modern marriages, "the change of the gay, laughing young girl, radiant with love and all aglow at the thought of union with her man, into the housewife of a decade [later]—complaining, fatigued, and disillusioned." Myerson also published the *Foundations of Personality*, an academic treatise that remained in print for decades, and the *Inheritance of Mental Diseases*. That may have prompted Murt to schedule sessions of his own.

Murt met with Myerson five times between January 2 and December 23, 1931. Oddly for an author and psychiatrist, Myerson advised Murt to throw away his diary and stop analyzing his own mind. Give up your "obsessive" reading of books on "neurosis, psychoses, manias and phobias," Myerson said. He diagnosed Murt as a "psychopathic personality." Whether Myerson ever told his patient that is unknown. He may not have, because what was to be done? If that was Murt's personality, then that was Murt's personality. The boy was not someone who would subject himself to years on the couch. Between sessions Myerson stayed in touch with Murt by letter.

Murt's visits with Myerson coincided with a major bout of depression sparked by the most ordinary source of trauma—his love life. A girl he was courting had refused to stop seeing other boys. So Murt fled. The act of travel, he discovered, drew his internal eye outward.

But the failed romance wasn't the sole reason for his departure. His sister Frances blamed their father, too. "Murton was sitting down to supper one night, and my father was cursing and swearing at him, and he got up from the table, and he didn't say anything, and the next morning I looked in his room and saw the bed was still made." Murt had disappeared.

They heard from him some days later when a letter arrived for their mother. "Dear Ma, I am desperate, and I think this is the last letter you will receive from me," according to Frances's recollection. "I hope the old coot lands in hell for all the tortures he has inflicted upon me. Don't worry, but this could be the last letter." In his pocket were two grains of morphine, four times what was needed to get high, and eight grains of the muscle relaxant atropine, about ten times the fatal dose.

After posting the letter in Philadelphia, he traveled to Virginia, where a high school friend, Saul Messinger, was attending William and Mary College. Alarmed, Messinger contacted Joe Millen. The threatened suicide of his son cut through Joe's obsessive self-pity, and he wrote, or rather dictated to his secretary, a lengthy apologetic letter that he asked Messinger to deliver. Joe even paid Myerson when the psychiatrist's bills arrived at Lawrence Avenue.

Murt also exchanged letters with the professor, who pleaded with him not to kill himself. "Nothing is so final as death. Don't do it."

Murt was not persuaded. On a cold February night he made his way to a deserted stretch of beach outside Norfolk, Virginia. There he intended to die. Or so Murt said later. In the dark he walked across the damp sand, toward the sea, as pain pressed in on his mind. He cried, stumbled, and wept again. He was about to capitulate to the black roar when "an emotional storm" swept in. His head quieted. He became alert and aroused, acutely aware of the waves, the dim starlight, the magnificence of the sea. Suddenly he felt plugged into the power socket at the center of universe and basked in the wonderful electric charge of mania.

Murt had read that "when you are very depressed . . . you substitute for that depression of inferiority one of superiority." So there on the beach he decided to transcend himself. He would command himself to not only survive, but succeed. Exactly how he did not yet know, but Murt was thinking big. "I must be a financier. I must be a master of industry. I must be on par with Columbus or Einstein."

Or as Murt later said more succinctly, "A change came over me. I decided not to croak myself."[12]

3

≡≡≡

The Tailor's Son

TOM LARBEY WAS JEALOUS. It did not make him proud, but there it was, and there was Abe Faber, the thin, curly haired, perpetually silent and solitary landlord's son, scooting about on a motorcycle. It was a gift from the boy's parents, and Larbey, a motorman on the Boston Elevated who earned $30 a week, knew he would never give such a present to his young child.

Larbey worked the night shift, piloting electric trolley cars along the steel rails that pressed outward from central Boston. The Elevated was at the heart of the city's transportation system, which seemed to grow as quickly as the number of Irish, Italian, and Jewish immigrants who filled its cars. It was steady work, but a home was unaffordable with a wife and four children. So in 1925 he rented the second floor of a triple-decker from Philip and Rose Faber.

A motorman's salary did allow for one of the new, inexpensive radios being manufactured especially for the home, so on dry, clear evenings he carried his vacuum tube set onto the back porch and hooked up the 80-foot antenna wire that looped back and forth beneath the wooden ceiling. On the porch above, Abe Faber was doing the same. Halting conversations ensued, and soon Larbey realized the boy, though only fifteen, could explain how the radio waves were bent in the atmosphere, and how to best align the antenna and tune the receiver. He knew how to maintain the lead-acid batteries and could even calculate which of the glowing tubes were most likely to burn out. Larbey learned all that bit by bit, whenever the unpredictable boy saw fit to speak. Abe refused to look the older man in the eye and mumbled when Larbey asked a question.

And he had this twitch. Some neighbors said it affected the right side of Abe's face, others said his shoulder. It came and went.

In the mornings Abe's father, Philip, rode the trolley into the financial district, where he worked in a tailor shop sewing jackets and trousers. He was a quiet, reticent man who labored with a speech impediment. His wife, Rose, was a nervous, fretful woman, perpetually worried about her son. Each day, up until the day of his arrest it was later claimed, Abe carried his mother's homemade lunch to work or school. Despite Philip's modest job, and perhaps with the help of more affluent relatives, the couple owned two adjacent triple-deckers on the north end of Blue Hill Avenue in Dorchester. The three-story wooden buildings, a family, or sometimes two, to each floor, were a hallmark of greater Boston. Philip and Rose lived with their son in the rear half of the top floor at 148 Blue Hill Avenue and rented out the other units.[1]

NO ONE EVER CALLED ABE by his first name, which was Morris, given to him on October 14, 1909. Abraham was his middle name. Later he acquired a second nickname "Abel." By contemporary standards his parents were old when he was born. Both were immigrants from Lithuania, a small nation on the Baltic Sea then part of the Russian Empire. Philip arrived in 1893, when he was eighteen. He and a brother, Hyman, opened a tailor shop. Rose Selzer immigrated in 1891 at age eleven. When Abe was born, she was thirty years old, four years younger than her husband.

It was not an easy pregnancy, and Rose was told either she or the baby might not survive. When Abe arrived, he was "black at birth," she said. The attending doctor dipped the newborn into two pails of water, the first one hot, the second one cold. "Then they wrapped him up in a sheet and put him in a drawer until he came to life again," she said. The dunkings were likely intended to stimulate the infant's circulation, and the drawer substituted for a cradle.[2] Rose never had another child.

In 1910 the family settled into an apartment on Wayland Street in Dorchester, on the edge of Boston's Ward 14. Political geography made that the city's Jewish ward. Rectangular, it ran along the eastern side of Blue Hill Avenue from South Boston all the way to Mattapan.[3]

In the 1920s three-quarters of Boston's residents were either born overseas or the children of immigrants. The Irish, Italians, and Jews occupied distinct ethnic neighborhoods and competed, with varying degrees of success, for the political and economic power held by Boston's Brahmin elite and the Yankee business class. Wayland Street was near the heart of the

Jewish section of Blue Hill Avenue, or "Jew Hill Avenue" to less proper Bostonians. A half dozen Orthodox synagogues were within walking distance, and Yiddish was the native tongue of most every adult. Faber neighbor Ida Goldberg was one of the few immigrant women living nearby who could read and write.[4] Neighborhood men worked as bricklayers, delivery boys, an "innersole maker" in a shoe factory, a tailor, a bookkeeper, and a grocery store clerk. The wives kept house—a full-time job when stoves were coal-fired and refrigeration was a block of ice. Shopping was a trip down Blue Hill Avenue with stops at the baker and the dry goods merchant and haggling with vegetable and fruit peddlers selling from horse-drawn wagons. Peanut butter was sold in scoops laid down on waxed paper, and pickles were ladled out of wood barrels. The kosher butchers did their work in full view of customers. The Jewish immigrants embraced America, but there were limits to their assimilation. When one butcher introduced "traife," or non-kosher meats, his shop window was smashed twice in a row. Soon a sign went up announcing new owners and henceforth only kosher beef and chicken.[5]

The Fabers left that behind when they moved a half mile north in the 1920s. Their new neighborhood was not a "better" one, but it was mostly non-Jewish. Philip and Rose may have believed that Abe would find it easier making his way in America by growing up where English was the common tongue and Easter the spring holiday. Perhaps the move would have worked with a different son.

Abe made no friends in his new surroundings. He had a father with a speech impediment and a fretful mother who kept to herself, and he prayed in synagogue on Saturdays rather than in church on Sunday. His isolation did not pass unnoticed. "His conduct was a topic of everyone in the neighborhood. They always wondered why he was so distant," said Larbey. "You would say, 'Hello Abe' and he would walk along and never say a word."

By 1927 Larbey had realized that proximity with Abe would never improve the boy's sociability. The seventeen-year-old clumped down the stairs, slammed doors morning and night, and dodged every attempt to open a conversation. "He would twitch his face and go away from you," Larbey said. Abe played no sports, either at school or on the streets at home. He ignored the Red Sox and the Boston Braves. He never chatted up the neighborhood girls. Larbey's teenage daughter, Lois, said, "He would always have his head down, and never look anybody square in the eye." She said it was his mouth that twitched, and the twitch was "very noticeable."

Philip described him as "kind of afraid of his shadow . . . He was a different kind of boy entirely from other boys." Not everyone saw that side of Abe. Some neighbors said he was so polite they wished their own children would emulate him.

Around the time he completed high school his mother suggested he see a physician. "I think there is something wrong with your head, or you wouldn't act the way you do." Abe was not pleased.

"Look in the mirror," he replied. "If there's something wrong with my head I must be crazy, and I think there must be something wrong with your head, too."

Abe was also a Jew, which meant he had to choose his sidewalks carefully or risk running afoul of toughs who took Sunday sermons too literally. Jews and Irish Catholics mostly settled around their own synagogues and churches. Theodore H. White, the journalist catapulted to fame by his account of John F. Kennedy's election, *The Making of the President*, was a few years younger than Abe when he grew up on the south end of Blue Hill Avenue. "The local library lay in such an Irish district, and my first fights happened en route to the library," he recalled in a memoir. "After one last bloody nose battle I was given safe passage by the Irish boys." He observed that the better-off "lace curtain" Irish "were, if not friendly, at least not pugnacious."[6]

As Abe's high school graduation neared, Larbey had already guessed that the boy would not be joining his father at the tailor shop. Family life on the third floor was a daily diet of unpleasantness. Abe was perpetually resentful and treated his father to a stony silence. Against his mother, Abe waged a daily skirmish. Larbey would first hear her voice, too soft to make out the words, and then Abe's loud, harsh response: "Don't bother me!" But Abe was her only child, and leaving him alone was not possible. Abe would warn her, "If you don't go away, I'll strike you!" though he never did.

So the neighborhood raised a collective eyebrow upon learning that the boy had made the grand leap across the Charles River to the limestone campus of the Massachusetts Institute of Technology. "If I didn't know of his going to his school," Larbey said, "I would have took him for a little abnormal man."

The motorcycle was a reward from his parents. On the morning Larbey later described to a jury—a recollection offered as proof that the boy's mind was never quite right—he awoke to discover that the coal-fired kitchen stove needed refueling. He picked up a steel bucket and descended into the cellar to fill it with hard black anthracite, delivered by the ton each month, and found himself staring in astonishment at Abe's motorcycle. Or what had been Abe's motorcycle. The boy had disassembled the machine piece by piece. The handlebars, brakes, spoked wheels, gas tank, engine, transmission: all were laid out across the floor. "I asked him what he was going to do with it," said Larbey. "He didn't give me an answer."

A month later, a vehicle emerged from the cellar, though of what sort Larbey was uncertain. It had two wheels in the front and one wheel in the back. A registration plate was screwed onto a fender, and Abe drove the contraption onto the street. Frantically manipulating the controls, he sped up and down the block. And while Abe did not confide in the motorman, he told a high school classmate that three-wheeled cars were the future of automobiles, and he was going to create one. He was going to invent something. It was his life's goal.

WHEN MIT ADMITTED 450 NEW STUDENTS that fall, four of them came from Jewish Dorchester or Roxbury: Leo Green, David Goodman, Jacob Gordon, and Abe. Gordon was Abe's best friend, and maybe his only friend, in college. Four was a large number of students from the small area, given that some Jews believed MIT limited Jewish enrollment to 5 percent of the student body. The Boston boys arrived as MIT was completing its transition from an engineering school churning out graduates to operate America's factories into an institute devoted to pure and applied scientific research.[7]

Every freshman enrolled in the same set of classes: "descriptive geometry," the mathematics used to represent three-dimensional objects in two dimensions, English, history, more mathematics, mechanical drawing, physics, and "working drawings," which taught students how to produce schematic diagrams a machinist could turn into a three-dimensional object.

A similar set of courses was required for sophomores, and military training was mandatory both years. Students were taught parade ground drills, marksmanship, map reading, and the rudiments of military engineering. In junior year they were eligible for an advanced ROTC program that commissioned graduates as second lieutenants in the U.S. Army Reserve. Enrollment wasn't automatic. Officer candidates received a daily 30-cent payment for "rations," which the army acknowledged was a major reason 76,000 students were enrolled across the country. Over the course of a year, 30 cents a day added up to a $100 a year, equivalent to 25 percent of MIT's annual tuition. In return, the army required six weeks of training for two summers and courses on artillery, battlefield engineering, and chemical weapons.

Abe and Jacob Gordon applied and were accepted. Perhaps they needed the financial help or shared an enthusiasm for things military, but the two had also grown up in a world where "Jewish courage" was commonly considered an oxymoron. ROTC service was a rebuff to that stereotype. Abe also found an unexpected gratification in firearms training.

Handling the hefty, powerful rifles and handguns was a tactile pleasure for him, as was assembling and disassembling their precision parts. There was a satisfying "click" as he snapped each bullet into a magazine. Even though the student scientists were unlikely to ever see the inside of a trench, they were trained to shoot and service the World War I–era Springfield bolt-action rifle, a .45 caliber pistol, the ubiquitous .38 revolver, and Colt's specialized target-shooting pistol, the .22 caliber Woodsman. Like the .45, it was a semiautomatic weapon with a sliding receiver, but the smaller rounds made it easier to handle in competition. With concentration and precise control over his breathing and twitchy shoulder, Abe consistently delivered a bullet to the bull's-eye. Soon he was considered one of the four best marksmen on campus.

At an ROTC summer training camp, Charles S. Draper, a new MIT research assistant, saw Abe in action. Draper, who would become a legend in aerospace engineering, "marveled" at Abe's accuracy with both pistol and rifle. "He was a good shot with any sort of gun," Draper told a professor.[8] On campus Abe was a frequent visitor to the student firing range, prompting a teacher to say it was Abe's "only known recreation." That was not entirely accurate. Abe had also joined a frat.

Most of MIT's twenty-nine fraternal organizations served a particular ethnic or religious group. The newest was Sigma Omega Psi, whose members were mainly working-class Jewish students from greater Boston, and it was the smallest when Abe graduated in 1931. The thin roster required each frat brother to manage a portion of the house's affairs. Abe was named treasurer, no doubt the least desired job, as it was the single post that entailed actual work.

Abe performed his role too enthusiastically. He declared that a planned dance, that year's major social event and a chance to chat up Jewish girls not just from the neighborhoods but from colleges throughout Boston, had to be canceled because Sigma Omega Psi couldn't afford the indispensable refreshments.

The other students disagreed. Dorchester boy Leo Green let Faber know what was what. There would be a social. "I took it upon myself to explain matters to him," said Green. "It was very simple. He just acquiesced to it." The frat members were already wondering about Faber and girls. One brother was notorious for reciting "sexy stories," and at the start of a "lecherous" yarn Abe always got up and walked away. Gordon attributed his friend's prudishness to mere shyness.

In fact, Abe was pleased that MIT had only a half dozen or so female students. It made college more professional, as the boys always showed off when girls were around, Abe complained. Women also frightened him.[9] While some seemed to like him, he became helplessly shy trying to converse. "I was afraid they were waiting until my back was turned to laugh at me." In high school a girl from one of Boston's wealthier sections had fascinated him. "She wore beautiful clothing. She smelt of perfume, she had an innocent sweet face and hair the color of copper." They studied mathematics together, meeting after school to pore over textbooks. But she dropped him after passing a major exam. Years later, when Abe faced death, the slight still rankled.

At MIT he did show an interest in the opposite sex as a subject of scientific inquiry. That required fieldwork. In the yearbook for Abe's class of 1931 only one woman's photograph appears. It is of Helen Delight Moody, who had transferred as a sophomore from the University of Denver and graduated with a general engineering degree. Her nickname was "Dee." She had a bright, shiny smile, and if her path ever crossed Abe's she likely concluded there were better opportunities elsewhere.

For the boys on campus a convenient sexual outlet was the compensated sort. It was not difficult to find a professional willing to have paid sex with a college student, as between MIT and Harvard there were thousands of single young men all wondering when they were going have sex for the first time, if not the next time. Abe partook "purely for a scientific purpose," he later said.

By ordinary standards his experiment was a failure.

After three encounters, presumably necessary to familiarize himself with the mechanics of coupling, Abe concluded that intercourse was repellant. "Disgusting," was the word he later applied to it. Granted, sex with a prostitute was not the best introduction to physical intimacy, an experience naturally suffused with a fear of imminent embarrassment. And Abe's father may have passed on an aversion to sex because of his own youthful experience with a prostitute, details of which would be whispered about in court. On the other hand, the fact of Abe's three assignations suggests that he was not repelled by physical contact per se. Perhaps his dedication to the scientific method overcame, momentarily, a struggle with sexual repression. Or perhaps he preferred men.

Abe never admitted to having sex with a woman again. That did not, however, mean he never fell in love.

In the interim he made a friend.

She was Rose Knellar, a jewelry store clerk from Dorchester, whom he met during his sophomore year. She was seventeen with a serious demeanor that appealed to Abe. The irritable parts of his personality aside, Abe had great potential as marriage material. Only 7 percent of Americans his age attended college, and Abe was at one of the best universities in America or the world. Knellar acknowledged that Abe was not as romantic as other boys. If she wanted a kiss, she had to ask. "He didn't throw his arms around me," Rose said. "Most of the affection came from me." They had a chaste friendship that evolved into a chaste courtship, even after he presented her with his fraternity pin with the understanding that they would eventually marry.

Abe's success at MIT came in the classroom. The end of sophomore year in 1929 was the time to choose a major, and at that moment no field was more celebrated than aeronautical engineering. While the Wright brothers had flown twenty-five years earlier to worldwide acclaim, and the World War I fighter aces who daringly piloted wood and cloth biplanes became national heroes, America's aeronautical industry went into a slump after the war. The situation overseas was dramatically different. The Germans were flying the first all-metal transport plane—with wings of aluminum rather than fabric painted with resin—and the Italians had built an eight-engine flying boat. Scheduled passenger services were in operation. Those achievements were undergirded by burgeoning scientific research and industrial development, as manufacturing modern aircraft demanded sophisticated, material engineering and major strides in engine development.

In America, virtually the only scheduled flights were those paid for by the government to carry the U.S. mail, and they became known mostly for the large number of pilots killed: thirty-one of the first forty airmail aviators died as they flew their rudimentary aircraft through storms and freezing rain.

Then in 1927 Charles A. Lindbergh made the first transatlantic crossing by air, in thirty-three hours of solo flight. He became a hero, and his achievement shook the nation out of its aeronautical lethargy. At MIT, aircraft engineering courses were suddenly popular. Students had use of a new, four-story aeronautical laboratory that was the product of an unusual philanthropic effort led by the second and third generations of heirs to a mining fortune established by a nineteenth-century Swiss immigrant, Meyer Guggenheim.[10]

The family is better known for endowing the New York City museum, but Meyer's grandson Harry had served as a navy pilot in World War I and, after a tour of Europe in the early 1920s, returned alarmed at America's aeronautical backwardness. He persuaded his father to create a $5 million research fund, which proved crucial for the development of the cockpit instruments necessary to "fly blind." Without that technology, a pilot whose view was blocked by clouds, fog, rain, or snow was soon likely to be a dead pilot.

The breakthrough flight came on September 24, 1929. A holder of two MIT graduate degrees, army major James H. "Jimmy" Doolittle, climbed into the rear seat of a two-place open-cockpit biplane and, with a canvas canopy blocking his view, took off, flew fifteen miles, and landed, all the while using only his instruments as a guide.

At MIT it was all very thrilling. The undergraduate aeronautical engineering major, dating only to 1926, was overwhelmed with applicants. Facilities were still limited, and jobs remained few, so enrollment was limited to thirty students a year. "It is probable that a relatively small number of engineers can be absorbed each year," MIT administrators announced, "but these must be of exceptionally high quality." They were chosen by the program's small cadre of professors, and in the fall of 1929 one of those lucky few was Abe Faber.[11]

It should have been the doorway to the rest of his life.

Abe's teachers literally wrote the book on aeronautical engineering. Abe's adviser for his senior thesis was Joseph S. Newell, the coauthor of *Airplane Structures*, published in 1928. It sold 49,544 copies before it went out of print in 1954—a remarkable demand for such a specialized textbook.

Newell taught Faber structural engineering from February 1930 to his graduation in 1931. He found much to admire, and he chose Abe and three other students to spend the summer of 1930 working at the Viking Flying Boat Company in New Haven, Connecticut. Abe was employed as a junior draftsman but did not capitalize on the chance to socialize with the esteemed Newell. The professor was puzzled. "He would leave when the work was over at the end of the day and very frequently go his way," said Newell. If the MIT contingent attended a Hollywood film after work, Faber declined to join them. "We would see him the next morning." Newell's professional admiration of Faber endured despite those quirks, including, the professor noted, Faber's habit of refusing to look directly at him during a conversation. Instead, "very frequently he would turn his head and drop his eyes."

Faber's ability also led to a friendly relationship with Professor Shatswell Ober, an expert on aircraft engine development and wind tunnel testing who coauthored another seminal text in the field, *The Airplane and Its Engine.*

On June 9, 1931, Faber was one of 437 undergraduates to receive a diploma and walk off the stage into what were the worst years of the Depression. Employment was uncertain, though some students still had money for luxuries, as the graduation edition of the *Tech* student newspaper included a large advertisement by the White Star passenger line offering "Fun on the rollicking way to Europe" starting at $105. "Any kind of merriment made on a moment's notice," it promised.

Faber's summer work experience paid off, however, and he secured a job with Viking at the respectable salary of $20 a week. Viking was owned by industrialist Robert W. Gross, who in the fall of 1931 was forced into bankruptcy. After only three months on the job Abe was laid off. Gross quickly bounced back. In 1932 he purchased the bankrupt Lockheed Company for $40,000 and transformed it into one of the nation's largest aircraft manufacturers. But Abe was back in Massachusetts and living with his parents.

His career may have been stymied by his religion as well as the economy. There was widespread anti-Semitism in the engineering and aeronautics industry, acknowledged but not condoned by MIT faculty members.[12]

Abe returned to MIT in February 1932 and enrolled in a postgraduate class on engine development theory with Myron S. Huckle, a balding, bespectacled instructor who grew friendly with his quiet student. The research required them to spend three or four days a week together in the lab. Before long Huckle invited Faber to help him on a private experiment, an attempt to build a gasoline engine that could run on diesel fuel as well. Huckle also invited Faber home for dinner. His wife was put off by Abe's twitch. That did not bother Huckle.

"I never remember hearing him swear, never saw him smoke. I never got the impression that he had any bad habits." Huckle thought Faber had an inferiority complex, but as they spent more time together, he realized Faber's quiet demeanor hid an arrogant streak. Huckle initially shrugged it off. Abe was not the first smart Tech student to conclude that he knew more than his professors.

Toward the end of 1932 Huckle noticed that Abe displayed a new self-confidence, as if he were willing himself into a different personality. Nevertheless, with Huckle's recommendation and in the face of what the teacher called the "handicap" of Abe's religion, his student secured a job teaching airplane power plant and electrical theory to students at the New England Aircraft School. It was run by a Boston University professor who described Abe as "the most inoffensive chap you could imagine. I should have said he had the character of a mouse." That job paid $12 a week, a slim salary for a Tech grad.

At the same time Abe became convinced he could develop a faster, less expensive method for reclaiming used crankcase oil. The existing practice was to send dirty engine oil back to a refinery, where it was reprocessed in much the same energy-intensive way as crude straight from the ground. Abe was experimenting with a simpler filtration system. He was joined by another Dorchester MIT grad, David Goodman, and the two of them set up a laboratory in the attic of Abe's house. Whatever progress they made wasn't enough to satisfy Goodman, who abandoned the effort in mid-1933. And whatever newfound self-assurance Abe had was insufficient to persuade Huckle to invest in his oil reclamation scheme. Technology aside, Huckle believed there was no way to turn a profit on the venture.

The nation was now at the nadir of the Depression. Nearly one-quarter of the workforce was unemployed, and the stock market was down 85 percent from its 1929 high. Spirits got a boost when Franklin Delano Roosevelt took office in March 1933 and moved fifteen major bills through Congress, including banking reform, securities regulation, public works, and relief programs, though none offered any immediate help to Abe, as he had lost his teaching job, perhaps because of the economy, perhaps because he had trouble maintaining classroom discipline. To outward appearances he was, nevertheless, bearing up well. He continued with his oil reclamation experiments, he had a room over his head and meals provided by his parents, and he was certainly not the only young man, or young MIT graduate, in such straights.

But in his head Abe was simmering. He had followed all the rules, he had received a first-class education, and he neither smoked nor drank. When was society going to do something for him? he wondered. One answer was provided by his old acquaintance Murt Millen, who told him that society was going to do nothing.

"Society couldn't even fix me up with a living, such as it had taught me to expect. That is legal society couldn't. Lawless society did—lawless society in the person of Murton Millen!"[13]

THE TWO HAD MET as students at Boston English High and stayed in touch while Abe was at MIT. During their moments together, Murt derided college as a chump's game. "Murt took it for granted at the start that the cards were stacked against him," Abe wrote later. "He quit school early, and while I was grinding away at MIT, he was having a good time. He thought I was a sap for studying."

Murt might have thought Abe a fool for hitting the books nights and weekends, but Murt's life was more than an applause line short of a success. Early in 1930 he took what would be the first of three trips through the states of the Old South, returning home to tell his sister Frances of the pleasure he found in the warm, damp climate.

In the fall he went to work for David A. Morey, the owner of a "decorative advertising" company that designed and installed department store displays. Morey was of two minds about his new hire. Sometimes the owner saw flashes of "brilliance." But those moments were outweighed by periods of laziness, unhappiness, and indifference. A year into the job Murt announced that arranging mannequins and designing store windows weren't for him. From the outset it was an intriguing career for Murt to have considered, as professional window decorating in the 1920s and 1930s was regarded as the province of gay men.

Murt was next hired as a chauffeur by a doctor and a dentist. That job didn't last, as Murt again fell into a depressive slump. The dentist explained that he let Murt go for fear of what he might find inside his car one morning.[14]

Money kept coming from somewhere, however. There were rumors, always short of proof, that Murt drove for the bootleggers who floated illegal liquor ashore on Cape Cod.

The cash Murt had he spent on cars. Other times he stole them. He and Irv operated a crude mechanic's shop in the backyard of their Lawrence Avenue house. Their customers were neighbors looking for a cheap repair or folks feeling sorry for Irv. Irv did most of the work while Murt, when not bouncing from one job to another, cobbled together what he boasted would be a new class of race cars, the "Millen Special." When he returned home after his revelation on the Virginia beach, he set to work on the project in earnest.

"He was so different," said Irv. "He came back so full of pep, and so full of ideas, and he had a lot of schemes, and I thought he was great. I worked for him. He had the ideas."

Murt mounted a 16-cylinder engine on a Ford chassis and installed aluminum alloy pistons, believing the lighter weight would be rewarded by an increase in horsepower. The vehicle's appearance did not impress his mother. "They made the most ridiculous car you ever saw. The wheels, one painted blue and the other painted black . . . Murt thought it was the most wonderful thing." As for herself, "I was ashamed to have it in the yard. The junk in the yard was bad enough."

By the fall of 1931 Murt was ready to enter an invitational meet in Rockingham, New Hampshire, where amateur drivers and mechanics competed for a chance to race against nationally known professionals. Organizers set a stiff set of requirements. Applicants had to show they could work as a mechanic in the pits, fueling and repairing other cars. They also had to show they could handle a car at high speed around the oval track. Murt succeeded and obtained a temporary professional race car driver's license and a spot in the Columbus Day lineup.

Overeager, Murt pushed his car to the starting line too early. When the gun did go off, Murt led the pack for four laps, momentarily beating professional drivers with professionally prepared cars. Then the engine blew, probably because of the aluminum pistons. Around him the other, better-designed and better-financed cars raced past.[15]

"That is where I got an idea that the best way to get money was to get it." Steal it, is what he meant. "It's a good way. The bunch on Wall Street do get it that way, Insull and that bunch of crooks," Murt said, referring to the British-born American businessman Samuel Insull, accused of peddling worthless stock to gullible investors. "The bankers steal it anyway. Why not steal it from them?"[16]

Initially, the early end to his racing hopes sent him back into a downward spiral. Murt climbed into his Chevy and headed south again, the first trip since his manic-depression revelation. Travel was an effective distraction from his mental gloom. The journey placed him in a new world every day, full of new possibilities.

And driving a car provided a flood of visual and aural stimulation that demanded attention. The day-to-day difficulties of piloting a vehicle across rural America were often daunting. More than 15 million cars plied American roads in the late 1920s, but the vast majority were in the North and the West, and many were still crude machines. Hydraulic brakes didn't appear until 1922, and automatic transmissions were available only in luxury cars. To travel 1,500 miles Murt would have loaded his car with spare tires and spare parts, tools, food, and even bedding. If he didn't make it to the next town by the end of a day's travel, he camped by the side of the road. And that road was probably still dirt, or mud after a rainstorm. By the end of the 1920s only a fifth of American highways had a solid surface, and the proportion was lower down South. The only paved interstate highway was a two-lane roadway that connected New York City to San Francisco.[17]

The journey to Louisiana swept away Murt's psychological tumult. Each day he had to find gasoline, figure out the route with the smoothest surface, and decide where he was going to get his next meal. The daily tasks prevented him from obsessing over the darkness hovering in his mind. But the relief was never permanent. From Louisiana he wrote home, "I am sitting on the banks of the Mississippi. I am going to take my shoes off and walk and walk." To ensure that his letter was sufficiently alarming, he added, "I don't think you'll hear from me again. I guess this will be the last letter."

It was a hollow threat. In late 1931 Murt walked back into the house on Lawrence Avenue. In 1932 he and Faber reconnected. Soon they were in almost daily contact.

In an era when adult children remained at home until marriage, a custom reinforced by Depression poverty, parents were intimate with the doings of their children, and children with the lives of their parents. Families shared a single bathroom and cooked in the same kitchen. Eating out was a rare event. Wives and mothers or daughters were expected to make meals for the entire family. Communication was largely face-to-face or by letter. Telephones were commonplace, but they were almost always located in a common space like the kitchen or hallway, making confidential conversations impractical.

So when Murt wanted to catch up with Abe, he drove up Blue Hill Avenue and walked up three flights to the Fabers' apartment. If it was the evening or a weekend, Abe's parents were home.

They found Murt's presence alarming.

"I don't think that boy is in your company, and I don't like the looks of him," Philip Faber told his son in English still stilted by the Yiddish of his youth. "Please, Abe . . . do me a favor . . . don't go with him. That boy is not a good type."

If Rose or Philip heard the telephone ring and found Murt on the other end, they hung up. Their son was out of work—a setback, it was true—but he had an MIT degree and yet was hanging out with this mope. Soon Murt came face-to-face with the angry father.

"You ain't fit to go with my boy . . . I want you should go out of my house and leave my boy alone."

Murt gave Philip Faber a stare. "He just looked at me. He didn't say anything."

Later, Abe tried to reassure his father, but Philip was adamant. "Now listen . . . I have experience. I am a man. I am your father. I have seen young fellows. You are a college boy. Pick a college boy. Don't pick a boy like him." Philip's plea was not well received.

"You make me sick," his son replied.

Abe's parents were also perturbed that Murt was a child of Joe Millen, he with his reputation as a loud, unpredictable, and brutal man. Joe had recently trotted down to the Roxbury police precinct to file a criminal complaint against Murt and Irv for "sponging off" him. More disturbing was that Joe himself had run afoul of the law.

When Prohibition took effect in 1920, Joe joined a class of entrepreneurs who exploited a loophole allowing alcohol to be sold for medicinal purposes. Drugstores experienced a flood of prescriptions naming alcohol as the treatment of choice for a host of ailments. Providing the medicinal booze was a business on the thin edge of legality. Nevertheless, Joe established the Baystate Wholesale Drug Company. It had only one product.

The shady practice might have evaded the notice of his neighbors but for Joe's propensity to sue his business partners. He went to court claiming a former associate had cheated him out of a barrel of whiskey. For that he was seeking $100,000 in damages.

Then on April 16, 1931, Boston police found what they called "the base of supply and distributing point for alcohol and beer in greater Boston." Officers initially thought they had merely discovered a bootlegger's cache when 1,000 gallons of pure alcohol and 2,000 gallons of beer were found inside a trolley garage converted into an automobile storage facility. The interior of the "car barn," as the papers called it, was a confusing maze of vehicles and partitions. So police went back for a second look and literally stumbled over an electric wire. It led to a hidden room in the building's rear, inside of which they uncovered a distillery of nearly industrial scale. The sophisticated installation included fabric-lined walls and ceilings to prevent telltale odors from escaping into the neighbor. It worked well. "The alcohol . . . fumes were so strong that the police were affected after remaining in the room a short time," said one report.[18]

The newspapers had a field day, one report calling it the "most elaborate and best equipped distillery plant and brewery found in recent years." The landlord, the papers noted, was Joseph Millen of Roxbury.

Five people were arrested on site. Joe claimed ignorance—he was just the landlord—and escaped with a mere $500 fine for "unlawfully manufacturing intoxicating liquor."

So Philip Faber was immensely disquieted to see that his son was now at Murt Millen's beck and call. "I used to hate him," he said.

Abe felt quite differently.

4

======

Everything
I Cannot Do

ANOTHER UNHAPPY FATHER was Joe Millen. His problem was Abe, who he saw almost every day now, and sometimes at dawn in the upstairs hallway.

In early 1932 the entire Millen family was still living at Lawrence Avenue, though Joe's position in the home was teetering on the untenable. Enraged at his wife yet again, Joe struck her in the face with a telephone receiver. His sons were no longer intimidated by his bulk and temper, and this time Murt and Irv threw him out of the house. Carolyn's injury healed in a few weeks, and Joe hoped the incident would slide from everyone's memory, though he didn't forget that his oldest daughter, Frances, had cheered the boys on as they manhandled him through the front door.

His banishment lasted three months, and on his return the usual uproar resumed. Contributing to the tumult was Joe's fixation on uneven black splotches mysteriously defacing a wooden column on the front porch. The marks increased in number day by day and soon had disfigured almost the entire surface. Eventually it dawned on Joe that, as odd as it seemed, he was looking at scuff marks from a pair of shoes. Someone was climbing the column. The marks began a couple of feet from the bottom and ran up to where the column met the flowery, Corinthian-style cap that undergirded the porch roof. Joe was dumbfounded and demanded an explanation. "Who are the lunatics climbing on this post?"[1]

Irv clued him in. The lunatic was Abe. He would arrive shortly before midnight, usually after dropping off his girl, Rose. He parked his car, walked up the steps, and hopped up onto the front porch balustrade. He wrapped his hands and feet around the white column, and shimmied upward until his head almost bumped the roof beam. Then he reached out, grabbed the wooden rain gutter, and swung his legs up and onto the porch roof. From there it was a few steps to Murt's window. It was a regular thing, Irv said.

Which was why Joe later discovered Abe padding about the house one morning. "What do you do?" Joe demanded. "Stay here all night?" Abe said no, lowered his eyes, and mumbled a few words. Joe was at a loss. He pondered the advice the psychiatrist, Myerson, had given him after the Virginia crisis. Ease off your son, Myerson said, let him grow up as he sees fit. Easy for him to say, Joe must have thought.

Once, he strode right into Murt's room but didn't find what he feared. "My surprise was they were talking about different experiments."

Abe's refinery experiment was still active, and Murt was working on his 16-cylinder race car. They talked automobile engines in conversations on Roxbury and Dorchester street corners. Just as Abe had taken apart the motorcycle to build his three-wheeled vehicle, so, he discovered, Murt was tearing apart and reassembling engines for the Millen Special.

"He had a great mechanical knowledge . . . of engines, which I admired," Abe said.

Abe knew the theory behind the internal combustion engine, its metal alloys, and high-temperature lubricants, but Murt in his backyard workshop had mastered practical mechanics and a surprising amount of sophisticated engineering, even if his Millen Special engine had blown up. "He tackled problems that I thought almost impossible for a fellow with his education, yet would come through successfully," Abe said. "There were many men in my class that weren't as good as Murt, even though they were graduates from MIT."[2]

That wasn't all Abe found appealing. "He was an all-around good athlete . . . He was physically strong and not afraid of anything," Abe said. "He always finished what he started to do, no matter how long it took him."

Abe struggled as he realized that Murt's skills made him feel deeply inferior. "He could do almost everything that I could not do." What had he gained from his academic success? He had no real friends, unless he counted Rose, and for her he felt no passion. The person he wanted to please, and whose respect he sought, was Murt. "I felt an attraction towards him," Abe said. When his life was about to end, Abe put it this way: "I cannot deny that Murt made my mind his slave."

In conventional terms Abe looked more "American" than Murt. His features were more refined, and mimicking movie star Clark Gable, he grew a thin mustache. Whether it made him look mature or mousy was debatable. Murt had a larger nose, a tougher-looking face, and a facial structure that bespoke Jewish genes from the eastern European ghetto. Nevertheless, Murt's strengths went beyond physical appearance. "He was a go-getter, and could make people do what he wanted them to do," Abe remarked. "I could not do that.

"He was the kind of fellow you'd like to put your arm around his shoulders and walk off with," Abe added. "I felt as if he was the only real friend I ever had."

IN THE MEANTIME Joe's businesses were dissolving. The easy money his enterprises threw off in the 1920s was long gone. In 1931 he filed for bankruptcy, declaring $29,493 in debts. After the car barn raid, he gave up the auto storage operation. Across the country the construction industry was sliding toward catastrophe. Home building was down 80 percent since the '29 crash. Millions of workers saw their wages cut. Boston was readying soup kitchens, and farm families could barely afford to purchase the seed needed for crops to feed themselves.

Amid the chaos of Joe's home, the older children were making something of themselves. Harry toured the East Coast playing jazz and big band music. Frances was an office manager and was active in ward politics, with the Democrats, of course. Mary was married to a musician, which Joe disliked, but at least marriage fit his plan for his children. A baby was on the way too, his first grandchild, who would be named Gloria. Joe's youngest child, Idalyn, was still in high school. That left Murt and Irv as the focus of his attentions. He had reluctantly comprehended that Irv was beyond any remonstration. With the boy's twitches and grins, and with a mind that operated a beat too slow, Joe knew there was little he could do to push Irv into his version of a proper life.

Murt was a different matter. He was smart, but willful. Joe thought that his son deliberately defied him. "Sometimes I would get out of patience and I would tell him, 'you dumbbell!'

"Or I might call him a lunatic." That his boy remained unmarried at age twenty-two violated the norms of Joe's peasant upbringing. "I mean, he didn't have no use for women at that time. He never associated with girls that I know. In fact, he hated them."

Joe was proved wrong as 1933 wore on. Murt started spending time with Freda Siegan, a neighborhood girl and typist downtown. She spent time with Irv, too, who Murt was now referring to as his "henchman." With Murt she went to dances and took drives to the beach. Certainly he was not like other boys, but that was the attraction. "The second time that I had gone out with him he showed me the palm of his hand, and he pointed to the lifeline. He says, 'See that line? You know what that means? I am going to live only until 25 to 26.'"

Despite his oddities, Murt had a car and some money, and he was fun. He cared little for what parents or society said to do or not do. "Everything was an experience to him," she said.

Toward Irv, Freda was touchingly sympathetic. "It was very hard for him to talk. If he wanted to say something he would start to stutter and get confused. He could not get anything out of his mouth." Yet when not on the spot Irv proved capable of extended monologues. Irv wanted to be heard. "He would get up on chairs and pretend he was an orator and recite, wave his hands in the air, in the motion, more or less, of a man going through gymnastics, with statements that were entirely incoherent," said a relative.

Irv's social awkwardness extended to women. When Freda first met him, Irv flirted with her by flicking drops of water into her face from a glass on a restaurant table. It was schoolboyish, she thought, before she realized that Irv did not trust himself to speak. At least he smiled. Others were not as amused by him. A girl up the street by the name of Foreman was pursued by Irv in his awkward, misunderstood way. He was not unattractive. At nineteen he was well built, with strong features and a thick shock of brown hair, but the twitch and the stuttering and the odd grin scared the girl. Irv could not grasp that she found his attention disturbing. In the end, Murt confronted the girl's father and, according to the complaint filed with police, pulled out a gun and threatened to "put him on the spot if he tried to keep Irving away from his daughter." The incident never went further than the precinct desk blotter. Irv agreed to look for female company elsewhere.

Freda thought Irv was harmless and that together the brothers were a hoot. "I thought they were interesting, different."

Rose, though, was becoming uneasy. The friendship she and Abe had established at MIT took a more serious turn when, shortly after his graduation, Abe gave her his frat pin, sort of the equivalent of an engagement ring, but not quite. They still saw each other four or five times a week, but evenings after a date he more and more frequently stopped at Lawrence Avenue on his way home. "He seemed very much attached to [Murt]," Rose said, "very much, and there were occasions when he would drop everything, practically, and go right ahead to Murt." The new friendship did little to alter Abe's churlish behavior at home. His unpleasantness often poked through his muted moodiness. Rose came to dread visiting his parents, as Abe unleashed an acid tongue on his father after Philip made remarks that other young men would shrug off as irrelevant parental commentary.

He threatened to strike his parents, but never did. Nor did he hit Rose. "Maybe he would push me, or something," she said.[3]

That summer Abe was required to spend two weeks on active duty at the Middletown Air Depot in central Pennsylvania, a grass landing strip and engine maintenance base nine miles south of Harrisburg. His fellow MIT grad from Dorchester, Jacob Gordon, was posted with him.

There was little to occupy them when they were not on duty, and Abe didn't join the other ROTC officers drinking in nearby speakeasies or chatting up the local girls. But Abe's taste in films was similar to America's, and his favorites were the gangster movies produced during an inventive, controversial era in American cinema that was about to be ended by a new Hollywood standards code.

Films from the late 1920s and early 1930s included hitherto unseen nudity and violence, and if the good guys won, the bad guys seemed to have more fun. Hollywood's portrayal of heavily armed criminals, whose real-life counterparts were actually roaming the country between Chicago and Texas, infuriated Americans who saw their nation becoming unrecognizable. Particularly notorious, and playing in Harrisburg that summer, was the Howard Hawks film *Scarface*. It starred Paul Muni as "Tony," who decides to move up the gangster career ladder by knocking off his various bosses. By the film's end Tony has reached the top, has slid down the other side, and is gunned down by police.

Abe was impressed. Not with Tony's criminal accomplishments, which he found lacking, but rather with the potential return that might come with better planning and execution. Abe mulled over the cinema gangster's failings and on the way back to the barracks commented to Gordon, "Some man with brains could do a really good job on that." "Poison gas" might be a useful tool, Abe added.[4]

THAT FALL MIT RESEARCHER HUCKLE concluded that Abe's self-assurance had grown to overreach when Abe announced he was applying for the vacant job of state airline inspector. Massachusetts was in the midst of regulating the increasing number of scheduled flights, and passenger safety was a priority. Abe was supremely unqualified for the job. "I was quite surprised that he, not even being a pilot, should apply," said Huckle. True, he had earlier encouraged an insecure Abe to "feel he could overcome everything," but aircraft inspector? "The obstacles appeared insurmountable to me."[5]

There were two other unusual events on the MIT campus around this time, though Huckle didn't connect the dots until much later. First, the test vehicle for his engine experiment was stolen, abruptly ending more than a year of research. Huckle reported the theft to the police, to no avail. Huckle later said an officer suggested looking look for the missing vehicle in Roxbury, at a home owned by a fellow named Millen.[6]

Then on the morning of November 1, 1932, an ROTC sergeant arrived at the MIT firing range to discover that the bottom panel of the entry door was missing. Inside, a steel gun locker had been pried open. Six .22 Colt Woodsman pistols were gone, along with seven thousand rounds of ammunition. Police were informed, but more than a year would pass before the thief was found out.

5

1175 Boylston Street

LESS THAN A MONTH elapsed from the first evening Norma Brighton saw Murt to the moment when her stomach turned tight and her breath quickened and she realized she was in love. It was as much hope as reality.

Their second date was on a Wednesday, the first day of her senior year in high school and three days after their drive back from Nantasket. Murt took her to a film, probably at the 1,500-seat Colonial Theater, which had opened five years earlier on East Central Street in Natick. Afterward, he parked on the dirt road leading to Nonesuch Pond and climbed out to meet her father. That could not have been by his choice. The elder Brighton was polite. After Murt left, "he didn't say much about him, except that he seemed all right," said Norma. She was annoyed by her father's lack of enthusiasm. She and Murt set another date for Friday.

Her return to school meant an awkward conversation with Bob Rogers, a handsome, square-jawed young man, who had starred with her in a high school production of *Pygmalion*. That had led to a high school romance, though her father disapproved of Rogers, too. He had given her a ring, a significant gesture in an era when high school graduation was often followed by marriage.

Bob couldn't compete with a fellow from Boston, though. Murt was "polished and mature," Norma thought. He taught her how to smoke cigarettes and gave Norma her first drink. He had a car, and when he drove her from Natick to Newton and Brookline and then Roxbury, Norma drank in the passing neighborhoods, each with a glimpse of life beyond the pond in Natick. In Roxbury she met Murt's family. He gave her a nickname, "Kitten," and had it engraved on a white gold and platinum cigarette case as a gift.

"He began to take me out regularly, and I was in love," Norma said.[1]

The reverend seethed. His politeness had been merely good manners. His daughter was dancing, smoking, and, he feared, drinking. She was going out alone with a boy in a car. "I tried desperately hard to warn her against that sort of thing," he said. Norman was deeply unimpressed with the young man. He was of a different religion, his family came from a different culture, and he slouched into Norman's living room, sat in the overstuffed taupe armchair, and barely spoke. Norman was particularly dismayed by the light in Norma's eyes.

NEITHER OF NORMA'S PARENTS were natives of Des Moines, Iowa, where she was born in 1915. Norman Brighton was born in Surrey, England, and immigrated to Canada in 1905 at nineteen years of age. He studied theology at Toronto University, transferred to Drake University in Des Moines in 1911, and graduated from Oskaloosa College, sixty miles to the southwest, where he was ordained a minister of the "Disciples of Christ." Also known as the Christian Church, it was founded in the early nineteenth century as a response to the "dogmatic sectarianism" dividing the nation's Protestant denominations. His first pastorate was in Des Moines, where he met Margaret Smith, recently arrived from New Brunswick, Canada. They were the same age, and they had Canada in common. Norman may well have been charmed by Margaret's high spirits, and they married.

The reverend's next congregation was in Fargo, North Dakota. When World War I broke out, he became an army lecturer, "drilling soldiers in poise, deportment and the psychology of leadership," according to an account he gave the newspapers.

In 1919 the family came East, and the reverend became pastor of the St. James Street Christian Church in Roxbury, just north of the Jewish neighborhood. Three years later his marriage fell apart. Divorce was an anomaly in the 1920s, and the divorce of a reverend and his wife—with children at that—was nearly unheard of, so the split-up was fodder for the newspapers. In court, Margaret claimed the reverend beat her, and she received a divorce on grounds of cruelty.[2] Brighton family members dispute that; they say the reverend felt obliged to initiate legal proceedings because Margaret's increasingly erratic behavior alarmed his congregation. Whatever the truth was, and the latter version may be closer to it, Margaret won custody of the three children, and Norman was ordered to pay $30 a week in alimony.

In 1927 Margaret and her children lived in the Allston section of Boston on a tree-lined street along a trolley line. The rear of their apartment building opened onto a park, an ideal location for the children. Margaret talked the landlord down from $70 to $60 dollars a month—still a stiff rent—by noting that she was "lawfully a widow." They did not stay in Boston for long. Somewhere during the Brightons' travels, Margaret met Oscar Clinton, a farmer from Manhattan, Montana. Clinton's first wife, Cora, had passed away and he was left raising two sons under the age of ten. He appears to have come East twice to court the divorcée. Clinton proposed, and Margaret accepted, only to learn that she needed Norman's permission to take Norma, only twelve, out of state. Permission was not forthcoming, and the custody dispute ended up in court. "They told Norma to tell the court I wasn't good to her," Margaret said. Clarence, seventeen years old, and Thelma, sixteen, went with their mother, but a Massachusetts judge declared, "The little girl does not wish to go to Montana to live with her mother, but prefers to stay in this state with her father."[3]

Norma thought living with Dad was fine. "I cried at the thought of her [mother] going away from me, but I didn't want to go to Montana. It seemed like the end of the world . . . I was so upset about everything that I got hysterics in the court," she said, "and they had to carry me out." When father and daughter reached Norman's home, a consolation prize was waiting, a puppy she named Tippy. Norman's daughter was pleased. "I thought I owned the world," Norma said.

The girl's fear of Manhattan, Montana, turned out to be warranted. Located twenty miles northwest of Bozeman on flat, thinly populated farmland, the town was home to barely five hundred people. The isolation was not easy for a woman of Margaret's peripatetic temperament. Or perhaps blending two sets of children proved more difficult than expected. Thelma soon fled back to Massachusetts to keep house for her father and sister. Clarence stayed with his mother, but her marriage to Clinton frayed within the year. Mother and son returned to the East.

By then Norman Brighton's uneasy relationship with his children was entering a new phase. He was still an ordained minister but had given up his active ministry to attend law school at night while he managed an auto dealership during the day. He was also courting a young immigrant from Scotland who worked at a delicatessen where he and Norma took meals.

Polite chitchat about the menu turned into lengthier conversations. Norman was pleased when the woman, Muriel, hit it off with his daughter, who was soon referring to her affectionately as "Mu." By 1929 Norman had a new wife. Thelma may not have warmed to her stepmother, and father and older daughter were already clashing over what constituted a proper social life for a teenage girl. Norma later said her sister was "in love and she wanted to get married." Whatever the reason, Thelma quietly packed her bags one day and disappeared. There were no good-byes. The seventeen-year-old was just gone. She was not heard from again for five years.

TWO WEEKS AFTER THEIR MEETING in Nantasket, Norma announced that Murt was taking her to a dance at Lake Cochituate, and the reverend found his limit. He "commanded" that she remain home, and a furious argument erupted. He warned her that she was embarking on a path that would "lead to unhappy consequences." As they argued, his frustration spilled over and the reverend wished, out loud, that he had never gained custody of Norma. That he regretted the last five years. That she should have stayed with her mother.

Norma said his wish could now come true. If he'd rather she live with Margaret, she would move "the next day." In the morning her stepmother, Muriel, tried to mend the breach, but Norma was beyond persuasion. "I just kept saying I wouldn't live in Nonesuch out in the country and not be able to do a few of the things that I thought a girl my age ought to be allowed to do. And when Murt came I threw my clothes in his car and he drove me off."

At her mother's apartment in Tewksbury, Norma's plan was quickly dashed. Margaret had no interest in taking in the eighteen-year-old, and she told her daughter to "go home to Natick" because her home was too small for two adults. Norma insisted that going home was not an option. Her father did not want her in his house. A compromise was reached when Margaret promised that if Norma did return to Natick, she would write her ex-husband and "make arrangements" for Norma to eventually move in with her.

Perhaps Margaret turned Norma away because a third option was standing in front of her. At some point Murt may have volunteered to have Norma stay with his family in Roxbury. Whatever the case, Margaret turned to Murt and told him, "You be careful of my little girl," and he said, "Yes, Mrs. Brighton, I will."

When they left Tewksbury, if it was indeed for Natick and not Roxbury, Murt changed Norma's mind by promising $25 for a room in Boston.[4]

That evening Murt walked into the family home with the beautiful teenager. Carolyn Millen was kind, and told Norma that her anger would exhaust itself and she would return to her father in a day or two. For now, she could share a bed with Idalyn, Murt's fifteen-year-old sister. The two girls hit it off, and on Monday Norma drove downtown with Murt. He rented her a room in a four-story town house on Hemenway Street, a short walk from Fenway Park.

As rain from a tropical storm whipped the state, Norma began job hunting. In the depths of the Depression, this did not prove easy. That very week, Boston mayor James M. Curley arrived in Washington to pitch a $19 million public works package to President Roosevelt. It included construction of a new subway line, which Curley hoped would employ three thousand people. But he wasn't the only mayor or governor seeking federal help. So desperate was the nation, and so worried were Americans by the unrest they saw roiling Europe, that Congress established the Civilian Conservation Corps to sop up a few hundred thousand of the millions of unemployed men. In return for bed and board and $30 a month, they planted trees, built national parks, and restored eroded farmland.

In that world of struggle, Norma had little chance of finding employment. She hadn't graduated from high school, and her only work experience was a few days of waitressing in New Hampshire. The shop owners she approached had laid off friends, family members, and longtime employees in the three years since the '29 crash. Norma knew she had no skills, no money, a mother who had turned her away, and a father to whom she was too proud to bend a knee. That left her dependent on a guy she had known for a few weeks. Was she really in love? She wondered what he wanted.

It was not sex. Or not only sex. Or at least not right away. Norma spent two or three nights of that first week at the Millens' house, sleeping in the bed with Idalyn. When she did stay at Hemenway Street, Murt was back in his own bed at Lawrence Avenue. "He was very proper," she said. A week later, Murt found her an apartment on St. Stephen Street, also a short walk from the Fens. Then he proposed marriage.

Murt made his offer to Norma at the end of a particularly unsuccessful day of job hunting. She was uncertain. Norma replied that she was young and was not sure she loved him quite that much. Murt was not dissuaded. Before long, after spending another day vainly knocking on doors, "I think I began to cry just because everything seemed so upset, and Murt put his arms around me and kissed me. I said I would marry him." They had known each other for five or perhaps six weeks.

Around this time Norma finally met Abe. One day Murt pulled his car over as they were driving past the Faber home on Blue Hill Avenue. Norma saw a "tall fellow with curly hair and a small, black mustache, and quiet." Murt announced their planned marriage, and Abe offered congratulations, but didn't sound like he meant it, Norma thought. That surprised her. "He was Murt's best friend," she recalled. "I expected he would be more excited." She might also have wondered why a whole month had passed before she met the man Murt described as his "best friend." Abe was "pinned" to his girlfriend, Rose, so Murt's going down the same path should have been met with a hearty slap on the back. Instead, Abe evinced no happiness.

No wonder. Norma was slowly realizing that she had replaced Abe as the emotional center of Murt's life—and at Murt's deliberate choosing. Abe was now a distant second best. There would be no more nighttime shimmies up the front porch.

Norma listened as the two men discussed plans for the store, and she saw that Murt dominated the Tech grad. "Abe put everything up to Murt for his decision."

Rose Knellar was much friendlier. The two girls met over a chow mein dinner at a Chinese restaurant, where Rose offered job-hunting advice and promised to keep a lookout for potential leads. Norma's luck didn't change, but Murt stepped in with cash. He also bought Norma a ring and a fur coat that cost $245, half the price of a new car.

The radio shop opened in early October at 125 Columbus Avenue, a block south of the luxurious Statler Hotel, the tallest building in Boston at 155 feet at its completion in 1927. Another landmark was immediately across from the shop, the granite, medieval-looking National Guard Armory of the First Corps of Cadets, with a history dating back to a colonial militia founded in 1741. The prestigious location was part of the partners' plan, as they were not selling tabletop radios to clerks and mechanics. They were catering to the brand-new, burgeoning field of business and government radio communications, and the newest segment in that field was mobile radio.

It was an industry the nation's police helped create. Detroit began equipping patrol cars with one-way radio receivers in 1930, initiating a transformation in police work as great as the arrival of the automobile itself. Within a year fifty-one communities, from small towns to big cities, had either installed or were purchasing radio broadcasting systems. In another year the number rose to two hundred.[5] Some departments called the radio-equipped vehicles "scout cars" and fit them out with bulletproof body panels, submachine guns, and tear gas. With an antenna atop police headquarters, officers were no longer limited to walking a beat and trusting that luck would send a criminal across their path. Nor were they tied to the corner call box connected to a downtown switchboard. A patrol car with a radio receiver could reach a crime scene minutes after a victim called police on a telephone. For the first time it gave police a chance of actually interrupting a crime in progress or catching perpetrators as they fled. In Boston the police commissioner balked, but the Massachusetts State Police was one of the first state law enforcement agencies to adopt the technology.[6]

Of course, the wrong side of the law was paying attention, too. In October 1931, Chicago police discovered that members of Al Capone's gang monitored police broadcasts on a modified shortwave receiver. Two years later, seven thieves invaded a safety deposit vault in downtown Chicago and listened to police broadcasts while they cracked open the steel drawers and stole $50,000.

Selecting the right collection of parts and designing and installing a communication system required real expertise. Abe opened the shop with money and help from another Roxbury man, Joe Rothberg. He knew the retail and wholesale business, and Abe's MIT diploma set them a step above other shops. Indeed, the name emblazoned across the glass storefront was "Faber & Co." As for Murt, he told Norma his job was "radio technician." Later he described himself as Abe's "chief salesman." It was an inside joke, but closer to the truth. As crime increased, so did the demand for communication gear. Apparently robberies were good for business.

But renting the store, stocking the shelves, and paying for Norma's apartment and gifts had seriously reduced Murt's cash roll, so the Box Office Boys went back into business.

They took advantage of another revolutionary development—multilane, limited-access highways. That fall Massachusetts opened the last stretch of the new Boston-to-Worcester roadway. The $5 million project featured four lanes, two east and two west. Work was speeded by modern earthmoving equipment, despite complaints that the state should be paying people rather than buying machines.

Others said that the project was too modest. County commissioners, chambers of commerce, and town officials along the route fought to have the state Department of Public Works put in six lanes. They failed, but nevertheless the four lanes allowed an automobile driver to speed from Boston to Worcester and back at upwards of 65 mph. So many people started going so fast that the number of accidents ballooned and the state Registrar of Motor Vehicles issued a statement warning drivers they risked being "severely penalized" if they didn't slow down.

One of the people speeding back and forth was Murt. The new highway allowed him to stretch his horizons to his newest target, Worcester's Palace Theater, the city's largest. It had three thousand seats and boasted marbleized columns, mirrored walls, and giant chandeliers. Plaster-cast adornments mimicked those of an ancient Roman villa. Murt did not intend to go in with guns drawn. Ticket receipts were stashed in the office safe, and Murt's idea was to get into the safe and out of the building without raising an alarm. Irv was his sole accomplice, but two were enough for a kidnapping.

By October 8, a Sunday, Murt and Irv had staked out the theater, identified the manager, Ralph W. McGowan, and tracked him to his home fifteen minutes away on the city's southwest corner. That night when McGowan arrived home with his wife, the brothers were waiting. The couple was forced into the Millens' car, and Murt proceeded to interrogate McGowan. Where was the safe, exactly? How could they best get to it? Who had the combination? According to what McGowan later told police, he convinced Murt that he did not have the combination and that only his assistant manager, Robert Portle, could open the steel box.[7]

If McGowan thought that would discourage the Millens, he was wrong. Murt started the car, and at gunpoint McGowan directed them to Portle's home, fifteen minutes in the opposite direction. They arrived to find it dark and unoccupied, so all four waited for Portle to return. Then he, too, was forced into the car and all five drove back downtown to the Palace. On the way Murt learned of another problem: rumors of a possible robbery had been circulating, maybe as a result of the brothers' reconnaissance, so police had put a patrolman inside the theater office.

It was well after midnight when the car pulled into an alley. Murt, Irv, and the three hostages entered through a side door and immediately collected a fourth hostage, night cleaning man Charles Gary. All were marched up to the second floor, where Officer Michael F. Morrissey was locked inside the office. A threat of violence solved that problem. A gun was jammed into Portle's back, and he talked Morrissey into opening the door. As it swung back, Murt and Irv shoved their way in, using the hostages as a human shield. Morrissey surrendered his weapon, Portle opened the safe, and Murt and Irv collected $4,500—proceeds from the entire weekend box office. It was a much better take than what they'd scored at the Oriental. The now-five hostages were locked in a closet, and Murt and Irv departed with the cash and Morrissey's revolver. Hours elapsed before the five managed to break free, and by that time Murt and Irv were back in Boston. Worcester police were at a loss but theorized, "A well organized gang from Boston or New York was responsible."

Murt began spending money the next morning when he plunked down $550 on a new maroon, four-door Chevrolet with a straight-six engine. The latest model boasted 60 horsepower and could zoom along at a top speed of 70 mph.

Norma had use of the car and on occasion drove it to Medford, five miles northwest of Boston, where her father was managing an automobile deal-ership while completing course work at Suffolk Law School. She wanted his advice on her pending marriage. Perhaps she wanted to be talked out of it, as she knew her father would try to do. But she never worked up the courage to go inside. Instead, she circled the block and returned to Roxbury. Perhaps she was stopped by the knowledge that the very act of approach-ing her father was an admission of error. On one occasion she drove out to Nonesuch Pond to have a conversation with her stepmother, but no one was home and she ended up leaving a note on the door.

But if she couldn't reach out to her father, neither did he attempt to contact her. Norman knew where his daughter was living, and soon his ex-wife sent him a letter announcing the pending nuptials. The next time he saw Norma was five months later, when she called on him to rescue her from the New York City police.

As for Margaret, her marital advice reflected the era's social standards. Norma had taken money and gifts from Murt and was living in an apartment he paid for. Margaret told her daughter, "When you've gone this far you certainly ought to marry Murt."

"She said it was the best thing for me to do, since I borrowed money and cannot pay it back," Norma said, and that it "looked bad" that she was "driving around in a car alone with Murt." Margaret also said she had received a letter from the reverend declaring that he did not want Norma in his home.

Some days later Margaret met Norma and Murt at North Station and together the three drove to Lawrence Avenue to meet Murt's family. Lonely in her Fenway apartment, Norma had been spending most nights in Idalyn's bedroom. Like her daughter, Margaret thought Carolyn Millen was "very, very nice." Joe apparently was not to be found. "We had a talk about nationality and religion, and agreed it didn't make any difference. I stayed to lunch and Murt and Norma took me home," Margaret said. She bought her daughter a peach satin wedding dress and placed an announcement in a Boston newspaper "so her father would see it."

On October 24 Norma and Murt obtained a marriage license and rented a furnished apartment at 1175 Boylston Street. One block closer to Fenway Park, it overlooked the Boston Fens, a freshwater marsh near the Charles River. Norma purchased towels, a trash can, and, with her mother, a comforter for the marriage bed. Margaret introduced her daughter to co-workers at the state hospital, who gave Norma a collection of silver spoons as a wedding present.

Happiness was harder to find. "All this just seemed to make the thing more inevitable and make me more frightened," Norma said. She wanted to get away and think. "I told him I was going to take a trip to New York. I know he was hurt, and a look of anger came across his face." But he drove her to the ship—there was regular steamer service to New York—kissed her goodbye, and told her to stay at the Lincoln Hotel in midtown Manhattan. The ship arrived in New York the next morning, and Norma took a taxi to the hotel. She dropped off her luggage and window-shopped along the streets of Manhattan. She inquired unsuccessfully about a job at a dress shop, and then returned to the hotel to get a manicure and hair wave. Sometime that afternoon she decided to go ahead with the marriage and went to bed that evening without leaving the hotel.

The room phone awoke her at six o'clock. It was the front desk announcing that a Mr. Murton Millen was in the lobby. Should they let him up? Murt had driven down from Boston to bring his Norma back. Perhaps there was an emotional reunion in the hotel room. Perhaps Norma was merely resigned. She packed her bags and went downstairs, and that night he dropped her off at the Boylston Street apartment. Idalyn was there, and the two teenagers slept while Murt returned to Lawrence Avenue.

The next day was a Saturday. Murt came over in the morning and they went to buy kitchen utensils. As Norma shopped for a flour tin and salt-and-pepper shakers, he walked off to make a phone call; he returned to tell her they were getting married that very afternoon. A justice of the peace would meet them at the Canterbury Hotel on the other side of Kenmore Square, past the ball park toward downtown. There was no time for her to run back to the apartment and don the peach dress. Abe and Rose showed up as witnesses, the words were said, and they were a legal couple. No one else attended, nor had anyone been invited. The honeymoon was dinner and a movie and a drive back to Boylston Street to start married life.

Murt had to have been pleased with himself. He'd just pulled off a big score, and not a smidgen of evidence was linked to him. He could work, when he wanted, at the new radio store—maybe they would even make some money—and he had married a woman who drew admiring stares on the street. Well, maybe she was more of a teenager, Murt admitted to himself. But still.

They washed and dried themselves with the new towel set and climbed into bed together for the first time, perhaps naked beneath the new comforter. What happened next wasn't what either of them expected. The night did, however, lead to the murder of four men. The first death came three weeks later.

6

Sex and Death

IT WAS A DEAD-END STREET that got Ernest W. Clark. It might as well have reared up and slapped him down, punishment for surviving the first volley of shots from the black Packard. Bleeding from two bullet wounds in his left arm, Clark staggered to the sidewalk as the automobile sped north on Blossom Street in Fitchburg. A passerby ran to his aid, and together they turned to seek help.

Then the sedan came screaming back downhill.

Clark had been on his way home from his job at the Iver Johnson Company store in Fitchburg, where he sold handguns, shotguns, bicycles, and motorcycles, all manufactured in a row of two-story factory buildings along the Nashua River that sliced through the city. Named after its nineteenth-century Norwegian immigrant founder, Iver Johnson was particularly proud of the "automatic safety hammer" it built into each revolver. The design made it impossible for the hammer to strike the firing pin unless the trigger was pulled, reducing the risk of an accidental discharge. Drop the gun, snag the hammer on a coat pocket, or even whack the hammer with a hammer, as the firm boasted in its advertisements, and the weapon would not fire. One magazine advertisement showed a young girl sitting up in bed, her doll on a pillow, a revolver in her lap, and a text block above her head that read, "Papa says it won't hurt us." In 1901 the firm suffered a spate of difficult publicity when another immigrant, anarchist Leon Frank Czolgosz, pulled the trigger on an Iver Johnson .32 caliber revolver, bypassing the safety hammer and assassinating President William McKinley.[1]

On December 11, 1933, Clark was behind the counter of the store in downtown Fitchburg. He was a thirty-seven-year-old World War I veteran who had driven ambulances in France for the 26th Infantry Division. At about 6:15 p.m. he closed the shop, locked the front door, and turned east along Main Street, beginning the mile-and-a-half walk to the bungalow he'd recently purchased for himself, his wife, and their three-year-old daughter. After a few blocks he turned left onto Blossom Street, slowing his gait as the road slanted uphill, and noticed a Packard sedan following behind. It pulled up next to him, and the driver leaned out. He asked how to find 15 Blossom Street, which Clark thought was an odd question because he didn't believe that address existed. The driver explained he was from out of town and confused. A door opened. Murt was behind the wheel.

"He wanted me to get in the machine and show them the way. That seemed kind of suspicious to me and I refused," Clark told police from his hospital bed later that night. "The fellow at the wheel didn't say anything. He slammed the door of the car and the machine started away." Then he heard a "pop." And then another.

There were three, or maybe four, people in the car, Clark said. He recognized none of them, which was not surprising as the passengers had driven in from Boston. They had reconnoitered the downtown area a day or two earlier and had walked into the store to inspect its stock of firearms. The plan was to kidnap an employee at gunpoint, force him to open the store, and then ransack the display cases for weapons and ammunition. But Clark's nervous refusal to enter the car foiled the scheme. Now Murt was not only angry but embarrassed, too, for with him, and watching his plan fail, was Abe.

This was Abe's first crime. Until that evening he and Murt had palled around, talked engines, experiments, the radio business. Abe knew Murt was robbing theaters and stealing cars. It's likely he served as a sounding board for Murt's criminal plans, for during their long evenings of conversation Murt and Abe concluded that they were smarter than the average thug, and the average cop. The newspapers showered publicity on bandits who were singularly unimpressive to Murt and Abe—high school dropouts mostly. Not like Abe, with his officer's commission and MIT degree and four years of training on how to break a problem into parts, evaluate potential solutions, and integrate the best into an answer. "I'd like to have your scientific knowledge, professor. I'd make some history. These gangsters just talk tough. They don't know anything. An educated man could laugh at the law," Murt told Abe. With meticulous planning and a dose of ruthlessness, they would do well. They could stay ahead of the police, Murt said. They talked about creating an "empire of crime." Initially, it was mostly Murt's idea. He had no lack of confidence. Like any novice criminal, Murt believed he could fashion a career that did not end in arrest or death. He had been knocking over movie theaters, stealing cars, and robbing stores with only his brother Irv as an accomplice, and yet law enforcement had no leads or links to Lawrence Avenue. So why not go bigger?

Murt found the act of crime exhilarating. Sure, it was scary at the start, but then it turned fantastic. In those moments Murt became a new man, a superman as the philosophers said, transcending good and evil. "Isn't it great, Abe? Don't it make you feel powerful?" he exclaimed.[2]

When he found Abe dismayed at the loss of his teaching job, Murt explained how he had overpowered his own depression. "He got the idea that he should go out and live," Abe recalled. Murt preached the gospel to his friend. "That's the thing, Abe. You've got to live. You can't think about abstract things all the time. That's what I'm doing. I do what I feel like. I live."

For inspiration Murt looked to the bandit gangs crisscrossing the Midwest and traveling north and south, from Illinois to Texas, gangs with guns riding roughshod over the police. John Dillinger had done well. He took $10,600 from an Ohio bank in June 1933, and though cops nabbed him a short while later, in October he broke out of jail and robbed the Central National Bank in Greencastle, Indiana, of $75,000. He was now vacationing in Florida. Clyde Barrow and girlfriend Bonnie Parker started their criminal career in 1932 — their murder toll was nearing a dozen — yet in November they escaped yet another trap, this one set by police outside Dallas. Lester Gillis, who had adopted the pseudonym George Nelson and was called by strangers "Baby Face Nelson," made off with $25,000 in jewelry during a 1930 score, then $4,600 from a bank robbery, and $18,000 in jewelry stolen from the wife of the Chicago mayor. True, he'd been arrested, but in 1932 he escaped and went right back to the bank-robbing business. Just a few months ago he had robbed a Minnesota bank of $32,000.[3]

They danced around state and local law enforcement, and even the new Division of Investigation set up under President Roosevelt to fight the surge in interstate crime.

All those fellows, Murt and Abe realized, had criminal records stretching back to their teen years. Police had mug shots of them and fingerprints, and some cops had met them and could try to calculate their next step. But Murt, Irv, and Abe were anonymous. Law enforcement did not know they existed.

Abe admired Murt's toughness and boldness, and he wanted some for himself. And he wanted to reclaim a piece of the emotional territory Norma had usurped. Joining Murt in crime was the way. Life had failed him, and he was angry and lonely. He did not love Rose. He did love Murt.

Plus, they all needed the money.

The radio shop was struggling, and Murt's proceeds from the Worcester robbery were almost exhausted. He had underestimated the bankroll necessary to support a household. But for bigger crimes he wanted heavier weapons. Murt and Abe ruled out purchasing guns legitimately for fear police could trace a spent bullet or cartridge. So they would steal them.

Yet now this Fitchburg store clerk was embarrassing Murt, and inside the car Abe was watching the plan fail. With other pedestrians nearby, it was too risky to jump out and drag Clark into the backseat, and it was too late to break into the store and loot the display cases. They were stymied. But who was this dull, ordinary clerk to stand in Murt's way? So as Clark turned away, a burning sensation ran up his left arm.[4]

Pop. Pop.

A block away Perry Wilson, the city's cemetery superintendent, was on his way to a church supper. He saw the Packard pull away and ran to assist Clark. The two men had gone hardly a block when the Packard suddenly reappeared and rolled to a stop in the street.

Murt hadn't known that a left turn off Blossom led to a dead end. To reach the road back to Boston, they had to return the way they came, and as they did Clark reappeared before them in the early evening darkness. Murt opened the door and said, "Both of you better get in here."

Wilson turned and ran. Clark, still stunned from his wound, was about to follow, but "before I could move they started to fire again."

The thing was, Clark was laughing at him, Murt said later. Maybe not literally baring his teeth in derision, but that's what Murt saw in in his mind's eye, this nobody foiling his plan. And jeering at him. So Murt opened up. As the shots rang out, Irv too raised his weapon.

Clark didn't remember being struck by nine .22 caliber bullets. A tenth gave Wilson a flesh wound. Clark was hit in the groin, twice in the back, in the ankle, in the head. No single one of the small-caliber projectiles killed Clark. But together, they caused Clark's death three days later.[5]

He was the first person Murt murdered. It is unlikely he had climbed into the stolen Packard, gun in his jacket, intending to end a stranger's life. But Murt's life had moved in that direction. He had entered the world with a mind ill-suited to empathy, a inclination magnified by the mental and physical violence at Lawrence Avenue. Beatings were what Joe knew, and Murt lacked the psychological resilience that enabled his siblings to manage their father and survive their upbringing and go on to flourish, in some fashion.

Murt couldn't whack the old coot. And now he was embarrassed and failing in front of his friend. And then there was his wife. She was beautiful and warm, and they were not having sex.

So he iced Clark.

Afterward, Murt was undisturbed by the killing. When Clark's demise was published in the Boston newspapers, Norma overheard Abe and Murt discussing the crime. Abe told Murt that they "shouldn't have gone back and got him."

Murt saw the brighter side. "For my first job I'm a good shooter," he said.[6]

Clark was laid to rest on Saturday, December 16, at the Rollstone Congregational Church. He had immigrated from Plymouth, England, at the age of four, was raised in Hartford, and moved to Fitchburg after the war to marry Marion E. Bidmead. Their daughter was Helen Louise. The funeral attracted a crowd, and not only because of the shocking manner of his death. Clark had mastered amateur moviemaking, and as a projectionist he "was much in demand by fraternal and service organizations," the *Fitchburg Sentinel* reported.

Meanwhile Fitchburg police chief Thomas J. Godley's dogged investigation was going nowhere. Godley thought he had a lead when a police officer from neighboring Athol said he'd witnessed a black Packard running a stoplight and hightailing it eastward. Under careful questioning, he described the car as a 1932 Packard model 901 with a spare tire suspended beneath the rear window. With the assistance of a former Massachusetts governor and current Packard dealer, Alvan T. Fuller, Godley obtained a list of all the hundreds of 1932 model 901s sold in New England. With the help of police from across New England, each address was checked. The effort came up dry. The Athol cop was wrong, They were looking for the wrong car.

The Packard they should have sought was a model 900 with two spare tires on the running boards.

That Packard had been stolen the previous fall on Providence Street in Boston, a block from the main entrance to the Statler Hotel and a short walk from Faber's new radio store, where its owner had parked to attend the annual Harvard-Dartmouth ball. More than 1,500 people attended, and extra police officers were detailed to handle the traffic. Murt and Irv watched as the autos poured past the radio store and parked every which way on nearby streets. By next morning the car was gone, already secreted in a wooden garage behind a row of houses on Brinsley Street in Dorchester. Murt had rented the unit under the name of "Nelson." It cost $21 every three months, and Murt or Irv was always careful to pay on time.[7]

Another impediment to Godley's investigation was the seeming lack of motive. Why was a store clerk, with no known enemies and no criminal record, gunned down on the street?

WHEN CLARK WAS MURDERED, it was three weeks after Murt and Norma's wedding. The marriage had not yet been consummated. Their first night in bed together was a failure, and weeks later they had yet to have intercourse. Murt blamed his wife, who may have found vaginal penetration too painful. Or perhaps Murt found an erection impossible. "It made him angry," Norma said, and "it made me nervous."

What Norma knew about sexual relations when she first climbed into bed with Murt is unknown, and her parents gave conflicting answers on whether they had discussed the facts of life with their daughter. Formal sex education was all but unheard of. America was more than a decade away from the first Kinsey report, *Sexual Behavior in the Human Male*, which made the best-seller list in 1948. Diaries from the 1930s show that young women rarely discussed sexuality among themselves. In a study of college students by two women newspaper writers, three-quarters of the 772 girls who participated said they were virgins. Among the others, 11 percent reported having had sex with a steady boyfriend, 9 percent were "experimenters," and 3.5 percent were "sowers of wild oats," including one woman who said she had slept with twenty men.[8]

Of the entire group, only forty-six said they had had intercourse in high school.

Predictably, the boys claimed more sexual experience, with half saying they had lost their virginity. The authors classified 21 percent of the boys as "hot bloods," meaning they slept around, too.

Sex out of wedlock was becoming more commonplace, however, as economic conditions forced couples to put off marriage. Young people were leaving farms to live in the big city, where parental supervision was nonexistent. Then there were cars. "The automobile has extended the range of freedom of action," which one writer said meant an increase in the practice of "hot petting." Or, as the *New Republic* put it, they "nibbled at the sweet fruit of intimacy without daring to pluck it from the tree."

Norma's descriptions of her life during the first weeks of marriage vary. In one account she said they were happy until Christmastime. Later, when she was attempting to rebuild her reputation, she said the marriage went off the rails early on. One day her mother was visiting and pitched in to clean the apartment. She set about straightening up the bedroom and had worked her way over to Murt's side of the dresser when he walked in and saw Margaret amid his belongings. He reacted with a snarl. "I don't want anybody sticking their noses into my things."

Norma was surprised and hurt and later chided Murt for his behavior. That wasn't how she was raised. "I may not have been contented at home, but at least we will always be civil to each other," she told him. The back-and-forth escalated into a full-fledged quarrel until Norma delivered a withering rebuke. "I'd rather be home with Dad!"

"Is that so?" Murt asked. He grabbed her by the hair, dragged her into the bathroom, grabbed a piece of soap, and shoved it between her teeth until it settled firmly in her mouth. It was punishment for talking back.

That moment "killed every bit of affection I had," Norma said.

Although Norma gave this account two years later, in far different circumstances, Murt no doubt did go wild over what he feared Norma's mother might discover stashed in that bureau drawer. And he probably did use the soap.

Much else of what she said about Murt's odd behavior is also likely true. Sometimes when a jazz tune came on the radio, she would find him dancing about in a frenzy, flinging his arms left and right. He got out of bed at two in the morning for hour-long walks. Sometimes he tried to persuade her to accompany him. He gave her books on psychology to read, which she admitted she didn't understand, and he once told her, "You're too dumb to live."

One Sunday morning he gave Norma a $10 bill to buy a newspaper, only to lock her out when she returned from the store. She had spent money on groceries after he had expressly ordered her not to. As Norma stood in the hallway, Murt yelled through the closed door to return the food if she wanted to get back in. Neighbors looked out to see what the ruckus was about. An elderly woman invited Norma in. After hearing the story, she fetched an ironing board. It was long enough to reach from her kitchen window across an air shaft to Norma's living room window, which was open a crack. Norma started crawling across on her hands and knees and was halfway there, 15 feet above the ground, when Murt saw her, jiggled the board, and shut the window. Norma crawled back. Finally a janitor arrived, thought it was all a joke, and let her in with his pass key. Norma walked straight into the bedroom with the packages and closed the door. "I stayed there about half an hour. Murton was in the living room, and sat there silently. 'Well, when do I get my paper?' he finally called out."

But Norma gave back, too. When he told her that she'd taken marriage vows to "love, honor and obey, I kind of said they don't say obey any more, and he glared at me and said, 'Oh yes they do and you will!'"⁹

Norma acknowledged that Murt had another side. "He took a queer pride in me. He always liked me to look nice, and he was not being stingy about spending money for my clothes." He helped her pick out dresses, and while he was often jealous when he caught other men looking her over, at other times he was proud, telling her, "Other men look at you, so I figure I have good taste."

They socialized with Millen relatives of a similar age. A woman who later married one of Murt's first cousins doubled-dated with the couple shortly after their marriage. "He seemed perfectly normal, like you and I," she said decades later from her bed in a nursing home. As for Norma, a bit of envy emerged. "She wasn't that pretty!"

But, unsurprisingly, their sexual failure rankled the couple. They went to see doctors—Murt to his physician, Norma to hers, who after an examination came up with a solution. "He said I could have an operation, but it would cost $150, and Murt said he couldn't afford it," Norma said. That reaction, from a man who was spending money on his wife's clothes, giving her the keys to his new car, and knocking over movie theaters, seems the response of a man who did not want to hear that he was not man enough to make his bride a woman without a doctor's help.

The nature of the operation the doctor recommended, or whether Norma ever had it, is unknown. A guess is that their marital problem stemmed from what Murt's street corner acquaintances would have called Norma's "cherry." Her hymen may have been too thick for natural penetration, an unusual but by no means unheard-of condition. Or else Murt, finally in bed with his new wife, found himself unable to perform. Given the surgical recommendation, it was likely the former. The solution is an incision in the shape of an X or Z. It is a simple outpatient operation, and depending on the patient, recovery can be complete in four weeks.

Or a couple can forgo the scalpel, just keep trying, and hope for the best. While he fumed, Murt planned another crime.

7

I Look Like Who?

IT WAS NEARING MIDNIGHT when the four drunks hailed Clement Molway's cab. Massachusetts had voted to repeal Prohibition months earlier, but federal law wouldn't change until two-thirds of the states agreed to go along. That wouldn't happen until December 5, 1933, so this October evening Molway's boozy passengers announced that they were hunting for a speakeasy located on Essex Street in Chinatown, near the Boston Common.

When he found it, Molway was rewarded for his navigation. Three of his passengers invited the cabbie in for a round of drinks. The fourth, the drunkest of the lot, remained passed out in the backseat. Molway didn't mind, since if the fellow couldn't walk, it meant another fare before his shift ended.

One drink became a few before Molway, twenty-two years old, stepped back out onto the sidewalk and started down the street toward his cab. Curiously, the rear door was open. After another step or two, Molway realized that two strangers were inside rolling the drunk. As Molway yelled and broke into a run, the men looked up, grabbed what they could from the drunk's pockets, and sprinted down the street.

Molway reached his taxi seconds later, only to realize that there was a third bad guy, because a gun was suddenly stuck in his ribs. At that moment a police car came around the corner. Molway thought he was saved until the cops decided to arrest everyone in sight. Molway was fingerprinted and photographed and jailed. He was sprung a day later when the cops finally sorted it all out. His photograph, however, remained glued in the department's mug book.[1]

That was why Molway and a slightly older fellow cabdriver, Louis Berrett, found themselves getting arrested on January 5, 1934. Molway was staying at Berrett's apartment and walked in that night to find five detectives with their .38s drawn and pointed at him. The cops drove them to the Brighton precinct house and to the cabbies' puzzlement proceeded to turn them over to three other cops from Lynn, a mill town on the North Shore.

At 2:00 a.m. they appeared in front of Chief Inspector William H. Kane. He had spent fifteen years as the top detective in one of the toughest towns in New England. As Lynn filled with factories in the nineteenth century, it acquired a reputation for bars, brothels, and corruption. "Lynn, Lynn, the city of sin: if you ain't bad, you can't get in!" went one doggerel.

Surrounded by big, angry cops who refused to say why the cabbies were in custody, the young Molway started to panic. Each cabbie was taken into a separate interrogation room, knocked about a bit, and ordered to account for his whereabouts on the previous Tuesday, January 2. Molway was cooperative. Berrett, twenty-nine, offered only a few specifics, perhaps because he wasn't with his wife and child but out with his girlfriend. He gave Kane an "offhand" account, which Kane didn't like. "This is a serious matter. You had better tell me this hour by hour and be sure you are right," he told Berrett.[2]

A chastened Berrett provided a detailed account of where he had been and what he had done the day after New Year's. Then Kane demanded an account of his movements the next three days, too. When Berrett was finished, Kane had filled five pages with notes, yet still hadn't told Berrett why he and Molway were in custody. So Berrett asked again. When he heard the answer, "I got goosefish all over me."

Berrett and Molway were murder suspects, Kane said, and Berrett suddenly realized what crime he and Molway were suspected of. Stories of a robbery and murder, outrageous and daring, had filled the Massachusetts newspapers all week. "Boldest Hold Up in History of Lynn Police" was the headline in that city's *Daily Evening Item*.

"You don't believe I did it?" Berrett exclaimed. He had not been in Lynn. He had no police record. And he had an alibi.

Kane studied the cabdriver. "We don't know who did it. Someone did it. You might've done it, or he might have done it," Kane said, and pointed at another detective, "or I myself might have done it. But someone did it."

At 8:45 a.m. on Tuesday, two men had walked through the side entrance of the Paramount Theatre in Lynn's downtown. One man carried a .22 caliber pistol, the other a .32 caliber revolver. The weekend had been cold and stormy, and the street outside was covered with fresh snow, but the morning started sunny. For the past three days, crowds had flocked to see the feature film *Prize Fighter and the Lady*, a vehicle for three actual prize fighters, Max Baer, Jack Dempsey, and Primo Carnera, and one actress, Myrna Loy. The theater had opened in 1930, and with 2,300 seats it was the largest on the North Shore.

The two men entered the dimly lit main lobby, where janitor Michael Ford, an Irish immigrant and former IRA soldier, was beginning his work day. "Where's the manager?" the men asked. Ford said he wouldn't arrive for a few hours, and one intruder started toward the office. Ford moved to intervene but found a gun in his back and a voice in his ear saying, "Don't make any noise."[3]

The theater had a large cleaning and maintenance crew, and that morning eight employees were scattered about preparing for the afternoon showing. One of them, Harry Condon, walked up from the basement just as Ford was being led into the office. A gunman grabbed his shirt, but Condon wiggled free and dashed down the hallway toward the glass doors that opened onto Union Street. His flight abruptly ended when the other gunman raised a pistol and shot him in the shoulder. Condon fell and slid across the floor, in pain but not fatally wounded from the .22 caliber bullet. Bleeding, he and the other workers were rounded up and forced into the manager's office. One hostage, who operated the theater's basement boiler, warned that the holiday weekend ticket receipts had already been deposited. There was no big store. "I think you are making a mistake on this thing. There is only a few hundred dollars," he told the men.

There was a more pressing problem, however. Only the assistant manager, Stephen Bresnahan, could open the safe, and he was at the theater's Salem office and not due back for hours. The gunmen were also told that a couple of "state inspectors" usually appeared on the first business day of each month. Instead of scaring the bandits off, this gave them an idea. Chief janitor Leo Donahue was put on the phone to Bresnahan. With a gun in his face, he said the inspectors had arrived, already had questions, and wanted Bresnahan to return immediately. The manager said the trolley would take an hour. The gunman who shot Condon turned to the hostages and warned them not to attempt to escape. "If you fellows get fresh, you'll get what that fellow outside got."

Everyone settled down to wait. One bandit asked a cleaning lady, Hazel Dutch, if a police officer who had worked as a security guard the day before would be in before noon. Dutch realized this was no spur-of-the-moment crime. Then the gunman asked how often the beat cop walked in. "We haven't killed any cops for a long time and we just love to do it. If any cop comes, let him have it. No questions," said the man with the pistol.

Just then a postman pulled open the glass doors, walked into the lobby, and, as he did every day, headed to the office. He was reaching for the doorknob when a man appeared out of the gloom and stretched out his hand. The postman delivered a sheaf of envelopes and walked out. "He didn't seem to be excited or anything, and I never suspected there was a holdup being staged," the mailman recalled. About that time a third gunman arrived, described as skinny, with a shotgun and a black silk handkerchief masking the bottom half of his face. The robbers apparently made no attempt to lock the main doors opening onto Union Street.

So the parade of visitors lasted all morning.

After the mailman departed, C. Fred Sumner walked in. He was an employee who posted theatrical bills around town and transported film negatives to and from the movie house, and the gunmen couldn't turn him away without arousing suspicion. He was sixty-five and cantankerous. An argument began in the lobby. Perhaps Sumner objected to being taken hostage. Inside the office the hostages heard voices, a sharp exchange of words, and the start of what sounded like a fight. Sumner yelled, "Stop it, stop it," and two shots rang out. A voice said, "I got him with a .22." His body fell near a drinking fountain. It was 9:30 a.m.

Again, the shooter was lucky. No one outside heard the gun go off, including two police officers who minutes earlier had watched Sumner park his car.

The gunman now wondered aloud about the assistant manager, Bresnahan. "What's keeping that monkey? If he don't come along pretty soon it will be too bad for you people."[4]

At 10 a.m. a delivery man with a load of fuel oil for the boiler knocked on the side door. He recalled that a strange man cracked open the door and said to go ahead and fill the tank that was out back.

A few minutes later employee Jack Kane, an assistant to Bresnahan, walked in smoking a cigar. He was smiling at some private joke, and one watching gunman declared, "I don't like his looks."

"Why don't you give it to him, then?" said another. Instead, they added him to the crowd staring at the wallpaper.

At 10:15 a.m. Bresnahan finally appeared and was greeted by a revolver. He was led to the safe. A lamp was switched on to illuminate the dial. The numbers were spun, the handle was turned, and everyone saw that the boiler man had told the truth. There was no big score, only $159 in coins and a $20 bill. A gunmen ordered Bresnahan to empty his wallet. He had $4.

At that moment the Union Street doors opened again, and this time William W. Jaeger, an advertising man for the *Lynn Item*, strolled in. As he made his way into the lobby Jaeger was brought up short by an armed man. But the interior was "semi-dark," and Jaeger had just come in out of bright sunlight, and he couldn't make out the man's face. The gunmen rummaged through his wallet and took $12.

The hostages, now numbering eleven, were shoved into a cloakroom and told to count to ten before opening the door. They counted to fifteen. When they emerged, they found Sumner lying in a puddle of blood, his face bloody from a beating and a bullet in his brain.

A half hour later, a passenger in a black sedan zigzagging through traffic on Memorial Drive in Cambridge opened fire on a slower-moving car blocking the way. Passersby got the license plate number. Whoever was inside was mighty angry, all agreed. Later that day Lynn police said that same car had been used by the Paramount Theatre killers. The plates, however, were stolen. The only leads would come from the hostages. They had seen the killers' faces.

The brazen hostage taking, and poor Sumner's murder, demanded action by the state. On Wednesday, Massachusetts governor Joseph B. Ely told reporters that he had ordered state police to "get out and get the bandits." Ely declared there was evidence that the heist was the work of a master criminal also involved in the Fitchburg slaying and that that crime was connected to the Worcester movie theater robbery. Or so it seemed. There had also been a spate of bank robberies in Brookline, Quincy, North Easton, and Turners Falls, a mill town in western Massachusetts. All in all, $100,000 had been stolen since September. Police thought they might all be linked. Ely assured residents, "I am cognizant of the situation and did not like to see our citizens shot down by an organized band of ruthless bandits. I want it stopped. The similarities in the holdups and murders indicate that the same gang is responsible. I plan to institute a concentrated drive to rid the state of these gangsters."[5]

The only hard evidence in police possession was a ballistics test that showed the weapon used to kill C. Fred Sumner in Lynn was the same one used to kill Ernest W. Clark in Fitchburg. Public pressure on police and politicians was intense. On Friday, Lynn mayor J. Fred Manning announced that police would install a radio "call system" in city patrol cars. The Lynn hostages were driven to Boston to browse the largest collection of mug shots in the state. There was much hemming and hawing. The light inside the theater was bad, the hostages said, everyone was scared, and most had had only a brief glimpse of the bandits' faces. One wore a mask. But a consensus grew around one photo in the "rogues gallery": Clement Molway's.

Kane and a team of detectives questioned Molway and Berrett until 5:00 a.m. before breaking for a nap and returning for a 2:00 p.m. lineup. The night's work left the detectives convinced that Molway was involved, but "the inspectors seem less confident that Berrett was one of the bandits than they did when they were brought in," according to the Lynn paper. So the lineup would tell. It was a very intimate affair. Each hostage walked alone down a line of eleven men, looking at each face-to-face. To identify a suspect, the witness reached out and touched the man's shoulder. When it was over, at least six had fingered either Molway or Berrett or both.

The next week the cabbies were indicted for murder, along with a John Doe whom police hoped to arrest soon. A shotgun-wielding line of police surrounded the courthouse for Molway and Berrett's first court appearance. The trial was set for the first week in February. But unhappy murmurs arose from some officers. For starters, the ballistics evidence showed only that the Fitchburg and Lynn crimes were connected. It was not proof that Molway or Berrett was involved in either. Was there evidence that they had traveled to Fitchburg? The investigation had not turned up any guns, cash, or a car. A search for fingerprints inside the theater yielded nothing. Others noted that immediately after the robbery two of the men were described as having "dark complexions," while both Molway and Berrett had the "light complexions" of northern Europeans. Boston police sergeant Arthur Tiernan, who led the team that seized the cabbies at gunpoint, came away believing they knew nothing of the crime.[6]

The truth of the matter was that Molway and Berrett were innocent. The three men inside the theater had been Murt, Irving, and Abe. The shooter was Murt. So far, that was still their secret.

MURT AND ABE READ THE PAPERS with fascination. At the radio store they exchanged whispers. It was a relief that police detectives had fixed on the cabbies, if a bit of bad luck for the two fellows. They were angry that there was no money, though much of their plan had worked. They left no leads for police, and their identities remained a mystery. But $200 wouldn't go far. They needed a big score, Murt and Abe concluded, and they still needed heavier weapons.

8

A Thompson

PREVIOUS ATTEMPTS TO EXPAND their arsenal had ended in failure, and not only in Fitchburg.

Murt's first scheme some months earlier went awry outside the National Guard armory of the 101st Engineer Battalion, a four-story brick building conveniently located just down the block from the main entrance to MIT.

August 23, 1933, was an unusually cool summer day that topped out at only 68 degrees. Late that evening Captain Frank E. Lodge and Lester Mason, the civilian armorer in charge of weapons maintenance, locked the doors at the end of their workday and walked toward their parked cars. They were likely discussing the uncertain weather, as a tropical storm was working its way up the Atlantic coast, and so failed to notice the automobile tailing them until it pulled alongside and they were staring at two drawn guns. They were forced into the backseat and ordered to put their hats over their faces and keep their heads down. They were surprised again when, after seizing the armory keys, the kidnappers didn't tie them up and raid the gun lockers but instead started driving aimlessly around Cambridge.

In the front seat the two kidnappers debated how to best get in and out of the armory with the battalion's dozen machine guns and ten thousand rounds of ammunition. As Lodge and Mason listened intently from the backseat, they realized the two young men knew the layout of the armory, where the arsenal was, what it contained, and that Mason always carried keys to the weapons lockers.[1]

Thirty minutes later the car and its prisoners returned to the armory on Massachusetts Avenue. Inside in the front Murt and Irv remained uncertain how to proceed. As the car idled, they suddenly worried aloud that the unattended cars in the armory's employee parking lot would attract police. Lodge was ordered to get out and move his automobile out of sight. He also was warned not to make a break for it, as the kidnappers had him covered with their pistols.

That did not dissuade the captain. In a demonstration of bravery spoiled only by his disregard for Mason's safety, Lodge sprinted away after he spotted a police officer on foot patrol. Murt and Irv sped off with the armorer. Mason had to have been relieved when they pushed him out, unharmed, a few blocks away. Police found the car abandoned nearby on Portland Street. It was, of course, stolen and offered little in the way of clues. All Lodge and Mason could say was that the kidnappers were young and wore trench coats.

The incident made the front pages of the Boston newspapers, and the alarm it raised grew the next day when it appeared that the same two perpetrators, who were indeed Murt and Irv, turned up in Quincy and used the same technique to try to rob a National Guard armory in that town. Once again they surprised two men, Captain Robert Knapp and his brother, Corporal Ralph Knapp, as they sat in a parked car chatting after work. But the Knapps were fast talkers. They convinced the Millen brothers that there were no machine guns inside, only artillery munitions, so the bandits tossed those armory keys back to the Knapps with a warning they would be "burned up" if either contacted the police. One of them, probably Murt, added that the bandits were planning to "get" a fellow named Lodge for talking to the Cambridge police.[2] The Knapps ignored the threat, but once again police didn't get much of a description of the robbers. The Knapp brothers could only say that the two armed men had "dark complexions," by which was meant they looked southern or eastern European.

By the following weekend Murt was at Nantasket Beach, and his interest in robbery was supplanted by his interest in Norma.

NOW IN JANUARY 1934, the need for a weapon more fearsome than a .22 caliber was urgent. Going after real money meant going after a bank, and that required weapons to intimidate employees and repel pursuing police. They could try to rob another armory or locate a source in the underworld. A third solution was found in a newspaper story. The annual auto show in Boston's Mechanics Hall was opening that month, and among the exhibitors were the state police, who planned to demonstrate that law enforcement was up-to-date and ready to face any threat.

Twenty-three vehicle manufacturers set up displays in the 110,000-square-foot exhibition hall along Huntington Avenue. Auto industry sales had dropped every year since 1929, and Detroit was hoping that 1934 would mark a turnaround. Enthusiasm was high in the wake of the large crowds at the New York City auto show earlier that month.

The show opened on January 20, and sure enough, the first day's attendance broke records. The vehicles were laid out in elaborate floor displays, the centerpiece of which was a multistory Chinese pagoda surrounded by luxury automobiles. One vehicle present was the innovative Chrysler Airflow, the first mass-produced car developed with wind tunnel testing for aerodynamic efficiency.

Abe, Murt, Irv, and Norma took in the sights during a scouting trip. Norma had come along, not as a potential participant in the robbery but in the hope of having a serendipitous conversation with her father. Norman Brighton managed the Chevrolet dealership in Medford, northwest of Boston, and she hoped to find him working the company display. He wasn't.

The state police exhibit was on the basement floor and included an impressive collection of weapons: four riot guns, two belts of shotgun shells, tear gas grenades, tear gas launchers, various handguns, and sophisticated shortwave radio gear inside a mobile command center. There was also a Thompson submachine gun with a hundred-round circular magazine.[3]

On the afternoon of January 26, Abe bought a ticket to the show and made his way into the basement. There he unlocked a window and loosened screws fastening an exterior screen. Waiting upstairs were Murt and Irv. They left the hall, dined out nearby, then returned to the Brinsley Street garage, where they climbed into the Packard, and drove back downtown. It was after 1 a.m. At the Mechanics Building the trio watched the cleaning crew depart and then parked the Packard on a loading ramp at the rear of the building. Irv removed the screen, climbed through the window, and opened a door for Murt and Abe.

At 1:50 a.m. watchmen Lucien Kerkian and George Mason were in the basement on their rounds when three armed men stepped out of the dark. The hapless guards were ordered to face the side of a truck. One robber held them at gunpoint while the other two bandits pulled apart the state police exhibit. They found four shotguns in the radio truck. The remaining weapons were locked in a wooden case. This proved no impediment. Kerkian and Mason were struck by the robbers' unhurried calm as they removed the guns and a police radio set. Then the watchmen were tied up. The bandits departed quietly by the rear entrance.

Murt, Irv, and Abe drove the weapon-laden car back to Dorchester. Most of the armaments were stored in the Brinsley garage, but the Thompson submachine gun was taken to Lawrence Avenue and hidden under Irv's bed.[4]

That afternoon the *Boston Globe* put out an extra edition with "EXTRA!" emblazoned across the page. "Trio Raid Police Arms Exhibit at Auto Show," read the headline. "Hold Up Watchmen and Escape with Shotguns, Bombs and Revolvers Owned by State," read the subhead. One story reported, "The auto show holdup and robbery was one of the most carefully planned crime[s] with which police have had to cope in years."

Embarrassment only grew when state police, checking the serial numbers of the stolen shotguns, discovered that eight riot guns were also missing from a storeroom in the Massachusetts State House. No one thought that the Mechanics Hall crime and the missing State House shotguns were linked. Nevertheless, the robbery was only the latest in a string of similar crimes that police feared was the work of organized criminals or radical political organizations. There had been the two unsuccessful attempts to rob Guard armories, along with one successful effort in Woburn, where thieves made off with three Browning automatic rifles, the weapon favored by the Bonnie and Clyde gang. Early in January a gun shop in downtown Boston was robbed of fifteen handguns, and police intelligence sources reported that competing criminals in Boston were about to start a gangland war.

"Notorious Bandits Ready to Wipe Each Other Out," blared a headline in the *Boston Post.*

On January 29 Bostonians awoke to learn that city police had thrown a cordon of officers around the department's headquarters building. Inside, an officer guarding the third floor weapons storeroom was ordered to shoot to kill any intruder. A day or two later the arms and ammunition were moved to a vault on the first floor. "That any police department anywhere would have to take such precautionary measures against gangland is something, officials admitted last night, of which no policeman anywhere perhaps ever dreamed or any fiction writer ever imagined," said the *Boston Post.*

The near panic followed years of tumult across the country. In March 1933, Roosevelt had ordered the nation's financial system shut down for a week; he euphemistically termed the shutdown a "banking holiday," but everyone knew it was really a desperate effort to avoid a complete collapse of the financial system. Beggars and hobo camps were a common sight in every big city. Then there was the seemingly endless success of bank robberies and killings. Two groups of criminals emerged. One had business as their primary interest, be it bootlegging, gambling, or prostitution. They were in it for the long term. The second group made no pretense of providing a "service." They were robbers and killers. This small number had an outsized influence on American popular culture. The names are as well known today as Roosevelt's: John Dillinger, "Pretty Boy" Floyd, "Baby Face" Nelson, Bonnie and Clyde, and "Machine Gun" Kelly.

They operated in the same Midwestern states where armed bank robbery had all but been invented amid the upheaval following the Civil War. The first daytime bank robbery in American history took place in Liberty, Missouri, on February 13, 1866, when bandits pistol-whipped a cashier and made off with $60,000 in bonds, paper currency, and gold and silver coins. During their escape they killed an innocent passerby. Frank and Jesse James might have been among the bandits.

That crime wave lasted through the 1870s. Now the same territory was the stalking ground of bandits thriving on the availability of motorcars, highways, and automatic weapons. Some also had the sympathy of ordinary citizens who watched, helplessly and angrily, as they lost their homes and farms to foreclosure.

In September 1930, six bandits stole $2.8 million in cash and negotiable securities from the Lincoln National Bank in Nebraska in what may still be the nation's largest bank robbery ever. Soon thereafter five armed robbers, two carrying Thompson submachine guns, raided a Chicago bank and made off with $40,000 while a fifth member waited outside in a getaway car.

Bank robbers struck cities where the crime had previously been unheard of. In Rochester, New York, a bank lost $3,000 in 1932. Fortunately, the bandits overlooked $20,000 sitting in nearby cash drawers. On the way out of town, they "evaded a network of every available city and county radio-equipped police automobile," the Associated Press reported.

Some bank robbers said that economic deprivation drove them to pick up a gun. In July, Bloomington, Indiana, experienced its first bank robbery when a man made off with $574. A physiology professor from a local college trailed the bandit to a gas station twenty miles out of town. The two ended up in conversation, and soon Roller Spice, a young farmer, agreed to surrender. Spice told officers he had robbed the bank to halt a foreclosure on his father's farm, the Associated Press reported.

In McLeod, Oklahoma, a nineteen-year-old man made off with a mere $500 from a local bank but garnered national publicity when he used the cash to charter an airplane and fly to Nashville, Tennessee, not to escape but to see his sick mother. Or so he told police.[5]

At the end of that year the leading bank insurance company, the National Bureau of Casualty and Surety Underwriters, confirmed that the bank robbery business was booming. In 1922 its insurance losses amounted to 16 percent of the annual premiums paid by its insured banks, a figure that in 1932 mushroomed to 104 percent. The underwriters were losing money, and rates were raised. Robberies were most common in Midwestern and Southern states, including Florida and Georgia. Minnesota was another contender, and bankers in Illinois might have wondered why they, too, were not on the list.

Bank robberies in Massachusetts remained rare. Then came the crimes cited by Governor Ely. On October 2, 1933, the Brookline Trust Company lost $35,000 to bandits. On November 10, armed men took $20,000 from the First National Bank in Easton, twenty-five miles south of Boston. On December 4, another $20,000 was taken from the Wollaston branch of the Quincy Trust Company, and on December 13, robbers hit a bank in Turners Falls, on the western side of the state just south of the Vermont border. They made off with $23,000. Also in December, robbers staged a street corner holdup and took $13,518 from the treasurer of the Tri-Mount Clothing Company in Roxbury.

Murt, Abe, and Irv decided it was time they got their share.

Their initial plan was ambitious: three holdups, in quick succession, on a single day in the affluent Boston suburb of Wellesley. They figured police would converge on the first bank robbery, giving them a clear field for the next two bank heists. But during a scouting trip Murt decided the Needham Trust Company was a more convenient target. It was a small brick bank on Great Plain Avenue, the main east-west thoroughfare through town. Perhaps Murt knew it from driving to and from Natick, as he and Norma once stopped at a corner drugstore there for hot chocolate. Needham was not far off the Worcester-Boston highway, which would provide a fast route in and out of town. And it was home to large textile mills, which meant cash payrolls at the end of each week.

They started to prepare in earnest.

Murt found that the eleven-pound machine gun was remarkably comfortable to carry for short periods of time. He could nestle it in the crook of an arm, and at only 3 feet long it was easy to swing onto a target. The hundred-round drum magazine did make keeping the weapon aimed an effort, particularly on full automatic. Fortunately, the .45 caliber rounds produced less kick than a rifle cartridge.

Developed during World War I under the auspices of General John T. Thompson, the weapon was the army's first effective submachine gun. Thompson wanted a quick-firing gun that a single soldier could use to clear a trench of enemy troops. It wasn't very accurate over 50 yards, but then that wasn't the point. Murt called it his "typewriter," a nickname based on its "clackety" sound and coined by Prohibition gangsters.

Abe had trained on the Thompson, but it was Murt who took effective possession of the gun. Somewhere, possibly in the woods outside Boston near the town of Weston, he may have practiced assembling and disassembling and shooting the weapon. It was a finely made piece of machinery. The stock was furniture-grade hardwood, and as with all early-model Thompsons the internal mechanism was machined out of the best steel. Different models had slightly different characteristics. Murt's was a Thompson model 1928, which fired up to six hundred rounds a minute, meaning the magazine could be zipped clean of rounds in ten seconds.

Events would show that he was able to fire it single-handedly—a skill police investigators found impressive, particularly during a long burst of fire when Murt had to fight the gun's recoil.

The gang constructed a new, false license plate for the Packard, but curiously decided to use the very vehicle already seen by witnesses in Worcester and Fitchburg. They also installed the police radio lifted from Mechanics Hall. No radio was ever installed by the Packard dealer, so Abe did the electrical work from scratch. He did it too well.

In the 1930s automobile radio reception was plagued by buzzy static generated by electromagnetic pulses produced by the ignition system and spark plug wires. The solution was a "suppressor," a resistor that, as its name implies, reduced noise from the high-voltage signals. One model was introduced in 1932 by the Arthur H. Lynch company of New York City. It was a cylindrical device attached to the car's distributor. Abe had purchased a supply during a trip to New York City, and Faber became one of the few shops in greater Boston, if not the only shop, to sell the "Lynch suppressor."[6]

The radio also needed a power supply. It was easily connected to the auto's electrical system, but the stock battery and charging system were unable to handle the added demand. So a custom-made, high-capacity lead-acid battery was bolted into the battery box in the passenger compartment.

While the rechargeable battery dated to 1859, in 1934 the technology was still limited by relatively crude materials and rudimentary electrical systems.

The basic science, however, remains the same to this day. Thin lead plates are submerged in diluted sulfuric acid, called the electrolyte. Inserted between each plate is a sheet of nonconductive material known as a "separator." When the car is started or the radio is turned on, power is generated as ions move through the acid from the negative plates to the positive plates. The reverse occurs when the battery is charged. The charge and recharge cycle can be repeated, but eventually the components deteriorate, and a battery can short-circuit and cease holding a charge.

The "separator" slows that down. Batteries are designed so the negative and positive plates cannot touch. However, debris created during the charge and discharge cycle can create a "bridge" between adjoining plates that causes a short circuit, much like what happens if a mechanic with a wrench simultaneously touches the negative and positive terminals. The separator plate allows the ions in the electrolyte to flow back and forth but blocks a direct flow of "live" current between the differently charged plates.[7] In the 1930s, separators were often sheets of hard rubber, sometimes perforated and sometimes woven through with cotton threads.

Others were made of thin panels of wood.

There was also no such thing as a "maintenance-free" automobile battery. Batteries were expensive, and neither durable nor reliable. When, rather than if, a battery failed to hold a charge, its owner took it in for repair at a nearby battery shop. In 1934 there were dozens in and around Boston. One of them was at 37 Blue Hill Avenue in Roxbury, and on January 24, 1934, Irving Millen was one of its customers.

He arrived in a Chevy and out of the backseat lifted an unusually large, three-cell lead-acid storage battery. It was failing to hold a charge, Irv told shop owner Alfred LeVierge. He placed the 60-pound battery on a test stand and ran a current through the positive and negative terminals. One cell was indeed shorted out. LeVierge opened up the battery, pulled out the damaged cell, and showed Irving that the lead plates were intact but the rubber separators were damaged and had to be replaced. Irv told him to do the work.

On January 27 Irv returned with Murt. LeVierge had removed the damaged separators, made by the Prestolite company, and replaced them with larger separators called a "J" type. They were made of wood, not rubber, and stood about a half inch taller than the stock Prestolite parts.[8] The brothers paid the bill. They may have noticed that their name on the paperwork was misspelled as "Miller." Murt and Irv returned to the Brinsley Street garage and bolted the battery into the Packard.

By now the gang had decided a Friday morning robbery would be best, as extra cash would be on hand for payday. At 9:21 a.m. every weekday, a commuter train was scheduled to stop at the Needham railroad station immediately to the bank's right. The train, usually a half dozen cars or so, remained there for only a matter of minutes, but during that time the motionless rail cars would serve three purposes: the tracks ran across Great Plain Avenue and the final few cars of the motionless train always stretched into the roadway, blocking the view of the center of town; road traffic would be halted by the crossing gates; and any patrol car racing up from the police station would have to make a roundabout detour. The train lent an added measure of safety.

On January 31, 1934, Irv and Abe drove to Needham along the new Worcester highway, reconnoitering the route and pausing in front of the bank. Abe may have gone inside. Two days later, early on February 2, 1934, Murt and Norma rose at about seven o'clock and drove from Boylston Street to Lawrence Avenue. Norma stepped out to spend the day with Idalyn. Inside, Irv wrapped the Thompson in a blanket and carried it downstairs. Abe was waiting out front.

Snow had fallen the night before and was coating the highways. The morning papers said the price of milk would drop a penny to 10 cents a quart, while in Portland, Maine, a gang was threatening to kidnap the mayor's children. As Murt, Irv, and Abe climbed into the Packard, the temperature hovered just below freezing. They were dressed in overcoats, and Abe readied his mask. Needham was about thirty minutes away. The town had a population of eleven thousand and a police force of twelve officers.

9

The Snow Turned Red

CHARLES STEVENS WAS KNEELING on the wet street, changing a tire on his family's produce truck, when the Packard slowly drove by, heading west on Great Plain Avenue. Stevens paused and stared because the Packard was a rich person's car and so out of place among Needham's Chevys and Fords. Years later, Stevens recalled that as he turned his head a fellow in the car tossed off a "smart aleck" comment about the poor sap toiling in the slush.[1] The fellow was probably Murt.

The Packard crossed the single railroad track that sliced through the west side of town and stopped in front of the redbrick Needham Trust Company. Stevens heard the 9:21 a.m. commuter train rumbling toward the station, and the railroad crossing gates started to descend across the avenue. The engine and passenger cars of the train appeared and screeched to a halt next to the bank. There was little majesty to the one-story brick building. The flanking columns at the entryway were of poured concrete rather than stone. There were two windows in the front and a row of windows on the right side looking out over the railroad tracks, the station, and the rail cars now blocking the street.[2]

Inside, a lone teller glanced up to see a skinny stranger with a pencil-thin mustache stick his head through the doorway and then walk into the vestibule. He stood for thirty seconds scanning the empty lobby and then ducked back outside. After two years behind the cash drawers, John D. Riordan knew all the regular account holders. The bank had been open since 8 a.m. but had seen few customers, so Riordan was assembling stacks of cash for the Friday payrolls. It probably was not a job he had planned to have at age thirty, though by now he had become adept at making small talk with shopkeepers and housewives. A graduate of Boston Latin and Harvard College, and a member of the Crimson's football team, Riordan had no doubt hoped to be working in a downtown Boston financial house. But he graduated just two years before the crash of 1929, and in the new decade banking wasn't a growth industry.

Abe was pleased that there were no customers inside. He signaled Murt and Irv, who were waiting in the car, and then pulled his mask up over his nose. Behind him Irv bounded up the steps with two of the stolen MIT target pistols jammed into his pockets. Abe toted a sawed-off shotgun. At the car, Murt slipped out from behind the wheel carrying the Thompson. It was only a few steps off the street and into the lobby. They were not seen, except by a taxi driver who at that moment pulled up at the crossing gates, glanced to the side, and stared in disbelief at the three armed men. Stevens, his view blocked by the train, had turned back to work on his truck.

Stenographer Elizabeth Kimball was the first person inside to spot a weapon. The twenty-four-year-old was holding a pen and notebook to take dictation from the youthful-looking bank treasurer, Arnold Mackintosh. She was seated next to his desk in the central lobby and had a prime view of the small interior. On this cold morning, in out-of-the way Needham, it seemed unimaginable to look up and see a man in a mask waving a shotgun in the air. Behind him appeared a second man, his face undisguised, who carried a dangerous-looking weapon of the sort she had seen only on Saturday afternoons in the newsreels. "Stick your hands up!" the fellow with the shotgun shouted. A third man, shorter, thicker, holding a pistol, added incongruously, "No fooling!"

The masked man turned to Mackintosh. "If anything goes wrong here and you're part of it, you're going to die."

The bank was laid out around the lobby. Immediately to the right of the entrance was a conference room that doubled as an office for the assistant treasurer, Ernest Keith. One of its windows faced the single track separating the bank from the train station, and once the train departed for Needham Heights it would offer a clear view of where Great Plain Avenue intersected Chestnut Street in the center of town. On the left side of the lobby, where Riordan stood, were the teller cages, and at the end of the room was the vault, where an elderly, mustachioed man with the grandiose title of vault guard sat unarmed. In the rear, in her own office with a glass panel door, was Ada Mary Gaykan, the bookkeeper. In just a moment she would throw all the bandits' plans awry.

The three spread out. Mackintosh obeyed Abe's command and remained at his desk, in his chair, with his hands in the air. But despite the three ominous men within arm's reach, Kimball sprang out of her chair and rushed across the lobby into the conference room. To the young assistant treasurer she cried, "There's a man out there with a gun!" Murt followed in her footsteps. He walked in, waved the muzzle of the Thompson, and ordered the couple to stand facing the front wall. Murt pushed Keith's desk away from the window, giving himself unimpeded access to the glass panes. For the moment at least, the crossing barriers and train blocked his view into the center of town, as it would block any police rushing from the police station only two blocks away on Chestnut Street.

In the lobby Abe and Irv moved toward the teller cages. The immediate impediment was Walter Bartholomew, the seventy-five-year-old vault guard in a chair behind the iron grillwork. Gray-haired, Bartholomew had begun his work life in the 1880s as a clerk in a New Hampshire drugstore. His Needham bank job largely involved clicking open the metal gate as the tellers and clerks walked back and forth from the lobby to the rear offices and the vault. The pay was minimal, but he was inside and warm. Old-age insurance, later known as Social Security, remained a dream of the new president.

Now Bartholomew was being shouted at by two armed and nervous men. Irv, the one with curly hair, yelled, "Throw up your hands." Abe, with a ferocity he had not learned at MIT but perhaps had been taught in ROTC, spat out, "Open the door, you son of a bitch." The obscenity jolted Bartholomew. He obeyed, and Abe and Irv got access to Riordan and the teller cages.

The bank was only 29 feet deep from foyer to vault and 38 feet wide, meaning that everyone was almost within arm's length of someone else. Except for Mary Gaykan, who sat in a rear office minding the books. Neither Murt nor Abe, and certainly not Irv, thought to scout the back rooms. Gaykan suddenly heard the commotion punctuated by Abe's shouted obscenity. She jumped to her feet and peered into the lobby, where she saw Irv, pistol in hand, heading toward the cash drawers.

A decade earlier, when she was twenty-six and still known as Ada Mary Morton, Gaykan journeyed from Needham to Brattleboro, Vermont, and on a Tuesday, after the Labor Day weekend, married Martin Edward Gaykan, an Armenian immigrant and furniture store salesman from Boston. He was thirty-one, and his native language was Turkish. A justice of the peace officiated. They were both old for a first marriage. Mary Morton's romance with the foreigner suggests she was a woman unfazed by social convention. It showed an independent streak that served her well, because she did what no one else had had the willingness, or opportunity, to do. Gaykan stooped over and punched the alarm button. Then she crawled under her desk.[3]

The gong was inside a square iron box bolted to the bank's brick exterior. When it sounded, storekeepers, workmen, and shoppers within earshot instinctively glanced up but evinced little other reaction. The bank had a history of false alarms, and policeman Forbes McLeod, two blocks away, was neither worried nor startled. He had started his day on the west side of town on crosswalk duty for children on their way to elementary school. He walked two miles to the town square and arrived about 9 a.m. The red light on the police call box was unlit, so there was no need to telephone the station. Around him businesses were opening, and no doubt he was trading good mornings with the shop owners when the alarm clanged. McLeod started down the street. He passed Model's Men's Store and the Mobilgas service station with the red Flying Horse logo. He was walking, not running. He moved toward the passenger awning parallel to the train tracks. By now the train was pulling out of the station, though the crossing gates remained down. Charles Stevens was still fixing the tire but paused to speak to the policeman, telling him about three well-dressed strangers inside the Trust Company. McLeod listened to him but did not draw his .38 revolver, tucked inside his heavy winter greatcoat but accessible through the right pocket.

Clearly, he did not hear the shotgun blast that exploded across the bank lobby when Abe, startled by the alarm or annoyed by a delay, pulled the trigger on his weapon. For a split second the bank was filled with a 150-decibel sound wave that reverberated off the stone, steel, and plaster interior. Lead buckshot pockmarked the rear wall and dented the metal trim around the vault. A ricochet smashed a bone in Bartholomew's upraised hand. Blood spurted out. Smoke floated toward the ceiling. Abe swung the weapon toward Mackintosh—did he see some untoward movement?—and shouted, "Face the wall!" At the teller cage, Irv jumped at the Harvard grad. "The money!" he demanded. Riordan pointed to a metal cash box on the floor. Irv picked it up and passed it to Abe, who flipped open the lid and saw a row of empty cash drawers. He slung the metal box back at Riordan. "If he doesn't give it to you, slug him," he said to Irv.

The husky Ivy League athlete, his fingers already dirty from sorting bills that morning, faced the thin, gangly MIT graduate. Irv was only inches away, pointing a handgun at Riordan's midsection. Years later Riordan would become chairman of a Boston bank, marry, and raise three daughters, and now he did the smart thing. He reached down and produced a second metal box. Inside was $4,000. Irv passed it to Abe.

They were happier, but both knew that there was more cash on hand to meet Friday's payrolls. So again Abe confronted Riordan. The "big money," he demanded, or else that jumpy fellow with the pistol will "plug you."

To demonstrate the risk, two rounds erupted from Irv's .22 Woodsman. The bullets whipped past Riordan's midsection. With that, Riordan pointed to the unoccupied, locked teller cage next to him and said it contained bundled cash. Irv broke a small glass pane in the cage door but was unable to force the latch. He pointed his handgun at Riordan, who got the idea. With his weight bending the cage's frame, Irv pried loose a metal stanchion and slipped the latch free. Inside was a cash box with $10,000. Riordan lifted it up and handed it to Irv.

In the meantime McLeod had walked west along Great Plain Avenue and emerged into view as the last train car departed from the station. A couple striding toward him passed by the bank entrance and then spoke a few words to the patrolman. He reached for his holster. He was only a few steps away from the tracks when Murt spotted him, perhaps 25 feet from where he stood in the bank window overlooking the train station and center of town.

"Here comes a cop!" Murt yelled. Voices replied from the lobby. "Get him," said one voice. "Spot him off," ordered Abe.

McLeod headed across the steel rails, angling toward the bank entrance. The crossing arms were still down, forcing McLeod to duck underneath. He was just returning to his full height, less than a dozen steps from the bank, when Murt pulled the trigger.

The Thompson's firing pin detonated the first cartridge. Gas from the exploding powder propelled the lead bullet out of the barrel and kicked the bolt backward, extracting the empty shell. A powerful spring flung the bolt forward, and the machined steel picked up a fresh round from the magazine and slid it into the chamber. The weapon kicked in Murt's hands as each round exploded out. The small office was electric with smoke and shards of glass. Murt was shooting right through the window. Six bullets punched holes in two lower panes.

Three bullets slammed into McLeod. Two struck the right side of his abdomen and passed through the width of his body. One tore up the flesh just under his skin but hit no vital organs. The second was dreadfully effective. It mangled his pancreas, intestines, and kidneys, and as it exited McLeod's left side, his abdominal cavity filled with blood. The punch of the bullet to his midsection brought his shoulders down, and the third bullet flew into his back, just above his right shoulder blade. It traversed the upper lung, plunged deeper into the center of his body, and he collapsed.[4] It had all taken perhaps a second.

From his seat in a municipal truck stopped at the railroad crossing, Harold Vincent didn't understand what he was seeing. The town employee had arrived at the crossing just as the bank alarm went off and had glanced toward the station when McLeod fell onto the tracks, writhing in pain, his knees pulled up to his chest in an involuntary reaction to the ripping anguish in his midsection. Vincent jumped from the cab and as he tried to lift McLeod off the ground saw blood drip from McLeod's winter greatcoat. At 230 pounds McLeod was too heavy. Vincent looked around and called out for help.

Murt backed away from the window. He saw assistant treasurer Keith lean over to look out and snapped, "Get back there." He turned to Kimball and said, "You too or I'll drill you both." The bittersweet smell of gunpowder drifted around Murt as he left them staring at the wall and darted into the lobby.

Bartholomew's wounded hand was dripping blood as Abe and Irv stuffed the cash into a steel box. Cradling the Thompson in one arm, Murt motioned Mackintosh out of his chair and with his free hand pushed the treasurer toward the door. Abe, the ROTC lieutenant, glanced at Riordan and turned to Irv. "Get the big guy and take him along," he said. The two bank employees were hustled toward the door. Murt stepped quickly out of the bank to the driver's door as the scared and confused Riordan and Mackintosh were pushed down the steps. Irv ordered Riordan into the backseat but then changed his mind. "There is no room for you here. Stand on the board."

In the biting cold Riordan's bare hands grabbed the metal frame of the open rear window, and he wedged his feet on the 6-inch-wide running board beneath the door. In front of him Mackintosh stepped up and grabbed the front windshield.

Abe and Irv scrambled into the rear seat. Between them lay the cash box. Before Murt climbed into the car, he turned toward the railroad tracks and let loose a burst from the Thompson, shattering shop windows along Great Plain Avenue. Then he laid the Thompson on the empty front seat, settled himself behind the wheel, and pulled away.

Behind them a small crowd gathered around McLeod's wounded body. As Murt steered the Packard into a left turn off Great Plain Avenue, Riordan spotted a high, thick mound of snow cleared from the sidewalk. He tensed his muscles and leaped off the running board, hit the ground, and rolled under a car. Behind him he heard a shot from Irv's .22 caliber pistol, but the teller rose unhurt. The .22 slug buried itself in a bunch of bananas waiting to be unloaded from a grocery truck. Murt completed his turn and kept the Packard moving over the slippery road at a surprisingly sedate 25 mph, much to Faber's worry. They passed large lots and single-family homes as Murt took two more lefts, headed north onto Chestnut Street and toward the highway to Boston. The Packard would have seemed just another black auto picking its way down a slippery street if not for Mackintosh perched on the running board, still wearing only his suit jacket, hanging on in fear. But he nevertheless was astonished at the route they were taking. "You damn fools! You're going right through the center of town," he said.

A voice from inside the car told him it was none of his business. "We're running this. You just hang on."

Murt's route indeed took them past every official building in town. The hospital, the police station, and the fire station on Chestnut Street, and then through the town square and past the town hall. Word had spread by now, and soon the fire chief and a police lieutenant scrambled into a car and attempted to overtake the Packard. In a few minutes Murt was piloting the car past the sprawling new two-story high school that was Needham's pride, the almost new library opposite it, three churches, and on into Needham Heights.

The neighborhood is indeed a bit higher than the rest of the town. A fire substation was built there in the nineteenth century, specifically to take advantage of the elevation. The bronze and steel pumpers were drawn by a team of horses, so placing the station where the animals could gallop downhill toward a fire was common sense.

Now the telephone rang on the second floor of the wood frame firehouse, and Lieutenant Frank Salamone picked up the receiver. Outside, a lone firefighter, Timothy Coughlin, had paused while shoveling snow to talk politics with the police department's Needham Heights beat officer, Frank Haddock. Townspeople described him as a "cop's cop." Like McLeod he was a crack shot. Indeed, the night before both men had received awards for their marksmanship. Once Haddock had commandeered a car to chase down a fugitive and while steering leaned out, aimed carefully, and shot out a rear tire on the fleeing vehicle. Another time he responded to a brawl at a Heights dance hall, and when he stepped into the doorway, tapping his night stick against the palm of his hand, the fight immediately ceased.

Their conversation was interrupted when Salamone burst out the door. The bank was robbed, he yelled. Shots were fired, McLeod was hit, hostages were taken, and the bandits were headed right their way. He spoke for no more than a few seconds, because a car with a man on the running board suddenly came plowing down the street.

At the same moment Murt saw Haddock. From his spot on the running board, Mackintosh heard Murt say, "There is a cop ahead." Haddock started walking toward the road, realizing who must be in the dark car. He clawed at his revolver, but Mackintosh waved his hand, signaling to Haddock not to fire at him. "I thought Haddock was going to shoot and I would get it. I didn't think I would get out of Needham Heights alive."

Murt absorbed the scene from behind the wheel. Cold air was rushing past him, and even as he fought to keep the Packard on the road, he took his right hand off the wheel, picked up the Thompson, stuck the muzzle out the front window—the windshield opened from the bottom—and fired a long burst. Despite the moving car, the running man, and the slippery road, Murt's bullets hit Haddock and Coughlin.[5]

Coughlin first heard the chatter of gunshots and saw Haddock collapse. He started to move toward the fallen man when he felt a blow to his leg and then a kick in the stomach. He ran 10 feet and collapsed. Later, residents counted twenty-two bullet strikes in a brick wall facing the fire station. The

Packard disappeared toward Boston, and Salamone stared at the two men on the ground before him. Blood turned the snow red as Coughlin writhed in pain. Haddock was hit in his right thigh, but a bullet had also struck his lower left abdomen and exited through his back. Blood was pouring out. At home he had four children.

A half mile farther down the road, the Packard slowed and Mackintosh jumped off.

Then the black car disappeared.

PART II

10

Dragnet

THURSDAY HAD BEEN A GOOD DAY for Needham police chief Arthur P. Bliss. In the morning he had motored into Brookline for the annual meeting of the Massachusetts Police Chiefs Association, where he was elected vice president. It was recognition for his work organizing a teletype and radio system linking thirty-nine police departments in and around greater Boston.[1] The radio component was still a year or two in the future—the Depression was again forcing municipal budget cuts—but the teletype system was largely in place. For the first time, one police station could transmit a printed message to every other virtually instantaneously.

The *Boston Globe* took pains to explain why that would be useful in the case of, say, a murder: "The registration number of the murderer's automobile, descriptions of the car, the men, or their identifications can at a moment's notice be sent to all the departments." The teletype had a typewriter-like keyboard where an operator punched out the message sent over dedicated telephone lines. The system was faster and more accurate than making multiple telephone calls and far more reliable than two-way radio. And there was a typed record.

Bliss had a machine in his office, but the operating cost was pricey at $50 a month. As finances worsened town selectmen declared it expendable. It was another blow to the chief, whose salary had been cut 15 percent a year earlier.[2] Bliss resorted to telephoning police in nearby Dedham, who were kind enough to tap out Needham's alerts and bulletins. But on this Thursday, Bliss could happily tell his fellow chiefs that the selectmen had been shamed into restoring the teletype link by Norfolk County district attorney Edmund Dewing, who denounced the cut as a false economy. In a few days, or perhaps next week, the teletype would be back up and running.

It could not be too soon. The Mechanics Hall theft monopolized the chief's meeting. The association president, Chief Edward J. Tighe of Revere, called on each police department to help recover the guns before they were used in a crime, but he nonetheless dismissed a widely held belief that the thieves were part of a sophisticated gang. No, Tighe declared, the Mechanics Hall theft was the work of "punks." He wagered that they did not even know how to use the weapons.[3]

The next morning Bliss discovered that Tighe was at most only half right.

The first telephone call came into the Needham station at 9:34 a.m. Police and firefighters occupied the same brick building on Chestnut Street, next to Glover Memorial Hospital. The town's small fleet of vehicles included an ambulance, toward which Bliss now dashed, running out the door and sliding his way into the driver's seat. He frantically worked the choke and throttle until the vehicle started and spun out of the lot. Bliss turned right and had barely traveled a block when he saw a truck headed toward him, filled with men waving their arms. It flashed by, and Bliss turned around and followed it to the hospital entrance. He arrived in time to help lift McLeod's still-living body out of the truck. The two had served together for a decade.[4]

In the hospital, nurse Helen Clarke cut away the wounded officer's clothes. A bloody .45 caliber bullet fell out of his coat onto the floor, and she bent to pick it up. Outside on Chestnut Street the black Packard, with Macintosh still on the running board, motored by, heading north.

McLeod murmured a few words: "I didn't see anyone before they got me."

Bliss later elaborated: "He said he didn't know what had happened. He didn't know where the shots had come from."[5]

Bliss had no time to ask anything more because the police department's small switchboard was suddenly flooded with a new round of calls, this time from Needham Heights. The fire department's telephone was ringing, too. Callers reported gunshots in the Heights. Dozens of rounds, in fact. Bullets had cut down two uniformed men and pockmarked a brick wall facing the road.

Bliss was now inside an inconceivable nightmare—it had been a quiet, snowy morning just minutes earlier. He climbed back into the ambulance, and this time he drove a few blocks before another band of frantic men, in a car coming the other way, waved him back. Again, Bliss turned around to the hospital. He ran inside just as Haddock was laid out and the nurses began cutting away his clothes. A moment later another car turned into the hospital's entrance, this one carrying Coughlin.

For the time being all three men were still alive, but the hospital staff needed help treating the gunshot wounds. At 9:45 a call was placed to Arthur H. Kimpton, a Boston City Hospital physician and pioneer in the science of blood transfusion. He arrived at 10:15, but despite his reckless drive on the icy roads it was too late for McLeod. The officer had not lived an hour. Dr. Kimpton made a cursory examination of Coughlin, determined that the firefighter's wounds were unlikely to be immediately fatal, and concentrated on Haddock, who was bleeding fiercely. Volunteers lined up to donate blood for a succession of transfusions. The fire department's Lieutenant Salamone, whose blood type matched Haddock's, gave until he fell unconscious.

With no teletype, the first news of the shootings and robbery was relayed to the Dedham police station by a telephone call at 9:43 a.m. The teletype operator there pounded out a message immediately picked up by Newton police, who broadcast the alert over their new radio transmission system: "Holdup by three men of the Needham Trust Company. In car Mass reg. 304-210 headed towards Wellesley."[6]

Among those listening were Murt, Abe, and Irv.

More details were broadcast minutes later: "There were four men in that car, and the man with a machine gun got in the front seat and placed the gun on the seat and drove the car." The source of that information must have been Riordan, who had jumped off the running board.

Police conducted a quick check of the license plate number and learned it was fake. "The owner was contacted by phone and he states that the plates are still on his car." Police did broadcast a description of the getaway car.

"Were in a pointed Packard sedan, apparently a new car, with a pointed front."

The gang was speeding east on the Worcester Turnpike back toward the Brinsley Street garage. Just as the traffic slowed at a construction site, the first dispatch crackled out of the stolen state police radio Abe had installed. It was time to start covering their tracks. "We pulled into a side street and removed the plates on the car and put others on," Abe said. "We drove carefully and directly to the garage in Dorchester, parked the car there and took the small car," referring to Murt's Chevrolet. The three men carried the Thompson and the $14,500 in the bank's metal cash box. At Lawrence Avenue, Abe took the money upstairs to Irv's bedroom and Murt followed with the Thompson, wrapped in a piece of cloth. He hid it under Irv's bed. Then they turned on a radio, cranked up the volume, and divided the money three ways.

Downstairs, Norma and Carolyn Millen prepared lunch as the scratchy radio signal boomed out. "You could hear it even though Irving's door was closed," Norma said. Carolyn called up and said food was on the table, but received no response.[7]

In Irv's bedroom Abe put his share of the cash in a briefcase and asked Murt to drive him home. After dropping off the briefcase, Abe returned to work at the radio shop. His partner, Joe Rothberg, noticed nothing out of the ordinary.

In Needham, hundreds of people filled the town square as news of the crime spread. Almost everyone knew every officer on the force, at least by sight, and many were on first-name terms with the bank tellers and clerks. In the initial confusion, it was hard to sort out exactly who had been shot and who was unharmed. At the Emory Grove elementary school, Arnold Mackintosh, Jr., "was quietly called out of the room and sent home" by worried teachers, a classmate recalled.[8]

By noon catching the killers was the sole objective of law enforcement. The robbery and stolen cash were irrelevant. The extraordinary, even feverish response of Massachusetts police was triggered by the attack on fellow law enforcement officers. Bay State police who had watched the carnage endured by county sheriffs and local police in the Midwest had long feared such violence in their state. The Needham crime was said to be the first submachine gun bank robbery in state history, and that very day Boston police had distributed a circular warning that "Pretty Boy" Floyd, the Midwestern bank robber and killer, was reportedly scouting targets in the Northeast.

Boston's seven competing daily newspapers amplified the outrage. As dozens of police joined the hunt for the killers, the newspapers dispatched carloads of their best reporters. The first on the scene was the well-connected and well-known *Globe* reporter Joseph Dinneen. Not only did he live in Needham, but his next-door neighbor was a town policeman. He arrived at the bank by 10:10 a.m. In 1931 he had profiled the Needham department in a lengthy story comparing small-town police with those in a big city department. He told the story of a woman who called to complain that neighborhood bullies were harassing her son. She was connected directly to the chief. Bliss suggested she teach her son how to fight. "You don't want to make a sissy out of your boy. Make him stand on his own feet."

Standing on their own feet was just what the Needham police were now struggling to do. When Dinneen walked into Needham Trust, he found "two town policemen, dazed and still trying to comprehend that two of their companions and associates had been shot down." He was writing about men he knew. He began walking up and down the street, speaking to witnesses and taking notes. "The town was in a state of panic. Stores and business offices were closed. Residents barred themselves in their houses, fearing a return of the bandit car," he wrote.

As he went from shop to shop, buttonholing the clerks and merchants, Dinneen metamorphosed from an observer to a participant in the investigation. When he stopped at the Stevens brothers' grocery store, a block from the bank, "a truck driver, unloading bananas in the town square, handed me a bullet that fell from a bunch as he dropped it from his shoulder to the floor."

From Dinneen's hand the .22 caliber bullet made its way to the state police ballistics expert, Captain Charles G. Van Amburgh.[9]

Not only was Dinneen collecting evidence—and soon made capturing the killers his top priority—but his mere presence pumped up the intensity of the media onslaught in time for that afternoon's editions. One reporter arriving immediately after Dinneen was Lawrence Goldberg, the top crime reporter for the *Boston Post*.

Also on the scene was state police detective Lieutenant Michael F. Fleming. He had been at district attorney Dewing's office in Dedham when word of the shootings came in. Fleming had served twenty years as a Brookline police officer before joining the state force in 1917 and was soon to turn sixty years old. An affable, bookish man who was popular with reporters, Fleming was one of a small band of talented state investigators who answered directly to the commissioner for public safety, Daniel Needham. (His was another name that caused confusion among the public and out-of-town reporters.)

Not far behind were two other state police detectives, John F. Stokes and Joseph L. Ferrari. The Boston Police Department dispatched four patrol cars carrying a ballistics expert and two assistants, a fingerprint expert, and a photographer. They were on the road within an hour of the teletype alert.

Sightings of the black Packard were already being reported. In Rhode Island police rushed to throw up a roadblock at the state line after a Massachusetts motor vehicle inspector spotted a large black car speeding south. But spotting the right large black car was nearly impossible because witnesses had given police six different versions of the license plate number.

By noontime Lieutenant Governor Gaspar Bacon had conferred with Daniel Needham and announced, with remarkable optimism, that he had reason to hope the killers would be caught by the morning. If not, he would convene the Governor's Council and vote a reward. In the meantime, Bacon put up $1,000 of his own money. Reporters asked if the stolen state police submachine gun was used in the robbery. Needham didn't believe so but said that one of Fleming's jobs was to ensure that spent bullets and cartridges at the scene were collected for ballistics tests. Early that afternoon, two state legislators announced a bill mandating life in prison for illegal possession of a machine gun.

That evening Needham selectmen voted their own reward of $1,000. They also helped organize a citizens committee to assist the families of the three victims. By the end of the day they had raised $500. A $75 contribution came from New York City via telegram, and the town's American Legion post, where both men had been members, threw its weight behind the fund-raising effort. "Let us share and lighten the burdens of others as generously as our means will permit," one member told the *Needham Times*. But in private conversations, bitter accusations were already flying back and forth. They would surface in the following days as the perpetrators, the "machine gun killers" as they were named by the newspapers, eluded capture.

On Friday afternoon and into the evening, police scrambled for a lead. An off-duty Needham officer, Howard Mills, had passed by the bank the very moment the robbery was under way and noticed the Packard. He didn't recognize the car, and instinct prompted him to scribble down its license plate number. Like the others, it turned out to be a dead end.[10] By the end of the day speculation was rife that the perpetrators were from the Midwest, where brazen hostage taking and the killing of law enforcement officers were nearly commonplace. Police sources told reporters that the crime was too violent and too well planned to have been committed by anyone without experience in that sort of mayhem. The man considered most likely to be the culprit was Floyd, whose picture was splashed across the next day's Boston papers. Floyd was known to force hostages onto the running boards of his getaway car to discourage pursuing police.

The team of state police detectives scoffed. Fleming thought the bandits were local. "*True Detective* magazine stories which describe crimes minutely are a regular school" for criminals, he told a Needham newspaper. Fleming cited a particular story that detailed Floyd's methods and suggested it was an inspiration for the Needham bandits. "They had profited from Floyd's lesson by using two bank employees as shields in their getaway."

Fleming also told reporters that the descriptions provided by Mackintosh, Riordan, and other employees, and now plastered across the front pages of the Boston newspapers, were so contradictory as to be useless. The more information police received, the more the bandits varied in height, girth, age, and skin tone.

By Saturday Boston police believed that the perpetrators likely came from within the city's criminal subculture. They latched onto a known bandit and holdup artist named John Curran, alias Carroll. He was arrested, interrogated, and charged with another crime, robbing the Wollaston bank in October. Some news accounts said that he had also been "partially identified" as one of the Needham robbers. But within a day he was eliminated as a suspect. Over the weekend other detectives theorized that members of the once-fearsome Jerry "the Pole" Gedzium gang were back in action.[11] "The Pole" had been executed three years earlier, but fingerprints supposedly recovered from the bank and descriptions by the victims had "tentatively identified" former gang members as the perpetrators. But no fingerprints had been found. The experts from Boston found one palm print that might have belonged to the machine gunner, but nothing else of use. And the palm print matched nothing in the Boston files.

The Saturday *Globe* ran a credible story from a Needham real estate agent. He told investigators that a couple of days earlier, three well-dressed men arrived at his office and announced that they wanted to buy a home. The agent drove them around and fielded inquiries about the recently built redbrick police and fire station. The potential clients wondered out loud about the number of patrolmen and asked how much money the town had saved by closing down the police teletype. They ran across McLeod that day, and the police officer commented afterward that the trio looked like "tough guys."

As Bostonians mulled over Dinneen's account, Governor Ely, aboard a cruise ship in the Panama Canal, sent a telegraph endorsing a $20,000 reward, the largest in state history. Adjusted for inflation, it amounts to $350,000 today. Boston police organized a statewide roundup of all "known criminals." The initial sweep through the city turned up thirty people, and by Sunday some 125 suspects were in custody for questioning. The dragnet's results were striped across the front pages of the region's newspapers and were the top story on the newly created Yankee radio network, the first effort by regional broadcasters to organize an independent radio news entity.

A variety of theories about the perpetrators popped up—no surprise, as a hundred city detectives without any real leads were combing Boston's underworld of stickup men, numbers runners, armed bandits, drug dealers, pimps, and involuntarily retired bootleggers. Essentially, the cops were shaking the tree in hope of finding someone who knew something. In the *Boston Post*, a photograph of a roomful of men holding hats over their faces ran alongside three columns of newsprint detailing each potential suspect's criminal history. A *Boston Evening American* front page declared that the probe had reached the city's financial district. "Banker Grilled in Hunt for Needham Bank Mob," the headline said in inch-high type.

That was Stokes's doing. He was running down a theory that since the Needham bank and the recently robbed Brookline and Quincy banks were all part of an "association affiliated with a Boston bank," the group's executive director was, just maybe, the brains behind the guns. The article was on more solid ground when it described what the Needham bandit trio missed—a $70,000 shipment of cash to Needham Trust from the Boston Federal Reserve normally made on Thursday but unexpectedly delayed. The *American*'s number may have been high, but more detailed reports in other papers seemed to confirm that Murt, Abe, and Irv just missed a really big score. Stokes had wondered if the banker provided the gang with the expected date of the shipment in return for a piece of the take.

THE REPORTERS WERE PLEASED that Stokes was on the job, as he enjoyed jousting with the press and was sometimes a useful source, if rarely quoted on the record. Bespectacled and round-faced, with his red hair almost gone, Stokes, forty-five, liked to play the good guy in an interrogation. His father, Thomas, immigrated from Ireland in the 1880s and married another transplant, Mary.[12] They had five children. John was the second oldest. He began his working life as a steamfitter's apprentice and won appointment to the Cambridge Police Department in 1911. Stokes was an avid reader—he was a particular fan of European detective stories—with a gift for observation. He enlisted in the U.S. Army near the end of World War I and emerged as a second lieutenant, an impressive leap out of the enlisted ranks. In 1921 he passed the entrance examination for the Massachusetts State Police detective division. The new unit was to be an expert sleuthing force, and its members typically had a decade or more experience doing patrol and investigative work in a municipal department. With his nearly three years in the military, Stokes had barely seven years in police work but was chosen nonetheless. He didn't hide his pleasure. "It was like making the first team," he said.[13]

Stokes worked important cases. He solved the murder of a woman whose body was found in three pieces scattered about Middlesex County—her head was in a suitcase floating in a river. When the ten-year-old daughter of a banker was kidnapped and held for $250,000 ransom, Stokes was ordered out of his sickbed to interrogate a suspected accomplice.

Stokes's opening gambit was a plea for help. He knew almost nothing about the case, he explained, and wanted to hear both sides of the story. He was trying to be fair. The man told his version and then, very mildly, Stokes asked to hear his story again. And again. And again. Soon the man was contradicting himself and finally yelled, "There is nothing more I can tell you!" There was, Stokes yelled back. The name of the kidnapper! He handed the man a pencil and paper and told him that if he couldn't bring himself to say it, he could write it. The man wrote down the name of his brother, the banker's chauffeur.[14]

It was an impressive performance, and some local police gave Stokes his due. Others felt their toes had been stepped on.

BY SATURDAY MORNING investigators were pursuing reports that a "colored janitor" at the bank had a side job as a numbers runner, which meant he had a connection to the Boston underworld. Was the janitor the inside man? He was sweated by Needham police and eventually cleared.

Late Saturday night word came that Haddock was dead. He had remained in critical condition since the shooting, and doctors had warned that there was little hope they could repair the ripping wounds from the

Thompson's bullets. His wife, Helen, and a brother, Joseph, were at his side when he died at 10:25 p.m. Timothy Coughlin the firefighter was given so-so odds.

ON BLUE HILL AVENUE that Sunday afternoon, Rose Knellar arrived at the Faber apartment for a visit. She was cute and pixyish, with her short dark hair, sharp features, and clear skin. She lacked Norma's striking good looks and the younger girl's self-absorption.

Midway through her visit, Abe walked in and quickly pulled her aside. In his hands was a heavy, squarish package wrapped in a thick layer of old newspapers and magazines, the corners and edges reinforced with tape. He handed it to her. It was a present, he explained, for their eventual wedding. Rose was taken aback. "It was the first time he ever gave me a package," she said later, insisting she meant that fact in "the strongest" way. "It was the first package he ever gave me."[15]

Now Abe told her that "we" had received an early wedding present, but steadfastly refused to say who the gift was from. "Put this away where it will be safe. We're not going to open it or look at it until our wedding day. Then we'll look it over. Be sure now that you don't lose it and whatever you do, don't open it." Perhaps they would be married in June, he said.

She followed his instructions and the next day carried the bundle to her job at a downtown jewelry store and locked it in the company's safe. Inside was $3,580 in cash, or three-quarters of Faber's $4,800 cut.

Murt and Norma spent their weekend at the Boylston Street apartment. Murt was restless. When not pacing he was bent over a psychology book reading, "or pretending to read," Norma said. Sometimes he wrote in a small black notebook, and once he wrote a letter he didn't mail. On Sunday Norma was shopping for dinner at a corner delicatessen when she glanced at the news racks. The papers were filled with stories about the Needham investigation. Back at the apartment, she mentioned the coverage and the killings. "Really?" Murt inquired mildly. "Did you read the paper? Oh, you don't want to read the papers."

"He said it casually. I remember because I thought he was being pretty coldblooded."[16]

The single-digit temperature Sunday night warmed slightly in time for McLeod's Monday morning funeral. The ground was still snow-covered, and the temperature was in the teens even at midday. McLeod's father, James, watched his son lowered into the frozen earth. With him was his other son, George, and his daughter, Margaret.

James McLeod emigrated from Scotland in the late nineteenth century to become a stonecutter in Quincy, where Forbes McLeod was born on January 1, 1898. The family soon moved to Needham, where his father worked indoors as a stock clerk. James remarried following the death of his first wife, Sarah.

Forbes McLeod worked as a machinist after high school until World War I. He served in combat and was awarded the Croix de Guerre by the French government and in 1924 joined the Needham police force. Off duty he played goalie for a local soccer team. Two years later, on April 7, 1926, he married Margaret Elizabeth Delaney. Her parents were from Canada and Northern Ireland. They had no children.[17]

The town's businesses closed for the funeral procession, which started at the McLeod home, traveled down Great Plain Avenue and through the town center to St. Joseph's Church. Bliss led the surviving members of the Needham police, followed by a detail of town firefighters. Officers from nearby departments staffed the Needham station and patrolled its streets. Other police joined members of Needham's American Legion post and lined the church's front steps as the crowd waited for the cortege. Inside, the pews overflowed. News reports said that 2,500 people stood silently outside in the freezing weather. They were witnesses to Margaret McLeod's inconsolable grief. At the end of the service, she was all but incapable of walking. A photograph shows a slim woman, her body warped in anguish, being led out of the church by men grasping both her arms.

Her husband was buried at Calvary Cemetery in Waltham.

A few hours later came news of the first break in the case, courtesy of Dinneen's banana bullet.

According to Dineen's account, state police ballistics expert Captain Van Amburgh returned to his lab on Friday after the shootings and immediately examined the bullet. Van Amburgh used a comparison microscope, a type invented in 1925. It had a single eyepiece connected by a series of lenses to two separate, but side-by-side specimen trays. One bullet was placed in each tray, and the lenses combined the two images to show a single, side-by-side magnified view of the bullets. It made ballistic comparisons fast and accurate. The instrument had been famously used to absolve Chicago police of any role in the 1929 St. Valentine's Day Massacre.

Van Amburgh's comparison microscope was perched on a dirty, stained wooden desk piled high with papers and files. Next to it was a file cabinet, cartridge boxes stacked on top. Van Amburgh must have immediately noticed the caliber of the projectile caught by the bananas. He had worked on the Lynn case and knew that that murder weapon fired a .22 bullet. And he knew that a weapon of the same caliber had killed Ernest Clark in Fitchburg two months earlier. Now here was yet another .22 bullet.

Van Amburgh studied the banana bullet's grooves and ridges, known as "lands," and compared them with the bullet on the second tray, the one taken from Clark's body. He flipped on a desk lamp and angled it to highlight the details. Peering through the eyepiece, he saw that the Needham bullet matched the Fitchburg bullet. Both had been fired from the same gun.

That wasn't all. The banana bullet also matched the bullet removed from the body of C. Fred Sumner, the Lynn bill poster. So the weapon was fired at all three crime scenes. Van Amburgh was even able to suggest to police the specific make, a Colt Woodsman. At least that was what the *Boston Evening Globe* breathlessly announced in its Monday afternoon edition, attributing its scoop to Daniel Needham.

The news report received particular attention from the two attorneys defending cabdrivers Molway and Berrett, because on the day of the Needham bank robbery the cabbies were in jail under lock and key. If the report was true, and it was, and if the Needham bandits had carried the very weapon used at the Paramount Theatre, had the wrong men been arrested by Lynn police?

Maybe their clients really were those rare beasts, innocent men.

FRANCIS HADDOCK'S BURIAL SERVICE was held in the same Newton church where he had married Helen Frances "Nell" Callanan in 1919. His early life was not easy. Haddock's mother, Nelly, emigrated from Canada in 1883 as a young girl and married William I. Haddock. They had two children who died in infancy. A son, Joseph, born in 1891, survived, as did Francis, born in 1892, and a daughter, Florence, who arrived in 1894. By 1900 Nelly was a single mother. Her husband had been involved in an "altercation" that subsequently required him to flee Massachusetts on a stolen horse. He never returned. Then Nelly passed away from influenza in 1901, and her children were separated and raised in what amounted to a series of foster homes.[18]

Francis Haddock joined the army in World War I and was discharged with the rank of sergeant. He worked as a shipper at a local knitting mill and was appointed to the police department in August 1920. Soon he was Needham's first motorcycle officer. The two-wheeled machines were useful for patrols and cheaper than cruisers. He was a handsome, imposing man, with blue eyes and brown hair. He could handle himself if patrol work came to a fight. Townspeople knew that he was an officer not to cross, as proved by the oft-repeated dance hall brawl story. In spring and summer he grew vegetables and flowers. Planting the family garden was an annual project and a tradition passed on to his children and grandchildren.

On the day Haddock was taken from the Church of Mary Immaculate of Lourdes for burial, he left behind four daughters: Phyllis, seven; Dorothy, nine; Helen, ten; and Mary, fourteen. None were allowed to attend the funeral mass or interment, presumably in an attempt to shelter them from the raw grief. There were dozens of other Needham children present, as Haddock had organized a school-crossing guard program. Hundreds of residents filled the church.

After the service the funeral cortege wound its way back to Needham and passed by the Heights fire station. The fire bell was tolled. A "traffic squad" of the students trained by Haddock lined up in a salute. A legionnaire played taps as he was buried in St. Mary's Cemetery.

That night the board of selectmen voted Margaret McLeod a $1,000 annual annuity. Helen Haddock was voted $985, plus $200 for each of her children "until they become of age." They also voted to purchase "the best machine gun obtainable."

MEANWHILE, THE POLICE tried to capitalize on Van Amburgh's discovery, but with no success. The sweep of "known criminals," the toughs on the Needham real estate tour, and the Boston banker all proved to be dead ends. What appeared to be a lead—currency bearing serial numbers from the stolen cash was passed at stores in Stoughton, Wellesley, and Boston—fizzled when police learned that Needham Trust had compiled an erroneous list of serial numbers.

Public outrage and fear were genuine, however, and swept through the greater Boston area. In Swampscott, the police chief volunteered to teach town residents how to use a revolver. In Stoughton, police were issued Thompsons. In Cambridge, bankers met with the mayor and asked for officers to be permanently stationed in every lobby. The Malden police chief suggested bringing back the whipping post. A minister called for posting sharpshooters outside each bank. Daniel Needham mulled over plans to train teams of vigilantes "as a sort of Police Department auxiliary."

Norfolk County district attorney Edmund Dewing, whose jurisdiction included Needham, declared, "Something has got to be done, and done soon, about meeting the growing menace of organized banditry." On Saturday he predicted an imminent arrest but by Monday was far less optimistic. "All I can say at this time is that we are making progress and that we are expecting developments. We haven't given up hope of catching these ruthless slayers, by any means."

Or as the *Globe* shouted on Tuesday, "Major Clews Fail Police in Search for Slayers." "All Tips Traced in Vain," said the subhead.

Beneath that, a second subhead retracted the paper's Monday afternoon scoop. "Gang Not Linked to Other Crimes," it said. Inside on page 11 Van Amburgh "ridiculed" the earlier story. "There is absolutely no truth in it," he said, "and I deny every word of it."

But it was Van Amburgh not telling the truth. He had linked all three crimes, if not solely with the banana bullet, then via .22 shell casings collected at each scene.

Who wrote that Tuesday, February 8, *Globe* story is unknown. Like most newspaper articles of that era, it ran without a byline. While Dinneen may not have written the two articles—like anyone else he needed a day off—he surely contributed information. Or perhaps another reporter buttonholed Needham. Whoever the author was, the commissioner infuriated his detectives by disclosing that police had proof the crimes were linked, thereby warning the killers to ditch their weapons and flee.

There was also the matter of law enforcement politics. The *Globe* story had punched a large, public hole in the case against the cabbies, and the theater murder trial was due to start the following week. A commissioner of public safety undermining a district attorney's case in the newspapers was not done.

That same evening President Roosevelt's oldest son, James, appeared on Boston radio station WNAC to discuss the threat posed by armed and motorized criminals. Roosevelt said that the only lawmen actually feared by those gangsters were agents of the Bureau of Investigation at the Department of Justice, whom he called the nation's "sharpshooting force." Roosevelt praised "John Edgar Hoover," a man then little known to most Americans but busy creating what, in 1935, officially became the FBI.

However, unlike the situation in the Midwest, where armed robbers left long lines of the slain and casually crossed state lines, the succession of killings and robberies in Massachusetts remained a domestic affair. The investigation remained up to the locals.

11

A Fire in the Woods

POLICE HAD PROVED INCAPABLE of solving the Mechanics Hall theft, the string of movie theater robberies, or the highly publicized Worcester score. The Fitchburg cops had no idea who gunned down Ernest Clark, and in Lynn two innocent men were going on trial for the Paramount Theatre murder. No usable fingerprints were found at the Needham bank. Police were grasping at straws, hauling in all manner of well-known miscreants in the futile hope that one possessed a legitimate tip.

Maybe Murt and Abe weren't worried. But Murt had killed two cops.

Within hours of the robbery it was obvious the Needham police needed help. There was chaos at the bank and inside the department's headquarters. Bliss had just watched one officer die and was attending to another comrade who would soon follow. In the past thirty years there had been two recorded murders in town. As the bank filled up with local officers, Boston police, bank managers, and newspaper reporters, one witness described the Needham officers as "stupefied." A reporter inside the bank called them "dazed." It was a crime that was far, far out of their experience. The Boston fingerprint experts and photographers could help for a day or two, but were city detectives to be assigned for the length of the investigation? Clearly not. Unless the bandits tripped over themselves in front of a cop, the investigation could last weeks or months and crisscross the state, or indeed the country.

Some of the first investigative work in the hours after the killing was done by Dinneen and Goldberg. Dinneen's status as a Needham resident gave him easy entrée. Goldberg was the *Post*'s top crime reporter and no doubt was on first-name terms with the Boston officers. Goldberg joined Dinneen during his walk in the snow up and down Great Plain Avenue interviewing anyone who offered a scrap of information. The initial description of the bandits sent out over police teletype was compiled from information Goldberg and Dinneen collected.

They knew that police faced a formidable challenge and assumed that the state police's top investigators, nicknamed the "Aces" by the more inventive reporters, would take control. So the two reporters were appalled when they saw that the talented Stokes and his team were being sidelined. "For reasons best known to certain Needham police officials, and certain Boston police, the assistance of the state detective bureau was not desired," Goldberg wrote in a private memo.[1] He and Dinneen could not let that stand, and within a day of the shootings they buttonholed the town selectmen "and insisted that the state detectives be called into the case without any further delay." The selectmen and the town's business leaders all agreed. That inversion of a reporter's role, from observer to participant, was in later decades a firing offense.

Conflict had plagued the investigation from the outset. State police detective Fleming, in the Norfolk County District Attorney's Office in Dedham, was specifically assigned to assist with major criminal investigations. But Chief Bliss's first move was to call in the Boston Police Department, which had no jurisdiction in Needham. Fleming only learned of the crime from a reporter. Perhaps Bliss was turning to his friends in a time of crisis. Or perhaps he knew that the Boston police, no matter how much help they provided, had no authority to usurp control of the investigation.

Some infighting between law enforcement agencies was expected, given professional pride and inter-agency politics. But in 1934 that background noise was at symphonic levels because of a plan by Governor Ely to consolidate Massachusetts's 136 municipal police forces. The gubernatorial priority was vociferously opposed by almost every law enforcement agency not based on Beacon Hill.[2]

Ely's effort was rooted in a national police reform movement dating to a 1931 federal commission investigating why state and local law enforcement failed to effectively enforce Prohibition's ban on the production of alcoholic beverages. Public opposition to the law aside, the commission pointed out that short-staffed, untrained local police departments were fighting criminal gangs organized across county and state lines. It called for the professionalization of police — who were said to be all too frequently corrupt — with training, better equipment, and regional organization. In 1933 Ely named his own commission to examine Massachusetts police, and by that fall it declared that there was "a serious breakdown of law enforcement agencies in the Commonwealth in dealing with the situation," meaning modern gangsters with automobiles and automatic weapons. "Old law enforcement initiatives must be scrapped and new substituted."

Local police could get behind the call for new equipment and better training—though it took a direct order by the governor in January 1934 before the Boston police equipped patrol cars with radio receivers—but centralized control from Beacon Hill was another matter altogether. Ely also erred when he put a Boston University law professor, Frank L. Simpson, in charge of the commission. Criticism of the chiefs' life work from an ivory tower made the opponents of consolidation only dig in deeper. Individual careers and political fiefdoms were at risk. Was the state to eventually control hiring and firing? The controversy meant that when Stokes and Ferrari were charged with solving the Needham killings, high on their list of challenges was internecine law enforcement politics.

UNLIKE STOKES, whose disarming smile worked magic in an interrogation room, Ferrari, with an angular face and a prominent nose, often found himself cast as the "bad" cop. He wore thick, circular eyeglasses and favored double-breasted suits. His Italian immigrant parents ran a North End fruit stand. He joined the Boston Fire Department in 1905 and won an early commendation for rescuing two women caught one night on an upper floor during a wintertime fire. With the temperature at 10 degrees below zero, Ferrari made two trips up and down a wooden ladder to carry the women to safety. In 1909 he joined the city police department and was posted in the North End, where he was said to have arrested a murder suspect after only twenty-four hours on the job. On another occasion he jumped off a subway platform as a train was screeching into the station and saved a woman sprawled on the tracks. After twelve years in the North End, he became the first Italian American on the state detective force.[3]

By his own admission Ferrari was sometimes hotheaded, and so made a good match for Stokes. They had first met when Stokes was on the Cambridge force and chased a car thief into Boston. He walked into the North End station and was told to see Ferrari, who years later recalled that "Stokes looked me up and down, from head to toe, and then up again. Then he said, 'He looks like an honest man to me.'"[4]

In newspaper photographs Stokes had the appearance of a pugnacious beat cop, while Ferrari exuded a scholarly, diffident air, more that of a librarian than a cop.

Stokes and Ferrari worked major investigations of all types but inevitably ended up specializing in murders. And while other state police detectives were permanently assigned to specific counties to help local prosecutors with major criminal cases, Stokes, Ferrari, and other members of the detecting bureau, based in Room 24 at the State House, worked directly for the commissioner of public safety and had the entire state as their beat.

The political infighting was one of two factors that powerfully affected the course of their investigation. The other was Dinneen and Goldberg. They were talented investigators with access to people who would not talk to a cop. In their eagerness to catch the killers—and get a story, no doubt—they effectively became agents of the state police. This relationship was unofficial, and not always amicable. Both sides wondered at times if the cooperative effort was more effort than cooperation. But it was fruitful.

THE DETECTIVES AND REPORTERS shared an intimate world. The reporters worked out of a two-block stretch of Boston's Washington Street, nicknamed "Newspaper Row" when it was home to eight papers in the 1890s. In 1934 the Row with its narrow five- and six-story buildings was home to the *Post*, *Globe*, and *Transcript*, with the other major dailies scattered nearby. Presses were located on the first floor or basement, and reporters, editors, typesetters, advertising clerks, and salesmen were crammed into the upper floors. When magician Harry Houdini needed to publicize a new stage act, he strung himself upside down from a rope stretched across the street. Wrapped in a straitjacket and chains, he escaped as the crowd watched. As newspaper editions were published from morning through evening, the street was alive nearly twenty-four hours a day. The Row had its own bookies—one was called "Army" because he had only one arm—and a specialized coterie of nighttime peddlers for the reporters and pressmen who slept during ordinary shopping hours. Speakeasies dotted the street and surrounding blocks during Prohibition.[5]

Newspaper Row's cachet was boosted by its neighbors. On the northerly end was the Suffolk County Courthouse, the state's Supreme Judicial Court, and the golden-domed State House. On the southerly end was the city's financial district. So at breakfast, dinner, and supper in the evening, and for drinks almost anytime, the reporters and editors were joined by cops, judges, bankers, lawyers, innumerable clerks, criminal defendants, and any number of elected and appointed state officials. The judges knew the defense lawyers, the defense lawyers knew the prosecutors, the police knew the reporters, and good reporters like Dinneen and Goldberg knew everyone. And everyone's boss, too.

Dinneen and Goldberg may have been particularly useful in an era when most police officers were untrained and hired on the basis of how hard they threw a punch or whom they knew. The reporters' investigative skills could be matched by few officers outside of Boston. Indeed, there is no record that any of the ten remaining Needham officers played a significant role in the gang's eventual capture.

Within a day of the bank robbery, Dinneen and Goldberg ceased competing and began working together as a team. They shared information, knocked on doors together, and soon were trading information and making deals with the state police. They trusted each other, because on a number of mornings either man could have awoken to find himself scooped by his erstwhile partner on the biggest crime story of the decade.

Dinneen was born in Dorchester in 1897, the son of Irish immigrants. He learned shorthand in high school and had three years of law school before serving in World War I. He started off working at the *Globe* library in 1922, was moved to the copy desk in 1923 and then into street reporting. He had a facility for words and an eye for detail. Sent to report on the bankruptcy and annexation of a factory town actually named Millville, Dinneen led his story with "Millville, February 19 — This Dateline Dies." While he made his living working for newspapers, Dinneen had greater literary ambitions and in the 1920s wrote his first book, a classic novel of Boston politics titled *Ward 8.*[6]

Goldberg was a year older. His family immigrated from London shortly after his birth, and as a youth he hawked the *Boston Post* to commuters at North Station. He attended journalism school at Columbia University and won a Silver Star while serving with the Yankee Division in France during World War I.[7] He returned to the *Post*, this time as a reporter, and was on the team that won a Pulitzer Prize for reporting on the original Ponzi scheme, a scam run by supposed financier Charles Ponzi, who lured investors by promising to double their money in ninety days. By the 1930s Goldberg was the paper's top crime reporter. Like Dinneen's, his college education was atypical for reporters of that era. He sported a pencil-thin mustache and had acquired a reputation as a "fast talker . . . and master of the one-liner."[8]

Now the two reporters set up shop in the basement of a home owned by Thomas E. Norris, a Needham attorney who had already established a citizens committee, initially intended to raise funds for the officers' families. But the committee quickly became alarmed at the disorder of the official investigation and so reconstituted itself as a group of "vigilantes." By Haddock's funeral on Tuesday morning, the committee members had pooled their personal resources and hired the Burns International Detective Agency, the firm favored by bankers and industrialists. Dinneen and Goldberg cooperated with the vigilantes, too. A flood of tips poured in to the private detectives, and the best were pursued. All were fruitless.

A FEW HOURS AFTER THE LAST SHOVELFUL of earth covered Frank Haddock's coffin, Murt and Norma drove to Lawrence Avenue for a lunch of corned beef and cabbage. Since Friday afternoon Murt had rarely ventured outside the Boylston Street apartment. For this trip he replaced his usual brown overcoat and with a blue one, ordinarily saved for special occasions. He also wore a hat, which Norma had rarely seen him do. The couple were joined at the table by Carolyn, Irv, and the family's youngest child, Idalyn. After the meal Murt and Irv disappeared into the attic. Carolyn wondered why her son wasn't at work on a Tuesday.

Murt and Norma returned to the Boylston Street apartment in time for supper. While she was in the kitchen preparing the meal, Murt disappeared. He returned thirty minutes later and announced they were leaving. "Get your coat on," he ordered. In the darkness they returned to Lawrence Avenue, picked up Irv, and then headed north on Blue Hill Avenue to collect Abe. Then Murt spun the Chevy around back south and five minutes later stopped at the Brinsley Street garage. It was another bitterly cold evening. Irv was blowing on his hands and rubbing the back of his neck. Norma shivered as Abe climbed out of the backseat. A few minutes later he returned behind the wheel of the Packard.

Murt and Abe had been spooked by the very *Boston Evening Globe* story that Van Amburgh so vehemently denounced as untrue. The two carefully tracked newspaper coverage of their crimes and kept a file of clippings at the radio shop. That single front-page article with its bold headline was the first indication that the investigation was making real progress. If a link between Fitchburg, Lynn, and Needham was no longer just speculation but underpinned with facts, then even Irving recognized that there was a hard-to-hide piece of evidence connecting all three crimes—the black Packard. "It was too dangerous to have the car on our hands," Faber said.

The Packard with its distinctive "shovel nose" grill had been described by witnesses, and the trio had to assume that some resident of a triple-decker overlooking the concrete block garage had glanced out the window and noticed the Packard backing in or driving out. They had to get rid of the car before a good citizen turned squealer. Murt had driven the stolen vehicle sparingly, but he did occasionally motor to Lawrence Avenue and take Norma for a ride. Neighbors had noticed, as Packards were purchased by families on Beacon Hill or in the Back Bay, not by Roxbury tradesmen and shopkeepers.

The "Light Eight Model 900" at Brinsley Street was introduced in 1932 as an affordable alternative to the carmaker's regular luxury line. Its nickname came from the distinctive grill that swooped forward at the bottom to meet the bumper. It gave the car a modern, lighthearted touch. The stolen car had a second distinctive feature. To preserve the cachet of its more expensive stable mates, the stock Light Eight did not have the Packard's distinctive "speed emblem," the silver figurine of a woman with her arms pointing forward, that was mounted on other models atop the radiator housing. But the original owner had the statuette added. It was another detail a neighborhood kid crazy about cars was certain to notice, particularly given the reward money. "Fortune" was not too extravagant a description of $21,000 at a time when a skilled truck driver, or a novice newspaper reporter, earned $30 a week. After a bit of multiplication and division, a prospective snitch would realize that $21,000 equaled thirteen and a half years of weekly paychecks.

But disposing of the auto was not going to be as easy as stealing it. Disassembling it piece by piece was feasible, since the trio had the necessary skills and the tools, but Brinsley Street was not the place to use acetylene torches and power tools. They had no links to the underworld, so there was no junk man they could trust to take the Packard off their hands for a wad of clean, unwrinkled currency. Even a solution out of Hollywood—driving it off a deserted pier into Boston Harbor—was risky that February. The long stretch of freezing temperatures had frozen inshore waters. Soon, children were skating off city wharves and marveling at the steel freighters stuck to their berths.

Murt and Abe needed to make a quick, accurate analysis of their options. At that they failed. After sneering at the police for so long, Murt now realized that killing two cops placed him in a different class of wanted criminal pursued by a different class of cop. A capable mechanic, he had proved himself a criminal of some talent. But he failed to reckon how detectives in possession of the Packard could trace the auto back to him.

This was when Abe should have put his mind to work, trained as he was in methodical problem solving. But he either had too much faith in Murt or was tripped up by the personality traits his MIT professors saw, an interior life that swung from insecurity to overweening pride depending on a not necessarily accurate reading of the circumstances.

And both were probably panicked.

In this contest Stokes, Ferrari, and Fleming had the upper hand. Decades of dealing with liars, murderers, and con men—the best lawbreakers the people of Massachusetts could throw at them—had given them an impressive education in practical psychology. Abe outshone them in book learning, but the detectives far surpassed him in comprehension of their fellow human beings. The mind so adept at MIT struggled unsuccessfully to calculate the imponderables of this new world of crime. It wasn't quite like the movies.

Murt told Norma that he and Irv would ride in the Packard and she should follow with the Chevy. "Drive slow, and for God's sake drive good and don't lose us," he said.[9] The two autos crept out of the thickly populated neighborhood and motored past Franklin Park, the 527-acre masterwork of open space designed by landscape architect Frederick Law Olmsted, renowned for laying out New York's Central Park. Traffic increased as they turned onto the new state highway heading south to Providence, Rhode Island. The Packard pulled ahead and Norma could not keep up as it disappeared into the oncoming headlights. She pulled over to the side of the road and drove at a crawl until she saw a car idling.

Its door opened and Murt ran back to the Chevy's running board. "For God's sakes, what's the matter?" He was steaming. "He looked at me disgustedly," Norma said, and told her she had to keep up.

A few minutes later they were traversing the flat terrain that led out of Boston toward the low-lying Blue Hills to the southwest. The two automobiles started uphill and were navigating past woods and fields when the Packard turned left onto a narrow, snow-covered road.

Norma followed along as Murt pulled into a clearing. They were on Everett Street in Norwood. Norma overshot the Packard and was forced to make a U-turn at the entrance of a long driveway leading to a farmhouse with lights blazing from its windows. She began a three-point turn, but the Chevy became stuck in a snowbank. Out of the darkness Murt ran up, cursed her again, pushed her aside, and took the wheel. He powered the car out of the snow and drove to the Packard. He got out and walked up to the other two men. Norma could hear voices. "A lighted driveway? The goddamn little fool!" That was Abe.

She shivered alone in the Chevy as the Packard drove slowly away.

Murt maneuvered the big car down a small wooded track called Lily Pond Road. Perhaps he was confused by the darkness, because he did not travel far before pulling into a small clearing amid young evergreens and thin saplings. There the three men pulled apart the license plate and threw the pieces into the bushes. The police radio was removed and partially disassembled. They unscrewed the gearshift knob. Because they were rushed or anxious or merely sloppy, they left other evidence behind. Perhaps Abe assured them that nothing would survive the fire. He spread "percolate and chlorate" of potassium over the interior, a compound that was later a component of solid rocket fuel. A gallon of gasoline was splashed about the interior and the metal can tossed onto the floor. Then a match was lit, and the trio scampered back to the Chevy as the gas and chemicals exploded and blew out the Packard's windows. The blaze consumed the seats, the headliner, the door panels, and much of the dashboard, leaving the interior mostly ashes and scorched metal. If they were expecting the gas tank to ignite, it did not, and the engine compartment remained undamaged.

All four were silent for the first few minutes of the drive back to Boston. Murt was at the wheel, Norma next to him, and Abe and Irv in the back. The Chevy was small and the quarters were close. Abe now remembered what he should have recalled earlier, Norma later said. "We had that battery fixed," he murmured. Murt took his eyes off the road and jerked his head around. "For God's sake, why didn't you think of that before?" He had forgotten, too. They had to return, Murt said. Abe shook his head no. The car was burning and any evidence, including the battery, would be destroyed by the flames. If they returned they would have to wait until the flames were out and the heat dissipated. They couldn't risk someone coming by and wondering what they were doing hanging about on a cold night near a burning car. Irv agreed. "Don't go," he said. They didn't.[10]

Back in the apartment, Norma could not shake off the cold. "My fingers are so numb I can hardly use them. I lay in bed shivering. Murt took his time getting undressed. He stomped around the bedroom in a kind of trance, with that peculiar glassy expression in his eyes and his lower lip jutting out. When he finally got into bed beside me, for a second I thought I was going to let out a scream."[11]

In the morning she woke up with a runny nose. Sometime later Murt walked to the nearby delicatessen for a meal. On his return he carried a newspaper and dropped it on the kitchen table. A Boston paper had rushed out an afternoon edition, and on the first page was a photo of the burned-out Packard. It was surrounded by big men in overcoats.[12]

STOKES GOT THE NEWS that morning after it percolated up from a Dedham man, Henry Deloria, who spotted the scorched wreckage as he was driving back from his job on a local farm. He called the Norwood police and two officers rushed to the scene, followed by the state detectives, who were notified by Chief Bliss. A short while later the Needham taxi driver who had seen the getaway car identified it as the burned-out Packard. However, no one was fully convinced until a spent .22 caliber shell casing was found in the ashes. A short while later a .45 caliber cartridge turned up. A check of the vehicle's registration number showed, predictably, that the car was stolen.

In the early afternoon detectives had the vehicle towed to a Norwood garage, where it was given an initial going-over. One officer said that it looked like a radio had been removed. Stokes ordered it towed to Needham's municipal garage the next morning. He wanted the car disassembled piece by piece in the hope that some part or scrap of material could be traced to the killers.

The rest of that day was a continuation of the grind that had begun Friday and not let up. Maybe the car would break the case open, but at the moment its discovery forced police to follow up on a slew of rumors and reports of other abandoned vehicles and strange men in and around the Norwood-Westwood town line, a wooded area that conceivably could be home to a gangster hideout. That evening eight cars with twenty-five troopers descended on the Green Lodge section of Westwood with electric torches and shotguns. Other search parties went to Foxboro, Sharon, and a Boy Scout camp in another part of Westwood.

It was miserable duty. The highest temperature that day was 4 degrees. In northern Maine forecasters were predicting a temperature of 30 to 50 degrees below zero, and that week the Boston papers began running front-page lists of people who had frozen to death. One was George Baker, fifty-six, of Cambridge, who died inside the Park Street subway station "when he had sought refuge from the cold." Another victim was Michael Breen, fifty, married and living on Bunker Hill Street in Charlestown. He was "found frozen to death in a hallway at 218 Bunker Hill St., where he had apparently fallen downstairs after mistaking a neighbor's house for his own, next door and similar in appearance." The temperature was 18 below at 4 a.m., reported one newspaper.

While state police shivered in the woods, Newton officers caught up with a man atop the list of potential perpetrators. He was Joseph Castanino, a twenty-five-year-old Italian immigrant suspected of covering bets taken by the Needham Trust African American janitor, a man never identified by name in any report or newspaper story. Presumably Castanino had links to the Boston underworld, and detectives wondered if he was the "finger man" who identified the bank as a target for the Boston underworld. The public safety commissioner himself led heavily armed state troopers on a raid of Castanino's home. Police found a .38 caliber revolver, two boxes of ammunition, and a handful of shotgun shells but no Castanino. Newton police, excluded from that action, raided his house again the following night. The vigilantes would cite that as an example of one police agency not knowing what the other was doing. Newton police found evidence that someone had been cooking a meal before "decanting in a hurry," according to a story in the *Boston Globe*.

On Wednesday Castanino was tracked to his wife's sister's home in Newton, and that evening he was turned over to Stokes and Ferrari at Needham police headquarters.

Chief Bliss was present and so, probably, were Dinneen and Goldberg, because the next morning both the *Globe* and the *Post* ran front-page, virtually up-to-the-minute stories about the interrogation. The *Globe* declared that the "finger man" was quizzed "until an early hour this morning." The story and headline were careful to note that the man was only a "suspect," but the bold type and placement at the top of the front page promised otherwise.

The *Globe* did not identify Castanino by name, but the *Post* was not as particular. It also included his age and his sister-in-law's exact street address and claimed that he was "an alleged nigger pool operator." Whether or not that was true, Castanino had indeed been sought by Belmont police on a "minor charge," which probably explained his effort to avoid capture. Stokes and Ferrari's grilling crawled into Thursday morning. Needham Trust employees were called in, but none recognized Castanino.

His apparent innocence was more evidence that the "expert gang" theory needed to be revisited. Even after a flood of tips from police in New Hampshire, Rhode Island, and greater Boston, calls and letters from dozens of ordinary citizens, and raids on two dozen homes and businesses, no police department had a whisper of an actual lead. No one in the professional criminal class had any inkling of the perpetrators' identities.

For Stokes, Ferrari, and Fleming the frustration must have been palpable. As the sixth day following the robbery dawned, they had nothing. Leaving aside the matter of two dead policemen and a robbed bank, Commissioner Needham and his boss, Governor Ely, were about to use the Needham killings as exhibit number one for police consolidation. This was no time for their top team of detectives to be floundering.

BUT CASTANINO DID PROVIDE Stokes a clue, or at least an idea.

In Castanino's pocket was a receipt from a battery shop in West Newton, the town bordering Needham to the east. Stokes was nothing if not thorough and wanted the story behind the slip of paper. Castanino explained that the battery in his car needed fixing, so a week earlier he had dropped it off at the shop and rented a temporary replacement. Hence, the paper Stokes held in his hand.

Stokes studied Castanino and wondered aloud if the battery in the burned-out Packard might be the very battery that Castanino had rented. That would link him to the bank robbery. Castanino assured Stokes that it was not and that he was not connected to the crime.

It was easy to check.

By now it was daylight and Walter Mills, a floor covering salesman and the brother of a Needham officer, was poking about the station. He had a car and Stokes asked him for a favor. Would Mills please drive to Norwood, remove the battery from the burned-out Packard, and bring it to Needham. Stokes wanted to see it. Mills returned in an hour. Stokes looked at the battery. It didn't reveal much: it was merely big and black with a partially melted exterior. So Stokes asked Mills to take the battery and Castanino's receipt to the West Newton shop and find out if it had been rented to Castanino.

The fact that Mills rather than a Needham officer, a state police sergeant, or one of the detectives went on the errand suggests that Stokes doubted the battery's significance.

While Mills was away, the Packard arrived at the town garage. Detectives in suits accompanied by a mechanic in coveralls crawled around the interior, sorting through the debris. They opened up the engine compartment, pulled off the tires, and even took the tires off the rims, hoping to find a patched flat that might somehow be unique. Working with them was a Packard company mechanic, Henry Corcoran. As he poked through the engine compartment, Corcoran came across a small metal tube attached to the ignition system. It was a radio-wave suppressor, and its sole function was to reduce the static emitted from a car radio speaker.

It was not a standard part, and Corcoran carefully set it aside.

Mills returned that afternoon and announced that Castanino was in the clear. The shop owner merely glanced at the battery and declared that he had not rented it, had never seen it before, and would have remembered it because no one could buy that battery in a store. It had been assembled with parts from two different manufacturers. The internal cells containing the battery plates and the battery acid were made by Prestolite, while the outer case was manufactured by Hood Rubber. A battery man somewhere else had done custom work.

And custom work was traceable.

Now Stokes realized that the Packard battery could be the clue he sought. It was distinctive, and distinctive meant recognizable. Batteries were short-lived and unreliable. The bandits' Packard battery had to furnish a burst of current for the starter motor and then a steady flow of electricity to the radio receiver. The Packard's electrical system wasn't designed to cope with both demands.[13] Stokes figured the killers, who had gone to so much trouble to plan their crime and set up their automobile, would have ensured that the crucial battery was up to snuff. And unlike the Lynch suppressor, which a shop could have sold months ago, the battery was almost certainly serviced immediately before the robbery. There was a good chance, perhaps better than good, that whoever did the work would recall a battery constructed out of the unusual combination of parts.

That was the good news. The bad news was that "The Boston Directory" listed sixty-seven battery shops in Boston alone.[14]

This time telephone calls would not suffice. The battery had to be seen to be recognized. On Friday morning, February 9, state police detective sergeants John J. Canavan and Harold A. Delaney arrived at the Needham police station. Stokes showed them the battery and said that their first stop was going to be a Prestolite dealer in Boston by the name of Macomber's. Since the battery had been put together, Stokes said he now wanted it taken apart.

Arthur Rankin and John Suttie were at work when the sergeants walked in. They examined the thick, partially melted exterior and used a blowtorch to remove the rubbery compound sealing the top. That exposed the three heavy, square Prestolite battery cells. The two cells on the left were black and gray, and between each cell's nineteen internal plates was a dark-colored separator.

The cell on the right was very different. Indeed, it appeared to be brand-new. There were thin wooden separators, bright and almost white, and un-damaged by the acid. The battery had been repaired, and it was an unusual repair job. Rankin and Suttie explained that the right cell had probably shorted out, so the stock separators were replaced with wood slats of a type they did not recognize. It was original work by an inventive repairman.

It would be recognized by whoever did the repair, but that didn't reduce the number of shops to check. The detectives' task was the very definition of hit or miss. They could strike gold in thirty minutes—the next stop was Hood Rubber in Watertown—or they could trudge from shop to shop for days. The two detectives climbed back in their police cruiser and motored off.

Stokes, nevertheless, was glad for the news, because his day had begun badly. A headline on the front page of the *Boston Globe* declared, "Needham and Vigilantes Hire Own Sleuths." The ugly subhead explained why: "Dissatisfied with Police, Wealthy Citizens Form Secret Group to Find Bank Robbers." The police named in the article were the state police.

The work of Stokes and his team was "aimless and futile," the vigilantes' anonymous spokesman declared. "We do not want to argue," he said, "but we do want action. We expected action, but a week is gone by with much random investigating and no results."

The speaker was described as the group's secretary, who was likely Norris. He complained that the detectives were ignoring palpable leads, like the real estate agent's account of the three toughs who took a tour of the town. He complained that the detectives had ignored an entry in McLeod's pocket notebook giving a hint of those suspects' identities. He complained that police had not raided the Norwood-Westwood area days earlier.

The article does not have a byline, but it had to have been written by Dinneen. That he did not want his name on it is unsurprising. The story is a mishmash of information and reads as though it were written only to massage his source, the vigilante committee. It was important to stay on good terms with them. With their private detectives on the case, he had no way of knowing what they might turn up.

State and local police suffered more embarrassment the next day at the hands of three local teenage boys who scampered to Lily Pond Road after police finished their search. The three were avid readers of the true detective pulps and had decided to put their self-taught skills to the test. They scoured the packed, blackened snow where the Packard had burned. After carefully but fruitlessly poking about, they expanded their search to the fresh snow in the nearby woods. There they turned up one, two, three, and then four bits of cut-up license plate. One bore a smudge that looked like a fingerprint, though it later proved useless. Then one of the trio, Philip King, nineteen, noticed a small slit in the crust of an otherwise undisturbed patch of snow. Beneath the surface he found a bright chrome plate, about 9 inches long and 3 inches wide, inscribed with a serial number and the words "Bosch American Police Radio." That was the manufacturer of the radio stolen from the Mechanics Building.

King explained to reporters, "I figured that the bandits had this radio in the car, see, and all the time the state police were looking for them, they were listening in to what the state police was saying with their own radio. You get it?"

Murt and Norma did not see the story. By that time they were in New York City, having sex.

12

Finally

AS THE NORWOOD TEENAGERS combed through the snow, Murt and Norma climbed into their Chevy sedan and headed south to New York City. It was an all-day journey along the old Atlantic Highway, renamed U.S. 1 when the government started numbering long-distance roadways in the 1920s. From Boston they drove though Providence and New London, continuing along the coast through New Haven and into New York. Their first stop was the Coney Island rooming house where Saul Messinger lived with his brother, George. It was located on Mermaid Avenue, about as far south as one could get in the borough of Brooklyn without wading in the Atlantic Ocean.

Messinger had dropped out of William and Mary College after one year, briefly lived in Washington, D.C., and then gravitated to New York City, where he found a girlfriend, Elsie Rosenbluth, who had recently become his fiancée. He also decided to become a New York City cop. He passed the physical test and was scheduled to take the written exam on March 2.[1]

He was not home when Murt and Norma arrived. They left a message at the rooming house, then motored past the amusement park along the beachfront, and headed into Manhattan, where they rented one of the nine hundred rooms at the Hotel Chesterfield, just off Times Square.

It was 15 feet by 15 feet and furnished with two single beds separated by a lamp and telephone on a night table. Murt and Norma might have specified separate beds, or perhaps only singles were available. But that weekend they managed to fit themselves onto one.

Any account of intimacy as distant as those moments at the Chesterfield risks being no more than speculation, but there are scraps of information, if teased out and placed in context, that suggest Murt and Norma's brief physical life as a couple began this weekend, or in the few days immediately after the Needham killings.

Some evidence comes from Norma herself. At her trial Norma's attorney calculated that convincing the jury she had been a sexual innocent might sway the dozen men otherwise willing to brand her a fast girl, enjoying the company of a fast man, and a murderer to *boot*.

Norma took the stand and, with her eyes downcast and in a tiny voice, said that the first successful "sex act" between herself and Murt occurred three to four weeks before their arrest.[2] That would have placed their first physical intimacy, at least intimacy that Murt would have considered real sex, in the last days of January or during the first week or so of February. Norma's choice of words suggested she was referring to the same month as their arrest. The Needham robbery was on February 2. It seems fair to assume that before the crime Murt was too keyed-up to revisit the failures of his marriage bed.

Other evidence is present by omission from the five-part series Norma wrote, or rather had written for her, as the ghostwriter was clearly being paid by the word. The articles ramble on with overwritten, day-by-day chronicles of the weeks leading up to her arrest. But absent is any mention of those days in New York City, other than a few brief lines that incorrectly describe their trip as a dash in and out of Manhattan. The omission of any detail is telling, as those eventful days loomed large at both trials.

There was also this. Norma mailed a postcard with a photograph of the hotel to her stepmother in Massachusetts. The message was chirpy, even lighthearted. "Murt and I are staying here. Will be buying radio parts. Gee, I have a big wart on my toe and it's got to be cut. Oh, meeee! love Norma." She added a final note after her name: "A kiss for Dad."

Did sex change the nature of their relationship? It certainly eliminated a major point of contention. Tensions between the two had run high. Norma found that the man so charming and considerate during their courtship was less so once they were living together. Each discovered that the other had idiosyncrasies and odd habits that had to be tolerated. And Norma discovered that she had married a criminal. When she found this out would be much debated in the months to come.

MURT ARRANGED to meet Saul and Elsie on Saturday afternoon in the lobby of the Knights of Columbus Hotel at Fifth-First Street and Eighth Avenue, a four-block walk from the Chesterfield. They chatted in the lobby for a half hour until Murt moved the conversation to the Hotel Edison, five minutes and four blocks to the south, where his brother Harry had a room. After a short time in the Edison lobby Murt insisted that they return to the Chesterfield, where they met Norma.

Elsie had been eager to spend an evening in Manhattan with Saul's boyhood friend. She discovered that Murt called him "Buddy," but she found little else appealing about the man. He was oddly fidgety, like a fellow who thought he was being followed. The two couples went out to dinner and a film at Radio City Music Hall, which Elsie considered an unwarranted expense. At the end of the evening, she came away unimpressed with both Murt and his wife. "She was high hat, talking about clothes and beauty treatments," said Elsie, nineteen, who had graduated with honors from high school the year before. She lived in a tenement with her father, a tailor who wasn't finding much work. "I didn't like either one of them," she said. "They brag too much and talk too big . . . Norma kept talking about her clothes and what they cost and what she planned to buy."[3]

Except for Elsie's discomfort, Messinger thought it a pleasant evening. Murt behaving oddly was not unusual. His friend could be quiet and moody or loud and boastful. Messinger was relieved to see no trace of the angry, suicidal man who haunted his dormitory room in Virginia.

The next morning Murt took a call from Messinger. New York was experiencing its own cold and snowy winter, and Elsie had left the galoshes she wore into the city at the hotel. Saul said that he was taking the subway into Manhattan to retrieve them.

Murt and Norma were both in the room when he arrived. Norma was straightening out the odds and ends that spilled out of their suitcases as Murt began to talk. He was glad Saul had come by. After a few minutes of casual conversation Murt leaned closer. "Listen, have you been reading the Boston papers?" Messinger shook his head. Murt nodded. "Well, that's all right. I want you to help me out of a jam." See, he had held up a bank with Irv and "Abel," the MIT grad. "We had to shoot our way out. It was tough, but we could not do anything else," Murt told him.

Messinger looked at Murt and laughed. Was Murt saying he had killed someone? His friend had a boastful, blowhard streak and spun stories of fast cars and narrow escapes that Messinger knew could not be true.

By now Norma was listening to the conversation. "Don't talk so much, Murton. You are telling all you know." Murt shook her off and told Messinger that he needed someone to communicate with Abel in Boston. An intermediary. Murt kept talking. Either he wanted his friend to know just what he was getting involved in or he needed someone to confide in, or maybe he had to boast. It wasn't that he'd just fired a few shots in the air, said Murt.

Had he killed someone?

Well, maybe more than one. There was a dead man in Lynn—which Murt blamed on Faber—and "another job at Fitchburg."

Norma interrupted again. "Are you crazy, Murton? What do you want to talk so much for? Why don't you keep your mouth shut?"

Messinger thought that it was all a tall tale and that Norma was in on the joke. "I began to laugh. I figured that they had rehearsed the whole thing, with the idea that I would believe it. I did not for a minute pay any serious attention to them." He remembered when Murt had boasted that he drove 80 mph down a narrow Boston street. "I couldn't believe they were serious. Norma just sat there with her legs crossed, swinging one foot back and forth." He became even more dubious when he asked Murt, his friend now flush with stolen cash, for a loan to pay back rent. He needed $12. "Murton had only $2 in his pocket and had to get the rest from Norma and Irving. I figured then that his stories about being so desperate and getting a lot of money in a holdup were all bunk."

Nevertheless, Messinger agreed to pass Murt's letters on to Abe. Murt said that he would be in touch. Messinger left with the galoshes.

If Messinger dismissed the tale of a bank robbery and dead men as a macabre joke, events in the middle of that afternoon must have given him pause. At three o'clock, in quick succession, two telegraph messengers bicycled to his rooming house, each carrying a cable from Irv in Boston. Both telegrams said it was urgent that Messinger find Murt and have him call home. Sending two telegrams in a row, delivered by couriers, wasn't cheap.

Messinger telephoned the Chesterfield, only to be told that Murt and Norma had checked out.

Irv had already found them. They were now on a train to Boston, the Chevy stored in a Manhattan garage. Two newspaper reporters had visited Lawrence Avenue, Irv told his brother, and the old man wouldn't stop talking. "Then the reporters met me too," Irv said.

STATE POLICE DETECTIVES Canavan and Delaney began their weekend trying their luck at more battery repair shops. They skirted the Boston

Common early on Saturday, swung past the Public Garden, frozen over and deserted, its swan boats put up for the winter, and headed west one block. They stopped at 33 Newbury Street and carted the heavy battery into George Tufts's shop. He solved the puzzle that had stumped the Prestolite men. Those were "J-type" separators, he told the sergeants, and not very common. Tufts couldn't tell them who did the work but suggested that the detectives stop at Mack's Battery in the South End. Canavan and Delaney drove down to Harrison Street, where Mack's was located. Whatever they learned sent them back to the State House.

That morning the newspapers reported that the Needham vigilante committee was now working with another team of private investigators, hired by the American Banking Association. The detective work did not improve with the addition of more private dicks. They declared that the Needham robbery and four other bank heists were the work of a single criminal organization with tentacles reaching across the state. "Three of the men in the Needham car, according to the private detectives, are known to them . . . They feel that they were shortly closing upon them," said the *Boston Globe*. Clearly, the private investigators were obliged to show something for their fees.

In the State House, Stokes and his team were more concerned about five brass keys they had found scattered in the ashes beneath the burned-out Packard. Three were stamped "us," and after much legwork they proved to be master keys to the state National Guard's weapons lockers, stocked with pistols, rifles, and automatic weapons. While the keys were now in police possession, the bandits could have made copies. And how did they obtain them in the first place? The detectives feared that someone in the Guard, probably a Guard officer, was colluding with the "desperados."

That made quickly capitalizing on their best lead—the battery—all the more important. Traipsing around from battery shop to battery shop was an enormous and potentially futile task. Visiting each one of the shops would take weeks. A solution was proposed by Dinneen and Goldberg—let the newspapers print a photograph of the battery. Someone would recognize it, and that would be good for both their papers and the investigators. Initially the idea gained no traction, but Stokes quickly realized that he needed other police departments to join the battery man search. He decided to issue a bulletin describing the battery and asking police in the five-state region to start knocking on repair shops in their own towns. With that development Dinneen and Goldberg intensified their lobbying effort. They told Stokes that the Sunday newspapers offered the police their best chance. More than a million copies of the two papers were sold in greater Boston, trucked up to New Hampshire and down to Rhode Island. The story would be the talk of the battery trade, and if the sought-for repairman didn't see the article on Sunday, he would surely hear of it on Monday.

The commissioner was reluctant. He feared publication would only guarantee a dead battery man, killed by the bandits to foil investigators.[4] The argument went back and forth. Stokes sided with Dinneen and Goldberg. All knew that Molway and Berrett, the two cabdrivers charged with the Paramount Theatre murder, were scheduled to go on trial Monday. It would be embarrassing if the cabbies were innocent and convicted because the detectives were slow to solve the McLeod and Haddock killings.

But Needham wouldn't budge, so Dinneen and Goldberg returned to their telephones and began calling battery repairmen themselves. According to Dinneen, they were "halfway through the D's" when Needham changed his mind. Stokes had finally convinced him that publication was a bet worth taking. The detective sat down and crafted a cable for transmission by police teletype. It went out at 4:01 p.m.

> To all stations:
>
> Added info Needham Bank job: please check battery repair shops for the following. The battery which was contained in the Packard automobile, which has been positively identified as the car in which the bandits that killed officers Haddock and McLeod of Needham, is described as follows:
>
> A 19 (thin) plate battery with a Hood Rubber case with Prestolite plates. One of the cells was recently re-separated with "J"-type separator.
>
> Will all cities and towns please check all battery repair shops for any information regarding the same.[5]

For good measure Stokes included a description of the five keys found with the burned-out Packard.

Stokes handed a copy to Dinneen and Goldberg, who quickly discovered that the editors they worked for weren't enthralled with the lead-acid battery storyline. Perhaps it was because Stokes insisted on releasing the photo to every Boston paper. The story was no longer an exclusive.

The *Globe* did run a front-page story on the status of the case, but the battery description did not appear until the reader flipped to the inside page and read halfway down the column. The top of the story repeated the stolen National Guard key disclosure from the Saturday edition.

The *Post* relegated its entire update to an inside page, presuming that continuing coverage of the bitter temperatures would attract more readers. Now that large portions of Boston Harbor had frozen over, there were unsurprising stories about youths running out on the ice and then falling through, sometimes being rescued and sometimes not. So, at least in some editions, the day's Needham story was buried, and the battery details were buried even deeper.

The Sunday papers hit New England street corners and doorsteps before dawn. At 1 p.m. the call came in.

It was to Dinneen, and it was from his wife.

Various accounts exist of the events that occurred later that afternoon and evening. Goldberg's was the most detailed, but better written was Dinneen's in *Harper's* magazine. That article mostly told the story of the falsely accused Molway and Berrett, but it included a lengthy aside on the hunt for the battery man. Dinneen could not have resisted. That episode, on a freezing winter afternoon, was one of the most rewarding, frightening, and exhilarating in Dinneen's journalistic career.

Helen Dinneen's full-time job was raising the couple's four children, ranging in age from five to thirteen, so she was at home on Oak Street in Needham when an excited friend called to say that she had just received a very odd call from her own husband. He was William Greene, and he sold dried and unprocessed whole-grain corn from a shop in the Meeting House Hill neighborhood of Dorchester. Greene told his wife that a nearby business owner had just burst though the door grasping the Sunday edition of the *Boston American*. It was opened to a photograph of a lead-acid automobile storage battery. Its top had been sliced off to reveal bright, new separator plates. "I repaired that battery," declared the man in the doorway.

His name was Alfred LeVierge.

He was once an electrician, at Hood Rubber ironically, but as the Depression wore on he ended up pumping gas and fixing cars. In the early 1930s he went to work at his brother's battery shop. After a time Alfred struck out on his own, though the brothers cooperated closely. Indeed, they worked on the Packard battery together.

Dinneen learned much of that later. Now, speaking to his wife, he had a more important question.

Did LeVierge say who asked him to fix the battery?

"Yes," said Helen, "a guy named Miller on Lawrence Avenue in Roxbury."

Dinneen hung up the phone and picked up the telephone book. He found dozens and dozens of Millers, but no listing for a Miller on Lawrence Avenue in Roxbury. Dinneen walked over to the table in the *Globe* newsroom on top of which rested "The Boston Directory." In its 2,514 pages it listed the head of household, spouse, address, and occupation of virtually every adult in Boston. It was cross-referenced by name and street address, so with one he could find the other.[6]

Directories were compiled for almost every major city in the nation. They were of such value to police, salesman, reporters, political campaigns, and anyone else who wanted to know who was where that many publishers rented rather than sold the volumes. In Boston the annual hardcover edition sold for $25; the leather edition cost $29.

Dinneen had only a street name, but that was sufficient.

On page 2,276 of the 1933 volume were four columns beginning with the homes and businesses on Laurel Street and continuing through Lauriat, Lauten Place, Lawn, Lawndale Terrace, Lawnwood Place, Lawrence Street, and finally Lawrence Avenue. The first address was "7 Blumenfeld Abr tailor" followed by "9 Kaplan, Israel" and "11 Vacant store"; then Dinneen's eyes swung to the final, far-right column, where he saw "39 Millen Jos."

Miller. Millen? Of course. That had to be the one.

It looked like battery man LeVierge was the real deal.

It was 2:15 p.m.

"The break had come," Dinneen wrote. "There was nothing to do now but to call the police and get a ringside seat at the arrest." Dinneen reached Captain Michael Barrett, the acting commander of the state detective force and Stokes's boss. The conversation was short and sweet.

"The battery in that Needham car was repaired by Alfred LeVierge of

Dorchester for a Joseph Millen of 39 Lawrence Ave. Better get a squad car out there. Goldberg and I are leaving now."

Barrett replied with a tired "Okay." Unfortunately for him, this Sunday afternoon telephone call was perhaps the hundredth such tip to cross his desk since February 2. In the past ten days Barrett, like the rest of the squad, had gotten little sleep and certainly not a weekend off. Barrett took down the address, made a note summarizing Dinneen's message, and stuck it on the pile with all the other tips.

DINNEEN AND GOLDBERG considered how to proceed. They decided to wait. They did not want to arrive before the police, as it seemed unwise to go knocking on the door of a desperate cop killer before the cops did. They left twenty-five minutes later with Goldberg driving.

When they turned off Blue Hill Avenue and motored up Lawrence Avenue, the reporters were puzzled and then disappointed. The street was empty. There were no police. Dinneen figured they had waited too long and the detectives had made their arrest and departed. If the drama was over, there was still work to be done. Maybe someone in the Millen house would talk. It was difficult to predict a family's reactions. Sometimes parents and siblings wanted to plead the accused's case, other times the door was slammed with a shout to get off the property, and on rare occasions someone would throw a punch. Reporters were like cops, however, in that they usually didn't have to worry about getting shot.

The house was on the right, faded white and yellow, in the middle of the block. Dinneen and Goldberg walked up the stairs and found the front door ajar. Dinneen pushed it open and saw "a short, squat man of about 55 with a gray stubbly beard" descending the interior stairs. He was tugging at his suspenders.

"Who you looking for?" the man asked.

The reporters suddenly realized that they were not late; the police were. In their surprise the mental list of questions they had compiled momentarily vanished. What if the killers were inside? They were now faced with the task of delicately extracting themselves. But they had to say something.

The obvious question popped out.

"We are looking for Joseph Millen."

"I'm Joe. What do you want?" said the man with the suspenders. That was followed by the next obvious question. Did he own a black Packard? No, said Joe. His car was a Chevrolet. But the query led Joe to conclude that the two men in suits and ties and fedoras, desperately exuding confidence, were agents from the Registry of Motor Vehicles. Law enforcement, but not quite police. That misapprehension was fine with Dinneen. "I submit that a little plain and fancy lying under the circumstances was permissible," he later wrote. It provided them a cover for the string of questions that came flooding out.

Did he have any sons? Yes, said Joe, three — Murton, Irving, and Harry — and no, they couldn't speak with them. "The boys ain't home. Murton, he's gone to New York with his wife. Harry, he's in New York too; and Irving, I don't know where that boy is but he ain't in now."

Goldberg asked about Murt's wife. Perhaps the *Post* reporter also dropped a word or two of Yiddish, because the father became more talkative. Yeah, Murton was married, Joe said, and in a voice Dinneen described as "indignant and profane" complained that his son "married a Gentile." The ceremony wasn't conducted by a rabbi but a justice of the peace. His name was Sam Thorner, an assistant district attorney in Suffolk County. Perhaps the registry agents knew him? The reporters actually did and nodded yes. Joe talked on about the radio business Murton ran with a fellow by the name of Abraham Faber, a neighborhood kid who had graduated from MIT. The conversation was interrupted when a woman's voice from inside the house yelled at Joe in Yiddish. Goldberg cocked his head to catch the words and at the same time spotted, on a table down the hallway, in plain view, the ammunition magazine of a semiautomatic pistol. He figured it was time to go. Once outside, Goldberg translated.

"She's bawling him out for talking to us about Murton and Irving. She told him he's crazy and will get them into trouble. She said something about keeping out of the cellar."

In Goldberg's account, the reporters brazenly told Joe that they were there about a crime. They asked him if his sons had ever patronized LeVierge's battery shop. No, he said. Joe insisted that they were "law-abiding boys and never in trouble." That weekend Murt was "out of town on business with his wife and brother Harry." He told them that Faber lived on Blue Hill Avenue and that he and Murt were "very chummy." Goldberg said that when the woman, whom he identified as Joe's daughter Frances, yelled her "emphatic warning," the conversation ended with Joe Millen saying, "My boys are not mixed up in any robberies and murders, if that is what you're trying to find out."

As the reporters walked back to their car, a Chevy pulled up. Inside were two men. The young driver identified himself as "Irving Nelson."

Dinneen and Goldberg knew that this was not the moment to stop asking questions.

Irv's use of the pseudonym was short-lived. He soon told the reporters that neither he nor his brother owned or operated a Packard, and even answered a question about firearms—neither had any. Irv contradicted his father and told them that Murt was "around the corner with his girl."

Goldberg concluded that Irv was an inventive but transparent liar. "His questions and answers during the interview convinced the reporters that he was hiding the truth. In reaching this conclusion then and there we gave consideration to his conduct at the time, suspicious discrepancies in his replies and statements, his omissions, his false statements, the natural reluctance . . . and his desire to volunteer evidence in the Needham bank robbery killings." Irv said that one perpetrator was "Bad Eye" McGinnis, a known killer from Providence. The small man in the car with Irv, Edward Frye, said little.

Once again the conversation was ended by Frances. She appeared in the doorway and "excitedly warned him against talking to us anymore" As he started for the house, she informed Irv that "New York is on the telephone."

The reporters' next step was to talk to the neighbors, though first they probably got into their car, drove around the corner, and parked nearby to mislead anyone watching from the Millen home. They knocked on doors up and down the street and stuck their heads into local shops. Joe was contradicted on a key fact. The Millen brothers had indeed been seen driving "a big black Packard sedan." Sometimes it was operated by a "pretty girl," they were told, though the car was seldom parked at the house overnight. No one much liked Murt or Irv. "Bad eggs," said one man.

Back downtown, late that afternoon, the reporters called Thorner, who had married Murt and Norma. As a favor he went to his office and pulled Murt's marriage records. He remembered the couple. He was uncomfortable performing an interfaith marriage, what with Norma being the daughter of a clergyman, but he knew Murt's older sister, Frances. So he agreed.

Thorner gave the reporters the couple's address, 1175 Boylston Street. Dinneen and Goldberg must have wondered if it could really be true that a
Jewish murderer was married to a minister's daughter.

By now it was the evening of Sunday, February 11. The obvious next
step was to go back to their respective newspapers and write a story for the
following day's front page. But mulling over exactly what they would write
may have made them reconsider. What could they say, exactly? That they
found a man, or maybe two, who at one time had possession of a battery
later found inside the burned-out Packard? What did that prove? And did
they really know that for sure? They had not spoken with LeVierge, only
relied on a secondhand account. Sure, Joe and Irv lied to them, but that
wasn't illegal. If pressed, the reporters could cobble together the available
facts to suggest that a Millen was somehow involved, but that was far short
of putting anyone in the car with guns on February 2. And who was Abraham Faber?

Dinneen and Goldberg realized that they faced a dead end. What were
they going to do next, knock on Murton Millen's apartment door and get
shot? "After much debate," Goldberg later wrote, the two decided to report
back to Stokes.

But first, Goldberg made a telephone call.

In an extraordinary paragraph he describes a conversation that leads to
only one conclusion: someone living at 39 Lawrence Avenue was informing
on Murt and Irv.

> Reporters Goldberg and Dinneen went to a telephone and communicated
> with a certain party whose identity cannot be revealed for obvious reasons.
> Reporter Goldberg had conferred with the party earlier in the day and
> had made certain requests of this party. This party informed reporter
> Goldberg, upon being called the second time, that a telephone call had
> been put in from the Millen home to the Knights of Columbus Hotel in
> New York City, the Lincoln Hotel, and to a Coney Island home. The
> conversation was between members of the Millen household and a man
> answering to the name of "Murton." The conversation was a warning
> that "police were checking the battery of the Packard sedan repaired at
> LeVierge's." The conversation also revealed that "Irving is leaving for New
> York right away."

Who could have known those facts?

Certainly not the police. Surely not the Burns detectives. Neither yet knew the Millen family even existed. It was someone who had overheard the telephone calls. For that there were only two possibilities. One was that Goldberg had a source inside the telephone company who tapped the telephone. It is not inconceivable, though it is unlikely, that after Dinneen and Goldberg discovered the 39 Lawrence Avenue address but before they left their offices, Goldberg called the source and asked that person to listen in on any phone calls from the Lawrence Avenue address. But this was a Sunday, tapping a telephone was illegal, and it wasn't as simple as clicking a switch in the central office.

The only other possibility was a family member. Present at the Millen home in Boston that day were Joe, Carolyn, Frances, Mary and her husband, Harry Goodman, and Idalyn, a teenager in high school.

The likely candidate was Frances Millen. She was involved in local Democratic politics and had organized receptions for local candidates during which she could have met Goldberg. That was probably how she knew the assistant district attorney who married Murt and Norma. The Millens' neighborhood on the Roxbury-Dorchester line was also surrounded by many of the city's largest Jewish synagogues, and Frances was a talented, experienced vocalist who sang with a variety of Jewish choral groups. In 1933 she was a soloist in the Temple Israel choir, a venerable Boston institution founded in 1854 by German Jews. Temple Israel in the 1930s was home to an "Americanized" congregation with a reputation for discouraging membership by Russian and Polish immigrants with their Yiddish language and "shtel" culture. It could well have been the synagogue Goldberg attended, if he attended synagogue with any regularity, as it is hard to imagine the hard-charging reporter taking time off for Friday evening or Saturday morning Sabbath services. He may have shown up for the major Jewish religious holidays.[7]

Nevertheless, Frances Millen and Goldberg could have known each other. If she knew that her brothers were up to no good, might she have felt compelled to seek advice? Why not approach the well-known Jewish crime reporter? Goldberg would have eagerly promised her anonymity in return for information.

The other possible source was Harry Goodman, Mary's husband. The couple had a four-year-old daughter, Gloria. At that time he was a self-employed music teacher, a job that did not generate much income. His wife did not work, and they had no choice but to live with her parents, much to Harry's dismay, as he thought little of Joe and less of Murt.

Members of the Millen family probably knew that Murt and Irv were skating close to the edge of the law. If Harry suspected that his brothers-in-law had graduated to murder, he could well have worried about the well-being of his wife and young daughter. However, no connection between Harry and Goldberg has surfaced.

But all that is speculation. The identity of the person Goldberg says he telephoned remains unknown.

AFTER GOLDBERG HUNG UP, he and Dinneen walked to Room 24. They asked if the detectives had any news on the battery, for if they had by now found LeVierge, the reporters would be off the hook and might even get a story. Instead they were told "nothing yet" and so were obliged to fess up.

Needham and Stokes pulled them into a side room and listened with growing unhappiness as the reporters recounted their day's work. The detective and the commissioner were, Goldberg wrote, "very much disturbed." But the reporters said they had called Barrett. It was not their fault if he ignored the message. Anyway, a now furious Goldberg declared that Barrett's inaction had put the reporters' lives at risk. Barrett, who had walked into the room, snapped back, "I can't send a squad of men out on every wild tip that comes into this office."

"You'd rather let us walk empty-handed into a machine gun nest?" Goldberg replied.

Needham interjected. "You shouldn't have gone there . . . You are guilty of obstructing justice."

After trading more recriminations, Stokes and Needham asked the reporters not to print any news about the battery, the Millens, or the LeVierge brothers—not until police gave the okay. The reporters agreed. Needham later made the same request of other newspapers as their reporters got wind of the battery story from Boston police sources. "Editors of all Boston papers were communicated with and were requested temporarily to withhold publication of these facts," said a 1935 state police report. "All of the newspaper editors promised to do so. All kept their promise." Police told the editors that premature publication would foil their investigation. It was also true that disclosure of Barrett's failure to follow up on the tip, thereby allowing the reporters to discover the battery's owners before the police, would have embarrassed the detectives and Governor Ely just as he was pushing his police unification bill.

THE FIRST OFFICIAL INFORMATION on the LeVierge brothers reached Room 24 later that night when Dinneen and Goldberg had already departed.

After Alfred's excited declaration at Greene's shop, the battery man buttonholed a beat officer, who took down his statement at 1:00 p.m. LeVierge said that a man came to his business on January 24 to have the "end cell of the 19 plate J-type stub handle battery repaired and the battery recharged." The customer returned on January 27 and "said at the time the battery was used in a Packard automobile." He described the man as "26 to 30 years, 5'11", Jewish, 150, slim build, wearing a light gray soft hat, dark suit, and dark overcoat."

The patrolman filed his report, noting that the city detective bureau was contacted at 3:45 p.m. and told to immediately forward the information to state and Needham police.

That didn't happen.

Out of carelessness or pettiness, Boston police did not call the State House until late that night, after Stokes and Needham had spoken to Dinneen and Goldberg, Fleming wrote in a report to his superiors.

By then the reporters had made their way to Boston police headquarters to tell their story again, along with an additional tidbit. "We were sure of instant cooperation since this information we had would give them an opportunity to beat the state police," Dinneen wrote with unusual candor.[8]

The tip they had not given to Stokes—they may have forgotten in the stress of the moment—was Murt and Norma's Boylston Street address copied from their marriage license.

"We were not walking into a second machine gun nest if we could avoid it," Dinneen wrote.

13

Ambush

STOKES AND FERRARI finally spoke to the LeVierge brothers on Monday morning. The men, who had already told their story to friends, family, and the Boston police, told it again. The brothers were reading the Sunday paper at their separate homes when, at nearly the same moment, they recognized their own handiwork staring at them from the newsprint. They met, studied the photograph together, considered the $21,000 reward, and decided to contact police.

The young, curly-haired man who had arrived at Alfred's shop had introduced himself and lifted a battery out of the back of a small coupe. It would not hold a charge, the man explained, and he needed a quick repair. Three days later he returned for the battery with another man, whom Alfred said he recognized now as Murton Millen, with an "n." Frank vouched for the identification.

The LeVierge brothers were certain the battery Stokes had pulled from the Packard was the battery they had repaired. It had the same nonstandard exterior box and, more important, the oversized wooden separators the LeVierges had installed. Each separator was fashioned from Port Orford white cedar, a chemically resistant, porous wood valued for its ability to withstand battery acid while allowing ions to move between the positive and negative panels and so generate electric current.[1]

Mere possession of the battery did not make the Millen brothers the killers, yet their identification by the battery man forced the detectives to finally revise their theory of the case. The proposition that veteran gunmen had committed the robbery and killings of McLeod and Haddock was perhaps very wrong. Instead of hardened thugs, the likely suspects were two young men, and maybe a third—since they did not know what to make of Abe. None had a criminal record, and all three belonged to a Boston ethnic group considered least likely to harbor street bandits and gunmen.

Murt, Irv, and Abe's religion did not preclude membership in a criminal gang, but nothing had been found linking them to the largest and best-known Jewish criminal organization in the Northeast, a syndicate until recently run by Charles "King" Solomon. He was another middle-class Jewish boy, also the son of Russian immigrants, who grew up working in his family's Boston restaurant at the turn of the century before deciding that life in the streets was more to his liking. Within a decade "King" Solomon was deeply involved in illegal gambling, narcotics, and bootlegging.

On January 24, 1933, the "King" was having dinner with two female friends, one blonde and the other brunette, at the Cotton Club, a small music and dining spot on Tremont Street. When Solomon rose from his table to use the washroom, four men sitting in another corner of the restaurant got up and followed him inside.

The "King" emerged moments later with one bullet through his neck, another in his chest, and a third in his abdomen. Nonetheless, he walked out unaided and announced, "I have been shot." He asked the maître d' to get a doctor and then added, "Perhaps you would be able to get a cab and send me to the hospital." Solomon survived long enough to whisper, "The rats got me." Thousands turned out for his funeral. The restroom shooting marked the high point of Boston's Jewish mob.

Stokes and Ferrari also had to consider a Millen connection to the better-known Jewish mobsters in New York City. They included "Dutch" Schultz, born Arthur Flagenheimer, and Jacob "Gurrah" Shapiro, one of the organizers of Murder Inc., founded in the late 1920s by a consortium of Italian and Jewish gangsters. The two ethnic groups were usually criminal competitors, which was bad for business, so in November 1931 the Jews and Italians sat down to halt the intra-criminal bloodshed. At the end of the meeting Bugsy Siegal, the gangster who created Las Vegas, is said to have declared, "The Yids and the Dagos will no longer fight each other."

But the Millen brothers and Abe were neither mobsters nor Capone-type gangsters. They were not involved in gambling, loan sharking, prostitution, or drugs. They did not aspire to run a street organization. They merely wanted money.

ON MONDAY AND TUESDAY Boston police and state detectives searched the Millen home and interviewed family members. Carolyn repeated a cover story concocted by Murt and Irv—that the brothers had merely repaired the battery for a customer whose real name they never learned. Days later, "gangsters" showed up at Lawrence Avenue and warned the family against cooperating with detectives. Or else. So Murt and Irv fled.

The search was futile, but legwork produced stories of the Millens' rough edges. Joe Millen's bootlegging conviction surfaced, as did his sour reputation among other contractors. The old man's persistent legal corner cutting, however, could not be laid on his sons and was a far cry from machine gun murder. Both brothers had a penchant for ignoring motor vehicle laws. Neighbors on Lawrence Avenue convinced police that Murt, in particular, was trouble.

Abe was another matter. Stokes and Ferrari knew that almost anyone could become embroiled in crime given the right set of circumstances, so Abe's academic pedigree was no free pass. But he was low on the list of probable killers. While the two detectives quizzed the LeVierge brothers, it was Canavan who was dispatched to Faber's radio shop on Monday. He was greeted by Joe Rothberg, Abe's partner, who confirmed that the Millen brothers were employees. They were on a job and expected back that afternoon, he said. Abe was not present, but presumably he told Rothberg what to say if anyone inquired.

Rothberg brought to the partnership previous experience in the radio business. He had invested $750 worth of parts and equipment, and Abe contributed $1,300 for rent and tools. The money may have come from his parents, from his short-lived teaching job, or maybe from the proceeds of a holdup. Both partners signed the store lease, and Rothberg believed that Abe was in for the long haul. "He insisted the business be run 100% proficiently and honestly, because we had all the intention in this world of making a successful business out of it," Rothberg said. They billed themselves as wholesalers, and when Rothberg tried to make extra money selling parts at retail he was scolded by Abe.[2]

Canavan staked out the store until the 6:00 p.m. closing. Murt and Irv never appeared.

As for Abe, in a state police memo Fleming said that he was "sent for and interviewed at our office in the state house" on Monday. "From him we got a description of the car which the Millens were using."[3] There is no other reference to that meeting in any other document, newspaper account, or trial testimony. Presuming the date of the meeting is correct, Abe must have said nothing to turn suspicion toward himself. Tellingly, neither Stokes nor Ferrari bothered to speak with him.

That benign neglect vanished within twenty-four hours as the detectives came to appreciate the importance of the Lynch suppressor. At a meeting late on Monday, Henry Corcoran, the Packard mechanic, handed the suppressor over to the detectives and noted its sole use as a radio static suppressor. Clara Hartigan of Newton, owner of the stolen Packard, confirmed that she had never installed a radio. The Lynch suppressor was not widely available in Boston. But which shops stocked it? Detectives had already compiled a list of radio supply houses in the greater Boston area. The dismayingly long tally ran to three single-spaced pages, and even at that was missing Faber's radio store, as it had opened only in October.[4] But thanks to Dinneen and Goldberg's conversation with Joe Millen, the detectives knew of its existence and location. Now they wondered if Abe Faber sold the part.

On Tuesday morning at 9:15 a.m. Ferrari stepped over the threshold of green and white five-sided tiles and opened the glass door of Faber's shop. He shook hands with Rothberg and then faced a thin, diffident mustachioed man. "I was introduced to Faber as the proprietor," Ferrari said. He opened the conversation with a bit of misdirection. Ferrari asked if the store stocked automobile radio condensers, which were used to tune in specific radio frequencies. Faber showed him two different models. After a bit more chitchat, Ferrari asked if the store also carried radio noise suppressors, specifically the Lynch make. "And he says he did carry them. I asked him if he had any in stock. He said yes. I asked if I could see one, and he said yes, and he showed it to me," Ferrari said.[5]

Ferrari rolled it over in his hands and saw that it resembled the part from the Packard. "I asked him if the Lynch suppressor could be bought anywhere else in Boston, and he said that he thought there was only one place that they could be had," a shop near the North End. As the conversation neared its end, Abe tried a bit of misdirection himself. There had been a recent break-in, he told Ferrari, and a police band radio set was taken. Perhaps he was suggesting that a Lynch suppressor was stolen, too. Ferrari thought he seemed very eager to help out and wondered about what it took to get the $20,000 state reward.

Before the day ended, Stokes also appeared at the store with some follow-up questions about radio electronics. More likely, Stokes wanted to get a look at this fellow Faber, now of increasing interest to the investigators. Afterward, the detectives remarked to each other that Abe seemed "just ordinary." He conversed calmly, with an occasional smile. The only odd aspect they noted was his twitch.

But they must have suspected something, because they never asked the obvious questions: Did Abe sell a suppressor to the Millens? Was one missing from his stock? Did he know anything about the bank robbery?

For Abe, the meetings with Ferrari and Stokes were bad news. They meant that he was cemented in place. The police knew that he knew Murt and Irv, and Abe must have realized exactly why they inquired about the Lynch suppressor. If he disappeared now, he would essentially label himself a suspect in a cop killing.

THAT LABEL was all but officially applied to Murt and Irv Millen that evening. State police sent out this bulletin on Tuesday at 11 p.m.: "Wanted for questioning by state police in connection with a robbery at Needham Trust Company in Needham, February 2, 1934, and murder of officers Forbes McLeod and Frank Haddock of the Needham Police Department. Irving Millen, 20, 5′10″, weighing 155 pounds, slim build, whose address is 39 Lawrence Av, Roxbury and his brother, Merton Millen, 25, 5′9½″, weighing 160 pounds, slim build, whose address is 1175 Boylston St., Boston."[6]

The message clacked into the District 16 station house on Boylston Street near Massachusetts Avenue, only a few blocks from Murt and Norma's apartment, where sergeant Charles F. Eldridge was on duty. Despite the late hour, accompanied by two other officers and not bothering with the niceties of a search warrant, Eldridge rushed over to 1175 Boylston Street and persuaded the building's janitor to let them into the apartment. They found dressers packed with personal belongings, and books and magazines scattered about the living room. A clue finally appeared when Eldridge upended a trash can and saw a stamped, sealed, but never mailed envelope addressed to "Saul Messinger, Mermaid Ave., Brooklyn, N.Y."

Until then neither police nor detectives had ever heard of Saul Messinger, and nothing linked the Millen brothers to New York City other than the comment overheard a few days earlier by Dinneen and Goldberg—presuming that they had told police of Frances's remark. Even if they had, where would police start to look in America's largest city? Now that was a problem solved. Eldridge carried the letter back to his station house, and his commander dispatched the envelope to the detective bureau with a recommendation that it be forwarded immediately to Stokes and Ferrari.

That never happened. One reason is that the bad blood between Governor Ely's administration and local police had turned truly poisonous.

On the same Sunday that Dinneen and Goldberg visited the Millens home, state attorney general Joseph E. Warner appeared before a group of North Shore businessmen and declared that McLeod's death was the result of the officer's faulty training. Running up to the bank without first calling for help from other officers was "a foolish piece of police work."

Warner was a Republican, but his remarks put him squarely in the Democratic governor's police-unification camp. An experienced politician now in his second term, he did not mince his words, which were widely reported in the Monday newspapers.

"The killing of the Needham police officer could've been avoided if these men had received the proper training. Instead of rushing up to the bank when he heard the alarm, the officer would've notified the station house of the robbery and then taken a point behind a tree, wall or house.

"Another officer would soon have their entrance covered, likewise hidden from view, after hearing from the first officer. They would have had a chance to halt the escape of the bandits when they attempted to leave the bank and at least an even chance in the gunfight."

His critique of the dead officer was enough to generate outrage among police, but Warner wasn't done. Police officers across the state were woefully undertrained and frequently undeserving of the title, he said. "Today we are giving him a uniform, a gun, and a club and call[ing] him a policeman. Ridiculous! He is but a uniformed man walking about. He is not equipped to cope with banditry. The Needham police job was a foolish piece of police work."

It was not a question of courage, he said. "There would be fewer police killings if the police were yellow. They are not, they are walking to certain death time and again."

And dead officers did not discourage the criminals.

"The underworld must be laughing quietly at the futile efforts made by police departments to halt them at work. They are certainly not frightened of us."

The resulting furor need not be guessed at, though privately many officials would have agreed with Warner. Chief Bliss's response appeared in Tuesday papers. He accused the elected attorney general of, shockingly, playing politics. As for the complaint that his men were insufficiently trained, Bliss gave the only response he could, which was to cite McLeod's bravery. "This policeman happened to be a war veteran. Trained in the use of guns and taught never to waver in the face of duty—to respond at once to an alarm call for assistance."

The outcry helps explain why Sergeant Eldridge's superiors did nothing with the new clue. Why rush to make the state cops look good? For two days the letter sat, untouched, on a desk inside the Boston detective bureau. Neither Stokes nor Ferrari was informed. The envelope was finally delivered to Chief Bliss on Thursday.

He didn't tell the state police about it, either.[7]

THE TUESDAY NIGHT BULLETIN released Dinneen and Goldberg from their promise of confidentiality.

On Wednesday morning the public read about the Millen brothers for the first time. Stories appeared in most of the major newspapers, some sympathetically describing the brothers not as potential perpetrators but as potential victims. "Needham Slayers Nab 2 as Hostages," the *Boston Daily Record* declared on its front page. The *Record* was one of two papers published in Boston by William Randolph Hearst. The other was the *American*, and between the two they represented nearly half the newspaper circulation in eastern Massachusetts. The *Record* described the brothers as mechanics who had had the bad luck to repair a battery for the bandits and so had seen the killers.

"Hot on the trail, police believe that the brothers would be able to furnish them with the identities," the paper said. As "key witnesses" the *Record* declared, police feared the bank robbers would "silence them forever."

The *Globe* story said police worried that the brothers had been kidnapped by the Needham robbers. Carolyn Millen was quoted repeating Irv's tale that he and Murt met the killers while working on their auto. The papers said she told police that two strange men came to the Lawrence Avenue home and told her they "had" her sons and would "get" the rest of the family "if there was any trouble."

Goldberg in the *Post* was less sympathetic and declared that the two Roxbury brothers were "wanted for questioning in connection with the murders and robbery." In unemotional language he wrote that the police did indeed fear that Murt and Irv had been slain by the bank robbers and then offered a remarkably positive portrait of the Millen family. Irv was said to have "a reputation above reproach all his life." Murt had "never been involved in any trouble with the authorities and has enjoyed an irreproachable reputation." Joe Millen was described as a well-known Boston contractor, and Goldberg called him "active in Roxbury affairs for many years." Perhaps Goldberg did not want to speak ill of the possibly dead. Or perhaps he wanted to preserve his source.

Not a single article had yet mentioned Abe Faber or hinted that Murt was married.

LATER THAT DAY Stokes, Ferrari, and Fleming made their own visit to unit 3 at 1175 Boylston Street. They had received a tip that the Millen brothers were back in town, though from what source is unknown. The detectives left behind their .38 revolvers and armed themselves with powerful .45 caliber semiautomatic pistols. The building janitor let them in and probably told them that Boston police had searched the premises the day before. The three detectives positioned themselves inside the apartment so they had a clear view of the doorway and a modicum of protection if weapons were drawn. Then they sat down to wait. The teletype bulletin had produced no firm leads, but scraps of information were filtering back to the state detectives. So they waited and listened for a knock on the door or the sound of a key in the lock.

It came in the early afternoon. The door opened and standing there was a short, stout teenage girl. She was Idalyn, the brothers' seventeen-year-old sister, and she found herself facing three drawn pistols.

Idalyn knew that her brothers were up to no good. She was probably sent to scout for the very detectives now facing her in the doorway, because at that moment Murt and Irv were parked outside with the Thompson. Their location may have been some 200 yards south, where Boylston meets Park Drive, and the three-way intersection would allow for an easy getaway or a quick dash past 1175 Boylston with the engine screaming and the Thompson chattering as the detectives emerged into the cold air. The only thing was, Stokes, Ferrari, and Fleming walked out with Idalyn. The detectives later became convinced that Idalyn's presence had saved their lives. She was a shield, and she foiled Murt's plan to kill three more cops.

"I guess they meant to get us," said Ferrari.[8]

"That is probably so. We went to the place and could have been put on the spot," said Fleming.

Up in Lynn, cabdrivers Molway and Berrett were thinking much the same thing, though the people gunning for them were the district attorney and his investigators. They were going on trial for murders they did not commit.

14

Certainty

MICHAEL FORD, a small, thin-faced man with reddish hair and a thick Irish brogue, raised his right arm and pointed across the courtroom, past the reporters scribbling on their pads and the public benches packed with spectators, to where Clement Molway and Lewis Berrett sat. It was those two, Ford said, "that man on the right and the man on the left." It was Berrett who had manhandled poor Harry Condon at the start of the Paramount Theatre robbery, and it was Molway who moments later shot Condon in the back as the janitor made a break for the doorway.

Ford was certain, and said so with a self-confidence that withstood four hours of cross-examination.

Wasn't it too dark in the theater to make an identification? "It would've been—for anyone not accustomed to it," Ford replied. He coolly conceded he couldn't recall the color of Molway's suit or whether he wore an overcoat or even whether Molway had worn glasses. "I didn't bother with those things. I only took a good look at his face, because that's what I wanted," said Ford.[1] He couldn't forget. Berrett had pushed him into the theater office at gunpoint and punched him in the jaw for not moving fast enough.

Ford's account launched five days of testimony, which the cabbies listened to with a combination of stunned amazement and dismay. A succession of witnesses, none of whom they had never met, and none of whom had ever met them, calmly assured the world that the defendants were indeed robbers and killers. Molway and Berrett found themselves grappling with a kind of reality-induced vertigo. "I suppose they thought they were right, but some of them were tough on us," Berrett said. "All the time they are testifying I'm saying to myself, 'They're lying. They must know better. I was never there. They must know better.'"[2]

The case was followed by readers all over New England. Defense attorneys Charles E. Flynn for Berrett and John P. Kane for Molway waged a two-pronged attack on the prosecution. One was undertaken in the county courtroom; the other was in the Boston newspapers. The attorneys diligently lobbied the reporters arriving in Lynn. Flynn and Kane insisted that their clients were innocent. The cabdrivers had not robbed the theater, they had not shot Condon, and they had not beaten and put a bullet in the head of Charles F. Sumner, the bill poster who interrupted the heist and paid with his life. Their clients had solid alibis, and a slew of witnesses were going to take the stand and prove that on January 2, 1934, both men were in Boston, going to a repair shop, picking up passengers, eating breakfast. No way could they have made the forty-minute drive north to Lynn, spent two hours holding the eleven theater employees hostage, and then fled south in time to be back in their cabs by noon as the prosecutor claimed.

The Essex County district attorney, Hugh A. Cregg, had it wrong and was going to face an embarrassment like the one he suffered last summer. That was when Cregg prosecuted housewife Jessie Costello for poisoning and killing her fire captain husband.

A talkative, self-promoting exhibitionist, she eagerly took the witness stand and ran circles around Cregg. Even after admitting to a much deplored affair with a police officer—she apparently liked men in uniform—which Cregg named as the motive for the murder, the jury acquitted her in only ninety minutes. Afterward Costello announced that she was interested in a film career.

Her triumph—and Cregg's defeat—were splashed across newspapers from Maine to California, and the ex-defendant was the subject of two long articles in the *New Yorker*, a magazine not always attentive to murders in the hinterland. All in all it was a good story, and reporters wondered if Cregg wasn't blessing them again. The cabbies' trial promised to be one of those rare occasions when two sets of seemingly credible eyewitnesses stood before a jury and, under oath, laid out two very different sets of supposed facts. It would be left to the jurors to make a decision that would, quite literally, mean life or death.

Ford was followed by Mary Cleary, the cleaning woman who said she'd seen Berrett close up under the light of two 100-watt bulbs. He had promised her that if she posed no problem, "I'll treat you right. If you don't, you'll be sorry."[3] She also gave the first description of the mysterious third man still sought by police: tall, with a thin, sharp face, and dressed in what looked to be a military uniform with a leather strap crossing his torso from shoulder to belt.

Condon himself then took the stand and named Berrett as the man who grappled with him moments before a second bandit shot him.

"He took hold of me and wanted me to go in the office," Condon said. Condon resisted and the two men ended up in a shoving match. Then Condon turned to run. "The next thing I knew I got shot in the shoulder. I don't know where the shot came from." Condon fell, was pulled up, and "I was told to go in the office. Berrett told me."

The wound in his shoulder was painful, but the small, low-powered .22 caliber bullet did not reach any vital organs. The bandits bawled him out, though Condon was not sure who said what. "You damned fool! You will know when to stop the next time," one said. Another added, "You poor bastard, it's too bad you got beat up but you'll know better next time."

By the end of the week ten eyewitnesses had testified. Two of the ten positively identified both Berrett and Molway. Five identified one or the other. Three witnesses said they couldn't definitely identify either man.

"It was murder. Only I was the one being murdered," said Berrett. "It got to the point where Molway and I would try to laugh at it. Then we would get serious again. I'd try to make a wisecrack, but some of the time I couldn't do it."[4]

No one could say who shot Sumner. The hostages inside the manager's office only heard shouts, a scuffle, the crack of a gun, and a thump. But it didn't matter. Cregg's eyewitnesses testified as they promised. They had told the truth, or rather the truth as they knew it.

NEITHER STOKES NOR FERRARI ever recorded the conversation they had with Idalyn Millen. The next day, Thursday, February 15, Murt was officially elevated to the status of a fugitive wanted for murder.

The announcement was made in a bulletin that went out over the teletype wires at 12:54 p.m.: "Further info re Murton Millen wanted by the Mass. State Police in the Needham Trust Company robbery and the murder of police officers McLeod and Haddock." With the use of "wanted," the police made clear that it was no longer a matter of just questioning him.

They gave his correct height, 6′1″, and described him as having black hair and brown eyes.[5]

No mention was made of Irv, indicating that the detectives had figured out the Millen who mattered was the older brother. Neither was any mention made of Abe.

More significantly, the bulletin publicly linked Norma to Murt for the first time.

Released to newspapers and radio stations after it was tapped out on the teletype, the bulletin named her as Murt's wife and included the names of her father, her mother, and even the date she and Murt filed for a marriage license. It described the automobile Murt was believed to be driving, a 1933 four-door Chevy sedan bought used the previous September. The bulletin closed with a request to the teletype office: "Will you please see that this is sent as far over the country as possible?"

Investigators also mailed copies of a letter signed by Daniel Needham to every financial institution in greater Boston—perhaps a hundred banks and trust companies—asking each to search its files for any evidence of an account or safety deposit box opened by Murt, Irv, or Norma.

"There is every reason to believe," the letter said, that "Murton Millen . . . had some participation" in the Needham bank robbery. It noted that he had recently married Norma and said "there was also some reason to believe" that Irving had played some role in the crime.[6]

Again no mention was made of Abe.

But he was not being ignored. As the state police secretarial staff ran dozens of envelopes through their manual typewriters, carefully addressing each, Stokes and Ferrari called Abe into their office.

It was a fifteen-minute walk from his shop on Columbus Avenue, across the Boston Common and up the short incline to the State House. The detectives occupied a small corner suite on the ground floor. Officially it was in the basement, but the rooms were above grade and large windows faced north and east. A series of thick, white columns lined the hallway. The floor was plain concrete. Above were the House and Senate chambers, the governor's office, and, most memorable, the golden, glowing Memorial Hall. Crafted from Sienna marble to honor the state's Civil War dead, it was a kaleidoscope of yellows, reds, and greens certain to stun first-time visitors into silence.

When Abe walked into the office, the detectives were surprised to see a woman accompanying him. She was Rose Knellar.

Ferrari led Abe into a private office and asked if he knew the whereabouts of Murt and Irv.

Abe said he did not. Ferrari mulled this over and replied that he had a request. "I'd received information that he had a photograph of Murt Millen, and I asked if I could have it." How Ferrari knew that is unknown, but more interesting was that he asked Abe for a copy. It was a high school photo; Abe's was not the only one. So how would Abe react when the police asked for his help?

Abe hemmed and hawed, and then refused. Ferrari said he could get the photo elsewhere. "Go ahead and get it," Abe replied.[7] Ferrari wanted him to help catch his own accomplice in murder! Was he suspected himself? Abe told the detective that while he did want to cooperate—really—he was being asked to betray a longtime friend. And why should he believe that Murt or Irv was the killer? "He didn't feel as though he was justified in handing it over," Ferrari said. Under oath the detective later insisted that Abe, despite his admitted friendship with Murt, was not yet a suspect. Perhaps. Or perhaps Ferrari wondered what would happen if he gave the bright MIT grad enough rope to hang himself.

While Abe insisted he would not deliver the photograph with his own hand, he did have a suggestion. He'd be more comfortable, it would seem less a betrayal, if there were a sort of raid. "He said he would not give it to us, but had no objection to our taking it," the state police reported.[8] An officer could pick it up at Abe's house. No warrant was necessary; only a knock on the door and it would be handed over. A trooper was dispatched to the Faber household, and late that night Murt's photo was distributed to the press in time for Friday's papers.

Abe was too smart by half. He ended up turning over the photo and at the same time convincing Ferrari that Murt was more than Abe's neighborhood chum.

Whether Abe told Murt that police had his photograph is unknown. The two men did, however, meet in Boston that night.

Murt and Norma had arrived back from New York earlier in the week following the telegrams and telephone calls from Irv. The couple actually stopped at 39 Lawrence Avenue for a few hours without being spotted and then spent early Monday morning at 1175 Boylston Street before realizing that it, too, was a poor choice of resting place. They left for a rented room at a Beacon Street hotel. By some accounts there was a Boston police stakeout at Boylston Street that Murt and Norma, now with Irv, had walked right through.

The next day, Tuesday, February 13, the trio rented a nearby apartment at what was then 117 Audubon Road under the name of "Mr. and Mrs. Clifton." Mostly they remained inside until late Thursday, the day state police obtained Murt's photograph.

After sunset they met Abe in the lobby of a building near Huntington Avenue. Abe carried a shortwave radio that he handed to Irv. Murt and Abe then stepped to the other side of a glass door for a hurried, private conversation and kept glancing back at Norma. She fidgeted uncomfortably. Abe left, and Murt led his wife and Irv to the top floor of the building, over a series of rooftops, and down to their new apartment.

Inside, Murt wrote a worried letter to Messinger.

"Dear Buddy: Sorry to have waited so long to write; things have been very very busy. Things have turned out badly lately and I shall have to await developments."

He enclosed a receipt for the Chevy left parked in the Manhattan garage and asked Messinger to retrieve a suitcase and a pair of Norma's shoes and store them until the couple returned to New York City. "Tell the garage man to hold the car until I call for it. Save the enclosed card very very carefully because I will probably come and send for it to enable me to take out the car." The Chevy would serve as a lifeline when it was no longer safe to travel by train.

"You will hear from us again — in the meantime take care of yourself."

He added, "Stick to the code. Yours, Murt."

Then he told Messinger to burn the letter.[9]

It was on that same Thursday that the trash can letter — the one with Messinger's Brooklyn address recovered by Boston police from 1175 Boylston Street — was finally turned over to Chief Bliss. He then made the startling decision not to pick up the telephone and call the New York City Police Department. Neither did he turn to the teletype and bang out an urgent message for the NYPD. Nor did he call Stokes or Ferrari, who had still never heard of Messinger. Instead, Chief Bliss sat down at his desk and wrote a letter to New York City detectives asking officers to ascertain Messinger's whereabouts. Then he mailed it. Then he waited.

No explanation of the chief's decision survives. But Bliss was certainly unhappy with the attorney general, the governor, and Daniel Needham, and perhaps at Stokes and Ferrari for seizing control of the case. No Needham officer was working with the state team. Bliss did give Messinger's name and address to the Burns agency, which contacted its New York office. Originally hired by the vigilantes, the agency was now working for the American Bankers Association.

Another day or two passed before Stokes and Ferrari were finally clued in. "We first learned of the letter when we called at the Needham police station one night and Lieut. Stokes asked Chief Bliss if there was anything new," Fleming wrote. "He then showed us the letter and told us he had written to the New York Police Department but had not received a reply."

Stokes also discovered that the Burns agency, following receipt of Bliss's information, had assigned two of its New York City operatives to locate and tail Messinger. So now Boston city police, New York city police, and Burns detectives were all working the same case—and not talking to the lead investigators, the Massachusetts State Police.

Nowhere was Stokes's immediate reaction recorded—though it had to have been cold fury—nor do any of the existing records name the exact day of his meeting with Bliss. It was probably Friday or Saturday, February 16 or 17. A hint of the anger that swept through the small team of state detectives can be teased out of the dry language of Fleming's account of a subsequent meeting Stokes had with the Burns agency's Boston chief. "He came to our office in the state house and the entire case, as far as we had gone, was discussed. It was agreed that we would work together and he would keep us informed of developments in New York."

While Stokes and Ferrari were grappling with that news, they also learned that the Millens had just avoided capture at South Station in Boston.

MURT'S PHOTOGRAPH appeared in the Boston newspapers on Friday, February 16. It showed the head and shoulders of a harmless-looking young man clad in coat and tie—a man with a distinctively long, narrow face and a prominent nose. By that afternoon Murt, Norma, and Irv were on their way out of town. Not only had they seen the photograph, but the state police bulletin had almost certainly been broadcast on the new radio news programs. And WNAC, a popular Boston station, had a special arrangement with the attorney general's office to air details of wanted desperadoes.

They packed three pieces of luggage, including two new black leather Gladstone bags reinforced by heavy leather straps. At about 4:15 p.m. Norma entered the building super's office at Audubon Street and asked to use the phone. Behind the desk was Matthew Murphy, an immigrant who had already noticed the pretty young wife. He knew Murt and Norma by the name of "Mr. and Mrs. Harry Clifton." When Mrs. Clifton appeared at his doorway "in kind of a hurry" and asked to use the office telephone to call a cab, he offered to drive her in his own car. Norma declined. She made the call and disappeared.

Murphy then sat down to read a Boston paper, an act he later insisted was out of character. "I don't bother with them at all. Sometimes I sit down and listen to the radio, and that's news enough for me," Murphy said. Papers piled up in the building everyday, cast aside by tenants or never picked up after delivery boys tossed them to the stoop. "I see them every day, but I never read them." Except on that day. And when he turned a page, he saw a picture of Murt Millen, whose wife, Murphy realized, had just called the cab.

"I went downstairs," he said, and "I went over to station 16."[10]

By that time the "Cliftons" with Irv in tow had already arrived at the Back Bay station in a Checker cab. The cabbie was Daniel Goldstein, who picked them up at 4:30 p.m. and covered the half mile to the station in fifteen minutes. On the way Murt complained about his taking a right onto narrow Westland Street instead of remaining on the Fenway. Goldstein told Murt that "Westland . . . was the best route to avoid traffic." Still, someone in the car complained about missing the 4:35 p.m. train to New York City. At the station Goldstein chose to apologize to the attractive Mrs. Clifton. "I'm very sorry you lost that train," he said. The lady replied with a smile and said, "That's perfectly all right." Goldstein noticed that one of the Gladstone bags was unusually heavy.

Inside was the Thompson submachine gun, two pistols, dozens of rounds of ammunition, and some gas grenades. There was also a sawed-off shotgun. Wherever the threesome landed, Murt was planning to do some work.

Goldstein had an easy time recalling the details because he was talking to Boston detectives within the hour.

This time the police had acted quickly. Murphy's tip prompted an urgent bulletin calling on city patrolmen to be on the lookout for a Checker taxi carrying two men and one woman. Goldstein, however, did not know where his passengers went or what they did after missing their train. Another urgent bulletin was issued asking officers to "keep a sharp lookout at bus terminals and railroad stations for a man wearing a brown suit, salt-and-pepper overcoat and a brown hat, who was accompanied by a woman with reddish hair wearing a white hat . . . The above-described man may be the person wanted in connection with the bank holdup and murder of two police offices in Needham."

Despite the multistate alarm the trio eluded capture.

By some means, perhaps a stolen car, they arrived in New York City on Saturday and rented a room at the Paramount Hotel near Times Square. Murt and Irv had a brief meeting with Messinger the next morning. Norma took a bath while they spoke. Murt wanted to make sure he forwarded letters to Abe.

"The police were after him for the Needham job," recalled Messinger. He was now convinced that Murt was indeed a bank robber and killer, but cooperated with him nevertheless. Murt told him that "he had no intention of being taken alive." To underline his resolution he flashed the revolver taken off the Worcester police officer the previous fall.

When Messinger was gone, Norma picked up a piece of Hotel Paramount stationary and wrote out the details of her false identity. Her maiden name would be "Clifton." Her parents would remain Norman and Margaret, and as "Norma Clifton" she would keep her genuine birthplace of Des Moines but would say that she had met Murt in Jefferson, New Hampshire.

Murt would be "Murt Nelson" from Montana. His parents would be "Ruth and Joseph Nelson."

Then they checked out of the Paramount and took a train to Washington, D.C. Murt's idea was to reach Florida.

THAT SAME SUNDAY Reverend Brighton walked into the Massachusetts State House and asked to speak with "Lieutenant Stokes."

The reverend was there on his own volition, prompted by the postcard Norma sent to his second wife and worried by reports of a young woman's murder in western Massachusetts. Some reports incorrectly speculated that the victim could be the girl tied up with the Needham bank robbers. The reverend sat down on a bench to await his meeting and found that he was sharing the lobby with Goldberg and Dinneen. They had arrived to check on any overnight developments and were immediately curious about the tall, thin man with the worried expression. The two reporters went over and asked why he was there. The man said simply that he was waiting for "the lieutenant." He declined to give his name. But because it was a Sunday, visitors to the State House were obliged to sign in at a side entrance. Dinneen and Goldberg walked to the register and saw the name "Norman Brighton."[11]

They were going to have a story.

Until then no Boston paper had identified Norma as a minister's daughter, though Dinneen and Goldberg, and probably other reporters on the case, knew that from her marriage license application.

The *Globe*'s first use of Norma's name, sans her father's identity, occurred in a brief sentence on Friday, February 16, the day she and Murt fled back to New York. "Murton, who disappeared with his wife and brother after the date of the crime, is alleged by police to have driven the death car," the paper said, and noted that "he was married to Norma Brighton, 19, of 1175 Boylston St." The inevitably titillating invocation of a "minister's daughter" did not appear until the following Monday, after the reverend was interviewed at the State House. The likeliest explanation is that newsroom standards at that time precluded dragging a minister into a scandal—he was, after all, unknown to the general public—until his daughter's role was clarified.

Now such restraint went by the board.

The reporters buttonholed the reverend after his meeting with Stokes, and the reverend talked. Stokes had assured him that his daughter was not the unlucky girl found dead.

And, yes, he had given the police Norma's photograph.

It appeared in the next day's papers. It was not particularly flattering and looks to have been cribbed from a high school yearbook. It presented her from the shoulders up. The image was blurry and indistinct, a copy of a copy perhaps. Her hair was brushed to the right in a mannish style. She did not yet look glamorous. Her smile in the photo was kind, and the caption noted that Norma was "a voracious reader of books." The *Globe* placed the photograph next to the headline "Pastor Tells Tragedy of Home Life—Both Daughters Gone and One Now Sought in Needham Case."

The *Post* front page declared, "College Girl in Bank Case. Minister's Daughter Eloped to Wed Millen—Sister Also Fled Home and Disappeared, Says Father."

Goldberg massaged his prose. "Mrs. Norma Millen . . . was revealed yesterday as a cultured daughter of a Boston minister and well-known American churchman who gave up her home and social position in search of excitement," he wrote. Goldberg correctly said that the reverend was the former pastor of St. James Christian Church in Roxbury and added that he was one of the "chief moving spirits of the American Christian missionary society." He also went beyond the facts to call Norma a Cornell University student who had been "prepared in the best finishing schools." The reverend disclosed to both reporters that his eldest daughter, Thelma, had disappeared from his home some years before. The reverend said he had undertaken a nationwide search but found no trace of her.

"I suppose it is some inheritance from myself or the mother, an impulse of restlessness and recklessness that has shattered my happiness as a father and turned my children away."

"I don't know why," he told Dinneen.

The reverend added that he had met Murt once but never knew much about him other than that he claimed to be a radio technician.

That afternoon in the State House basement the reverend was a font of information. He gave details of his education and upbringing, and apparently spoke so long that the reporters ran out of questions, as Dinneen finally resorted to just the sort of all-purpose, if nearly inane, question asked merely to keep a conversation going. Did the reverend have any message for his daughter?

"No," was the considered reply. "I am not a moralist or inclined to sentimental bosh. I have been a good father and try to do everything for my children. I do not want to preach to other girls, but I would like to have my daughter back."

15

Tear Up Carefully!

MURT, NORMA, AND IRV arrived in Washington, D.C., on Monday, February 19, and rented a $2 room at the Harrington Hotel, at Eleventh and E Streets, four blocks east of the White House. The next morning they let a furnished apartment in a small, four-story building on Sixteenth Street in northwest Washington. It had three rooms and a kitchenette. Murt and Norma took the one bed, while Irving slept on a divan in the living room. To the extent that they had a plan, beyond avoiding capture, it was to head south to Florida.

But they were in no rush. They scouted a potential bank job in Washington, and Murt announced that he wanted to indulge himself with flying lessons.

The robbery target was the Hamilton National Bank, where Murt rented a safety deposit box and stashed $4,730 from the Needham robbery. The next day Irv showed up at the bank to inquire about a job. The idea was to have an inside man. A bank vice president spoke with Irv and noted a "distinctive" face and a disconcerting personality. "He said he wanted any kind of job he could get. I had to refuse him."

Murt and Norma also wrote letters to Abe and to Murt's sister Idalyn and mailed them to Messinger. He put them in a second envelope and forwarded it to Abe from a New York City postbox. The idea was that if police in Boston intercepted the envelopes, the New York postmark would prove a dead end. The precaution was futile.

The letters to Idalyn, both signed by Norma, were deeply incriminating. They also showed that the teenager knew her older brothers were breaking the law. The first asked her to go to the 117 Audubon Road apartment they had fled after Murt's photo appeared in the newspapers:

Please go to apartment 11, 117 Audubon Rd., and take the radio home, the
food and candy and magazines also. Clean the place up. Make it look as
though we might return at any moment. If you are asked any questions, say
my cousin took sick, so we rushed back to New York for a short while.

Remember our name is Clifton. We are living there under the name of
Mr. and Mrs. H. Clifton of New York. You're our niece, if they question
you. Give a fake address. Try not to be seen or questioned.

The number of the suite is not on the door, but it is to the left on the
second floor as you get off the elevator. Hold key and don't lose it. The
gas bill under the name of H. Clifton is on hall table. Take it to the gas
company and get refund on the deposit we made. Please do my things up
in mothballs, also Murt's. Take care of the silver and comforter, honey; we
love those.

Send my black jacket dress and red pajamas and the bathrobe you got
from the tailor next door to Saul to hold for me.

Watch your step! We all send love. TEAR THE LETTER UP CAREFULLY.

The second letter corrected an omission in the first:

Sorry we forgot to send the keys. They are keys to 117 Audubon Road,
Suite 11. One is for the main door, the other for the apartment door. Please
follow Murt's instructions that I sent you very carefully.

Love, Norma, M. and B.

PS Please let my dad and mother know that I am all right, dear.[1]

Idalyn and Murt were bonded as older brother to younger sister, a link
fortified by shared enmity toward their father and sympathy for their
mother. That loyalty would be displayed again.

Norma also wrote, but did not mail, a letter to a New York publishing
house asking for the booklet on "charm and poise," to be sent to "Norma
Nelson" at the Washington apartment. Then she went shopping. She spent
$25 on a matching apple-green jacket and skirt, the jacket trimmed with
fur, along with silk frocks and lingerie.

It appears that Murt, Norma, and Irv were planning to make Washington,
D.C., a base of operations for some weeks, if not months. It might have been

better to keep moving south to Florida or perhaps west to California. But perhaps Murt felt safe. Irv would do what Murt wanted, and Norma—she was dependent on Murt. The three of them were using false identities. They were traveling by train, but Murt had cash for another car. Police had Murt's and Norma's photos, but the FBI was still a work in progress and it's "Ten Most Wanted" list was decades in the future. Abe did not know where the hunted trio were. Messinger in New York City knew how to reach them, but only by mail. He was a loose end, but only maybe. Murt just had to make sure that Norma did not mail any more postcards home.

Meanwhile, Murt applied for a student pilot's license and made an appointment with Dr. Bernard L. Jarman, an examiner for the Department of Commerce. On Friday, February 23, the doctor put his signature on the required medical examination. Norma later said that her husband attended at least one class. When he stayed away from home one night, apparently at an airfield, she wrote a cute note saying he was missed. Sometime during that week Murt also went shopping for a new car.

IN MASSACHUSETTS Molway and Berrett tried to save themselves from the electric chair.

Berrett took the witness stand first and painstakingly detailed where he was and what he did on January 2—when he woke up, where he had breakfast, who he spoke to on the telephone, which streetcar he took to the Central Cab Company's garage. He explained that he did not take a cab out that morning because he and a partner were arranging a new insurance policy. Berrett named four people he had seen or spoken with before noon, including his partner's mother, and another half dozen people during the afternoon.

Then he was set upon by Cregg, who chose to open his cross-examination with an attack on Berrett's morals. Cregg was going to prove that the cabbie was not only a murderer, but an amoral philanderer, too.

His first question before the all-male jury concerned Berrett's living arrangements. "You have said your home is in Malden?"

"My wife and youngsters live there," said Berrett.

"You call it your home?"

During his direct testimony, Berrett had referred to his Commonwealth apartment as his home and now Cregg was tossing that back at him.

Berrett did not reply.

Cregg kept pushing. "When you said you went home you went to 1152 Commonwealth Ave. You didn't mean that did you?"

"That's my home."

"But not the home of your wife and child?"

"There is a divorce pending," Berrett conceded.

"The night before New Year's, you were with a young lady?" Cregg asked.

Berrett said yes.

Cregg demanded to know her name. Berrett refused to answer, and his lawyer's objections were overruled by the judge.

Cregg was suggesting that a man who had left his wife to live with another woman was of sufficiently low character to be capable of even more heinous crimes. By the standards of the era it was a sensible, and quite possibly successful, courtroom tactic.

"A lady I know as Miss Hamilton," Berrett finally said, and admitted that they shared an apartment at 1152 Commonwealth Avenue.

And who paid the rent?

A seething Berrett said he did, but allowed that Hamilton helped out if he was short at the end of the month.

There it was. He had admitted giving money to a woman not his wife.

Cregg ridiculed Berrett's insistence that he had never owned a gun and had fired a weapon only once, years earlier during a July Fourth celebration. When Cregg declared it was impossible to believe that as a Boston cabdriver he had never armed himself, Berrett turned to sarcasm. He admitted the prosecutor was partly correct.

"I did have a cap pistol as a small boy," he said.[2]

Molway took his turn on the stand Thursday afternoon. His lawyer, Flynn, walked the twenty-two-year-old through the autobiography of an astonishingly harmless young man. Molway told jurors that he was the sort of fellow who helped his mother wash the dishes, had never, ever had a run-in with police, and was prone to fainting under stress. Molway, with a distinctive ski-slope nose, had a bit of the street urchin about him but spoke in what the *Boston Post* described as "the most gentle tones." It was a far different demeanor than that of the snarling gunmen described by the theater employees.

Molway admitted that he was miserably drunk on New Year's Eve. He tottered to his parents' home in Brighton, and even on January 2 he barely roused himself out of bed. That day began at 7 a.m. when he rose and took a trolley to the taxi company on Harrison Avenue in the South End. He climbed into cab 78 and drove off for breakfast at a nearby diner. He had coffee and toast, and gave the name of the counterman, Francis. Back at the wheel he was hailed by a customer at 8 a.m. and collected a 55-cent fare. Next he picked up two men near the State House and dropped them on Boylston Street. At 9 a.m. he parked at a West and Tremont Street taxi stand. There was no business, so at 10 a.m. he drove a short distance to a stand at Dwight and Tremont Streets and chatted with three other cabdrivers. He told jurors the first names of two and the full name of the third man.

Molway said that shortly after 10:15 a.m. he was back at the company garage filling the taxi's gas tank. At 11 a.m. he was at a tire repair shop at 588 Albany Street. Then he stopped at a taxi stand at Dover and Tremont Streets.

Molway was an excellent witness, his performance no doubt helped by the fact that he was telling the truth. When it became time for Cregg's cross-examination at 4 p.m., the prosecutor declared himself unwell and asked the court for a recess until the next morning.

As Cregg reviewed his notes that evening, Abe and Rose arrived at 14 Oldfields Street in Dorchester to play bridge with Jacob Gordon, Abe's MIT classmate. Like Abe, Gordon had failed to find a job in the field of aeronautics; whether it was because of anti-Semitism or the Depression was a subject of debate between the two. Gordon was now working in construction.

While they were best friends in college, they had seen less and less of each other since graduation. Partly that was the result of a natural divergence of interests, but Abe also spent more of his free time with Murt. Gordon lived a half mile from the Millen house, close enough to have heard the neighborhood gossip. He had advised his college friend, "[You] should not be with them so much." His advice was ignored, but the two still met for cards once or twice a month. This Thursday night's session was the first gathering since Murt's name and photograph had hit the newspapers.

As the cards were shuffled and dealt, the conversation turned to the bank robbery, the killing of McLeod and Haddock, and where the murderers—

the Millen brothers, the card players presumed—might be hiding. Abe assured his fellow bridge players that despite his friendship with Murt he had no knowledge of their whereabouts but guessed they were "probably in Florida." Gordon said that if he were Murt, he would flee to Mexico. There was no change in Faber's demeanor as they talked. Afterward, Abe drove Rose home.[3]

In the morning Cregg, now better prepared, had Molway repeat the details of his New Year's Eve dissipation. The cabbie affirmed that he drank himself into the gutter and reached his parent's home only with the help of a friend. Molway also conceded that he spent most of the morning of January 2 waiting for fares rather than actually driving, which the prosecutor said was suspicious.

Molway said it wasn't his fault there was no business. "The rest of the time I was available at taxi stands."

Cregg snorted. "You could have put the car in a garage and left it there all day."

Molway said that he had a written trip sheet. Cregg said that it could be easily falsified.

Molway objected. "The company has inspectors out checking up," he said.

"But it could be done," Cregg declared.

And no doubt it was a common cabbie ruse.

"Yes, it could be done," Molway conceded.

Molway was candid about the most incriminating fact, which was that he initially gave police a very different account of his whereabouts on January 2. The cabbie explained that when he was arrested by police on January 5 and interrogated into the early morning hours of January 6, he was scared and confused and mistakenly recounted what he did on January 3. Molway testified that he recognized his mistake within a day and told officers.

Both defense attorneys called a succession of witnesses to back up their clients' claims, but many were friends or family members, who, Cregg pointed out, had their own biases. One of Molway's passengers said that he picked her up at 8 a.m. and dropped her off on Beacon Street, where she was a maid in a private club, but admitted under cross-examination to being friendly with Molway's brother, who had driven her to court that morning.

The most compelling testimony came from a stockbroker, William L.

Cogghill, who testified that Molway picked him up at his home on Pilgrim Road, near the Fens, at 11:30 a.m. and dropped him at his office in the financial district downtown. Unlike Molway's other fare, this one had been dispatched from the Central Cab offices, and company records showed that Cogghill's secretary had indeed called for a cab. The dispatcher testified that he called the company phone line connected to the Dover and Tremont Street taxi stand and spoke directly to Molway.

If one believed Cogghill, his secretary's records, and the Central Cab dispatcher, it strained credulity to argue that Molway had left the scene of the killing in Lynn at 10:30 a.m., dashed fourteen miles to Boston, spoke to the dispatcher, and then coolly picked up his fare.

Cregg did his best. On cross-examination Cogghill admitted that he initially told police he did not recall his cabbie's name or appearance. Cregg left it to Flynn, the defense attorney, to ask Cogghill why he lied to police.

"I did not want to get mixed up in a murder case unless it was absolutely necessary," was Cogghill's sheepish reply. "It is not good for my particular type of business and it is inconvenient. I thought by being evasive I could keep out of it."

This was the first Judge Hammond knew of Cogghill's subterfuge. He was astonished. "You knew a man was charged with murder and you still were evasive to the police just for business reasons?"

"For selfish reasons, yes," he admitted.[4]

Testimony ended that afternoon. Molway and Berrett were returned to jail, and Judge Hammond told the jury not to discuss the evidence until court reconvened on Monday. Only after final arguments and his instructions, and only then, could deliberations begin. After two weeks of testimony and dozens of witnesses, the jurors had come to the painful realization that the entire case, the guilt or innocence of the two cabdrivers, rested entirely on eyewitness testimony. The prosecution had not offered any physical evidence connecting the men to the crime. There were no fingerprints, there was no gun, there was no getaway car. The defense had the cab dispatcher's written log, but it was a thin leg on which to rest Molway's acquittal. Otherwise, the entire defense rested on the testimony of friends and acquaintances of the accused.

The jurors were soon to face a stark choice—was the defense or the prosecution telling a story completely and utterly false? They could acquit the cabbies, but only if they concluded that all eight eyewitness had picked innocent men out of the police lineup. Each witness—a hostage!—would have to be mistaken.

And if the jurors voted to convict, they would be declaring that nearly two dozen defense witnesses had conspired to coordinate and fabricate the intricate details of their testimony. That would include the stockbroker, the president of Central Cab, who testified to the accuracy of the telephone dispatch records, and all the friends and acquaintances who had trooped to the witness stand. True, virtually none were disinterested, but who does one meet for breakfast or see at work if not friends and acquaintances?

All in all there was no way out. The jurors knew that deliberations and a verdict were inevitable.

But they were wrong.

IN WASHINGTON, D.C., Murt drove a new Chevy off the dealer's lot. The leather suitcase with the Thompson, the shotguns, and the gas grenades was checked at the train station. Most of the cash was left in the safety deposit box. Murt and Irv stuffed handguns in their overcoat pockets. They were taking a short trip. Norma came along.

16

========

*Guns in
Their Pockets*

MESSINGER HELD OUT for fourteen hours.

The first New York City detectives arrived at his rooming house early Saturday morning. The two said they were there for the home interview conducted with every department applicant, and so all three settled into the cruiser for an amicable conversation about Messinger's background. Afterward the cops thanked him, and Messinger walked back inside. Before long, the detectives returned. This time they numbered three, and they were not as pleasant.

"They tore the house apart. They opened up pillows and took the mattress apart and then one of the detectives bolted out of the kitchen and said, 'I got it, I got it!' And he had part of one of the letters that Murt had written to me from Washington," Messinger said.

Messinger was put in the backseat of the patrol car. The detective behind the wheel drove up and down Brooklyn streets as the others quizzed Messinger about Murt and his likely whereabouts. The cops were relaxed and easygoing, Messinger said. They had lunch, and they even stopped at a movie house to catch an early afternoon matinee. As the hours passed, Messinger insisted that he didn't know anything that the detectives wanted to know. "I said I haven't seen them for some time," he claimed.

Eventually, the squad car stopped at the Half Moon Hotel, a fourteen-story, Spanish-colonial style edifice on the Coney Island waterfront. The two Burns detectives had rented a room there, and now they opened it to the detectives. The idea was to keep Messinger out of a police station, where he might be sprung by an attorney.[1]

In the hotel the police "started in on me," Messinger said, though the New York City detectives insisted they never laid a hand on him and Messinger never offered any evidence of fists or a blackjack. As late afternoon turned to evening, the detectives decided it was safe to move to the Coney Island station house. Messinger remained silent, not caring that he risked quashing any hope of a career with the NYPD. So the detectives resorted to guile. Messinger was moved to a conference room with a view of the front desk. The door was left open, and Messinger watched the to and fro of a busy Saturday night. He was still watching when his girl, Elsie, was paraded into the station house, past the desk, and back toward the rear holding cells. She wasn't under arrest, but Messinger didn't know that. He saw his future wife, or maybe not his future wife anymore, in custody because of him. So he talked. Yeah, he was Murt's "mailman." He had forwarded letters to Abe in Boston. And Murt was in Washington, D.C.

It was 11 p.m. A detective called Boston.

In Room 24 Stokes picked up the telephone. He listened, then hung up and told Ferrari he was off to New York City on the midnight train.[2] He would grab a few hours' sleep in a Pullman berth as the locomotive rolled across Rhode Island and Connecticut. Stokes needed the rest. He had spent a long two days playing a cat-and-mouse game with Abe.

IT HAD BEGUN early Friday with a tip from the two Burns agents in New York. Messinger had posted a letter to Abe in Boston. Their source remains unknown, but an oblique reference in a state police document suggests that they had teamed up with federal postal inspectors. If a letter was arriving for Abe from New York, Stokes and Ferrari wanted to read it. They called Abe back to their office.

At each encounter during the past weeks, one or the other of the detectives had listened politely as the Tech graduate insisted he was eager to cooperate, really, except that he was reluctant to betray his old friend, which they had to admit was perfectly understandable. In any case, he didn't know much. Perhaps he could help, Abe told Ferrari, if he knew a bit more about the investigation. Ferrari had listened as Abe dropped "little suggestions" that his "deductive" skills might be useful.

Now Abe walked in and sat down.

Stokes called his interrogations "conversations." He disliked the former term with its suggestion of screams and brute force. So Stokes and Ferrari told Abe that they were speaking on a "strictly confidential" basis, thereby suggesting that they trusted him and so he could trust them. A letter was in the mail to him from Saul Messinger, the detectives said, and they had reason to believe that it contained a communication from Murt. Abe needed to turn it over to them.

Abe dodged. He asked to consult an attorney and called an acquaintance from Roxbury, Howard Kline. An hour later Kline and Abe conferred in a separate office while the detectives rounded up a stenographer. The stakes were rising. They did not want a defense lawyer claiming that the state police had interfered with the U.S. mail. Abe and Kline emerged, and Stokes began with a question that was more of a statement.

"We have an understanding with you now that it is perfectly proper for that letter to come into our possession?"

"The understanding is that you are supposed to get the letter," Abe said.

Was that a yes? Was that a question? Stokes wanted clarity. "That is, you have no objection to it?"[3]

Abe looked at his attorney. "That is right, Howard?" Silence settled over the room. Kline did not give a spoken reply. Perhaps he shrugged that it was up to Abe.

Stokes's request—it was not a flat demand, and the detective made no move to get a warrant—was a step too far. "Wait a minute on that," Abe said, and raised a new concern.

"If that was in court, how would it look?"[4]

The conversation ended inconclusively. Abe was allowed to return home.

NEGOTIATIONS RESUMED the next day, Saturday, at 1 p.m. Abe was at the radio shop when the detectives called, and again he walked across Boston Common and up the incline to the State House entrance.

At about the same time in Washington, D.C., Murt, Norma, and Irv climbed into the Chevy and drove north. Outside Baltimore they paused to telegram Messinger. They would meet him the next morning, Sunday, at the Hotel Lincoln. They had a reservation for room 616. In New York City the message was printed out and dispatched by bicycle courier.

It was delivered to Messinger's rooming house that afternoon, while he was in the hands of the police and while Ferrari was quizzing Abe in Boston.

FERRARI ASKED Abe when he had left home that Saturday morning.

Throughout the day Ferrari never raised his voice, and the detective said that Abe, too, never became excited or nervous or displayed any behavior out of the ordinary.

Abe said he left Blue Hill Avenue at 8 a.m. And what time was the mail ordinarily delivered there? Abe shrugged. He was at work when the postman arrived. Abe repeated his rationalization of yesterday. He wanted to help, but there were certain steps he wouldn't take. A compromise was reached. As with the photograph of Murt, Abe agreed that a detective could go to 148 Blue Hill Avenue, search the mail, and take the letter if it had arrived. His parents were not home. "He gave me the keys, and as a result of that I sent someone out there," Ferrari said. They waited. A sergeant returned and said he found the Saturday mail, but no letter for Abe.

The letter was still in transit. Stokes increased the pressure. Abe had to give them permission to intercept it before Monday's regular delivery. It was urgent. Abe made another call to Kline. "If you can get the letter we have no objection to it," the lawyer said when Stokes was handed the phone. The postal inspectors were told to be on the lookout.

Again Abe returned home.

It was Saturday evening, February 24, and in New York Elsie would soon arrive at the Coney Island police station, and Stokes would soon board the New York–bound train.

IT WAS AN UGLY, uncomfortable weekend for Stokes to be traveling. Boston streets had become impassable after a sudden freeze converted piles of slush into frozen mounds that could be dented only with a pick ax. Five thousand men were working to clear the snow and ice from the latest nor'easter, and after four days everyone was exhausted. Men hired from the relief rolls had begun their toil with inadequate clothes and in poor physical condition for the arduous labor. By now 2,500 were no longer fit for work.[5] And it wasn't an ordinary cold snap. The temperature plummeted an astonishing 26 degrees in three hours on Friday afternoon, and by 5 a.m. on Saturday it was 7 degrees above zero. The day's high was 12 degrees. Northern New England reported 10 feet of snow, and small towns around Lake Winnipesaukee in New Hampshire had given up trying to dig themselves out. They would wait for a thaw.

Conditions were little better in New York. The city had spent $1 million clearing its streets over the past week. On Sunday morning 54 mph winds and a temperature of 9 degrees greeted Stokes as he disembarked at Grand Central Station. Another 5 inches of snow were forecast for that evening.

On Mermaid Avenue near the Coney Island beach, the cold was savage and wet when Stokes and the NYPD detectives escorted Messinger back to his rooming house. Messinger's landlady, a Yiddish-speaking Russian immigrant with only a smattering of English, had been trying to get word to her tenant since Saturday evening. A "paper" had arrived for him, she told police at the precinct house. She was brushed off. But that morning when the detectives arrived they realized that what she called a "paper" was in fact a telegram—from Murt. The telegram he'd sent the day before from Maryland. It said Messinger should meet him at the Lincoln Hotel on Sunday at 11 a.m. Their watches told the detectives it was already 11:30.[6]

A scramble commenced. Messinger was pushed back into a squad car, and it sped into Manhattan, running stoplights with the siren blaring until nearing Times Square. At the hotel they found that luck was with them. Awaiting Messinger was another telegram from Murt, postponing their meeting until five o'clock. Murt, Norma, and Irv were already in the city—indeed, they spent Saturday night in the hotel, but had left their rooms that morning. It was time for Stokes to plan. There were four police officers: Stokes and three Coney Island officers, Lieutenant Charles H. Eason, Edmund O'Brien, and John Fitzsimmons. Also present were the two Burns agents, Benjamin A. Hall and James W. Smith. The hotel lobby before them stretched a whole city block. It was a lot of territory for six men to cover.

On a Sunday afternoon the Lincoln, on Eighth Avenue between Forty-Fourth and Forty-Fifth Streets, was packed with departing weekend tourists and incoming out-of-town businesspeople, despite a picket line thrown up by the Amalgamated Hotel and Restaurant Workers Union.[7] The union represented fifteen thousand waiters, cooks, and dishwashers across New York, and a month ago its members had launched a citywide strike. Mayor Fiorella LaGuardia intervened, and city health department inspectors began "raiding" the kitchens of the city's largest hotels, coincidentally also the ones employing the Amalgamated members. That included the Lincoln. As the New York Times said, "Officially the raids were a Health Department enterprise, but actually they had their origin in what the Mayor regards as the unjustifiable attitude" of the hotel owners.

Built of yellow brick with carved limestone panels running the height of each exterior corner, the hotel was what it advertised itself to be: economical but stylish and at an ideal location, near Broadway theaters like the famed Schubert just a half block down Forty-Fourth Street. In 1928, money was still sloshing through New York real estate, and the owners built the largest hotel in New York City, with twenty-seven floors and fourteen hundred rooms.

STOKES AND THE NYPD took over an eighth-floor room midday Sunday as Ferrari in Boston received a message from the Roxbury postal substation. The letter had arrived. Ferrari put a call into Abe and the MIT grad returned to the State House. Surprisingly, he was accompanied not by his attorney, but by his girlfriend, Rose.

The negotiation fell into the usual routine. "I asked him if he would go to the substation with me and get the letter. He says no." Abe said that Ferrari was welcome to the letter, but he would not hand it over himself. He told Ferrari that as a cop he must have a way to get it on a Sunday.

He did. Ferrari picked up the telephone, and a short while later a postal inspector walked into Room 24 carrying a surprisingly thick envelope. Not so fast, the inspector said as Ferrari reached for it. The named recipient, who was Abe, had to explicitly authorize delivery to a third person. Abe once more hemmed and hawed. Ferrari returned to the telephone, made a call, and handed the phone to the inspector. After a brief conversation with Abe's attorney, the inspector hung up and declared himself satisfied. Ferrari turned to Abe. Any objection, he asked? "No. Go ahead and get it," Abe said. Ferrari slit the envelope open.

Five letters and notes tumbled out. Three were written to Carolyn Millen, Murt's mother. The contents were never disclosed. Another letter was addressed to Murt's sister Idalyn. The contents of that also remain a mystery.

The final letter was addressed to Abe. It was very brief :

Dear Abel,

How you getting along? Things are just so-so with us. Please write or wire Buddy if anything comes up as I don't know where I'll be.

Please call by phone and see if storage for p.g. was received—$21—Sincerely,

Your chief sales mgr.

Ferrari read the letter out loud. "I asked Faber if he received a letter from anybody that was signed 'your chief salesman' who would be that party that would send such a letter. He says, 'That would be Murt. He does things that way.'"

Ferrari showed him the letter, and Abe nodded. "That's Murt's writing."

"Chief sales manager," Ferrari commented. "What does that mean?"

"I can't understand."

"Well, you ought to understand something that your chief salesman is sending you."

"I haven't the least idea."

Ferrari looked at him. "You want me to tell you what it means?"

If there was a moment when Abe could no longer deny that he had been outfoxed by the balding, eyeglass-wearing Italian American detective in the double-breasted suit, this was it.

"P.g. means police gun storage," said Ferrari. "$21 evidently is rent." The two men must have exchanged a look. Or perhaps Abe was staring at the floor as the court reporter tapped the keys.

"Now, you want to tell me where the storage is?"

"Could I talk with my attorney?" Abe replied.[8]

Kline showed up two hours later. It was a cold Sunday afternoon, and the puzzled attorney wanted to know "what it was all about."

Ferrari said only that his client needed to speak with him. Kline walked into the room where Abe was sitting and shut the door behind him. Fifteen minutes later he opened it and said Abe wanted to talk.

He was very straightforward. "I will draw you a diagram of where the p.g.'s are," he said, but added that he wanted to remain in the office while police went to the scene. Ferrari dismissed that out of hand. "It can be done quicker if you come along." Abe was still hoping to slide his way out. He might be seen, he explained, and it might put him in danger. Ferrari promised a car with curtains drawn over the rear windows. He called out to Fleming, and the three men, with a state police detective sergeant driving, climbed into a cruiser, the back windows curtained as promised, and drove to the Brinsley Street garage. It was 2:30 p.m.

THAT WAS WHEN IRV walked in off the icy New York City street and sat down in the Hotel Lincoln lobby. He wore a heavy overcoat, and a close observer would have noticed that the right pocket clunked against his thigh.

He had passed through the picket line and the smattering of police officers pacing the sidewalk to separate the strikers from the strikebreakers hired to work the kitchens and dining rooms. One of the cops was patrolman Pasquale Amoroso.

Stokes and the Coney Island detectives had worked out a plan. Their strategy was simple. Messinger was bait. They were, however, dismayed by the crowd and the lobby's layout and size. Not only was it a whole city block, but there were entrances on three sides for only six men to cover. And they could not know in advance which entrance Murt and Irv might use, or even if they would be together. They could not even be sure the meeting would still take place at five o'clock.

It didn't.

Stokes was on the eighth floor when a call came. Irv had arrived. Maybe. The New York City detectives in the lobby weren't sure. No police officer in New York had ever seen him in the flesh. They had no photograph, only Messinger's description. And the cops were careful to be careful. Two other officers were already dead, and these Millen fellows had to know that if—or once—they were caught, their future was a trial and execution. So to Murt and Irv a dead NYPD cop or two wouldn't count for much.

Stokes hung up the phone, dashed out of the room, and ran to the small art deco elevator. On the ground floor he found O'Brien, who pointed at a man in a thick, padded chair. The two detectives circled through the crowd of hotel patrons. Stokes headed toward the Eighth Avenue entrance and O'Brien moved to the cigar counter across the lobby. Stokes saw no sign of Murt or Norma, and studied the sitting man. It could be Irving Millen, he thought. Messinger would know for sure. Stokes took the elevator back to the eighth floor and collected Hall, Smith, Fitzsimmons, and Messinger.

Messinger got off at the mezzanine level and walked to the polished aluminum railing on the edge of the balcony. He looked down, and took out a hankie and blew his nose. That was the signal. They had the right guy.[9]

The detectives and the Burns men spread out across the lobby as Messinger walked down the curved staircase into the lobby and approached Irv. Stokes edged closer to Irv until he stood directly behind the chair. Messinger drew near and extended his open right hand. Irv began to stand, and as he reached his full height Stokes leaped the last few feet and grabbed Irv from behind, throwing his arms around Irv's chest and pinning his elbows to his sides. O'Brien grabbed Irv's right arm, and Hall gripped Irv's overcoat with one hand while his other searched for the pocket. Out of it came a .32 caliber revolver. Irv was strong and struggled against Stokes's grip. This was no time for half measures. Murt could appear at any moment. Perhaps he was already in the lobby. So O'Brien pulled out his revolver and hit Irv four times in the head with the butt of the gun, splitting Irv's scalp in two places. Irv went limp, and blood streamed down the right side of his face. He was hustled out of the lobby, pushed into the elevator, and taken to the eighth floor. It was all very quick. In the hotel room Irv was frisked and police found more than one hundred dollars in $10 bills. A Burns man began checking the serial numbers.

O'Brien wanted to know about Murt. "Didn't he come with you?"

For a mentally challenged fellow Irv was fast on his feet, even as blood dripped from the open wound on his forehead. "He is gone back, back to Harrington," giving the name of the Washington, D.C., hotel. Messinger walked in and in a move that was a half apology shook Irv's hand before returning downstairs. The police resumed quizzing Irv. A few minutes passed and the phone rang again.

Fitzsimmons had remained in the lobby, along with the Burns detective Smith, who now seated himself in a large soft chair. After Irv was led out, the New York officer told the lobby crowd that it was all over and not to worry. As the murmurs died away, Fitzsimmons selected a spot with a good view of the north and south doors and then he, too, sat down. He watched. A man and woman entered through the south doors, and Fitzsimmons saw Messinger begin walking across the lobby. A smile broke out on the woman's face, and the three met 10 feet from where Fitzsimmons was sitting. The men shook hands and "inquired as to each other's health," Messinger said later. The crowd in the lobby buzzed peacefully. If that was Murt, and it had to be, he was the gang's shooter, and this arrest would go no easier than Irv's. Probably harder.

Fitzsimmons watched and calculated the duration of the handshake, the size of the crowd, and the proximity of the woman, and he slowly rose from his chair.

"I walked to the side of Murton, I walked in front of him again, and I walked over to his right side." The problem was how to separate Murt from his weapon—Fitzsimmons believed there was a gun in his pocket—and do it before Murt could fire or grab a hostage, as he had done in Boston, Lynn, and Needham. The woman—and she was a looker, Fitzsimmons thought—gave him his opening. "Norma happened to walk about four paces away from him, to give Messinger a chance to talk," Fitzsimmons said.

He stepped closer and Messinger began to step back. Fitzsimmons felt for the revolver in his trouser pocket. "I drew it, pressed it to the right side of Murton, told him I was a police officer, and he was under arrest, told him not to make a move. If he did it was just too bad."[10]

The two must have exchanged glances. Perhaps Murt glimpsed the gun as it left the cop's pocket. Murt appeared to cooperate. He raised his hands, but as they reached shoulder height his right hand flashed down and grabbed for Fitzsimmons's gun. He wrapped his fingers around the barrel and pushed it away from his midsection before Fitzsimmons could fire. He bent the detective's hand back but could not break Fitzsimmons's grasp on the revolver's grip. The detective stuck out his right foot and tripped Murt, and the two of them were down, grappling on the lobby floor. Customers screamed and bolted. Fitzsimmons put a hammerlock on Murt's left arm and kept his fingers tight on the revolver as Murt tried to pry the .38 free. It seemed to Fitzsimmons they were sliding around the floor for almost a minute. Then he pulled the trigger. Later he said that he was only attempting to scare Murt, "to show him." But Fitzsimmons likely thought he had a clear shot at Murt's face, because as he pressed the trigger Murt glimpsed the movement and jerked his head back so only the burning powder blasting out of the muzzle scorched his nose. The bullet flew up into the hotel lobby woodwork. Murt was stunned but still moving.

There were two versions of what Norma screamed at that moment. One was that she yelled at the police officers, "Don't shoot him! Please don't shoot him." Other witnesses said that as Murt struggled with Fitzsimmons she offered her husband advice in words that were some variation of "Shoot him! Kill him! Let him have it!"[11]

Whatever Norma said, Patrolman Amoroso now loomed over the two men. Mayor LaGuardia had ordered police on strike duty to carry neither blackjack nor club, as the mayor was a friend of labor, so Amoroso grabbed a truncheon from Smith and brought it down on Murt's head.

He went limp. Fitzsimmons turned Murt facedown, climbed onto his back, and jammed his knee into the base of Murt's spine. More uniformed cops on strike duty poured into the lobby. The hotel customers had disappeared behind furniture or the marble trimmed columns.

Stokes dashed downstairs in time to see the man lying facedown on the lobby floor with two uniformed officers sitting on his back. Fitzsimmons, breathing hard, stood holding the pistol he had indeed found in Murt's coat pocket. They took Murt upstairs in an awkward, three-way dance because each of the killer's wrists was handcuffed to the wrist of a New York cop. Stokes took Norma into custody. It was a crowd in the small elevator.

Inside the eighth-floor room, a New York officer looked Norma up and down and called her a "trollop."

Police searched all three and pulled $1, $10, and $50 bills from the men's pockets and Norma's purse. The hotel doctor arrived and treated the brothers' bruises and cuts. A thick white bandage was wrapped around Irv's head, but the blood quickly seeped through, leaving a bright red, and then dirty reddish-brown, stain above his right eye. The "trollop" remark, if it was made, as Norma later claimed, did not dim her insouciance—or perhaps her self-absorbed compartmentalization—noted by police and reporters. On the way out of the hotel, with the brothers in handcuffs, officers allowed the pretty young woman to stop at a lobby kiosk and purchase a bar of chocolate.

IN BOSTON, the patrol car turned onto Brinsley Street and up a short, steep hill. Abe pointed at a string of garages to the left. In the first one on the right, he said, "you will find what you are looking for."

It was around 3:00 p.m. Leaving Faber with the driver, Fleming and Ferrari walked up the snow- and ice-covered driveway to the double wooden doors but couldn't see through the frosted, dirty windows. The detectives resorted to breaking off the lock with a sledgehammer. Then they shattered the ice blocking the door and pushed it partly open. Ferrari called to Abe, and all four entered. Boxes, bags, old signs, one with a giant arrow emblazoned with the word "DETOUR," spare lumber, and auto parts were scattered about. Ferrari noticed a burlap bag in the far left corner. It was large and looked to be heavy. He peered inside and saw a shotgun and cartridges, some in boxes and some not, along with a tear gas canister launcher.

He picked through other bags and boxes, and found the other shotguns missing from the Mechanics Building, along with tear gas grenades, shotgun shells, and .38 and .22 caliber handgun rounds. Ferrari also found a mask, a simple piece of cloth with a cord to tie around the back of the head.

Fleming's eye was caught by a wooden box with the word "Dynamite" stenciled on top. To one side of it was a bundle wrapped in newspapers and soaked through with what looked like grease. Fleming gingerly stepped over the box, bent down, and began to lift the soiled paper. Abe shouted for him to stop. "Look out for that! It is frozen dynamite. It is dangerous."

Dynamite is nitroglycerin mixed with diatomaceous earth, a soft, claylike rock. When frozen, the nitroglycerin crystalizes can become unstable. And it had been a very cold winter. Fleming stepped back. In the box and the wrapped paper pile were 209 sticks of explosive.

Ferrari and Abe did not return to Room 24 until early evening. The recovered state police weapons, with one obvious exception, were carried into the office.

"Can you tell me where I can find that machine gun?" Ferrari asked. Abe shook his head. "The only thing I can say is that it was not the gun checked at South Station. He must have it with him." Abe added, "The last time I saw it was underneath the bed in the Millen home."

The dance between Ferrari and Abe begun fourteen days earlier now ended. Ferrari nodded toward the collection of weapons. "Were these the guns that were used in the Needham holdup?" Ferrari asked.

Abe looked up. "Yes."

He looked very sad, Ferrari thought. "He said he was very sorry. He said he was very sorry for his father and his mother. And also Rose."

Abe asked, "Have I to stay here tonight?" He had to have known the answer before Ferrari said yes. They would be having another conversation in the morning.

"Well, I am sick and I'm tired and I want to go to sleep," Abe said. He was given a cot and put to bed in a cell. Newspaper photographers were allowed in to snap a photograph of Abe's head on the pillow, his eyes closed.

17

The Violet Depths of Her Eyes

OF ALL THE REMARKABLE EVENTS that transpired over the next eight days, the time it took to extradite Murt and Irv to Massachusetts from a cell on Manhattan's West Side, the most astonishing was that none of the suspects kept their mouths shut. Everyone talked, and for every interview or confession emblazoned across the news pages another was generated. The lawyers intervened too late, and so Murt, Irv, Abe, and Norma achieved the feat of making their impossible legal situation even worse. They were talking themselves into the electric chair.

To be fair, the four could not be expected to handle press, prosecutor, and police with the expert, wiseguy skills wielded by the likes of Al Capone, who with a straight face argued that he was a mere salesman with a product that was unfortunately illegal, if very popular. Nor did Murt, Irv, or Abe have the charm, swagger, and handsome good looks of a John Dillinger, who as Murt and Irv sulked behind bars, broke out of an Indiana jail with a fake wooden gun. Dillinger had acquired the reputation of a Robin Hood stealing from the very bankers who had plunged the nation into economic calamity. That whitewash was encouraged by those newspapers reluctant to kill a good story by pointing out his ever-increasing body count.

The Millen-Faber gang was in a lesser league. Irv could spin a yarn but not explain it. Norma displayed the usual preoccupation of a spoiled teenager — herself — and exhibited a dreadful naïveté. Abe had always thought Norma girlish, even for a girl. Murt's simmering anger and arrogance had undone his street smarts and daring. Abe was a mix of hubris and insecurity, and could not admit what he did not know. They were great copy. Almost overnight, the newspapers turned them into criminal celebrities.

In the weeks immediately after the Needham killings, Dinneen and Goldberg had the story largely to themselves. The Boston press busied itself with fresher tales of crime and punishment, particularly the February 22 execution of three men for the holdup and murder of a Somerville gas station attendant. They were the forty-fourth, forty-fifth, and forty-sixth people executed since Massachusetts had adopted the death penalty in 1898.[1] At the state prison in Charlestown, a stone's throw from Bunker Hill, they were electrocuted one after the other over the course of a single hour.

Starting that Sunday afternoon, Dinneen and Goldberg would face a mighty force of competitors from the *Boston Traveler, Boston Herald, Boston Transcript, Boston Daily Record*, the *American*, the Associated Press, and sometimes even the very proper *Christian Science Monitor*. Collectively, the newspapers sold nearly 1.5 million copies each weekday, so a big story was serious business. Dozens of reporters barged into what had been Dinneen and Goldberg's wholly owned territory.

The gunplay in a Times Square hotel made the front page of the *New York Times*. Its reporter, like all the others, took pains to take note of Norma. "Mrs. Millen," said the *Times*, "was well-dressed and pretty. She made use of her vanity case and lipstick" while in custody at the hotel and then "nonchalantly ate chocolate while the husband and his brother refused to answer questions.

"Later at headquarters she waited with the pert and unconcerned expression while the brothers were questioned further."

As the news rolled into Boston over the telephone and teletype that afternoon and evening, and as local police reporters picked up the scent of events at the Brinsley Street garage, reporters were dispatched to Roxbury, Dorchester, Natick, and New York City. Editors ordered their staffs to dig up whatever they could find about the various Millens, Fabers, and Brightons. Deadlines were rapidly approaching as the papers rejiggered their front pages for the news from Dartmouth College, where nine students in a fraternity house had been found dead that very afternoon, victims of carbon monoxide from a malfunctioning coal-fired furnace. Fortunately, from the standpoint of the Boston papers, none of the dead were from Massachusetts. Morning papers like the *Globe* were particularly rushed, while the Hearst's *Boston American*, which published in the afternoon, could update events on Monday morning and get a bump in newsstand sales.

It quickly proved nearly impossible to manage the sensational details flooding in from New York, Brinsley Street, and Room 24. Where to begin?

What to emphasize? Early to emerge was the stunning disclosure that Faber was an MIT graduate and commissioned officer in the U.S. Army Reserves. Abe wasn't a Harvard man, regrettable in terms of news value, but MIT was almost as prestigious. Stokes awkwardly declared, "Faber was a genius whose brain fashioned future killings and robberies which would shock the nation."

Editors sent clerks down to the newspapers' morgues to research the last time a Tech grad was arrested for bank robbery and murder. Apparently, "never" was the answer.[2]

That all three men were Jewish was treated so gingerly that the fact went unnoted by all the major papers until a Jewish legislator from Roxbury arose in the State House to praise the police and, effectively, excommunicate the trio. Making matters even more delicate was that one of the Jews had married a Christian, and a minister's daughter at that. Norma was always identified as a minister's daughter even though her father was working full time running a car dealership and had just completed course work for a law degree.

Even more surprising, if that was possible, was that all four "were totally unlike the desperate gunmen or gangsters investigators expected to find," as the *Herald* put it. Police and prosecutors were grudgingly impressed by the amateurs' criminal expertise, the paper added. "Few crimes have been committed with more foresight and skill," and "except for the clue afforded by the rental battery found in the burnt wreck the identity of the criminals might never have been known," it declared, quoting anonymous police sources.

The details of the battery, that curious clue, had to be pursued and explained. Ordinarily astonishing discoveries received short shrift amid the flood of news, like those 209 sticks of dynamite stashed in the Brinsley Street garage.

And what about the two cabdrivers on trial for the Lynn murder? Were they really innocent? And what about the murder in Fitchburg? Or the robbery in Worcester?

ON MONDAY MORNING Murt and Irv took center stage at the NYPD's fabled daily "lineup."[3] It was not a lineup as the term was ordinarily understood. It was instead a sort of daily intelligence briefing for city detectives. Each morning plainclothes officers gathered in an auditorium on the fourth floor of the headquarters building as nefarious criminals arrested the day before were interrogated. Each stood alone under a spotlight as a detective snapped questions. Where did he live? Who were his accomplices? What other crimes had he committed? The practice dated to the late nineteenth century, and even in the 1930s it remained an efficient way to disseminate the identities and modus operandi of the city's wrongdoers. Sometimes it was great theater, but the public rarely witnessed it and the press rarely described it. But that morning the New York police invited Boston reporters to attend as an unusually large crowd of five hundred detectives crowded in to see the cop killers.

Irv was led to the spotlight. He was disheveled and his head was still bandaged. He blinked and shivered as questions were lobbed at him through a microphone. Why was he in New York City? How did he come by the cash police found in his hotel room?

Irv blinked again. "That's a long story," he said, and launched into a partially comprehensible version of his alibi about the stranger with the auto battery. The stranger told him, "I had better go away for a couple of days," Irv said, "and I made a mistake or something about the battery, see? So he comes down to my house and tells me here's some money to get out of town.

"He said the officials were coming to arrest me on some charge because I shouldn't have given my proper name when I got the battery. He threatened to get me or my family if I didn't go away." Irv rambled on. The detective with the microphone was unimpressed. "Listen, Irving, have to get a better story than that."

"Well, I'm talking fast now," Irv said, and explained that the man returned again the next day, Irv having not yet left town, and gave him "$500 or $600" and another $2,000 the day after that. It was expense money, Irv said. Then the man showed up with a suitcase stuffed with weapons and ammunition for Irv to spirit out of town.

By now there were probably guffaws filling the hall.

"You mean to stand there and tell me that a perfect stranger came to you and gave the $2,000 and $500 to $600?" the detective asked. "Take him away," he said in disgust.

Murt was next. He flatly denied any role in the Needham robbery. Asked why he carried so much cash, Murt played the wiseguy. "Because I don't trust banks. They might fail. You never can tell."

There was a lengthy series of questions about the .32 caliber revolver. It was the weapon Murt took off the police officer during the Worcester movie theater robbery, and it bore the initials "WPD." Murt claimed that he purchased it from a stranger during an overnight stay at the Worcester YMCA.

He played semi-dumb when asked about the weaponry in the Gladstone bag, which was found checked at the Washington, D.C., train station. "I don't know anything about the machine gun," Murt said. "All I know is that there was some kind of a gadget in a bag that looked like a machine gun. I looked in and I said to myself, this is bad business, so I closed up the bag right away and I said it would be just too bad if I was caught with this machine gun."

Like his brother, Murt stuck to the story about the strange man warning them to flee Boston, which was again received with incredulity.

"You and your brother Irving are on your way to the hot seat," concluded the detective.

IF MURT AND IRV thought they had gained breathing space with their alibi they were mistaken, because just as their interrogation ended Abe's began.

It was in a small, quiet room at the Norfolk County Courthouse in Dedham. There was no spotlight, no microphone, just state police detective Ferrari asking questions. He now reaped the benefit of his slow courtship of the MIT student who had thought he could outthink the veteran cop.

Ferrari may have appealed to Abe's scientific side. It really was a sort of math. There was "X" collection of evidence proving Abe's guilt, and "Y" suggesting his innocence, and no matter how he did the calculation it all added up to a conviction, so now was the time to get out in front. It would go easier on him, Ferrari promised. At 11:12 a.m. Abe sat down at a table with Ferrari and Fleming and a stenographer. Listening in was Dewing, the Norfolk County district attorney.

It was the same courthouse where ten years earlier Italian immigrant anarchists Sacco and Vanzetti were tried and convicted of murder, a case that still bedeviled everyone involved. Ferrari had played a peripheral role, and neither he nor Stokes nor Dewing wanted a repeat of that controversy with these ethnic criminals. They were going to convict the Millen-Faber gang so carefully that no one would ever ask twice.

"Start at the beginning," the detective said.

"Here is the story. Murt got married. Murt was an automobile mechanic and, as I understand things, he and Irving always liked cars and their income wasn't any too great." Abe paused and looked at Ferrari.

"It might be better if you asked me questions to get me going on this," he said.

Ferrari refused. He wanted no leading questions appearing in the transcript. "You left off with his wages weren't any too great," said the detective. "Go ahead now and say what was said and what happened."

The version Ferrari heard was neither complete nor candid. Abe portrayed himself as a person acted upon rather than an actor.

Abe explained he knew Murt and Irv were pulling holdups, but he had nevertheless "kept my nose clean" until just weeks before the Needham job, when his best friend pushed him to participate. He could not explain his agreement. "I don't know why," Abe insisted, "but for some reason or other I finally found myself mixed up in it. They needed another man.

"It was like a bad dream to me, the whole thing. As soon as we went in there the alarm went off. I could hardly hear it. Then Irving ordered the teller to collect the money, and he jumped behind the counter somehow, he wanted to open the grill, and the fellow wouldn't open it or didn't open it fast enough, and I yelled, "Open it up," and when I did I had my shotgun down low and the gun went off and got the old fellow. It almost got Irving too. That was a big mistake.

"Then we went out. Murt and Irving grabbed a fellow each from the bank, and I walked out and they walked out."

Ferrari interjected, "Now I will interrupt you there, please."

Abe had skipped McLeod's murder. "Just before you walked out, and while the robbery of the bank was going on, where was Murton Millen?"

"Murt Millen was running around like a madman inside there," Abe said.

"With what in his hands?"

"With the machine gun. He ran to the front room."

"He ran into that front room?"

"And in back and howled at them and then back and forth again."

"Then what happened?"

"Nothing. Afterwards I found out."

Abe would not admit he knew that McLeod had been killed, or say it was he himself who shouted, "Get him." Ferrari pressed him.

"Did you hear some shooting?"

"I didn't hear any. I'm telling you the whole thing appears to me like a bad dream. I was in a daze."

"Did you hear anybody say while you were in the bank, 'Here comes a cop?'"

Faber said no.

"Or did you say it?"

"No."

Any other shots he heard?

"Irving fired a few shots. He said he dropped his gun and it went off. He forgot about the safety on it."

Ferrari moved on. "What happened on that ride through town?"

"Nothing," Abe said. "Just drove through the town. It appeared to me he was crawling through."

Ferrari was visibly displeased.

"Did you read the papers of the account of the crime?"

"Yes."

"Did you read where a half or three-quarters of a mile from the scene of the bank robbery another police officer was shot?"

"Yes," said Abe.

"Now I am asking you what happened on that ride through the town, using that to refresh your recollection."

Abe yielded again.

"When we came down the street there Murt yelled, 'There is a cop out there,' and the officer was drawing his gun . . . or at least he said so, or we thought so, and Murt picked up the machine gun and shot him right through the window." Abe admitted he fired a blast from a shotgun as the car sped away.

"Then we drove home," said Abe.

At 39 Lawrence Avenue they shoved the machine gun under Irv's bed and split the money.

Ferrari had a final question. "Was Norma Millen anywhere in this case? Anything to do with it?"

"She knew all about it," said Abe.

"In what way?"

"She knew Murt was interested in it. She knew it was going to be."

Had she told him that herself? "No. I know."

"You mean by some talk you all had together?"

"Yes," said Abe, conversations "in Murt's apartment . . . Irving, myself, Murt and his wife."

Abe's confession was relayed to the waiting reporters in time for the late afternoon editions. Ferrari's interrogation wasn't as thorough as it could have been. Neither he nor Fleming asked about, nor had Abe mentioned, the killings in Lynn and Fitchburg.

But Norma did.

Unlike her husband, she had avoided the indignity of a New York jail cell and the morning lineup. Stokes had contacted her father, and the reverend arrived in New York City before dawn on Monday to rescue the daughter who had fled from his home in September. He was led to the office of Assistant Chief Inspector John J. Sullivan. Waiting there were Norma and a gaggle of newspaper reporters and photographers—and not only the New York press. By now the Boston papers had their own reporters and photographers at the scene. The *Boston American* described the minister as a "tall, aged, care-worn man." The paper then shared the touching reunion with readers:

"'Daddy, I knew you would come,' Norma cried, her eyes wet with tears when she saw her father. 'I knew it. I need you so.

"'Oh Daddy, believe me, I didn't know anything about this.'"

The reverend addressed her as "Lovey," supposedly a childhood nickname. "'Lovey, child, I'm here right now and everything is all right. Tell me everything you know. You can trust me.'"

That version sounded a bit too good. The *New York Post* probably got the reunion right. Father and daughter embraced. "'How are you, dear?' the Reverend asked. 'All right, Daddy,' Norma replied."

They departed later that morning in the company of Stokes. Another gang of reporters waited when they stepped onto the platform at South Station in Boston. Norma looked particularly fetching and sophisticated, a grown-up at eighteen, wearing a pillbox hat and a veil of sheer lace.[4] Her face was expertly made up, and the expensive fur coat, the present from Murt, was open despite the cold. She had a gay hello for the newsmen.

She was whisked off to the State House detective bureau as Abe finished confessing in Dedham. After an hour or so inside, Norma and her father walked out with a state police detective.

The reporters yelled questions, and some gave their readers answers that may have had some connection to the truth. "I fell madly in love with Murt because of his deep voice, athletic build and gaiety," the *Daily Record* claimed she said.

Certainly, Norma had fallen in love with the press's attention, and the papers had fallen in love with her photograph, though the rewrite desk sometimes still got the color of her hair wrong. In one article the *Globe* described Norma as the "blonde bride."

Favorite photographs emerged. One was a shot taken inside the New York City police headquarters showing Norma holding Murt's hand as he and Irv stared glumly at the camera. Another photograph showed a glowing Norma on her return to Boston that afternoon, her eyes drinking in the cameras' admiration. In that photo her father is on one side steering icily ahead. Stokes is on the other side, wearing the expression of a man desperately wishing to step out of viewfinder range.

The prose moved from purple to red. From the *Daily Record*: "She has the power of 1,000 sermons in the violet depths of her eyes. Did Murton Millen steal and kill to make her smile that he might provide her with the luxuries of the great world outside her father's house for which she yearned?"

Photographers vied for fresh shots of the killer's wife to please editors who ran portraits of Norma in multiple poses. They collected shots of Norma reading a book, Norma feeding a pet bird, Norma hugging her father, Norma shopping, Norma sewing, and even Norma cooking dinner. The *Daily Record* ran a series of photos filling most of one page, each a close-up of Norma in a different mood: pensive, surprised, smiling, and beguiling. The *American* countered with three close-ups of Norma's lips, large and luscious and splashed across the page. No eyes or chin, just lips.

"Lips that kissed," read the first caption. "For three months Norma Brighton Millen's lips caressed the lips of her bandit bridegroom as he and his band robbed and killed."

The second was tougher. "Lips that told . . . Then the law caught up with the gang and now she has bartered the lives of the two Millens and Faber that she herself may go free."

The caption writer ran out of steam in the third. "Lips that keep on smiling. And with a smile . . . she keeps on telling of the deeds of high red crimes of banditry."

The captions were true, if purple. Inside the State House on Monday, or perhaps during the train ride from New York, Norma told Stokes that her husband, Abe, and Irv had committed the Fitchburg and Lynn crimes. It was not, however, a formal interrogation and no written record ever surfaced. But it would send Ferrari back to Dedham for another conversation with Abe.

The police and prosecutors in Boston did not yet know what to make of Norma. Daniel Needham was apparently persuaded by the minister. Needham told reporters that Norma seemed an innocent girl whose only failing was tragic misjudgment. Her legal situation was uncertain, he acknowledged. No statement yet made public linked her to any particular crime, and she couldn't be asked to testify against her husband. Abe and Irv were another matter. They discussed asking her to turn state's evidence. For now, the agreement allowed Norma to live at home with the state police detective keeping an eye on her.

After Norma departed, prosecutors and police from Lynn and Fitchburg assembled in the State House to discuss their next step. Daniel Needham fed expectations by announcing, "There will be more astounding developments later."

EARLY THAT SAME EVENING, news of Abe's confession reached Murt and Irv via an enterprising *Boston Daily Record* reporter, Bob Court. He discovered that a reporter could get access to the Millens merely by asking the jail guards; so he did. The brothers denied everything and said that they would willingly return to Massachusetts to contest the charges. Then Court disclosed that Abe had confessed — to the Needham killings — and named them as accomplices.

"Both boys looked at one another and appeared a little startled, and then Irving said, 'If Abe has done that, as you say, which I doubt, if he was beaten up and forced to make untrue statements, he is a liar if he involves either of us in any jobs of any kind.'" Murt's denial, as reported by Court, was less encompassing. "Abe is a liar if he involves my wife in anything. She is a swell little girl and has never done anything wrong in her life." Court then moved onto the Fitchburg killing, the Mechanics Building job, and the Paramount Theatre robbery. Did they do those? Of course not. Murt and Irv even denied renting the Brinsley Street garage.

Abe did not.

Late Monday evening the prosecutor in the Lynn trial, Hugh A. Cregg, showed up. Was Abe one of the Lynn killers? he asked. He had to know, because two men were on trial. Abe found it curious that Cregg was asking him to admit something that could only embarrass the prosecutor. "I'd rather be dead myself than send two innocent men to their deaths," Cregg said. "It is my duty to tell the jury everything that I know was truthful and that's why I am here with you now."

Cregg's claim of altruism brought a sarcastic retort.

"You're the funniest guy I've ever met," said Abe.

Nevertheless, the next day, Tuesday, February 27, Abe again sat down before a stenographer in the district attorney's office. This confession was strikingly different than his first.

Lawrence Goldberg from the *Post* was in the back of the room, probably a special courtesy from Ferrari.[5] In an unpublished manuscript he set the scene with a particularly unusual metaphor:

> A great wintry sky is visible through the window. Covered with perspiration, his rumpled shirt adhering to his body, his hair tangled and knotted, his eyes aflame, Faber is walking back and forth with the jerky gate [sic] of one suffering sinus trouble: he is down for a moment, then rises; then is down again; then rises.
>
> Faber flings himself into a chair. This time he fastens his eyes on the floor and wrings his hands. The minutes race by.
>
> "You're in deep, Abe. You know it. It's your only chance. Come clean and I'll help you get a break," Ferrari is saying. The detective's voice has no touch of anger or scorn. He is pleading.
>
> "All right, Mr. Ferrari. I'll take your word for it. You take care of me—if I tell you everything?" asks Faber, finally. He glances about him swiftly, as though he were startled by the sound of the words, and lowers his voice.
>
> The police stenographer begins to write. Faber expresses amazement at his decision to talk.
>
> "I don't know what's happened to me suddenly. Something inside of me must've snapped. I can't believe my ears. I can't realize what I'm doing or saying. I ought to laugh at you," he told Ferrari. "I used to laugh out loud every time I read in the newspapers about persons breaking down and

confessing to police. What was it that made them talk and admit anything, I used to ask myself. Weaklings, fools, morons, I'd say. Maybe it was the police third degree we hear so much about, but there's been no third degree stuff here. No one has been rough. There hasn't been any slugging with a rubber hose and there hasn't been any gouging out of eyeballs. You've been with me all the time; you haven't raised a finger. You haven't lost your temper once. You've been a gentleman. All other cops have been the same way toward me. What is it that's making me talk!"

That prelude was not included in the confession later released to the press. Did Goldberg massage Faber's comments as a way of thanking Ferrari?

Abe then waxed philosophical. He knew his confession placed him on the path to execution.

"Maybe it's because I need sleep. Maybe it's because I'm getting frightened—fearful of what's going to happen—I can't quite describe it. It's not fear of death; not that. As a student of science I haven't any fear of death. I know what life is all about. And I know what makes a mechanism go. It isn't the sort of fear associated with death. It's something—I don't know—it doesn't matter. There is a heavy constriction about my throat and neck—something heavy is weighing me down. I've got to get it off; I've got to give myself breathing space. I'll feel better then. I know what it means if I—I'm no schoolboy."

Goldberg wrote that Faber's voice was high-pitched and nervous. His lips were twitching, his skin was pale, and "his eyes are gleaming savagely."

What came next unveiled a personality that was cold-blooded and remarkably megalomaniac. It was never described by his professors, and apparently never seen by Rose. After confirming his longtime friendship with Murt, Abe described their meeting of minds.

"We feel the same way about a lot of things in life, and about certain ways of living. We shared the same belief that all that counts is money; that life is to be lived and enjoyed; and that without money there can be no living or enjoyment; that since money was that important, it didn't matter how it was obtained; that all that counted was to get it."

They formed "a business organization for the sole purpose of getting money," said Abe. "The Millens agreed with me that if we did certain things the right way and took no chances, we couldn't miss. We figured that if certain things were done, and done precisely, no police force in the world would be smart enough or fast enough to keep up with us."

Their agreement included a code of silence, a "no-talking" pact, now obviously expired.

The trio was to be ruthless. Faced with any obstacle, they would "remove that obstacle promptly—no matter what it was. That meant if anyone got in our way we would kill him—policeman, detective, man, woman, or anyone else."

He described their hunt for automatic weapons and then gave another reason they had 209 sticks of dynamite.

"We planned to blast our way in and out of certain banks," he said. "We planned to set up our own roadblocks if we were chased, by dynamiting the roads behind us." They selected an isolated stand of trees outside of Boston and set up their own shooting range. Faber taught the brothers how to field-strip their weapons so they could take them apart and reassemble them blindfolded. They practiced with .22 caliber pistols and .45 caliber semiautomatics. They preferred the .22's, Faber said. "They were more accurate and we never missed our targets with them."

That was proved in Fitchburg, where Clark was slain with a volley of .22 bullets.

"The Fitchburg shooting brought us three close together. It proved that we were going to act like partners ought to act in the future," Abe said. The police department's failure was encouraging. "They were looking for gangsters, hardened criminals with police records," Faber said. "Someone said he was able to identify one of the gunmen. That made us laugh. We'd never been arrested and police didn't have our photos. We figured the police were stupid."

Then came a new fact that caught the detectives by surprise: Norma was present. "Murt's wife was with us in the backseat," Abe said. Ferrari's eyebrows lifted, but he didn't interrupt. He would ask about the minister's daughter later.

When Abe turned to the Lynn murder, Goldberg wrote that he paused, leaned his head against his chair, shut his eyes, and cleared his throat before continuing:

"Murt told me one man had to be shot when he wouldn't do what he was told. Murt shot him. He got fresh when he got the orders and so he got killed. Another man tried to duck out of the place a few minutes afterwards and we had to shoot him down too. We also had to blackjack another man, employed there, when he didn't keep his hands up in the air like he was told to do."

Faber got the sequence of the shootings wrong. But the admission was what Ferrari wanted.

With that robbery behind them, the trio was ready for the big score. Their plan was to stage multiple bank robberies in a single town in quick succession on a single day. The target was Wellesley, the affluent bedroom community.

"We were going into Wellesley and stage three holdups of banks simultaneously. We figured this would help in the general confusion. It would be easy to catch everyone cold and we figured out that we would clean up with about a quarter million dollars." A robbery at one bank would bring all the police to that scene, leaving the next targets unprotected. "Everyone would be panicky except us."

But they switched to the single bank in Needham because of its location next to the rail line. They scouted the town, attempting to ascertain the number of policemen and whether there was a teletype hookup. "Most of the cops were old-timers; none of them was very good at shooting straight; they were all married." Faber claimed he sketched the bank interior. They calculated the take at $50,000. Anyone who interfered would be killed. "Our philosophy was the survival of the fittest. That's all life amounts to anyway. I've learned that. I'm convinced of that."

Now it had all fallen apart. Abe was stunned. "We spent so much time figuring things and being precise about things that we were convinced we wouldn't make any mistake or that there would be anyone smart enough to stop us, or catch us. We made allowances for everything. I can't understand how we made that mistake about the battery in the car we used in Needham.

"It looks like that was a bad mistake.

"Murt and Irving laughed it off, but I didn't. They said it didn't mean a thing. He said the cops would never trace the battery. I had a feeling that someone would."

Then Faber snarled, "Those fools. He didn't say a word to me about having the battery repaired. The stupid goddamn fools." The business partnership was now totally dissolved.

"They ran. They ran out on me and went to New York. They told me they had friends in New York who would take care of them in any trouble. Now I understand. Well, I'm all done."

He was again wrong.

For himself, his family, and Rose, a whole new reality was only beginning. He would endure it for sixteen months.

Abe's account of dynamite roadblocks and triple bank jobs pumped up the newspaper hyperbole even further.

"The Most Astounding Confession Ever Made to Massachusetts Police," said the Associated Press. "A Series of Holdups and Slayings Gigantic in Scope." Or as the *Daily Record* put it, "An Empire of Crime Unsurpassed in Fact or Fiction."

The next confession would be Irv's, followed by Murt's, followed by Norma's, followed by Joe Millen's declaration, with tears streaming down his face, that his sons were insane.

Murton Millen, Irving Millen, and Abraham Faber in April 1934 at the start of their eight-week trial. The photographer may have cracked a joke to get a smile. Abe remained grim-faced, as always. *Courtesy Trustees of the Boston Public Library / Leslie Jones Collection.*

Norma Brighton Millen outside her Natick home on February 27 or 28, 1934. She had turned nineteen three months earlier. *Courtesy Trustees of the Boston Public Library / Leslie Jones Collection.*

RIGHT Norma with her father, Reverend Norman Brighton, at the state detective bureau, Room 24 in the Massachusetts State House. Earlier that day Norma had returned from New York City. *Courtesy Trustees of the Boston Public Library / Leslie Jones Collection.*

BELOW State police detectives Michael F. Fleming, John F. Stokes, and Joseph L. Ferrari and Massachusetts Commissioner of Public Safety Daniel Needham in front of the train that brought Murt and Irv Millen back from New York City. *Courtesy Trustees of the Boston Public Library / Leslie Jones Collection.*

Needham police officer Francis O. Haddock, shot and fatally wounded as he approached the getaway car. *Courtesy of the Haddock family and Jeffrey Sadow.*

Needham police officer Forbes A. McLeod, mortally wounded outside the Needham Trust Company. *Courtesy of the Needham Historical Society.*

Needham Trust Company, February 2, 1934. Murt fired the Thompson through the lower-left windowpanes above the sedan. Officer Forbes A. McLeod fell mortally wounded on the snow-covered railroad tracks at the bottom right. *Courtesy Trustees of the Boston Public Library / Leslie Jones Collection.*

Investigators combing through the black Packard sedan after it was found torched on a dirt road outside Boston. Two clues survived the fire. *Courtesy Trustees of the Boston Public Library / Leslie Jones Collection.*

The fateful lead-acid storage battery. The battery cell on the right was repaired with nineteen wooden "separators" inserted between each lead plate. The separators gave police the clue that solved the case. *Courtesy Trustees of the Boston Public Library / Leslie Jones Collection.*

Detective Lieutenant Ferrari with Murt and Irv as they await a train to
Boston a week after their arrest in New York City. *Courtesy Trustees of the
Boston Public Library / Leslie Jones Collection.*

Louis W. Berrett, *left*, and Clement F. Molway, the cabdrivers erroneously identified as the Millens by hostages in a Lynn robbery and murder. Their trial was brought to an abrupt halt. *Courtesy Trustees of the Boston Public Library / Leslie Jones Collection.*

Massachusetts governor Joseph B. Ely presenting medals to Helen F. Haddock, *left*, and Margaret E. McLeod, widows of slain officers Francis O. Haddock and Forbes A. McLeod. *Courtesy Trustees of the Boston Public Library / Leslie Jones Collection.*

LEFT Rose Knellar, who was "pinned" to Abe Faber. The photograph was taken inside the detective bureau. Note the photo of Murt on the wall and the memo below it. *Courtesy Trustees of the Boston Public Library / Leslie Jones Collection.*

BELOW Reverend Norman Brighton speaking to reporters outside the Norfolk County Jail. He was always available to the press. He had earlier left the pulpit to attend law school at night. *Courtesy Trustees of the Boston Public Library / Leslie Jones Collection.*

Reverend Brighton, *left*, and Joseph Millen outside the Norfolk County Courthouse during the first weeks of the Millen-Faber trial. *Courtesy Trustees of the Boston Public Library / Leslie Jones Collection.*

Millen defense lawyer George Stanley Harvey (*left*), Commissioner of Public Safety Daniel Needham (*center*), and Norfolk County District Attorney Edmund R. Dewing (*right*) share the staircase leading from the county courtroom. Dewing flunked out of Dartmouth College but recovered to end his career as a Superior Court Judge. *Courtesy Trustees of the Boston Public Library / Leslie Jones Collection.*

Defense attorney William R. Scharton with Abe's parents, Philip and Rose Faber. To save his son, Philip claimed he carried a sexual disease that he had passed on to Abe. *Courtesy Trustees of the Boston Public Library / Leslie Jones Collection.*

Famed psychiatrists Smith Ely Jelliffe, *left*, and L. Vernon Briggs, *center*, with Murt and Irv's defense attorney, George S. Harvey. *Courtesy Trustees of the Boston Public Library / Leslie Jones Collection.*

The *Boston Evening Globe* captured all three events of February 25 and 26: the arrests in New York; the arrest in Boston, and the end of the Lynn trial. Abe is at lower right, hiding his face. *Courtesy of the* Boston Globe.

Irv, Murt, and Abe guarded by state police as they rush from the courthouse minutes after their conviction. Note the news photographer running alongside and the state trooper behind Irv raising his truncheon. *Courtesy Trustees of the Boston Public Library / Leslie Jones Collection.*

Norma Millen on her way to court in June 1934, after four months in jail. No longer looking glamorous, she dreaded the prospect of a trial. *Courtesy Trustees of the Boston Public Library / Leslie Jones Collection.*

Crowds appeared every day at Norma's trial. Here she poses for photographs after sentencing. A jail matron is on her right. *Courtesy Trustees of the Boston Public Library / Leslie Jones Collection.*

Abe, Irv, and Murt being transported from the Norfolk County Jail to the Charlestown State Prison in Boston after being sentenced to death. *Courtesy Trustees of the Boston Public Library / Leslie Jones Collection.*

Rose Faber being led out of the Charlestown State Prison after visiting her son. This may have been the day before Abe was executed in June 1935. *Courtesy Trustees of the Boston Public Library / Leslie Jones Collection.*

The electric chair at Charlestown State Prison in Boston. Through the doorway are three holding cells. The executioner would stand to the right. *Courtesy Trustees of the Boston Public Library / Leslie Jones Collection.*

18

The Girl
Talleyrand

BUT TUESDAY STILL HAD some hours to run.

Shortly after 7:00 p.m. Judge Hammond at the Lynn trial turned to face the dozen men seated to his left and uttered a remarkable instruction. "It may surprise you to learn that you have agreed upon your verdict. I instruct you now that as the name given by the clerk is read you return verdicts of not guilty."

No deliberations were necessary, and there would be no closing arguments—because the district attorney had given up. The jurors knew that unusual events were unfolding, as court convened Monday morning only to be immediately adjourned with no explanation. Whatever the jurors learned came from friendly court officers, as they had been sequestered in a downtown hotel since the start of the trial two weeks earlier.

Molway and Berrett had known for twenty-four hours that the district attorney's case was crumbling. Their breathless attorneys briefed them Monday afternoon, and the cabbies were seen merrily clapping each other on the back. They were returned to their cells for the night, though not locked in, and on Tuesday evening they were not handcuffed as guards escorted them into the packed courtroom. In less than an hour they were again free men. Judge Thomas J. Hammond first declared the evidentiary portion of the trial reopened and called two of the earlier witnesses. Berrett took particular pleasure in watching the once supremely confident head janitor, Leo Donahue, stiffly declare, "I desire to say that I'm mistaken in my identification of these two defendants." The theater manager, Stephen Bresnahan, who got his identification wrong despite having conversed face-to-face with Molway and Berrett, or rather Murt and Irv, or perhaps Irv and Murt, in the theater office, was a bit more voluble. "As a result of the pictures and statements showed me today in Dedham I feel sure that these two defendants were not at the theater that morning."[1]

It was an enormously embarrassing moment for prosecutor Cregg. For the second time in a year his prosecution of a murder case had ended in public humiliation. To his credit Cregg didn't attempt to shift all the blame to the Lynn police, though he did note that officers handed him a case with eight eyewitness identifications.

Tired looking, Cregg stood erect in the courtroom. "The identification had seemed certain," he said. How had all the witnesses been so wrong? Cregg blamed it on the frailties of human memory, specifically what he claimed was "the strong resemblance" between Molway and Berrett and the Millen brothers.

"I can see now how the witnesses who testified at this trial were mistaken," Cregg said, "and I have no fault to find with them."

He turned to the two cabdrivers but spoke as though they were not in the room. "I am sorry that they were apprehended and confined in jail and have been subject to the ordeal of such a trial."

The reporters and county court employees gossiped quietly, some expressing sympathy for Cregg, who was well liked despite this egregious failure to second-guess the Lynn police. Others probably noted he had been warned by the state detectives, friendly newspaper reporters, and, of course, the defense attorneys that the trial should be delayed until the Needham bank robbery case was solved.

At the close of Judge Hammond's remarks, the jurors voted and one by one declared Molway and Berrett not guilty. The two men were again free. Ecstatic family members gathered about and there was handshaking all around. Cregg walked up to give a face-to-face apology. Berrett was not so forgiving. When the prosecutor said, "I am sorry," Berrett ignored his proffered hand and turned away.

He remained furious at Cregg for forcing him to name his girlfriend from the witness stand. Berrett would have been in an even worse temper had he known the jurors were ready to convict him and Molway of murder. They had talked about the case among themselves during the trial, contrary to Hammond's repeated instructions, and were unimpressed by the alibi-based defense. "I tell you if we had been given the case last night it would've been curtains for Molway and Berrett," said one juror. Chimed in another, "I couldn't see much hope for the pair of them . . . It looked bad."

Had it really been a case of misidentification, or had the hostages, eager for revenge after the death of their co-worker and angry at their humiliation at the hands of the killers, agreed too readily with police officers who assured them they had the right perpetrators? Examining photographs of the four men side by side, it was difficult to see any similarities beyond age, dark hair, and the fact that all four were male. Molway had a rectangular face with a large bulbous chin, deep-set eyes, and thin lips. Berrett had the fair skin and features of a northern European Anglo-Saxon, characteristics that fit neither Murt nor Irv. Murt's face in particular was strikingly different, what with its long, narrow, triangular shape and distinctive nose. Irv's round cheeks were found on neither cabbie.

Molway and Berrett remained in the limelight for a few more days. Each wrote a first-person piece for competing Boston newspapers, and a production company signed them to reenact their tribulations live, onstage.[2]

Now the Boston press turned its full attention to Norma. The following morning, Wednesday, February 28, Daniel Needham released new excerpts from Abe's Tuesday confession, which eventually broached the subject of Norma. It gave reporters a brand-new narrative—that Norma, rather than an innocent girl enticed into crime by a Roxbury Lothario, was instead a knowing, even willing, participant.

During the drive to Fitchburg, according to Abe's account, she rode in the front seat next to Murt. She got out and waited on a corner as they followed the Iver Johnson clerk up Blossom Street. If the abduction had gone as planned, Norma would have sat behind the wheel while the men ransacked the store for arms and ammunition. "She was to sit in the car and act as lookout," Abe said. Instead, she was still on the downtown corner when the car screeched back to pick her up after the botched kidnapping. On the return ride, "Norma was informed that they shot somebody and she thought, or said, very little of it," Abe said.

He added a second damaging disclosure. Abe said Norma helped the trio torch the Packard. She drove the Chevy, Abe said, and even described the moment when it became stuck in the snow. Murt jumped out of the Packard and "was kind of angry about her being so dumb and going away up the road or something of the sort. I don't remember exactly. He didn't scream, but he was sort of cursing."

The new disclosures had the effect of "stirring the pot," in journalistic parlance. They rose to the top of the reporters' notes and were turned into new stories and headlines.

Goldberg was first to get a denial from Norma, probably because he was tipped off by Ferrari. He found Norma as she waited on Wednesday, February 28, to testify before the grand jury, which later that day indicted her as an accessory to robbery, and the three men for murder.

"'That isn't true,' she cried, but trembled visibly," Goldberg wrote. "'I was never let in [on] their plans. That's all a lie, and he knows it.'" Norma should have stopped there, but then the reverend should already have hired a professional for legal advice. Norma's panicked reaction was contradictory and incriminating.

"The first I knew anything about Fitchburg was two days before that man was killed there. Murt told me he was going to Fitchburg three days before the time he went there, with the purpose of buying some guns." So the innocent country girl knew that her husband wanted guns and knew that he was going all the way to Fitchburg to get them.

Instantly Norma realized what she had said and tried to conjure a fix. "He didn't tell me why he wanted the guns. He didn't tell me where he intended to buy them in Fitchburg." Goldberg pressed her. What did she say to him when she learned of the murder? Too polite, too intimidated, and perhaps a bit too confident not to answer, Norma said she had turned to her husband and asked, "Say, I hope you didn't kill that fellow that was shot there last night?"

So she thought her husband was capable of murder?

"I had no reason to say this other than it just happened to occur to me that he was killed there the day he was there."

She said Murt reassured her. "He just smiled when I asked the question and said, 'Who, me? Now dear, you know me better than that.'"

This was too much for Daniel Needham. The deal on Monday to allow Norma to remain at home was based on the presumption that Norma had no more than cursory knowledge of Murt's crimes, and that after the fact. Now she was described as an active participant in one robbery and murder, and an accessory after the fact in a second since she had helped to destroy evidence. A Congregational minister and state legislator from the western town of Ware released an open letter to Needham and Dewing demanding that Norma get no special treatment and expressing outrage that she was available for interviews and photographs. Norma was "enjoying the spotlight as she has been basking in the enjoyment of the spoils of crime." The publicity would only encourage "thousands of giddy and reckless girls" to follow in her footsteps. "Let us not forget that a refined-looking girl is the most valuable asset that a gang can have," he thundered, and then got right to the heart of the matter. "Sex and beauty must not be used to shield any person's guilt."[3]

Dewing made reassuring noises to the newspapers and announced that Norma was being held as a material witness. Her father put up the court-ordered $1,000 bond. The hearing attracted a large crowd of the curious, numbering in the hundreds, mostly women coming to see Norma. Among them was her mother, Margaret, who collapsed from the strain on the courthouse stairs as if on cue. She was uninjured.

REVEREND BRIGHTON UNDERSTOOD the dangers and opportunities presented by the Boston press. Certainly they were not going away. A half dozen reporters and photographers were parked outside his home on a daily basis. On Tuesday he had attempted to exert a measure of control by placating the reporters and photographers with a brief conversation. He offered the necessary glimpse of Norma, who poured tea as he explained to a handful of writers, "It is hard for her to readjust her ideas of her husband. Murt Millen was always a perfect gentleman in his behavior. He was unfailingly courteous and thoughtful and for that reason, it is difficult for Norma to see him in the new light which this investigation has set upon him." It was essentially the argument he had made to Daniel Needham.

By the next afternoon Abe's disclosures had rendered that version moot. A counter-narrative was necessary, and it had to come from Norma herself.

The reverend, forty-three, had grown up as mass circulation newspapers were born. The daily morning, afternoon, and evening editions and their large and aggressive news staffs—like those now standing in his front yard—owed their existence to the Linotype machine invented by a German immigrant in the 1880s. A skilled operator working the ninety keys needed only seconds to produce a line of type cast from molten lead. The machine not only cut costs and speeded production, but allowed the use of sophisticated and varied typefaces, which meant that newspapers could print department store display ads and cheap classifieds, the mainstay of their revenues.[4] Dozens of the machines operated simultaneously on the composing room floor of every major metropolitan newspaper. The price of a newspaper was sliced to pennies, making it affordable to virtually the entire working population of a city.[5]

Now newspaper readership was challenged by radio news. Sales of home radio receivers had reached a critical mass by the late 1920s, but initially local radio stations had no news staffs and relied on reports read from the morning papers. There was little competition for advertising dollars between the new and old mediums, but that was changing. In 1932 the newspaper trade magazine *Editor and Publisher* warned, "It is a major error for the press to build up the radio as a news instrument by sharing its news reports." Advertising revenue would follow, publishers were told.

In 1933 the national wire services stopped providing radio stations with news reports, and newspapers that once had allowed their material to be read over the air now boycotted local stations. Publishers accused broadcasters of "filching" their stories.[6] The stations fought back, and in 1934 a new type of programming debuted—scheduled radio news broadcast multiple times each day over local airwaves by local radio stations with local news reporters.[7]

For radio news the Millen-Faber case was a godsend, with its daily flow of breaking news. One update came within hours of the next. The newspapers could not keep up. Even the *Boston Transcript*, the *Boston Record*'s opposite in readership and content, felt it necessary to preface its coverage with a front-page display listing "Today's Developments."

Despite, or perhaps because of, that new competition, the reverend was witnessing a particularly vibrant era in the history America's big city newspapers. He understood that his daughter's youth and beauty, and his own honorific, "Reverend," was driving much of the coverage. He tried, as best as he could, to manage what the reporters wrote about his daughter and what photographs they took. To do that he had to act as his own press agent. Reporters found the reverend to be accessible and quick on his feet. Only rarely did he reply with a "no comment." In the ministry he had cultivated the skills of a public speaker by giving lectures on current events before Christian organizations, and he had offered motivational talks while serving in the YMCA during World War I. He later managed a series of car dealerships, which certainly demanded communication skills, and completed his course work for a law degree. He had even had some experience with an ugly press when he divorced Margaret Brighton twenty years before.

In the first days after Norma's return, he opened their Nonesuch Pond home to selected photographers, one of whom was Leslie Jones from the

Boston Herald and *Traveler*. (The newspapers were published under separate names with separate newsrooms, though they had the same corporate ownership.) Largely self-taught, Jones was a factory worker and a part-time freelance photographer until he lost two fingers in a 1917 accident. Fortunately, that same year the newspaper hired him fulltime.[8]

Jones was familiar to Norma and the reverend. Tipped off to Stokes's midnight train trip, he sped to New York City to take the famous front-page photo of Norma and Murt holding hands in the police station. He was at South Station when they returned from New York City, and later that day he was present when father and daughter emerged from the state police offices in room 24.

Now at the Nonesuch Pond home, Jones shot carefully posed photographs of the reverend standing over his daughter as she did needlework seated before the fireplace; as she held her dog, Lady, in her arm, fed a parakeet, and looked up from a thick, hardbound book that she was supposedly reading. She posed outside against the garage door with the small white dog and then picked her way down the snow-covered driveway with Lady on a leash. Most of Jones's Natick photographs show a smiling, merry, even contended Norma, but a few catch her unposed. In those the glow is absent; Norma is wary and tired and looks far older than her now nineteen years. Those photographs were never published.

On Wednesday afternoon the living room of the modest home filled with reporters from the *Boston Globe*, *Post*, *Traveler*, *Herald*, and *American*. The walls were lined with bookcases and artwork. On the shelves were texts by Milton, Cervantes, Homer, and Plato and volumes by Francis Bacon, the English philosopher who helped lay the groundwork for the scientific method.[9] There was a fire in the fireplace to take the edge off the cold.

Her father settled himself in a soft chair. Norma sat on the padded armrest, her legs crossed to one side. The reporters were given chairs and the performance began. As an exercise in damage control it was not particularly successful.

For starters, Norma declared her affection for Murt, who by the standards of a later age met the definition of a serial killer.

"Murton was nice to me," she said. "That's what I saw in him.

"I met him at a dance. I was wondering how I was going to go back to Natick the next day. Fortunately, I met Murton."

One reporter noted the reverend's eyes narrow. He interrupted, "You mean 'unfortunately,' don't you?"

Norma smiled faintly at the back of his head. "All right. Unfortunately then." Clearly, there was going to be no angry denunciation from a bride betrayed.

"I saw him frequently after that. I liked him. He was nice. He was very intelligent, no matter how he has appeared since. He was interested in psychology, so was I. I had been considering taking a course in it. I liked driving a car, and he had a car. I didn't have a car."

The reverend interrupted again. "I told her it would only lead to unhappy consequences, and I think she felt I had placed too much restraint upon her, but it was like pulling an elastic back. When she went she went with a bang. I think she was ignoring my constant warnings against going with the wrong people."

"You never imagined that you yourself can go with anybody wrong," Norma said from her perch.

"You resented it, didn't you?" he asked.

"Yes, I did."

"You did rather like excitement, didn't you?"

"Every young girl does," Norma answered. "I was sort of restless."

Some newspapers had by now assigned women writers to the story to offer an alternative to the otherwise totally male perspective. The *Traveler* assigned Sara White, a 1929 graduate of Radcliffe College whose work evinced sympathy sharpened by a reporter's cynicism. She compared Norma to Talleyrand, the French diplomat who played all sides to serve and survive under Louis XVI, the revolutionary Terror and its mass executions, Emperor Napoleon, and finally another king after the Restoration. He died in bed at age eighty-four.

White now said of Norma that despite the threat of indictment and trial, "the peril left her cool as ice itself. There was no tremor of fear, no catch of peril in this steady, almost cold, but restrained and low voice with which . . . she made her denial of criminal acts.

"She was the apex of a diplomatic triangle, a slender, beautiful girl, playing the opposing forces of parental affection and marital fealty with the suavity and dexterity of a Talleyrand."

Reporters pressed Norma on what she knew about the murders. Here

Norma took the advice of her father and for a moment retreated to reticence. "I heard them talking about crimes, but I never heard them talk in such a way as to indicate that they took part in them."

She flatly denied Faber's assertion that she was in Fitchburg. "Abe Faber lied. Abe Faber always hated me. I never liked him either.

"I didn't know they had gone to Fitchburg. I knew nothing at all about it." She turned to look at her father and here sounded like a wayward teenager. "Honest, Daddy, I was not in Fitchburg that night."

She conceded that she had driven the Chevy to Norwood and helped destroy evidence.

"Perhaps it's partly true I helped them escape after the Needham robbery," she said. "That's true, I did. I was told by Murt to drive the small car up there, but he was my husband and I only did what I was told."

Perhaps at that moment even she couldn't believe herself, as she continued, "Of course, I knew vaguely what must have happened, but I didn't understand it. I had suspicions but no real knowledge."

Dinneen from the *Boston Globe* gave Norma the benefit of the doubt, but the other papers didn't. In the *Traveler* White wrote that despite her denials, "she admitted, with the utmost casualness, that she knew a good deal about what her husband was doing."

The *Herald* described her as "admitting as casually as though she was discussing the weather that she assisted her husband and his two companions in escaping after burning the car used in the Needham robbery." The reporter said that she had "the piping voice of a little girl who knew not the import of what she said." White was more generous, describing her voice as "a modulated, musical soprano."

The interview turned to what Norma did for entertainment, but that, too, turned sour. "I like swimming and dancing," Norma said.

"Dancing, mostly," her father said. "That's a particular point of a disagreement."

So the topic came back to Murt, and Norma now so completely abandoned her father's game plan that she included kind words about Irv, too. Neither brother drank to excess, abused narcotics, used "vulgar language," or otherwise behaved "ungentlemanly."

With that the reverend agreed. "It's a queer trait in them," he said, for criminals.

Norma continued, "What I can't get, understand, is that Murt could shoot anybody. I hate blood. I'm still nauseated by that sight in New York. And Murton was always so sensitive to consider it. I know, when I was in New York I had a wart on my toe. It was painful and I had to have an injection of anesthesia. He stayed with me while the stuff was injected and I think he felt it as much as I did.

"He was very good that way." For example, "he knew I didn't like gangster movies and if you wanted to see one he would not make me go with them."

She was quiet when her father said his daughter smoked only when she was nervous and said nothing when the reverend added that she "never takes a drink at all." Norma gave her fingernails a close examination.

As the interview closed, the reverend declared, for the second time, that his daughter did not care for the man she married. "Of course she doesn't love him. She never did. She thought she did. Didn't you?" He faced Norma.

"I was attracted by him. I must've loved him or I wouldn't have married him," she answered.

The father shook his head. "You haven't got the vaguest conception of what it's all about."

As the reporters began to file out, he tried again. "You didn't really love him, did you, Norma? Of course you didn't."

"Dad, if I hadn't cared for him a great deal he couldn't have pulled the wool over my eyes. I'm not dumb."

Murt and Irv could not make the same claim, as their behavior crossed the line into recklessness. The brothers were in the same cell block at the Westside jail on Fifty-Third Street, five blocks south of Central Park. Coney Island detective Eason figured that since the brothers were talking to reporters, they might talk to him, too, though he would elicit a confession rather than an interview. Eason deduced that Irv was the more malleable of the two, though he did take a stab at Murt. Abe was spilling the beans, he told Murt. "Don't you want to have your say, too?" Murt was dismissive. "I'm behind the eight-ball now. You don't expect me to get myself in any deeper, do you?"

But he kept at Irv, and the next afternoon, Thursday, March 1, he separated him from his brother. Eason also gave Irv a chance to boast.

"How much did you get?" he asked. It worked.

Irv told him that it was $12,000 and not the $14,500 claimed by the bank.

He admitted to the Mechanics Building robbery and the Worcester theater heist, where the cop surrendered the "wpd"-engraved revolver.

"At first we were going to kill him," Irv said. "But he gave us no trouble and handed over his gun right away, and so we let him go." Told that the officer had recently died of a heart attack, Irv replied, "He must of died of fright then. I never saw a guy so scared. He almost dropped the gun in the first place. We took it because we were afraid that he would drop it and it would go off."

Irv brought himself up short and said that he only agreed to discuss the Needham job. Some accounts said that Irv claimed to have wielded the submachine gun, but all agreed that Irv blamed the murder of McLeod on McLeod.

"It was the cop's own fault. [Murt] fired some warning shots and the cop kept on coming, so he just gave it to them. If he turned around and gone back, nothing would've happened. He ought to have ducked," the *Herald* wrote.

According to the *American*, Irv said, "He was a fool to run toward the bank when the burglar alarm went off. Should've ducked behind a tree. What he should have done was run down a side street when he heard it, and he would be alive today. You know, a live coward is a lot better than a dead hero. That hero stuff is quickly forgotten."

Irv paused. His head hurt, perhaps from the blow in the hotel lobby. "Look, give me a chance, will you? You know I get dizzy spells and I can't think."

He had never finished high school, and it showed. When Eason asked if Norma helped them "dispose" of the car, Irv corrected him. "We didn't dispose of it. We burned it."

Irv resolutely refused to implicate Norma. "Why are you guys trying to put her in the middle? Listen, we will all burn before he puts the blame on her. Ask Murton," he said. "She didn't do anything with us. We used to call her and say, 'Meet us with the Chevy, Norma. We want you to drive us home.' And she would come and meet us. She didn't know anything about it."

Eason was surprised Irv said as much as he did. Why the confession? he asked. Sympathy for Abe, Irv said.

"You wouldn't want to see all three of us burn for that job, would you?" Irving laughed. "I'd like to save Faber. He's one hell of a swell guy." Irv said that he wanted to negotiate a deal so at least one of the trio would survive. "And that one to be saved will be Faber. He is an only son. There's more than one son in our family. Losing a son in our family wouldn't be so serious."

As Eason wrapped up his interrogation, Irv cautioned him, "Now, don't think I'll write that confession down or sign it, and if you testify that I confessed to you I'll call you a liar and say that I have never seen you."

The young man fell silent. During the conversation, he pondered his likely future and asked Eason a question.

"Say, how long does it take to die in the electric chair?"

MURT TALKED NEXT. Bob Court, the *Daily Record* reporter, showed up at the jail with another news clipping, this detailing Abe's confession naming Norma.

Furious that Abe had implicated his wife, Murt tried to minimize her role but ended up digging her, and himself, in deeper. "Faber told the truth" about the killings, except for Norma's knowledge, he said.

"My wife didn't know half of what was going on and she never got any money out of anything we ever did," he told Court. Of course, that comment could also be construed to mean that Norma did know half of everything they did.

Then he talked to a *Post* reporter and confirmed that Norma was indeed in Fitchburg, but was only along for the ride. Somehow Murt thought that would clear her. He was panicked, or ignorant. "Norma thought it was a business trip. When we got to Fitchburg we told her to go to a movie and that we would pick her up later." Murt admitted following the store clerk and getting caught on the one-way street. "I had to whip it around. Then we drove back and picked up Norma." Wasn't she in a movie? Oh. Murt thought fast. "We picked her up down near the theater."

Essentially, he confirmed Abe's claim. He did not blame Abe for his arrest.

"I'm not sore at Faber for squealing. He's afraid of the electric chair and wants to take life imprisonment. That's okay with me. He just had a yellow streak, that's all. And we know we are licked, and if he wanted to rat okay, why wasn't he man enough to protect my wife?" Murt told the newspapers.

By now Murt had abandoned any pretense of innocence.

"We know we are going to the electric chair, but we are going to fight it anyhow. Our defense will be criminal insanity." He proceeded to lay some groundwork, telling the *Daily Record* reporter that at seventeen he had struck his head during a construction job and suffered a second blow in an auto accident, which left him with violent headaches and "and a desire to do desperate things."

He also wanted the credit he felt was his due. Some Boston papers theorized that the MIT grad was the brains behind the gang. No way, Murt said. "Regardless of what anyone else tells you I will tell you, and Irving will tell you. I was the brains of the outfit.

"Every time we pulled a job I carefully laid out the plans and everyone had a certain thing to do. Everyone did it. That's why we were successful. Then after we did the job we would sit around and read the newspapers and see what was doing, and have a quiet laugh at the bulls."

Killing the two officers with the "typewriter"—as Murt called the Thompson, so nicknamed for its explosive, metallic "clackety" sound—was almost accidental.

"I saw a cop coming across the railroad tracks. I said we will be trapped in here, so I upped with the gun and let him have it. I intended to cut his legs off, but I wasn't used to handling that gun and it was about the first time I fired it, and I was nervous, too."

The idea of forcing hostages onto the running board was indeed borrowed "from the work of Pretty Boy Floyd."

From the bank, "I drove the car with the typewriter on the front seat. The other two boys in the back were covering the fellows on the running board."

As the Packard approached the fire station, he saw two uniformed men and thought both Haddock and Coughlin were police officers. "Up the road a ways I saw two cops. One of them seemed to be walking out to the street. I thought, hell they will telephone ahead. So I picked up the typewriter and resting the muzzle of the gun on the front windowsill, which was open, I letta blast. I just fired in the general direction. I couldn't aim because one hand's on the wheel."

His only remorse was for himself.

"We made the mistake when we shot those two cops. We never should've shot the cop. When you shoot anybody but a cop it dies down, but when you shoot a cop, everybody's looking for you. It never dies."[10]

ALSO FEELING REMORSE was Daniel Needham. On Friday, March 2, he admitted to reporters that Norma might not be the "misled country girl" she appeared to be immediately after the arrests in New York City.

Newspaper reporters noted that in her daily interviews Norma displayed a particular ability to fasten on whatever interpretation of events was preferable to her at a given moment. Her father told a reporter, "She doesn't realize sufficiently to be afraid. She is still convinced, with the childishness that can't be explained, that the man—her husband—is innocent. She's fully cognizant that the electric chair awaits these boys, but she talks about the electric chair as she talks about her pretty frock."

Nevertheless, Norma was aware that her circumstances were tenuous. "I'd die if they ever locked me up in jail," she said.

As the news coverage began reflecting Needham's second thoughts, Norma and the reverend did themselves no good by embarking on a daylong clothes-shopping trip on Thursday, which yielded photographs of a happy girl with an armful of boxes and bags. Her husband had killed four people, and she seemed oblivious to the tragedies inflicted on four families.

On Friday the *American* ran a front-page list of Norma's "lingerie seized in raid." The couple had planned to return to Washington, D.C., and left most of their clothes in the rented apartment. All were seized by police, who released an inventory to the newspapers.

Among the items the *American* listed in boldface were two brassieres, two pairs of "step-ins," a sort of girdle, three pairs of silk pajamas, one reducing belt, ten pairs of ladies' hose, four pairs of shoes, five pairs of gloves, and dresses in colors of blue, black, white, green, gray, green, and a "crêpe de chine" slip. There were also two pairs of bloomers. And there was "a vast collection of cosmetics, powder and rouge."

Out of fairness, the *American* also listed selected items from Murt's wardrobe, which included a brand-new three-piece blue suit, ten shirts, five toothbrushes, two sets of underwear, two jars of Vaseline, seven pairs of socks, five sets of silk underwear, two safety razors, eleven handkerchiefs, eight neckties, shaving cream, a pair of gray gloves, and a pair of black slippers.

Norma found the ruckus over her clothing foolish. "They do so much want to dress me up, don't they," she said. After one newspaper claimed her wardrobe in Washington was worth $1,000, she declared, "It embarrasses me to reveal how inexpensive they are.

"Murt never gave me lots of money. I asked him for small change as I have asked my father. Sometimes he gave me $25 to buy clothes. That was enough."

On Friday evening her father, stepmother, and brother visited friends in Newton for dinner. They returned home to find a state police lieutenant waiting. Norma had to come with him, right now, to speak with the detectives in Boston. Their car was trailed by a long string of autos filled with reporters. In Norma's lap was her fluffy white dog, Lady.

Waiting for her in the State House basement was a wall of photographers and reporters. More poured out of the cars that had arrived from Nonesuch Pond. A *Herald* reporter described the scene:

> Before her and behind her scurried photographers shouting to attract her attention, their falshbulbs gleaming in the shadow-filled corridors as they snapped their pictures. With reporters and police shoving around her, she was halted at the threshold of the office at which she was to be examined.
>
> At that moment an instant of panic seemed to seize her. She clutched her father's arm, patently befuddled by the series of questions that were shot at her by reporters. No longer did she answer laughingly, no more did her slow blue-eyed gaze move coquettishly from reporter to reporter.

Waiting in Room 24 were Stokes, Ferrari, and Fleming and their commander, Michael Barrett, who had ignored Dinneen's tip about the battery. Once again her father was allowed to sit in, partly because of his capacity as Norma's attorney. Even now the family had not sought a criminal lawyer.

In the next ninety minutes Stokes asked Norma at least fourteen times, and in as many ways, if she had been in Fitchburg the night of Clark's killing. The transcript of her interrogation was never released to the media or entered into testimony, but a copy was preserved in state police archive.[11]

"Did you ever drive to Fitchburg with Murt?" Stokes asked.

"Never," Norma replied.

"Did you ever drive to Fitchburg with Faber?"

"Never." But she admitted she knew Fitchburg was their destination that day. She had driven up to Faber's house with Murt, and both walked inside. "His mother was there that morning; he said he was going up for radio parts."

"Didn't he say he was going to buy a gun?"

"He didn't say he was going to buy a gun, he said he was going to buy radio parts. He told me that in front of his mother."

"Didn't you drive up to Fitchburg one day with Merton [sic], Faber and Irving, getting up there about six o'clock in the evening?" Stokes asked.

"No."

"You never did?"

"No, I never did."

Had she seen any of the Millen family since her return? Norma said no.

Stokes returned to Fitchburg. "So you say you never went to Fitchburg at all with Murton, Irving or Faber?"

"That is what I say."

"You never stopped in front of a sporting-goods store, you never stopped on a corner and waited for them to pick you up and then drive down to Boston?"

"No."

"Is that the truth?"

"That is the truth."

So she knew nothing and suspected nothing?

Norma admitted overhearing conversations between Murt and Abe that raised suspicions but never asked for any details.

As the interrogation proceeded, however, Norma seemed to know more than she was letting on. "I had some vague suspicions because of the discussion in the paper, things like that." She paused. " I don't know what to say, you ask me to implicate Murt."

Was she worried about implicating yourself? Stokes asked. Norma said no. Abe's accusation was simply revenge for her coming between him and Murt.

"I never took to him and he never took to me. He told me someday I would be sorry I treated him so lousy."

What did that mean? Stokes asked.

"I don't know unless he is living up to it now."

"He said after they killed that man you drove with them."

"As I am sitting right in this seat, and if there is a God in heaven, you can believe me or not, I didn't."

She was in the Lynn theater the night before the robbery but insisted that she knew nothing about the crime and thought nothing of driving up to Lynn for a movie. "We used to go every place, we like riding." Norma said that the next morning she called the theater shortly after 9 a.m. to inquire about her lost ring. If she did so, Murt or Irv would have picked up the telephone.

She admitted driving the Chevy the night the Packard was burned but said she was merely following her husband's orders.

"Did they ever discuss Ferrari's or Fleming's or my name?" Stokes asked.

"Only that you and your partner were the best detectives."

"Did you ever hear them say anything about shooting up the cops?"

"No."

"What do you think they were carrying guns for?"

"Shoot anybody that came after them." That was an honest answer that Norma tried to temper by adding, "I didn't see why bandits would shoot them."

And yes, she knew they had a machine gun; she'd seen it at Lawrence Avenue in what used to be Murt's bedroom. He told her he was hiding it for someone.

Her denials were unconvincing. When the interview ended, Norma was arrested in the state police offices on the hitherto undisclosed warrant charging her with being an accessory after the fact of robbery. That same night Rose Knellar was arrested for receiving stolen property. Rose was jailed with relatively modest attention. But a caravan of reporters followed Stokes and Ferrari as they drove Norma to the Dedham jail that already housed Murt. Norma, as was her wont, steadfastly ignored this new unpleasant reality. One reporter said she took the steps into the jail "jauntily as if she were entering a country club for a dance." Norma confidently said a few days in jail could not be "so bad," though earlier that week she had told the *Boston American* reporter that going to jail "would kill her."

Murt was still in the New York City jail when he heard the news from a reporter. "That's the end," he muttered, and slumped to the bench.

PART III

19

The Briggs Law

IN 1901 a very pretty Broadway chorus girl and artist's model met a very rich and very famous architect. He was forty-seven; she was sixteen. The predictable occurred, involving excessive champagne and, at the minimum, statutory rape.[1] Nevertheless, the middle-aged rich man and the teenager had a fling for some months, which, even later when she was wiser, the girl recalled with fondness. Her name was Evelyn Nesbit, and she became what the world would later call a "supermodel." Nesbit's image graced magazine covers, advertisements, and corporate calendars, arguably making her the nation's first pinup girl.

Later she was successfully courted by Harry K. Thaw, the unstable but wealthy heir to a Pittsburgh railroad and coal fortune. Nesbit made the mistake of telling him the story of her deflowering in the bed of the older fellow, Stanford White, who was renowned for designing the original Madison Square Garden. Thaw did not react well. While touring Europe with his soon-to-be wife, he rented a German castle, locked Nesbit into an upper-story room, and set about beating her with a rawhide whip. Nesbit found it unpleasant, and Thaw found that he remained obsessed with White. Upon their return to the United States, he approached White during a musical revue and shot him in the head.

Thaw's prosecution became the first "trial of the century."[2] And why not? White was America's first celebrity architect, Thaw was a scion of one of the nation's richest families, and Nesbit was beautiful. To dodge a death sentence, Thaw pleaded insanity. His trial was elevated from tawdry spectacle to a spot in the history books because he hired not only the best lawyers but also the ten best available "alienists" (psychiatrists to later generations) at a cost reported to have reached $10,000 a day. A collection of the eminent, the alienists included three future presidents of the American Psychiatric Asso-

ciation and the up-and-coming Smith Ely Jelliffe, a friend and translator of
Sigmund Freud and one of the first American proponents of Freud's theory of
psychoanalysis. The prosecution retained its own alienists, and a courtroom
"battle of experts" ensued. To psychiatrists on the outside looking in, the trial
was a profound embarrassment. They wanted to turn the art of psychiatry
into a science, but what was the public to think when eminent practitioners
examined the same man, reached diametrically opposed conclusions, and
were then flayed for their opinions in open court. Just as dismayed were
the many Americans who chaffed at the mere thought of an admitted killer
escaping the electric chair for the confines of a mental hospital.

The first Thaw jury deadlocked, and the second convicted him of insanity. Thaw was eventually released and continued his habit of beatings,
though now of boys.

Afterward a call went up from psychiatrists for "reform of the insanity defense in expert testimony." The idea was to end the spectacle of squabbling
alienists, which served to confuse rather than illuminate. Justice demanded
an impartial evaluation of a defendant's sanity rather than a diagnosis that
depended on the skill of an attorney, the size of a defendant's purse, and
the ignorance of the jury. A new system was needed to secure a purely
professional psychological diagnosis, freed from the pressures of lawyers
and money. And publicity.

Different states proposed different remedies. In Massachusetts a respected psychiatrist, L. Vernon Briggs, pushed through a law that bore
his name. Under the "Briggs law," the sanity of a defendant in a major
felony case would be evaluated by two independent psychiatrists. Their
confidential finding would be submitted to the judge, prosecution, and
defense. It would not be binding on either side—a decision without trial
or public judicial proceeding would violate the U.S. Constitution—but
the two experts could be called to testify under oath. The idea was that if
the psychiatrists concluded that a defendant was insane, all parties would
accept an insanity plea and a commitment hearing would follow, a lengthy
trial thereby being avoided. If the accused was declared sane, his or her attorney would forgo the complexity and expense of an insanity defense and
contest only the facts of the charge. The law's effectiveness, then, depended
on mutual respect and cooperation between the lawyers, psychiatrists,

the judge, and, of course, the defendant. The Briggs law was held up as a model for the nation. For thirteen years it worked effectively to eliminate the embarrassing battles of experts.[3]

Then came the Millen-Faber trial.

SPECULATION THAT MURT AND IRV would choose an insanity defense began within days of their arrest—Murt had proclaimed as much to reporters—and became a foregone conclusion when Joe Millen arrived in New York City to visit his incarcerated sons. On February 28 he held what would be his first, and next-to-last, press conference. Standing outside the West Side's Fifty-Third Street jail, Joe came right to the point.

"My sons are insane. There was insanity in our family and a first cousin of theirs, Fanny Millen, is now in the insane hospital. There is also an insane streak on their mother's side."[4] He said Murt was "always a funny boy" and complained that Norma had insanity in her family, too. "When you get two people like that together see what happens?"

Nevertheless, he continued, "I cannot understand it. I always took care of them and they couldn't have had a better father. Murton tells me that they were in the Needham robbery, that they didn't kill anybody. And now the cops are trying to blame all the robberies on them." Joe knew who was at fault. "That Faber was a bad egg. He was always fooling around with guns. He came to my home a year ago with the gun, and I told him I didn't want him around there."

Joe was genuinely anguished. "I can't sleep. I haven't eaten anything. I just sit to try to figure it all out. It is no disgrace to have insanity in the family, but we never had murderers."

As they awaited extradition, Murt and Irv tried to cheer their father by promising that, somehow, their predicament would be resolved and they would be free to return home. Joe knew otherwise. "I know how they will come home. They will come home dead," he told reporters. Not right then or that week, but eventually. It was a prescient conclusion. But then Joe was a smart guy and knew his way around a courtroom. His sons had confessed, if only to a newsman, and that miserable Faber had admitted it all to a cop. If his sons were going to live, albeit behind bars, they had to prove themselves insane. And time was already short.

JUSTICE IN 1930S AMERICA was not slow. Four days after the arrests in New York City the grand jury met at the Norfolk County Courthouse in Dedham, and Murt, Irv, and Abe were indicted for the murders of Forbes McLeod and Francis Haddock. A trial date was set for March 26, leaving the defense and prosecution only eighteen working days to complete their investigation, assemble a case, and line up witnesses. For the district attorney, Dewing, the task was relatively straightforward. He had Abe's confession and testimony from the witnesses inside the bank, firefighters at Needham Heights, and the state police detectives. He had a single scientific expert, the state police ballistician, who would testify that the bullets that killed McLeod and Haddock were fired from the Thompson submachine gun found in Murt's suitcase. For Dewing it was open and shut. The trio might be crazy, he thought, but they were not insane.

Norma was a more complicated case. Police and prosecutors were uncertain what to make of Abe's accusations and her denials. So Dewing hedged his bets and obtained two indictments. As mentioned earlier, the first charged Norma with being an accessory after the fact of robbery. The second indictment initially remained sealed. It accused her of being an accessory to murder.

Abe's family also moved quickly, though too late to prevent Abe from incriminating himself. The extended Faber clan pooled their finances and hired defense attorney William Scharton. Scharton had attended Yale University, graduated from New York University Law School, and opened his Boston office in 1905. After three decades of practice in Boston, he retained the aristocratic accent of his Virginia youth. Trim, slim, and always impeccably attired, Scharton was convivial and good-humored and the possessor of a sardonic, sarcastic wit he eagerly exercised on opposing attorneys. He came to public attention in 1912 while representing "Dakota Dan," one of two men claiming to be Daniel Blake Russell, the long-lost heir to an old Boston fortune. That trial lasted 164 days and boasted 140 witnesses. Scharton, unfortunately, lost. Jurors decided that the genuine claimant was the other fellow, dubbed "Fresno Dan."[5] One reason the case ran on so long was Scharton's famously lengthy cross-examinations.

His courtroom record improved, and by 1934 "Billy" Scharton was a respected criminal defense attorney specializing in first-degree murder cases. "His mere presence at the trial make[s] the case a bit spectacular," said the *Herald*.

A lawyer of Scharton's caliber was not cheap. Abe's parents had little money, but his uncle operated the successful downtown tailor shop, and other family members ran a marine salvage yard in Chelsea and had purchased a grand mansion on a prominent street corner. The firm had recently gained a small measure of renown when it helped outfit a ship for famed polar explorer Admiral Richard E. Byrd.[6]

Given that his client had already confessed three times—once in Room 24 and twice on paper in Dedham—Scharton knew that a successful insanity defense was Abe's only chance of escaping a first-degree murder conviction and death sentence. To start down that long road Scharton needed an expert witness with impeccable credentials, and so he turned to the same man Murt had consulted in 1931, Tufts University professor Abraham Myerson. In their first conversation after Abe's arrest the well-known neurologist and psychiatrist appears to have told Scharton about his five sessions with Murt. Perhaps misunderstanding exactly who Scharton was representing, Myerson disclosed that he had diagnosed Murt as a "psychopathic personality."

Scharton wasted no time calling in a flock of reporters. To most Bostonians, still unfamiliar with the language of psychiatry, that sounded like a diagnosis of insanity—legal or not—a conclusion Scharton did not discourage.

"It seems to me that boys who would go out and shoot to kill in the manner described must be crazy. They are certainly psychopathic," he declared. As for Abe specifically, "His whole manner, his bushy hair, his kind eyes, his almost feminine appearance make it impossible for that boy in his right mind to have had the remotest connection" to the killings. With a nod toward public opinion, Scharton was careful to add, "There is not the slightest excuse for that brutal, cold-blooded ruthless murder . . . but how can you style that crime with the peace-loving, earnest student?"

What Scharton certainly knew, and didn't bother to discuss with the reporters, was that even a psychopath was not assumed "insane" by a court of law.

There is no medical diagnosis of "insanity." The legal definition used in the 1930s dated to the nineteenth-century trial of Daniel McNaughton, a

Glasgow woodworker convinced that he was being harassed by spies allied with British prime minister Sir Robert Peel. His judgment no doubt warped by his paranoia, McNaughton staked out the prime minister's residence, only to mistakenly shoot and kill Peel's private secretary. At trial McNaughton was acquitted "by reason of insanity" and placed in a mental institution for life. The outraged public had wanted him hung. Inquiries were held, and a legal principle was developed known as the "McNaughton rule." It said that a defendant could be found insane—that is, not criminally responsible—only if the person was unable to distinguish between right and wrong and could not comprehend that his or her act was a crime subject to punishment.

Most American states adopted the McNaughton rule, though Massachusetts added a provision that even a defendant "laboring under partial insanity" was not exempt from prison or the electric chair if it could be proved that the defendant understood "the nature and character" of his or her crime and its consequence.

A defendant could suffer from mania, depression, psychosis, schizophrenia, or what was then called dementia praecox and still be punished for machine-gunning police officers. One could be mentally ill and still understand that killing a person was wrong. Nevertheless, Murt, Abe, and Irv were going to contend their mental landscapes were so warped they could not be held legally responsible for planning and executing the Needham bank robbery and killings. It was a remarkable claim.

This is the legal standard the Millen-Faber jurors would be told to apply:

> A man is not to be excused from responsibility if he has capacity and
> reason sufficient to enable him to distinguish right and wrong as to the
> particular act he is then doing; a knowledge and consciousness that the act
> he is doing is wrong and criminal and will subject him to punishment.
>
> Whether you call it a mental disease, or you call it a mental defect, in
> either case the disease or defect must exist to such a degree that reason
> is dethroned and the will overpowered. When we have the capacity to
> reason the law requires us to reason correctly, and if we don't we must
> stand the consequences.[7]

A prosecutor disputing an insanity defense had the same burden as always—establishing beyond a reasonable doubt the defendant's criminal responsibility—or sanity.

"Their legal responsibility ... must be proved to you by the government beyond a reasonable doubt" was the standard jurors had to follow. "If it [the government] has not in any case sustained that burden of establishing legal responsibility ... then these men are entitled to an acquittal on the grounds of insanity."

Even with the burden on the government, Scharton in particular faced a high bar, given that his client was an MIT graduate, aeronautical engineer, and ROTC officer, achievements that seemed the very definition of a sound mind. Scharton prepared a slew of pretrial motions intended to buttress his defense, but legal proceedings had to await the Millens' return from New York City.

SHORTLY AFTER NOON on March 5, Murt was handcuffed to Irving, who was handcuffed to a police officer, and all three awkwardly boarded the *Yankee Clipper* in Grand Central Station for the trip to Boston and the Norfolk County Jail to await trial. Once inside and seated in a private compartment, their handcuffs were removed and replaced with leg irons. The sartorial standards of the era demanded suits and ties, and now that Murt and Irv were cleaned up they looked to any passerby like ordinary, respectable young men. Lunch was sandwiches and milk, as knives were not allowed within reach of the brothers. Photographers standing at the compartment door were allowed to take a shot of their meal, and at stops in Connecticut and Rhode Island police officers boarded to congratulate Stokes and Ferrari on their detective work.

Much effort went into preparing for their arrival at Readville station on the outskirts of Boston. Rumors of lynch mobs and assassins had circulated for days, and Chief Bliss declared it would be unsafe for the brothers to appear in Needham. Stokes asked reporters not to disclose the train they were on or when they would arrive, but keeping either a secret was impossible, as by midafternoon more than a hundred state and local police had gathered at the Readville depot. About half arrived in uniform toting shotguns and were stationed about the platform. The remainder, in plain clothes, were scattered about the growing crowd to foil any attempt to seize the prisoners. Before long police estimated there were two to three thousand waiting at the station. The *Boston Daily Record* excitedly, and erroneously, predicted the crowd would reach twenty-five thousand people.[8]

The *Clipper* arrived at 5:35 p.m. Flares illuminated the early evening shadows for the newsreel cameras, lending the scene a yellowish hue. Murt and Irv, leg manacles removed and again handcuffed together, descended from the rear car. They had heard the rumors of a lynching, and were shocked and frightened by the crowd pressing toward the motionless train. A blast of boos and catcalls rent the air. Reporters said that the brothers attempted to twist their lips into a smile but were "plainly dismayed as the wave of hostility struck their ears." But the show of force intimidated the crowd, and Stokes felt comfortable halting the procession so the photographers and newsreel operators could get a clean shot of the prisoners.

Even a merely noisy mob was exactly what defense attorney Scharton wanted. He had announced his intention to seek a change of venue and a delay in the trial date, and both efforts would be helped by a dramatic display of public anger followed by over-the-top press coverage.

When the photographers had finished, Murt, Irv, and their police escort filled a half dozen automobiles and, with some twenty-four press automobiles following, made the two-mile drive to Village Street in Dedham and the granite Norfolk County Jail. Another three hundred gawkers waited. The brothers were given showers and were escorted down into the pit, a row of cells on the lowest level of the jail where Abe was already confined. News that the Millen brothers were coming left him nervous and anxious. Abe not only had rolled over — on all the robberies and killings — but worst of all had involved Murt's wife. He felt a sudden terror at the prospect of confronting Murt face-to-face. Murt, he had heard, blamed him for their arrests. Abe tried to shrink into the darkness. He asked a guard to extinguish the sole lightbulb near his cell before the brothers passed through the corridor, and when he heard them approach he had the guard stand in front of the bars, further blocking the view into his cell.

The next day the *Boston Post* declared, "Millens Calm and Defiant as Crowds Roar Out Their Hate." Inside a headline read, "Millens Fret at Comforts in Jail. Get over Fear of Lynching Once Inside Building — Demand Supper and Complained of Conditions."

The *Herald* had them convicted. "Millens Booed in Readville; Bandits under Heavy Guard Hurried to Jail in Dedham. Troopers and Boston Police Hold Jeering Crowd in Check at Station."

The *American* ran a front-page headline declaring, "'Let Bride Die!'

Plea of Widow." In a masterpiece of understatement the article said, "Mrs. Clark is very bitter against the two Millen brothers and Abe Faber, the actual slayers of her husband—she is even more bitter towards Norma Millen. 'What does this girl do now? She hides behind a pretty face as she disclaims all knowledge of the gang's operation and it seems as though she will get out of the whole thing.'"

The Millen-Faber gang had made Clark's wife a widow and a single mother with a three-year-old daughter. "Personally I think that she and Irving and Murton Millen and Abe Faber should be electrocuted. I could execute them myself," she told the paper.

THE LOOMING TRIAL DATE demanded the speedy appointment of the two psychiatrists required to conduct the Brigg's law evaluation. The selection was up to the state Department of Mental Diseases, which decided who better for such a high-profile case than Briggs himself? He was joined by Earl Holt, the superintendent of Medfield State Hospital. It had nineteen hundred patients and was one of thirteen state asylums that housed, and sometimes treated, some twenty thousand people classified as mentally ill.[9] (State institutions to house the insane were commonplace in every state, and often every county, until the de-institutionalization movement of the 1960s argued that the mentally ill would be better treated in small, neighborhood settings. Many ended up on the streets.)

Briggs and Holt did not delay. The day after Murt and Irv arrived in Dedham the psychiatrists were at the jail for their first examination. With them was Myerson, who was now working on behalf of all three defendants and would simultaneously conduct his own evaluation. The doctors returned the next day, and again the following Monday, after which they announced a confidential report would be submitted to the court. The date was not specified, but there were now only two weeks until the March 26 trial.

THE PRESS COVERAGE did not diminish even with all four defendants behind bars. There were always new developments and scraps of gossip. Rose Knellar was suddenly released on bail after Dewing concluded that she had no role in the killings and was guilty of no more than innocently accepting a package of stolen money from her fiancé. In return for having the charge dropped she agreed to testify for the prosecution.

Then jail officials discovered that a gang of Peeping Toms inside the walls had somehow found a way to peer into the small women's lockup. Informants inside the jail provided a running account of Norma's daily activities to the *Post*, *American*, and *Record*, all of which displayed an insatiable appetite for any smidgen of news. Stories reported what Norma wore, what she ate, what housekeeping tasks were assigned her, and her purported reluctance to soil her hands with a washrag and bucket. An anonymous benefactor sent Norma restaurant meals prepared by a local chef. Other sympathizers sent her packages of cigarettes and bouquets of flowers. The other inmates were jealous—no one did that for them!—and public outrage soon forced a halt to the special treatment. There were newspaper reports, quoting women prisoners released after Norma's arrival, that she planned to take advantage of her celebrity status to launch a movie career. At one point even the more proper papers like the *Herald* and *Globe* declared in astonishment that Norma had asked for a pedicure to touch up her painted toenails. The truth of that was never sorted out, but all agreed she was receiving written marriage proposals from strangers who had Murt already convicted and executed.

Stories in the *American* and *Record* became particularly unflattering, and the reverend displayed flashes of a new bitterness. During his daily visits to the jail, he found Norma weeping and told reporters that only now did she understand the full dimension of her misfortune. Not that she had committed any crime, he insisted. She was jailed because the prosecutor and judge bowed to calls for vengeance ginned up by the very press he and Norma had courted. "My daughter is in jail because of the public clamor," he told one reporter.

To another, he said, "My daughter and I talked, frankly, openly. What happened? Our words were distorted, our attitude misrepresented. The public, I fear, gained a misconception of my child." His anguish was genuine. His daughter was behind bars and he could not get her out.

"She's only a child, a mere child. Innocent, easily led in her affections and now involved in this great catastrophe. I don't blame the public for their reactions. I cannot blame them at all. This . . . bail set for Norma is [based on] the expression of the public sentiment against crime."

Adding to the circus was Norma's natural mother, Margaret. Jealous of the attention her daughter was receiving and probably needing to supplement her modest income as a state hospital nurse, she began writing a

THE BRIGGS LAW 215

series of autobiographical columns for the *Boston Traveler* and the *Boston American*, variously detailing her own life history, Norma's upbringing, her courtship by Murt, and their brief marriage. Margaret also discussed her life with the reverend and blamed him for failing to cope with Norma's "ardent" nature. Not to be outdone, the tabloid *Boston Daily Record* began running a daily illustrated history of Norma's life. A four-panel drawing across an inside page detailed one or another episode. It was much like a comic strip. The first appeared on Wednesday, March 7, and purported to describe life inside the jail. A panel showed her "joyfully donning her own frilly silk nightgown" and alluringly slipping it off her right shoulder to reveal the top of her brassiere. The next panel portrayed her stretched out on her cell bunk reading "romantic stories." In the third she was mingling with two other equally attractive female prisoners. In the final panel Norma grasped the cell door bars and pleaded to see Murt. "I want my husband. He is here, under the same roof with me, I want to see him right now, please," the text declared.

The illustrated version of Norma's story appeared almost every day over the course of the month. The crime had kicked off a full-fledged newspaper war. Not content with its illustrated history, the *Daily Record* one-upped all the Boston papers with an autobiographical series it said was in Norma's own words. For its front page debut, the composing room made a custom mold and cast Norma's signature in lead for the logo. On March 11 "Norma Brighton Millen" in a schoolgirl's careful handwriting appeared on the front page, in white on a black background, and underneath it was "I, Norma Millen, will tell my story exclusively." The series ran daily through March 27 and provided cash urgently needed for her legal defense. Norma wrote nothing about the crimes, and very little about Murt. Instead each brief article was a sad but romantic paean to her father, her seemingly lost youth, her first dress, her high-heeled shoes, and high school parties. Norma disclosed that at age seven or eight she was bedridden for a year following an operation to repair a congenital problem with the muscles surrounding her knees, which had interfered with her ability to walk. For a time she wore braces. Norma gave no specific diagnosis of the problem, but it apparently proved no impediment in later years. All in all, it was invaluable free pretrial publicity for her day in court, scheduled to come immediately after Murt, Irv, and Abe's trial ended.

ON MARCH 10 the defendants appeared in court for the first time to enter a plea of guilty or not guilty. The opportunity for a glimpse of the four flooded the courtroom with reporters and the streets with spectators. Dozens of state police lined the route from the jail to the courthouse, providing the tightest court security in state history. And, on that very day, newspaper reports offered a plausible explanation for Murt's odd decision to leave Washington and return to the Hotel Lincoln in New York City, where he was caught: Murt wanted to kill his friend Messinger.

Police sources said Murt concluded that Messinger was the final loose end. If he were dead, no one could tell police where they were or where they planned to go. All links to Boston would be severed. Messinger was going "for a ride in typical gangster fashion," police said. Murt intended to find a deserted spot in New Jersey, shoot his pal, and dump his body.

Was this true? There was a bit of circumstantial evidence. Murt, Norma, and Irv had left most of their clothes and most of the weapons in the rented Washington, D.C., apartment or in a suitcase checked at the train station. Clearly, they intended to return. No other explanation for their sudden return to New York ever surfaced. Yet no one, not the prosecutors, the state police, or the Boston police, ever went on the record with the accusation. It may have been only police speculation too good not to print. Perhaps Irv, who even behind bars remained talkative, had let drop the plot in a conversation with a jail guard. Unless, of course, Norma somehow knew and had told Stokes.

That same day the *Post* carried a brief interview with Joe Millen, who reiterated his displeasure with Norma. "I bet I didn't speak to her more than a dozen times all the time she was in my house," he said. "She was always laughing and playing the radio and dancing, and she called me 'Pop.' That used to make me mad," he added. "I didn't like the way she acted. She was too foolish." But the person he was really furious with was Messinger. He had betrayed Joe's hospitality. "He didn't tell how when his father was out of a job and his mother was dying he lived at my home, slept with my boys, ate the food I provided and was glad to get it. So, to thank us for all that, he goes and turns the boys in."

In advance of their arrival thousands of spectators filled the narrow streets around the rear of the courthouse; there a short flight of stone steps led up to a double door, where the jail van would disgorge the defendants. Hundreds more lined up out front to get a seat in the courtroom. Faber looked shocked as he was escorted out of the van and up the stairs, only a few feet from the booing crowd. Reporters wrote that his eyes darted back and forth and his jaws worked. In the courtroom, watching the trio enter, was Helen Haddock, clad in black.

After Murt, Irv, and Abe's perfunctory appearance—each only said "not guilty"—deputy sheriffs slipped Norma in unseen. Any hope that spectators would glimpse a glamorous, dashing gangster moll, or even the pretty young woman photographed earlier by the Boston newspapers, vanished when Norma appeared. Standing in the courtroom was a slight young girl, purposely dressed in a simple, almost shabby dress. Her eyes were red-rimmed, and she looked thinner than even a week ago. She answered the court's questions with a soft, childlike voice. She gave a slight smile when her father stepped up to her. Norma's new attorney, George A. Douglas, pushed for lower bail. Douglas complained that prosecutors were purposely stirring up public feeling against Norma, a complaint that backfired when Judge Brown held up a copy of the *Daily Record* bearing Norma's signature.

"Did you, Mr. Douglas, have anything to do with the release of the story of her life?" an angry Brown asked. And who got the newspaper's money? he wondered aloud. Douglas began to reply but Brown interrupted him. "I will save you the embarrassment of answering that question, but I want to serve notice, warning now that the publication of that story, or any such story, will be cause for an order hauling everyone connected with it into this court for contempt." It was a tough threat, but one he could not enforce. The stories ran and no one was charged with contempt. Norma's bail was set at $25,000, but word reached Douglas that if that sum was raised, she would be rearrested on the sealed charge of accessory after the fact of murder.

Despite the continuing fascination with all things Norma, a genuinely important issue was outstanding—who would represent Murt and Irv at the trial? Joe wanted one of his business law firms to handle the case, while his eldest daughter, Frances, and probably Murt, pushed for a firm that specialized in criminal law. But any decision depended in large part on the matter of money. Joe was broke, or at least didn't want to sell whatever assets he had to defend his children. Days passed without a decision. Finally Judge Nelson P. Brown took the unprecedented step of convening a special hearing inside the jail to resolve the issue.

At 2:00 p.m. on March 16, he met with Murt and Irv in the company of prosecutor Dewing, Joe Millen, and Frances. The transcript of the session is lost, but during it Brown concluded that the family could not pay for a legal defense.

He then spoke privately with the brothers and afterward announced he had persuaded a former Middlesex County assistant district attorney, George Stanley Harvey, to take their case. Harvey was reluctant to the extreme. The time involved would be daunting, the fee was small, and Harvey knew what damage the case could do to his law firm's ability to keep and attract new clients. Plus, he had previously run for district attorney and still had political ambitions. Nevertheless, Harvey, fifty-three, accepted the appointment and moved aggressively to join Scharton's effort to delay the trial, citing his own abrupt appointment as one reason. He also wanted to let the "inflamed public opinion" exhaust itself before a jury was chosen. Harvey asked for the trial to be moved back to April, and Scharton asked for it to be held on Cape Cod in mid-June. They pushed to have separate trials—one for Abe, another for the two Millen brothers. Harvey also hoped to get each of the brothers a trial of his own. Psychological testimony would differ, not to mention the facts—Murt had killed both men, while Irv had popped off a few rounds but hit no one.

Brown was sympathetic to a delay. He had leaned on Harvey to take the case and could not, in good conscience, force his handpicked attorney to begin the trial unprepared. Brown moved the start date to April 16.

That gave Briggs and Holt more time to complete their report. On March 23, a week after the original trial date, they handed copies to the judge and both defense teams. It was supposedly confidential, but one newspaper after the other ran stories declaring that the state examiners had found all three men sane. Judge Brown complained that the newspapers were, technically, in contempt of court. If that was so, which was disputed, he nevertheless, and once again, had no practical remedy.

Now the limits of the Briggs law became evident as preparations for a full-fledged trial on the insanity issue continued apace. The law's effectiveness had always depended on the cooperation of all sides in a criminal case, particularly the defense, and until the Millen-Faber case courtroom disputes over the conclusions of a Briggs law evaluation had been "almost nonexistent."[10] When defense attorneys did contest a conclusion of sanity, they almost always limited themselves to quizzing the Briggs law psychiatrists rather than calling in outside experts. Prosecutors had also rarely challenged a Briggs evaluation.

But in Millen-Faber the stakes were too high. If Murt, Irv, and Abe accepted the psychiatrists' conclusion, that would be tantamount to walking themselves into the death chamber. Not they, their families, or their attorneys would surrender the one defense—insanity—that could save their lives. The Briggs law did not, could not, supersede their constitutional right to trial or, most important, their right "to have compulsory process for obtaining witnesses" on their behalf. In other words, they could call as many shrinks as they liked.

And had the report declared the men insane, what then? In non-capital cases prosecutors typically accepted a Briggs finding allowing the judge to commit the patient to a mental hospital "until recovered." But this was murder. Had Dewing agreed to a plea of insanity and to forgo a trial, Murt, Irv, and Abe would have been committed to an institution for life—unless at some future date the state Department of Mental Diseases found them to be "without danger to others" and the Governor's Council agreed to their release. There would have been a chance, however slight, of their eventual release.[11] Public outrage would have forced Dewing to proceed with a trial and seek the death penalty.

PRESIDING OVER THE CASE was a veteran judge with a reputation for scrupulous fairness. Brown was a Dartmouth College graduate who went on to earn a Harvard law degree and now, in late middle age, was a pipe-smoking jurist known for pacing back and forth behind his bench, pausing to make concise trial notes that he later compiled into thick volumes as bookbinding was one of his hobbies. Another was drawing, and when seated Brown filled the pages of his notebooks with sketches of criminals, police officers, and attorneys. While most of the state was preoccupied with the Millen-Faber arrests in February, Brown narrowly escaped assassination while trying a murder case in Springfield, Massachusetts. The defendant's brother threw a bomb into the courtroom. It failed to detonate, though the bomber did shoot the county sheriff in the right leg.

The bomber was likely mistaken if he thought that his brother was not getting a fair trial. In 1925, after sentencing a murderer to death, Brown learned that the supposedly sequestered jurors had in fact been allowed to roam about unsupervised. He threw out their guilty verdict and vacated the death sentence. Granted a second chance, the defendant pleaded guilty to second-degree murder and, amid public outcry, was sentenced to life rather than the chair.

During the jailhouse hearing for Murt and Irv, Brown displayed much the same dedication to fairness with his decision that the state would pay for the defense psychiatric witnesses.

Another step by Brown was not disclosed for weeks, but it served to guarantee just the "battle of experts" the Briggs law had attempted to prevent.

In the hectic days after Harvey's appointment, the lawyer told Brown that in the face of widespread public anger, he was unable to find defense psychiatric witnesses within the large community of Boston psychiatrists. Those he approached said they could not risk their reputation or practice if, after an examination of the defendants, they felt compelled to declare the brothers insane and so help them escape the death penalty. Harvey thought he would have more luck if the alienists were seen to be obeying a call from the judge rather than a defense attorney.

Brown agreed and went a step further; he wrote letters to five prominent out-of-state psychiatrists: "I sympathize thoroughly with any qualified doctor's disinclination to become connected with either side of a case that has received so much unpleasant, and, I do not hesitate to say, such illegal and outrageously unfair publicity," said one of the letters. "Of course, I am not in the least concerned with the obviously hostile public sentiment, and I do not feel that the medical profession should be, no matter what crime these defendants may be otherwise guilty of. The law, which I am sworn to uphold, guarantees them not only a fair trial but a fair and qualified determination of their mental responsibilities. You will be rendering a fine professional and patriotic service, which, I am sorry to say, appears difficult to command from your profession locally."[12]

All five agreed to appear, even though Brown could not promise them a fee. Perhaps they could be reimbursed for expenses.

His decision to bend over backward to ensure that the killers received a fair hearing set the stage for what was to be the longest murder trial in state history. Before it ended, seventeen psychiatrists testified. A battle of experts indeed.

Brown's solicitousness for the defense only went so far. He refused to give the three defendants separate trials, denied any further delay in the trial date, and refused to move the case to another county despite the defense argument that "bias and bitterness" against the trio were "without parallel in this Commonwealth."

Brown said the county sheriff would call an extra large jury pool, and he promised to take whatever time was needed to select twelve men who would at least enter the courtroom with an open mind. "We cannot hope to secure a jury of people so ignorant of affairs that they have not heard of this case," Brown said. "So far as the evidence they have read is concerned, if you can call it such, they may have formed an opinion, but such an opinion may not render them unfit."

THE DEMAND FOR SEATS was so great that tickets were printed and distributed in advance to dozens of reporters and doctors, psychiatrists, neurologists, medical students, and social workers. Many of the psychiatric witnesses had national reputations. The trial promised to be a fascinating display of forensic psychiatry. The mind of a brilliant MIT student would be dissected in public, and so would the psyches of two brothers—a proceeding almost certainly unprecedented.

Other seats were set aside for police officers, Murt, Irv, and Abe's families, and even Norma's father and stepmother, as in-laws of a defendant. Newspaper artists occupied a row of their own, as photographers were not allowed inside. If each bench was packed, the courtroom could hold nearly three hundred people. A hundred of the seats were set aside for ordinary spectators.

In the courthouse basement, workers assembled rows of whitewashed cubicles, and telephone and teletype lines were installed so the reporters—from all over the nation—could send copy back to their newsrooms. Reporters on the competing Boston papers organized themselves into teams, with one reporter taking notes in the courtroom while a second dictated to a rewrite man or tapped out a story on a teletype. Telephone booths were set up so reporters calling their editors could hear over the din. A microphone was installed at the witness stand to transmit testimony into the basement. The *Globe* declared it a first in any courtroom and explained it to the readers thus: "It is said to be neither radio nor telephone, although it uses a microphone, no larger than a penny box of matches, which picks up sounds 50 feet away as well as it does 10 feet away."

TRADITIONALLY, PRISONERS WALKED the three blocks from the county jail to the county courthouse, but that was impossible with the Millens, and not only because of the large crowds of spectators that gathered each morning.

A few days earlier Murt had asked one of the state troopers on the special jail security detail to pass a few magazines over to Abe in his separate cell. The trooper picked up the stack but delayed dropping them off. So when Murt called out to Abe, "Look at page five," it was the trooper who flipped the magazine open to find a long list of numbers written with what looked like burned match stubs. It was a code, though not a very good one.[13]

The troopers figured out that each number represented a letter, but in reverse, so "Z" was represented by 1, all the way up to the letter "A," which was represented by 26. After a moment's work with pencil and paper they read this: "Abl thinking can make a break. Get me a saw somehow. Need cash for L."

The identity of "L" was never discovered.

So handcuffed together, then handcuffed to a court officer, the three defendants climbed into the back of a small covered, motorized wagon for the brief drive to the rear of the courthouse and the short walk up the flight of granite stairs. Once inside they sat, still handcuffed, in a rectangular, steel mesh cage in the middle of the courtroom. It was about 3 feet by 6 feet and constructed of metal strips woven together, like a laundry basket with an open top, and colored bronze. They were all but invisible to spectators at the rear. The front of the cage was almost the shoulder height of a seated man. Behind the judge were four bookcases stuffed with law volumes and, above his head, a clock. The jury was to the judge's left, the press on both sides, the lawyers in front of the cage. Behind it were rows of spectator benches. Large windows on either side of the courtroom let in the spring light.

Jury selection took all week. During one break, a court officer produced a bag of chocolate bits that he passed around to his fellow officers and the three defendants. Scharton tried to get the judge to ask the jurors if they were prejudiced toward Jews, but Brown refused, saying the usual list of inquiries would suffice. He did lecture the jury pool of 170 people that "racial prejudice" could play no part in deliberations. The *Globe* described Murt as conferring with his attorney in "a grave man-to-man fashion. When his younger brother starts one of his chattering spells, Murt inclines his head and listens gravely and indulgently as to a parent. If Murt wishes to speak to Irving, he frequently lets out a low-voiced 'Brudge' and the family nickname brings him Irving's immediate attention."

By Friday twelve men had been chosen, with a median age of fifty—women were not allowed on Massachusetts juries until 1950. Their names and addresses were public information, and as was common practice in that era, they were also printed in each newspaper, along with single and group photographs. The jurors would be sequestered for the length of the trial—and not in a hotel. They would bunk together in the second-floor grand jury room. Meals would be eaten at the Dedham Community House, an old stone mansion turned into a recreational center. As for showers and baths, those would be available once a week at the jail.

THE FIRST TESTIMONY was scheduled for Monday, April 23. Out-of-town sketch artists and writers descended on Dedham hoping to capitalize on the "woman angle." They would be disappointed, as Norma remained locked inside the county jail. But rumors circulated, and were then confirmed, that jail officials would allow Murt and Norma to meet for the first time since their arrest. The reunion would take place on Sunday afternoon, inside the central square connecting the jail's four wings.

When the moment came, a carillon at St. Paul's Church—separated from the jail by a graveyard—played "Now That the Day Is Over" and "An Evening Song." It was nearly 60 degrees and sunny.

Norma walked in wearing a white jail uniform dress and blue jacket, and sat with Murt at a small table. She mostly cried. The meeting was not private. Jail officials and police required Ferrari and George Douglas, Norma's attorney, to be present. Harvey was there, too. Murt and Norma were told not to whisper. Newspaper stories, based on accounts provided by Douglas and off the record by Ferrari, described Norma as "weeping hysterically at the start of the reunion" and at one point, as the bells rang, slumping onto a tabletop in a faint. Words were few and sentences were monosyllabic. "She did not rush into her husband's arms and overwhelm him with protestations of love as was expected," said the *Herald*. Outside were "nearly 1,000 curious Sunday motorists."

Douglas provided this approximation of the hour-long meeting:

NORMA: I am worried to death. Look at the spot I am in.
Murt kissed her. They sat down.
MURTON: I hear you hurt your knee. Is it all right there?
NORMA: Yes. It's—it's all right. (*Silence.*)
MURT: Reading much these days, Dear?
NORMA: Yes.
MURT: Well, read good books. Never mind those cheap magazines.
(*Silence lasting nearly five minutes.*)
MURTON (*as he saw his wife weeping into a handkerchief*): Are you feeling
    all right? Anything the matter?
NORMA: I'm terribly worried. (*Sobs.*)
*Murt waited a few moments and asked how Norma was getting along in the
    women's section.*
NORMA: Not very well. It's all like a nightmare. I can't sleep.
MURTON: You have bad dreams?
NORMA: Worse than that. I can't sleep.

When they parted, Norma left the rotunda first. Murt embraced her. She did not reply when he asked to meet her the following Sunday. That was one account. In another Ferrari told the reporters that Norma turned to her husband and said, "See what a spot I'm in." And Murt did not reply.

The jurors were already sequestered, and efforts were made to entertain them over the weekend. They attended a Red Sox–Yankees game at Fenway Park, where they saw Babe Ruth hit his second homer of the season before striking out in the bottom of the ninth. The Sox still defeated the Yankees 9 to 6. Also that weekend, in northern Wisconsin, FBI agents tried for the fourth time in a month to capture John Dillinger. The wild, chaotic gunfight resulted in the accidental death of an innocent man, shot by an agent armed with a Tommy gun. The G-man was stunned by what he had done. "I can never shoot this gun again," he said. Dillinger got away.

Judge Brown spent the weekend with his family and apparently went trout fishing. Scharton had a home and farm in Virginia to which he returned that weekend to consult famed attorney Clarence Darrow, who had saved the Chicago thrill killers Leopold and Loeb from a death sentence. There had been much talk that Darrow would take on an official role in the defense. That never happened.

Harvey had his own agricultural escape in Lynnfield, where he owned 225 acres of apple trees, peach trees, and grapevines. Many of the trees were in bloom. Prosecutor Dewing was the only one who admitted spending time behind a desk, in his case mulling over his list of fifty witnesses. By that weekend Dewing had simplified his task, and hopefully shortened the trial, by choosing to prosecute only one charge—the murder of Forbes McLeod. The outcome would be the same in any case: life imprisonment in an insane asylum or death by electric chair.

Unsurprisingly, the Millen and Faber families preferred that their boys live, if only in a cell. They sought that outcome zealously, even once they realized it meant destroying their own lives in public, under oath, on the witness stand.

20

The Price of Life

WHEN PROSECUTOR EDMUND R. DEWING stepped into the courtroom on the morning of April 23, 1934, he had been district attorney for seven months. He had not been elected but rather elevated from the rank of second assistant prosecutor to solve a political problem for his friend the governor. In his six years as an assistant, Dewing had tried one murder case worthy of news coverage.

Standing in the packed courtroom, the air already warm and motionless, Dewing must have once again run through the task before him. He had to convict three defendants, grapple with two defense attorneys, and cope with the unknowns of an insanity defense. All the while, his every move would be recorded in the notebooks of Boston reporters and their counterparts from the national wire services. In his favor was Abe's confession. Their planning was not the work of crazy people. Or so Dewing thought the jury could be convinced. Still, there remained Scharton and Harvey and their decades of trial experience.

Judge Brown may have been surprised at Dewing's apparent command of the Millen-Faber intricacies. Brown's great enthusiasm outside the courtroom was the Dartmouth College alumni organization. He had even married the daughter of a former college president. So Brown certainly knew that Dewing, too, had a history at Dartmouth.

Dewing's family traced its roots in the New World to the 1630s, when an ancestor settled in the Massachusetts Bay Colony. The family prospered over the next three centuries. In the late seventeenth century one ancestor won a land grant along the Charles River. In the eighteenth century Dewing's great-grandfather was an officer in the Revolutionary army. In the nineteenth century his paternal grandfather was a state legislator, president of the Lynn & Boston Railroad Company, and a skilled businessman who left his heirs the considerable fortune of $100,000. His own father was a builder and attorney who met an early death at age thirty-three. Nevertheless, family resources allowed Edmund Dewing to attend Monson Academy in central Massachusetts, a respectable if second-tier private preparatory school whose headmaster was, coincidentally, one "H. F. Dewing."

If Edmund Dewing's academic pedigree was short of first rate, he nevertheless had sufficiently good grades and the correct background to be accepted at Dartmouth College. Dewing was in the Ivy League. It was an achievement he boasted of for the rest of his life, from his appointment as assistant district attorney in 1927 (when the *Globe* noted, "He attended Dartmouth College") to his death in 1954 (his obituary said, "He was a graduate of . . . Dartmouth College").[1]

But his claim to have "attended" Dartmouth was correct in only the narrowest sense, and to say he graduated was seven semesters short of the truth. If Dewing did not repeat the exaggeration and error over the years, he never corrected the reporters who did.

Judge Brown must have heard the story: how Dewing was admitted in 1911, began classes in September, was "admonished" by the faculty in November, and was "separated" from the college in February. In other words, Dewing was expelled. His college transcript shows he flunked three of six courses during that single semester, earning a 46 in English I, a 40 in French I, and a 32 in Mathematics I. His best grade was a 59 in History I.[2]

That academic debacle did not prevent him from enrolling at Boston University, where he remained until completing law school in 1917. Dewing then joined the law firm of Ropes, Gray, Boyden, and Perkins. It was a stroke of luck, because also at the firm was attorney Joseph B. Ely, who by September 1933 was not only governor, but a governor facing a predicament to which Dewing was the solution.

Ely's dilemma arose with the death that month of long-serving Norfolk County district attorney Winfield Wilbar. As governor, Ely was responsible for appointing an interim prosecutor to serve until the next election, in November 1934. Under ordinary circumstances Ely would have named a fellow Democrat, but filling the district attorney's job with a Democrat would alienate the county's Republican legislative delegation on Beacon Hill.[3]

What Ely needed was a friendly Republican lawyer, a man he knew and who knew him and whose loyalty he could count on. A man who would protect his political flank in the important suburbs.

No one fit that description better than a certain Norfolk County assistant prosecutor, a former associate of his own law firm, a friend, and, happily, a Republican. Dewing was appointed on October 3, 1933. Within days Dewing returned the governor's favor by naming a Democrat as his first assistant.[4]

Fortunately for ordinary citizens, Dewing had learned to apply himself since Dartmouth. Even if reporters described him as "cherubic" and a "college boy"—he favored raccoon coats in the winter—he was well organized and well prepared at trial. In major cases he worked alongside police investigators, and in court he disdained emotional declamations or slashing attacks on opposing attorneys. He was uncomfortable with the charge and countercharge in the courtroom, of which Scharton was a master. Dewing wanted to convict with the facts.

WHEN COURT CONVENED at 11:08 a.m., literally the first spoken words came from Harvey, who moved to halt the trial. Harvey had filed a motion to transfer the case to federal court, contending that even with the carefully selected jury there was no way his clients could get a fair trial with the "existing bitter, tense, biased, prejudiced, partial, enraged and inflamed feeling of hostility . . . unparalleled in the history of [Norfolk] county."

Judge Brown listened to the arguments, looked down from his bench, and said, "Denied." Then he broke for lunch.

Jurors spent the afternoon climbing in and out of a county bus as they examined key crime scenes: the bank, the firehouse, the Brinsley Street garage, Lily Pond Road, where the car was burned, and 39 Lawrence Avenue. The judge, jurors, and attorneys walked into Murt's second-floor bedroom and then onto the front porch roof. They examined the railing, which was almost 3 feet high with a thick wooden balustrade. No matter how thin and nearly sickly Abe appeared in court, he had to have had strong legs and well-conditioned arms to have shinnied up the column, grabbed the gutter, swung his legs onto the roof edge, and then, raising one hand while supporting himself with the other, pulled his body up over the railing. It was, jurors saw, a fairly remarkable bit of acrobatics.

Dewing gave his opening statement the next day, which was memorable only for what it did not mention: insanity. As long lines again waited for a vacant seat in the courtroom, Dewing said—Faber's confession or not—he would show that the Thompson submachine gun was stolen and toted into the bank by Murt on February 2. He would prove that Abe had fired a shotgun, that Irv let loose two rounds from his .22 caliber Woodsman's pistol, that Murt shot and killed Forbes McLeod moments before the gang took two hostages and, on the way of out town, killed Haddock. He would show that the trio were identified after the newspapers published a photograph of the Packard battery and that Murt's friend Messinger helped catch him in the New York City hotel.

The word "alienist" or "psychiatrist" or even "physician" never crossed his lips. Dewing was letting jurors know that to him this was no more, or less, than a rock-solid case of robbery and murder.

As if to emphasize that point, the first person Dewing called to the stand was not a victim or witness to the killings but an engineer, who described the bank's interior layout.

The reporters must have groaned, but after a few such preliminaries, three Needham Trust employees testified and in quick succession identified Murt as the man who carried the Thompson. His sister Mary shed tears as she scribbled notes from a seat in the first row of spectator benches.

During the next two days a succession of witnesses described the scene at Needham Heights and the deaths of the two officers at Glover Hospital. On Thursday Chief Bliss carried McLeod's bloody coat to the stand. Harold Vincent, the town employee who ran to McLeod's aid, testified, "He was rolling around from side to side and drawing his knees up as if in mortal agony. I asked him if he could sit up. Through his teeth he answered, 'No.' I tried to pick him up, but I couldn't. Another man came and we both took him. I called for help and some men from the filling station came. They got him on the truck and into the hospital."

As the testimony was emblazoned across the front pages day after day, the line for courtroom seats grew longer. Crowds numbering in the hundreds, or thousands according to some reports, milled about Dedham's center. One entrepreneur sold helium balloons on the courthouse steps, and another arrived with a "truckload of educated dogs from Hollywood" for the edification of bored curiosity seekers unable to squeeze inside for the big show.

The start of week three, Monday, April 30, promised testimony both titillating and significant, and did not disappoint on either count. The first witness was Rose Knellar, the MIT killer's girlfriend, and she would be followed by Saul Messinger, Murt Millen's former best friend.

For months Rose had been besieged by reporters and photographers. She posed wide-eyed with a thin smile for the latter but took the advice of her attorneys and studiously ignored the former. Small, slight, dark-haired, she offered a striking contrast to Norma with her merry smile. Reporters' favorite adjective for Rose was "elfin."

As she walked into the courtroom, spectators saw a "dainty figure" in a simple black dress with three large white buttons sewn onto the bodice. Affixed to the fabric was Abe's MIT fraternity pin. Abe's foot twitched, but he was not seen to raise his eyes as Rose walked by the prisoner's cage on her way to the witness box.[5] Under Dewing's friendly questioning, Rose testified to what everyone already knew—Abe had given her a package of cash; she didn't know the contents and pulled off the heavy paper wrapping only after learning, on February 14, Valentine's Day, that Murt was wanted for the Needham robbery. She feared the worst, which turned out to be true.

Then it was Scharton's turn.

Dewing's decision to call Rose gave Scharton the opportunity to launch Abe's insanity defense even before the prosecution finished presenting its case. Both defense attorneys knew they could not merely claim that on a cold February morning their clients were suddenly unable to comprehend that an action—murder—caused a reaction—punishment. Scharton and Harvey needed to lay out the history of each corrupted mind and do it in a stark and convincing manner so the jurors just might revisit their ordinary moral calculations, because by that measure the three men in the prisoners' cage were guilty of first-degree murder beyond any reasonable doubt.

Scharton's plan had three elements. First, he would show that even with his MIT education and ROTC commission Abe remained the awkward, nearly un-American boy he had been as a child, teenager, and college student: disinterested in women, sports, and speakeasies and easily manipulated by the psychologically tougher, street-smart Murt Millen.

Second, he would show that both Abe's parents descended from families rife with mental illness.

Third, Philip Faber would testify that he, Abe's father, was to blame for his son's predicament. The tailor with a speech impediment had told Scharton that as a young, unmarried man he had contracted syphilis. He had sought out the available treatment and believed himself cured. (Though that could be no sure thing until penicillin arrived during World War II.) Philip told Scharton he had been given "permission" to marry by his physician.

But what if that doctor was wrong? What if Philip Faber had not been cured? What if Philip had passed the disease first to his wife and from her to his son?

Scharton provided the answer to that. Syphilis, left untreated, can eventually destroy the ventricular system, which carries the brain's cerebrospinal fluid. The result can be insanity. Scharton would argue Abe Faber had been born with congenital syphilis, inherited from his father, and now, twenty-five years later, the young Faber was suffering from the tertiary stage of the disease, insanity, which would soon be followed by death.

Philip Faber, of course, would have to take the stand and testify in open court that he had infected his own son. This was no small step. Syphilis in the 1930s was a signifier of moral dissolution. If Philip testified, his sexual misdeed would become known and be a permanent stain on his reputation. And even with that disclosure Scharton would still have to prove that Abe's mind was not just infected but, indeed, damaged and that syphilitic insanity drove the mousy MIT student to Murt and then to murder.

FROM ROSE KNELLAR'S CROSS-EXAMINATION Scharton wanted to get firsthand evidence of Abe's unmanly and unhealthy disinterest in the opposite sex. He needed to prove his client aberrant, but not a "pervert." It was a fine line. Any hope of stirring empathy among the jurors would vanish if they concluded that Abe actually had sexual relations with other men. Scharton also had to treat the poised, delicate Rose like a lady.

Scharton worked in from the edges.[6]

"Do you know of any other associates he had, except you?" he asked, apparently realizing as he uttered the words that his question was so vague as to be meaningless. "I mean, by way of company," he added.

Rose gave him a puzzled look. Scharton uttered a single noun.

"Women."

"Women?"

"Yes."

"No."

Scharton had to be sure. "Girls?"

"No."

Rose now knew where Scharton was going. "I know there was nobody else except myself."

Scharton stepped closer. "Had he shown any—from your observation of him, and contact—shown any great liking for women as a whole?"

"No. He didn't take any interest in women." Rose paused, not liking the implications of that flat statement. "In other women," she added.

Perhaps she only meant that Abe wasn't carousing. Scharton needed Rose to underline it.

"I have to repeat the question, because it might be important later on. As toward you, will you kindly, in your own way, so as not to disturb you at all, state what was his conduct toward you in relation to affection." He was asking if they ever had sex.

The question echoed in a hushed courtroom. Rose had spent four, by some measure six, years of her life with Abe Faber and in return was embroiled in a murder trial. Now she was being asked to acknowledge, before three hundred people, a third of them journalists ready to transmit her answer to the world, that the man she had chosen cared nothing for the fact that she was a woman. And do so by discussing her sex life.

"He was not very affectionate."

"What you mean by that?"

"Well, he would not throw his arms around me, and all that sort of thing."

"He didn't throw his arms around you?" Scharton said. He needed more.

"Most of the affection came from me."

He noted they were engaged. "Didn't it strike you as out of the way, the fact that he had not shown as much affection [as] you might have expected, under the circumstances?"

"He was different from other boys."

Scharton nodded.

"You know as to when he first met Murt Millen?"

It was a transparent but necessary transition.

Two years earlier, Rose said. And, yes, she knew about his nighttime climbs into Murt's bedroom window.

"Did you notice anything between Murt Millen and Abraham Faber that led you to believe that Murt had domination over him?" Scharton asked.

"Yes, I think I did," said Rose. "He seemed very much attached to him, very much, and there are occasions when he would drop everything practically and go right ahead to Murt Millen."

It sounded rehearsed, but Rose nevertheless made Scharton's point in the elliptical manner of the time.

After a few more questions she left the stand. Abe again did not look up. Had he done so, he would have seen Rose Knellar for the last time.

THE DAY'S DRAMA CONTINUED when Messinger took the stand. Spectators swiveled their heads to see a handsome young man with a casual, confident smile. He was prematurely bald and always wore a hat when photographers were present. Messinger had been held as a material witness in the Dedham jail since early March, though Dewing never clarified whether that was necessary to keep him safe or to ensure that he appeared at the trial. To reach the witness stand Messinger, too, had to walk past the cage where Murt sat handcuffed to Faber's right wrist. Murt rose into a half crouch, dragging Abe's arm up with him, and spoke in a murderous whisper, "You dirty rat!"

Messinger spent some five hours on the stand over two days. He confirmed his role as the "mailman" and described Murt's visits to New York with a particular emphasis on their meeting on February 10 in the Lincoln Hotel.

"After we were sitting there awhile Murton said he had robbed a bank in Needham of $12,000, and while he was in there, he said, a police officer came across the street pulling the gun, and he shot through the window. When he was driving away, he said, another officer came out in the street to stop them. He took a shot at him. He said he was going 80 miles an hour." Boom. There it was in a paragraph, though the 80 mph claim was a Murt exaggeration, and the dollar amount was less than what the bank claimed.

Messinger testified that when he next saw Murt, a week later, his friend pulled a .32 caliber revolver from his pocket, flashed it before his face, and told Messinger he would not be taken alive. Messinger was a good witness, and his role as the "mailman" allowed Dewing to introduce the letter intercepted by Ferrari at the State House.

Harvey was first to cross-examine him.

As Rose had done for Scharton so Messinger would do for Harvey—begin the defense case. Harvey's plan was simple—he would prove that the minds of Murt and Irv were psychologically warped by mental illness, inherited through both parental bloodlines, and further deformed by a brutal upbringing at the hands of their father.

"Was Murt unusual in any way?" Harvey asked.

"He was quieter than most fellows I knew . . . Even when we went to school, as I remembered, he was always the quietest boy in the room." Other students thought it odd. "I just took it as an actual fact. That was the reason I liked him," Messinger said.

Under Harvey's detailed questioning, Messinger said Murt first announced there was "something wrong with him" six years earlier. He became increasingly "melancholy," and for the first time jurors learned of Murt's breakdown and suicide threat in Virginia. Messinger, however, had been well briefed by Dewing and limited most of his answers to little more than a yes or no.

"He made some complaints to you about his condition from time to time while you were there?" Harvey asked.

"Yes," said Messinger.

"His mental condition?"

"Yes."

"Did you try to help him?"

"Yes. I tried to talk him out of it."

"There were others that tried to talk him out of it beside you, weren't there, Mr. Messinger?"

"Yes. There were."

"In other words, everyone, as near as possible. Is that true?"

"Yes, sir."

Harvey found it slow, painful going. He wanted a narrative, but he wasn't going to get it.

"How concerned were you, please? Tell us the story."

"Well, I tried my very best to try to talk him out of committing suicide as intended."

"And what did you do besides talking to him? Anything?"

"Well, that's all."

The longest answer Messinger gave on the subject was this: "He told me he hadn't decided in which way he was going to. Just that he was going to ride out towards Norfolk, Virginia, and just kill himself there but he didn't say what way."

Harvey had Messinger again describe his role in Murt's arrest, particularly the first few seconds in the Lincoln Hotel lobby as he greeted Murt.

"You had some talk with Murton did you not?" Harvey asked.

"Well, we just said hello. We inquired as to each other's health."

"Shook hands with him?"

"I think I did. I don't remember."

"You concerned about his health?"

Messinger could see where this line of questioning was going. "Well, not particularly."

"Shake hands with Irving?" Harvey asked.

"Yes, I did."

"You had known these boys for a great many years?"

"Yes, sir."

Harvey then unsheathed his knife.

"You had been a guest at their home?"

"I was, that is right."

And plunged it in.

"There in the hotel lobby of the Lincoln Hotel in New York, with these two friends of yours, you handed them your right hand of fellowship—the hand of Judas—is that right?"

Dewing jumped up, furious. Harvey was out of order!

Brown began to say he agreed, but at that very moment Harvey declared he had completed his cross-examination and, literally seconds later, Scharton stood to take his turn. He was not one to let a theatrical moment go wasted.

"I understand you attended William and Mary College of Williamsburg, Virginia?" he asked. Or perhaps it was more of a statement.

"Yes, sir," said Messinger.

"You didn't stay there long enough to learn anything about chivalry?" Scharton wondered aloud in his southern drawl as Dewing shouted another objection.

The day's testimony was captivating, even enthralling, from any perspective other than the prisoners' cage. Courtroom seats were filled by prominent local dignitaries, including Judge Brown's wife and Fitchburg's mayor and police chief. But the spectator who made the front pages was a Harvard University student, Franklin Delano Roosevelt, Jr., the tall, slim, nineteen-year-old son of the president of the United States. A retired congressman escorted Roosevelt into the courthouse, and Judge Brown received him in chambers. Afterward a deputy sheriff led Roosevelt into the courtroom, where heads turned as he settled into a special seat placed near the defense table.

Handsome and graced with a bright smile, the young Roosevelt was already fodder for Boston news photographers, much to his displeasure. He was the Roosevelt son most like his father in charm and personality, but only a few weeks earlier he had lost his driver's license after striking a pedestrian during a snowstorm, while driving without a valid registration. In Needham that morning Roosevelt slipped into the courthouse unnoticed by the photographers stationed at the front and back steps, but realized he was going to have to run the gauntlet on the way out. Negotiations were opened with the photographers, to whom Roosevelt proposed a deal. If he cooperated for a picture or two—and they ignored the group of student friends who accompanied him from Cambridge—would they let it go at that?

All parties agreed, and the following morning flattering photographs of the popular president's son appeared in the Boston newspapers. As for the trial, "I found it interesting, from a sort of legal point of view." He was considering a career in law, he told one reporter. "I may, you see. That's why I came. To get an idea what it's all about."[7]

SO FAR THE TRIAL had proceeded at a rapid clip. Dewing had only three major witnesses remaining—Ferrari, Stokes, and the state police ballistics expert—though that short list was deceiving. Ferrari's testimony would allow Dewing to enter into evidence Abe's confession. It was his first, self-serving version, but nevertheless it was clear, coherent, and rational, recorded by a court stenographer and signed by the defendant. In it was little hint of a crazy man. Scharton could not allow it in without a fight. He warned Judge Brown that he would move to have the confession ruled inadmissible on the ground that his client was insane, and an insane man's confession could not be admitted as evidence against himself. So when Ferrari took the stand on Wednesday, May 2, with a copy of that very confession Scharton arose. "I take exception," he said, but got no further. Brown knew what was coming. He turned to the jurors and, without explanation, dismissed them from the courtroom.

Brown suspended the trial and convened a special hearing on Abe's sanity. But not his sanity at the time of the crime. That was a decision only the jury could make. Brown was going to rule only on whether Abe was sane when he made the confession. It would be a sort of trial within a trial.

The Briggs finding that Abe was sane was only advisory. It did not negate Abe's constitutional right to argue otherwise and contest the psychiatrists' opinion, and so it could not prevent just the sort of complex, convoluted, time-consuming, and expensive legal wrangle that was about to start.

It was the middle of week three.

Scharton's first witness was Abe's mother, Rose Faber, fifty-five, a short, "highly strung" woman with "coal black eyes and jet black hair." The *Boston Post* called her a "pathetic figure" as she stepped into the witness box. "She was attired in a plain striped woolen dress and black turban, the same she has worn every day in court since the start of the trial." But she spoke in a strong, clear voice.

Scharton led Rose through a recitation of the family's psychiatric history. Her sister Lena had committed suicide by jumping from a third-story window. Lena's daughter committed suicide by jumping off a train platform. Grandparents buried in Russia were insane, and she had a brother who succumbed to crying jags. She herself was beset with incurable "nervousness" that made her "afraid of the dark, and when I would be in the next room I would imagine there was somebody in back of us, and I didn't care to live."

As for Abe, Rose described a mother's nightmare. He swore at her. He threatened to strike her. He was completely dominated by Murton Millen, whom she considered a thug, and ignored her pleas to end the friendship. Sitting in the cage, Murt broke into laughter at her description of infant Abe being dipped into consecutive buckets of hot and cold water. During a recess Murt grinned and whispered into Faber's ear but failed to draw him out of his corner of the cage. Abe never met his mother's eyes or glanced her way.

As Abe grew, he lurched from problem to problem. At four he was foaming at the mouth and rolling on the floor with convulsions that occurred weekly and lasted fifteen to twenty minutes. He complained of headaches and stomach trouble; he was always tired, always sickly; and "he would be afraid to be alone in the room." He never wanted to play with other children and never cared for sports. He wanted to be left alone, he wasn't a good sleeper, and he had a poor appetite.

He went to Hebrew school, and he had a bar mitzvah, though he did not believe in God. She tried to get him to see a physician. "I think there is something wrong with your head, or you wouldn't act the way you do," his mother told him.

As for Rose Knellar, who until now had been visiting Abe's parents almost every night since his arrest, her son behaved toward her with a remarkable coldness. If she tried to kiss him, "he would push her away from him."

It was a sympathetic, even touching, performance.

Then Dewing began his cross-examination.

Wasn't her son a graduate of MIT? Hadn't he passed his courses each year with ease? Dewing asked with false politeness. And did he not continue onto a postgraduate course? Hadn't he successfully completed the Reserve Officers Training Course, and wasn't her son the holder of a second lieutenant's commission in the U.S. Army Reserve? And wasn't Abe sent for specialized air corps training at the famed Mitchell Field on Long Island?

"You were quite proud of that, weren't you?" Dewing queried.

"Well, no," said Abe's mother, glad for an assertion she could finally dispute. "I didn't want him to be there." Too far from home, she said.

Dewing parried. "It showed that he had been in pretty good physical condition, didn't it?"

Scharton jumped up and argued that Faber's mother was unqualified to assess her son's health. Brown overruled him. Abe's mother gave the only answer she could. No.

"He wasn't in good physical condition."

Now the prosecutor said he was puzzled. Wasn't her son required to pass the rigorous physical examinations necessary to become a second lieutenant in the U.S. Army Air Corps?

Rose Faber was stuck. What could she say? Yes? Her son's defense demanded that he be a cringe-worthy example of unmanliness.

"I don't know."

Rose Faber had convinced the courtroom spectators of her mother's love.

THE FIRST MEDICAL TESTIMONY was from Arthur E. Austin, seventy-three, a retired Tufts University medical professor who said Abe had incipient "hyperthyroidism," or an overactive thyroid gland. The doctor explained the condition typically produced nervousness, irritability, weight loss, and trembling fingers. In response to leading questions from Scharton, Austin invented new symptoms and said Abe had a different version of the disease, and this type gave its victim "a false courage . . . indifferent to the results of his acts." That brought another burst of laughter from Murt.

Austin's most important testimony came when Scharton asked if he knew the result of a test for syphilis on Abe ordered by Scharton and performed by another doctor on the defense team, Ray H. Shattuck. The test was not yet introduced into evidence, but Austin answered in the affirmative. "There is a syphilitic taint."

WHILE UNTREATED SYPHILIS can render a sufferer insane, insanity is not immediate, or inevitable. Many infected adults remain asymptomatic their entire lives. For those not so lucky, symptoms of "general paresis" or "softening of the brain" can still take ten, twenty, or thirty years to appear—if ever. Even though only a small percentage of syphilis sufferers reach that stage, asylums were filled with tens of thousands of patients presenting symptoms of "neurosyphilis," the final stages of the disease when the parasitic bacterium destroys brain function. New York state reported that five thousand patients in its asylums were suffering from general paresis, with its hallucinations, delusions, loss of long- and short-term memory, loss of motor function, personality changes, and muscle weakness. So desperate was the search for a cure that in 1927 a German scientist, Julius Wagner-Jauregg, won the Nobel Prize in Physiology or Medicine by showing that neurosyphilis could be treated by "malaria inoculation."[8] Which was what it sounds like. The patient was injected with the malaria parasite, and the resulting fever—and other malarial effects scientists could not isolate—attacked the syphilis bacteria and forced the disease into remission. The malaria in turn was treated with quinine. It was not a cure-all, but the treatment was at least temporarily effective for some patients.

Congenital syphilis results when a mother infected with the bacterium passes it to her child. In 30 to 40 percent of those cases, the child is stillborn. A majority of the infected infants born alive die at an early age, and those who survive often display distinct physical characteristics, including deformed, "notched" teeth. The odds of an infant born with congenital syphilis attending MIT and passing ROTC physicals were slim to none. But did the jury know that?

Next on Scharton's witness list was Evelyn G. Mitchell, a Cornell University graduate who, independent of any formal medical training in psychiatry and neurology, declared herself a specialist in those areas. Dewing spent an afternoon challenging Mitchell's credentials before Brown allowed her to testify.

Relying only on the information provided by Faber's family and with no independent research, Mitchell declared that mental illness ran through previous generations of Fabers. "We have a tainted family tree on both sides." Her complete psychological diagnosis, after three lengthy examinations of Abe conducted in the county jail, was that Abe suffered from schizophrenia, emotional infantile fixation, a reduced libido, an Oedipus complex, emotional instability, a morbid personality, and insomnia.

Mitchell added that tests of Abe's blood and spinal fluid—ordered by Scharton—were positive for syphilis. Not just syphilis, but congenital syphilis. How could she know that it was inherited? Mitchell testified that Abe's father displayed "a syphilitic taint"—without saying how she knew—and therefore the disease had to have been incubating in his son, where it developed into "cerebral vascular neurosyphilis."

Mitchell conceded she had not seen Abe's actual test results; she only knew what the other physician, Shattuck, had told her. Abe's supposed neurosyphilis was congenital because Abe "had no history of infection, no history of primary or secondary symptoms, and the family history was positive in that regard." She made no mention of Abe's sexual liaisons with a prostitute. There was no testimony that Philip Faber's blood or spinal fluid had ever been tested for the disease.

Mitchell remained on the stand for most of two days. Her testimony included the results of an effort to measure Abe's emotional attachment to Murt by using a "sphygmotonometer," essentially an early form of lie detector. As Abe answered questions about Murt, his heart rate and blood pressure, what the doctor called Abe's "emotional reactions," were recorded on a revolving disk.

Mitchell testified that when Abe heard Murt's name, both measurements jumped, indicating "a deep emotional reaction."

"I never liked to touch anyone else," Abe said, according to Mitchell.

"I felt just satisfied to be with Murt." If Abe's defense required proving he was irrationally in thrall to Murt, just that sort of testimony was called for.

"I would do anything Murt asked me . . . even now. I believe in him. I believe in him yet," Mitchell said Abe told her. He was angry at Murt for marrying Norma. "I didn't want anyone to break us up." But he had apparently forgiven his friend. "I was just miserable until we made up. I felt as if something of importance was missing. I was awfully happy when Murt made up. I was careful never to quarrel again. I couldn't refuse him anything. No. I'm not afraid of him, but it is terrible when I think I have not pleased him."

In the prisoners' cage Murt laughed and shook his head. Abe remained slumped against the steel side.

What it all meant, Mitchell said, was that Abe had suffered the "final break of the schizophrenic" during his relationship with Murt and so incorporated his friend's identity into "half of his personality."

"Murt had all the things he lacked, all the strength, physically, all the mental incentive, all the go-getterism, and the ability to sway others.

"He simply took hold of Murt and identified with him . . . That was the other half of his personality, and from that time forth he had no right or wrong of his own," she said. "He is not hard-boiled because he does not feel sorry. He has not got it in him to feel sorry. It simply isn't there. The schizo can't admit to himself that he is wrong, or to anybody else, or he loses his personality."

With a flourish, Mitchell declared, "His superiority complex is overcompensated for the early inferiority, and in his case he is simply a moral imbecile."

Mitchell also explained why Abe grew a mustache in college. It was an eastern European Jewish thing. "To a Jewish boy, a mustache is an evidence . . . of manly prowess. He wants to be a big man."

Irv began to chortle.

When it was Harvey's turn, he asked if Mitchell had seen "anything in the nature of physical hypo-sexual relations between Abe Faber and Murton Millen." Scharton and Judge Brown both corrected the attorney. "Homo," they said in unison. The doctor answered, "I saw nothing to indicate anything of that sort." It was, she said, "a psychological affair."

What Mitchell's testimony did not do was prove that if Abe had syphilis—the blood tests had not yet shown they could survive cross-examination—he emerged with it at birth. So on the third day of psychiatric testimony Scharton called Abe's father.

The elder Faber took the stand for eighteen minutes. "A tragic figure," the *Boston Post* declared, noting that his speech impediment turned his English into a "foreign language." He was fifty-nine years old and had immigrated to America forty years earlier. Philip Faber testified to his insane ancestors in Russia, his son's coldness toward him, and his own dislike of Murt.

Then Scharton stepped close to the wooden railing of the witness box. He was joined by Dewing. Judge Brown walked over and bent down as Scharton turned to the elder Faber. The lawyer's voice barely rose above a whisper.

"Now, something that we didn't tell your wife. Now, you were treated for syphilis?"

"Yes," Philip Faber said, "twenty-eight years ago before I was married."

Faber said he had sex with a prostitute in 1906 and soon thereafter developed a rash. A physician treated him for a year with a "salve."

"But two or three years later I felt a kind of funny feeling again." That was about the time Abe was born. This time Philip said he received injections of "606," an arsenic compound that was the first medicine to effectively treat the disease. Philip provided no specific dates, however, possessed no medical records, and could not recall the full name of the doctor who treated him. There was no testimony that he ever had a blood or spinal fluid test. And, if Scharton was going to claim Abe's mind was being destroyed by congenital syphilis, he would also have to prove that his mother carried the disease. But first someone would have to tell Mrs. Faber.

SCHARTON NOW INTRODUCED Abe's test results, via Ray H. Shattuck, a psychiatrist and former director of a state "School for the Feebleminded." Shattuck testified that he took two samples of Abe's spinal fluid. One was sent to a state lab that operated at Harvard Medical School, and the second to the city of Boston's Board of Health. The results were inconclusive. The city result came back positive for syphilis; the state result came back negative. In the best of circumstances syphilis was difficult to definitively diagnose. Blood or spinal fluid tests were untrustworthy and always repeated, and the disease was referred to as the "great pretender" because its symptoms resembled common bacterial and viral infections.

Working on the theory that the best defense is a good offense, Scharton declared that the state lab had deliberately falsified its result. It was a conspiracy, he roared.

"I am going to prove that there is absolutely interference from the medical association of Massachusetts preventing any psychiatrists from having any real honest blood test report. It is a matter of conspiracy between them to prevent the defendants from having a fair and impartial determination of the various tests." He did not then, or later, offer any proof.

But he did have Shattuck order a second series of tests. To eliminate any potential bias, these samples were submitted under false names—Boston tested "Alfred Fall" and the state "Charles Brown." The Boston lab tested Abe's spinal fluid in three different ways and reported that one test was negative and two positive. That was definitive proof Abe was infected, Scharton declared. Later testimony showed that the state's results were also mixed.

But still unproved was when Abe caught the disease, if indeed he had it. That was a matter of opinion, and Shattuck had one.

"Was it hereditary, or was it obtained by promiscuous sexual intercourse with impure women?" Scharton asked. In other words, was Abe the victim of his own sexual activities, or his father's?

"I believe it was hereditary or congenital," Shattuck said.

"Well, you know it was, or you believe, or what?" Scharton wanted to know. "Can you make it any stronger than belief?"

"I have every reason to believe," was the best answer Shattuck could muster.

Shattuck also performed a traditional psychiatric evaluation and, like Mitchell, concluded that Abe was schizophrenic, "insane and unable to distinguish between right and wrong in the legal and medical sense of the word." And he was under Murt's domination.

The syphilis testimony was all but ignored by the newspapers, despite its central role in Abe's defense. It was the only aspect of the trial that went uncovered. Millen-Faber stories occupied the front pages of each Boston daily almost every day. Photographers snapped shots of each witness entering or leaving the courthouse, and whole stories were devoted to trial trivia, like the daily *Boston Post* column telling readers which lawyers' wives were in court, what the witnesses were wearing, and how the jurors spent their free time. Court scenes sketched by professional artists often filled half an inside page. The *Post, Herald,* and *American* printed lengthy excerpts from the trial testimony. In the afternoon papers, last-minute news phoned in from Dedham was set in boldface type and plopped above the earlier copy. Millen-Faber was the biggest story in New England, and it was covered in newspapers from coast to coast.

Syphilis was another matter, however. The disease was considered not only an illness but a mark of moral dissolution. It was considered a disease of illicit sex, and so an infected victim was undoubtedly sinful. Syphilis was not a proper subject for any newspaper meant to be read in a proper home.[9]

So the *Boston Post* offered one sentence about Shattuck's tests, without saying what he tested.

The *Boston Herald* quoted Scharton's question to Shattuck—"The report of the Boston Dispensary laboratory in the Wasserman test was positive?"—and Shattuck's answer—"That was positive"—but the *Herald* relied on the reader to know what the Wasserman test tested. (Discovered in 1906, it was the first useful blood test for syphilis.)

The *Globe* said Faber was alleged to suffer from "an inherited blood disease which may cause general paresis." One story on an inside page used the phrase "vascular neurosyphilis" but made no mention of its being congenital.

The papers were also unable to report on another question, because only Judge Brown and the stenographer were within hearing when Scharton leaned close to Shattuck and asked if Abe said "whether or not he had any sexual experience with a woman."

"Yes, on three occasions with a prostitute, and done for purely a scientific purpose," Shattuck replied, "and he had no desire and he was disgusted with it and never has done it since."

"He didn't like it?" Scharton asked, just to be sure.

"No."

No longer whispering, the doctor added, "His whole general makeup in one way suggested a female leaning, which in turn suggested some endocrine imbalance."

Would that make him more subject to domination by a male? "Unquestionably," the doctor replied.

Now Scharton wrapped it all up. "He never indulged in any sports as a boy, American boy, would do?"

"That's right."

"He disliked girls as a whole because they were not interesting?"

"That's right."

"He didn't smoke?"

"No."

"Didn't chew?"

"That's right."

"Didn't drink liquor?"

"That's right."

"Which is wholly abnormal in a youth today, is it not?"

"It seems to be."

"Were all these, what you might call tendencies of a normal youth, so far as your examination disclosed, absent?"

"That is true."

DEWING'S CROSS-EXAMINATION appealed to what he hoped was the jury's common sense. You've heard all this mumbo-jumbo, he said in effect; now consider what happened that morning in Needham.

Shattuck did not hold up well. An example or two will suffice:

"Would you say, doctor, that if he went into that bank with a gun, and took money, that he didn't know that he was doing wrong?" Dewing asked.

"I would say that he thought his act was all right," said Shattuck.

"He didn't know taking money with the gun was wrong?" Dewing repeated.

"Yes, sir, I would say that," said Shattuck.

"Would you say that he had the gun with him for a walking stick, doctor?" Dewing wondered.

"I don't know that he had it with him," Shattuck said. He hadn't been there to see. Dewing snorted.

"Assuming that he had that, would you say that he had it with him for the purpose of aiding him in walking?" the prosecutor asked.

"No, he had it with him to shoot something with," Shattuck lamely conceded.

"Now," said Dewing, "what about the mask? Why did Abe wear it into the bank?"

"I don't know why he had it on."

"You don't know?" Perhaps Dewing feigned astonishment.

Shattuck insisted no. "I don't know why he had the mask on."

Dewing had to be pleased. It seemed to him very obvious.

It was 4:00 p.m. before the doctor left the witness box. It had been a long day, but Scharton was not done. He called his next witness.

"Abraham Faber! Would someone unshackle him, please?"

A dozen uniformed state troopers leaped to station themselves about the courtroom. They locked the main doors as another trooper unlocked Abe's handcuff, freeing him from Murt, and immediately handcuffed Abe's wrists together for the few steps to the witness box.

Scharton turned to the judge. "I offer Abraham Faber as an exhibit on the theory that the best possible illustration of an insane person should be presented on the witness stand for all these eminent alienists to draw their own conclusions." He motioned to the row of psychiatrists and physicians filling a front bench.

Abe was wearing a light gray spring suit newly tailored by his father. He was not there to testify as a witness or as a participant in a crime. He himself was the evidence.

As Abe took the oath, Judge Brown took up his sketchpad and began to draw Abe's profile for his collection.

Standing, Abe leaned slightly forward, bracing himself with his hands on the witness box railing. Different listeners described his voice in different ways. One called it "clear, polite . . . of some refinement." Another said, "There is a petulant droop to his mouth. His voice matches his mouth. It is soft, weak, petulant—the sick whimper of the ailing." Most found Abe to be emotionless as he gave quiet, brief, to-the-point answers to his attorney's questions. He kept his head down, and sometimes his testimony was nearly drowned out by the sobbing of his parents in the front row.

Scharton opened with a Q and A about Abe's internal life.

"Do you appreciate that your father was hardworking? Ever show him any affection?"

"No, sir. Never. I just didn't have any feeling that way." Or for his mother, though? "I thought more of her than I did of my father." He didn't enjoy high school but discovered an early interest in electrical engineering that he shared with a fellow student, Joseph Rothberg, the same Joseph Rothberg who was now his partner in the radio shop.

He didn't want his parents at his high school graduation and felt no gratitude for his father's effort to put him through MIT. "Well, he brought me into this world. It was his duty to see that I was provided for."

Scharton moved on to sex. "Did you have the urge—what we call the instinctive feeling for the opposite sex, when you were 18 years of age?"

"No, sir, never cared for women."

"Never liked them?"

"Never."

"You could not get a thrill out of the presence of the good-looking girl?"

"No, sir."

"You have lost a lot! That was true of you right along?"

"Yes, sir."

"And later on, to give some vent to some feeling for either the purpose or experiment or otherwise?"

As if in code, Scharton was asking if Abe ever had sex. Clearly, he and Abe had rehearsed.

"Yes, sir."

"What was your purpose then? Was that an urge, was that purely for experiment?"

"Just as a matter of information." If there was no tittering in the courtroom, the crowd was extraordinarily restrained.

"And you didn't like it?"

"No, sir. Disgusting."

"Was that true all of your life until the time of your arrest?"

"Yes, sir."

That led to the question of Rose Knellar.

"She was a good pal, a good companion, but there was nothing sexy in our relationship."

The next question was no doubt also on Rose Knellar's mind.

"What was your idea, then, in going with her?"

"Well, she was a pretty good friend, loyal, which is about all that counts."

Guided by Scharton's leading questions, Abe said he felt "no obligations to anyone" and had no regard for public opinion, which he found "always wrong in my mind."

Scharton asked if Abe believed any act he undertook was correct because it was he who did it.

"I was always of the opinion, well, I am my own boss," said Abe. "I always felt as if what I did was right, and I always had a good logic behind it."

In the last seconds of the day's testimony Scharton asked Abe if he comprehended the difference between right and wrong.

"I always felt that I was right, and just disregarded other people's opinions."

But didn't he rely on the opinions of other scientists at MIT? "Well, that was just a start. But as soon as I learned more about the subject I generally found faults and discovered other things in many cases."

At that Brown adjourned until Monday.

It was an awkward, stilted performance produced from a second-rate script.

Abe reappeared for another forty minutes after the weekend to detail his affection for Murt, who he described as a well-built, athletic, smart young go-getter.

Scharton moved on to the Needham job. "Did you then understand what you were planning was against the law?" Faber's response was labored and wooden.

"Well, that wasn't considered at all. At least I didn't consider it. I was more or less doing a favor. In any event, it's all it amounted to me."

"Did you realize the consequence of the act?"

"No. I didn't give it a single thought."

"Did you give it since?"

"Well, no. Not to amount to anything."

"You have no appreciation even of your present position?"

"Well, once in a great while, it dawns on me, but otherwise I'm not aware of it."

He was unperturbed by the state detectives' questions and found Ferrari "a very nice fellow."

"I didn't have any feelings of guilt. I didn't feel as if he was searching for me, and if he was, I wouldn't have felt guilty."

What about when Ferrari asked to open the "p.g." Scharton asked. Did you worry then?

"No," said Abe, "I didn't think of myself at all."

"Had no thought of your own protection?"

"No."

"Or self-preservation?"

"No, I thought of Murt, but I didn't think of myself."

At this Scharton was suddenly puzzled.

"But how did you think you were going to help out Murt [by giving] this letter to the police department?"

Abe had tripped himself up.

"I don't know."

The moment was embarrassing for Scharton. A fundamental rule of courtroom lawyering is never to ask a question to which you don't know the answer, particularly when your client is on the hook for murder. Scharton had rehearsed Abe, so it's likely Abe who went off script. Scharton tried to recover.

"How did you think you were going to protect him by delivering certain things to the policeman?" Scharton asked before realizing his error. If his client admitted to protecting Murt, it amounted to admitting that he knew Murt—and he himself—had done wrong. Scharton turned to the court stenographer and asked that the question be struck. He was flustered, and his next attempt was incoherent. "In what connection, if you had Murt in mind, how did you associate your ideas, so far as he was concerned?"

"Well, I thought the letter was against him. I didn't feel that there was anything against myself."

"But how were you going to protect him?"

"I don't know."

And did Abe believe he himself had committed a crime?

"It is comparative. That is, it is relative," Abe said. "In my mind I don't think there is such a thing—just one man's opinion based against another man's opinion . . . One person might think something he had done was right and the next person might think it was wrong. The one that thinks it is wrong might say it is a crime." Abe did not think it a crime. So it wasn't.

"I always feel, always have felt, that whatever I do was right; always been that way."

Scharton probed little further. Abe's performance had been an unfortunate effort to sell a version of himself that did not exist. He would have a second chance later, when the jury returned. But now the reporters were eager to hear the cross-examination.

The round-faced prosecutor disappointed them. "No questions," he said.

Instead he called a witness, Stokes. Dewing needed only a few minutes.

How many times had he spoken to Abe Faber before his arrest? Four times, Stokes said, the first on February 13 at his shop. They talked about the Lynch suppressor. On that occasion Stokes asked him nothing about the Needham bank robbery.

The second time was on February 15. "We asked him if he had a photograph of Murt Millen. He said that he did. We asked him for it. He said he didn't feel justified in giving it, and he didn't give it."

The third time, on February 23, Stokes asked if Abe had seen Murt the day of the bank robbery and killings. "He said he had no recollection of seeing him."

Stokes also recalled Abe's conversation with his attorney friend as they discussed turning over the "p.g." letter, and quoted Abe verbatim: "If that was in court, how would it look?"

Dewing had only one more question. "Moments before you left for New York City on Saturday, February 24, did you ask him if he had any knowledge of the Needham bank robbery?"

"Yes," said Stokes.

"What did he say?" asked Dewing.

"He had not," said Stokes.

Abe's answers, as recounted by Stokes, were the statements of a man lying to save his skin.

The hearing continued for another two days, but Scharton's argument for insanity gained no further traction. On the morning of May 9, Scharton called the Millen family doctor, William J. Brown. He was another Tufts medical school graduate, in private practice for twenty-five years. Rose and Philip Faber had been his patients for more than a decade. He first saw Rose Faber in 1922 for headaches and a "general nervous condition." The doctor prescribed a "nerve sedative," vitamins, and sunbathing in the summer.

Scharton approached the witness box railing, and once again Judge Brown walked over and bent low as the attorney spoke in a whisper.

"Did you in your treatment of her suspect that she might have syphilis?" Scharton asked. Brown replied that Philip Faber had told him of his bout with syphilis, and so he had kept a close watch on both patients.

"I consider him quite all right after marriage, and didn't feel that he infected Mrs. Faber," Brown said. As a precaution, he treated Rose Faber with iodine of potassium but apparently never explained why. The drug's modern uses are as an expectorant or, in the case of radiation exposure, as preventative treatment for the thyroid gland.

Dewing followed up. "You say you are satisfied with your examination that Mrs. Faber was not, the disease was not communicated to her?"

"I never found any evidence of it," said the doctor. No blood test was ever performed on Abe's mother. Fortunately for Scharton, the jury was absent.

Dewing followed with his own psychiatric witness, Miner H. A. Evans from Boston City Hospital, who argued that Abe's insanity was a pose, an effort by a bright, sane, inventive mind to create an "insane" personality that could pass legal scrutiny.

On May 9, Judge Brown finally ended the hearing, noting that he had given Scharton "the greatest latitude, both as to time and amount and the nature of evidence submitted." Brown said that his opinion on the confession's admissibility would have no bearing on whether Faber was legally responsible for the bank robbery and murder, or if he acted "through an uncontrollable impulse due to mental illness." That remained for the jury to decide. His only concern was whether Abe was mentally "competent" when he confessed.

The judge spoke for about five minutes. His remarks were so convoluted that even Scharton and Dewing were left momentarily puzzled about what he had decided—which was that Abe understood the questions Ferrari asked and "the significance of his answers," and so was sane, or sane enough.

Brown turned to the court officers: "The jury."

The twelve men returned to their seats; Ferrari returned to the stand and read aloud Abe's words.

Over the next two days Fleming and Stokes appeared to add more details, and the ballistics expert, Van Amburgh, testified that the bullets that killed Officer McLeod were fired by the stolen Thompson.

Then Dewing rested his case. Four weeks had passed. The defense case now began.

21

Poor Soil

THE PAPER CHART purporting to trace Murt's and Irv's insanity from a peasant hut near Kiev to their home on Lawrence Avenue was placed at the front of the courtroom within easy view of the jury. On it were pasted squares and circles cut from different-colored paper arranged in rows and columns. The squares represented male Millen ancestors, the circles female. Interspersed were a few diamonds indicating a lapse in research and so were labeled "sex unknown." Lines connected each shape, and the color of each shape had a specific meaning. Purple represented a mental disease other than insanity. Orange indicated a chronic illness, and green represented cancer. Blue stood for heart disease. Red was for family members insane at some time during their life. Some forty-eight individuals were represented. The chart's author, psychiatrist Max Bennett, said it illustrated the psychological history of Murt and Irv's family back to their great-grandparents.

Seventeen of the shapes were red.

Bennett had earlier studied two dozen murderers at the state prison in Charlestown and was convinced a patient's ancestors held the key to an accurate diagnosis, though in this instance most of his information came from the Millen family itself, hardly a disinterested source. Nevertheless, the chart was a cornerstone of Harvey's strategy to show that when Murt and Irv entered the world, they already had no chance of a "normal" psychological life.

Testifying to validate Bennett's work were Joe's older brother, Israel, and an in-law, Abraham Zimberg, who had married a Millen cousin. The two recounted a lengthy history of insanity, naming two aunts, two uncles, two nephews, a niece, and a maternal grandmother on Joe Millen's side. On Carolyn's side was a brother who was said to have committed suicide at age eight and two others regarded as "mental cases."

Some of the testimony was heartbreaking. Zimberg, sixty-six, thin and gray-haired, described how four decades earlier in the Ukraine he had married Joe's first cousin. She suffered a breakdown and was institutionalized for a year. After they immigrated to the United States, she murdered one of their children and spent the next twenty-nine years in an insane asylum, where she died in 1932. "My heart is bleeding to make statements of that kind to my own wife," he said from the witness stand on May 18, weeping at his memories. Dewing noted, however, that the poor woman's bloodline was too far removed from Murt and Irv's to qualify her as an ancestor under state law. Joe's brother Israel, a frail seventy-five, spent a good part of one afternoon pulling names and recollections out of his memory. He didn't have much good to say about his sibling. "My brother Joe was a little cranky, you know."

During infrequent visits to Joe's home, Israel would break up the inevitable, and purposeless, family quarrels. "They didn't know themselves what they were fighting about," he said. If he couldn't stop the shouting and blows, he tried to limit the damage.

"I told him not to hit the boys in the head," Israel said. "Hit them somewhere else."

"I told him he was crazy, too."[1]

Twenty-four neighbors, co-workers, former employees of Joe's business, and a few friends testified, each with his own tale of a screaming argument, a suicidal Murt, or a smiling and clueless Irv. The public's attention waxed and waned depending on the witness. On some days the Millen-Faber story was buried at the bottom of the newspapers' front pages, and seats were available to any casual passerby. By the third and fourth weeks of May, the crowds returned to watch Murt and Irv's siblings and parents dissect the brothers sitting chained and caged before them. Only the youngest, high school student Idalyn, did not testify.

Joe's low repute in his own home was already known, but now his wife and children denounced him with a specificity and ferocity that summoned biblical metaphors. "The Millen family offered up the father today as a sacrifice for his two sons," wrote one reporter. Much quoted was elder son Harry's flat declaration: "The whole trouble was brought about by my father's behavior." Or this from Frances: "There was never a morning that my father did not tear my heart apart with his treatment of all the family."

Among the children's first memories was the sound of their mother shrieking under her husband's blows. Once he floored Murt with a punch to the face for accidentally damaging a staircase. Another time Joe grabbed a golf club, stationed himself behind a door, and prepared to ambush his oldest son, Harry. Only quick intervention by Frances saved her brother. They described their attempts to protect Carolyn by periodically expelling their father from the home. They did not explain why none of them moved out. Dewing posed that question once on cross-examination after Mary, the mother of a four-year-old, testified about the household's terrors. The twenty-two-year-old explained that she was a homemaker, her husband was a music teacher, and they could not afford to live anywhere else.

The newspapers gave the testimony banner headlines. "Millen Hears Family Brand Him as a Brute," the *Globe* said, putting the story back at the top of the front page. "Sordid Story Unfolded."

Beneath the headline was a carefully posed photograph of Frances with her arm around her mother, both looking relaxed and composed. Our brothers or sons, our father or husband, may be killers and a madmen, but we are not, the picture declared. After Murt and Irv's arrest, Frances had left her secretarial job to work full time with Harvey and her lawyer friend, Ida Fendel, to plan the defense strategy and dragoon witnesses. From March into April, Frances, aided by Mary, traveled Boston, begging family to testify. She succeeded only with Israel and Abraham but nevertheless must have been remarkably persuasive given what she was asking: appear at the most infamous murder trial in recent Massachusetts history and testify that the blood flowing through their veins incubated mental illness. Millen relatives feared that they were tainted by the crime and the courthouse spectacle and considered changing their last name. One cousin lost his job as a typewriter sales- and repairman when his employer concluded, not irrationally, that he didn't need a Millen representing his business to customers.

Frances succeeded ably by recruiting the most important witness, Joe Millen himself, who not only took the stand but took the fall.

He spent much of a day on the witness stand, a painful, arduous experience for lawyers and judge alike, though not for any predictable reason. It turned out that Joe could not shut up. He never gave a simple yes or no when he could squeeze in a monologue.

Once, when asked about a childhood blow to Murt's head—from an accident, not Joe's purposeful beatings—he explained where they lived, why they had moved there, what kind of home they rented, why he fired the family chauffeur, and whom he hired as a subcontractor. He was describing a flight of stairs leading to a lake when Judge Brown begged, "Can't we come directly to the injury?" Joe's monologues were not helped by his immigrant's English.

But Joe did what his children wanted. Perhaps Frances had told him it was his only chance of saving whatever remained of a family. Perhaps putting him on the witness stand was also her revenge. His testimony was self-serving and self-pitying, but he did blame himself for teaching his children that anger could be quenched with a fist.

"He used to do a lot of things that didn't please me at all," Joe said of his son. "He was nervous, and he was, I don't know. I don't understand his playing. I thought that nerves is a thing that you may be nervous, and may not, so I used to abuse him once in a while, give him a severe licking."

Harvey interrupted. You hit him more than once?

"Yes, I did, to my sorrow. I did quite a number of times." Tears rolled down his cheeks. "I am taking it on the chin. I am willing to take it."

Did he hit Murt on the head?

"A great many times. He would try to dodge, but I would manage to strike him." If Murt performed a household chore poorly, "I give him a couple of blows."

Yes, Joe said, he was banished from the house for four months after striking his wife, and in 1931 he had dared file a criminal complaint against Carolyn and his children "for assault and for abuse." Why? "I wanted to get them out of the house." A judge threw the case out of court.

By Murt's teenage years Joe was becoming alarmed at what he had made, and in 1931 or 1932 Joe told his wife and oldest daughter that "it was dangerous to keep him in the house and that we either should send him away or send him to some sanatorium or some hospital." Joe left it unclear if he feared that Murt would do violence to others or himself.

As for Irving, Joe had refused to believe that his son had a mental handicap. He put him to work at the Grove Hall car yard, where Irv let a customer depart leaving a forty-dollar bill unpaid.

"I gave him a good beating. He will remember it for a long time . . . I slammed his head. I cannot describe just how I beat him."

Harvey reminded him. Was it with a stick?

"Yes," Joe said. "It wasn't a very heavy stick, but it was good enough to knock him out.

"I could see that he was a boy that didn't realize what he was doing and he wasn't anybody I could talk to."

Dewing's cross-examination was uneventful—he wasn't going to prove Joe a normal fellow—though he made sure to bring out Joe's bootlegging conviction. When it was Scharton's turn, the lawyer had this exchange with Joe.

"According to the chart you had a great many insane people in your family."

"Yes, sir."

"Are you insane yourself?"

Joe mulled over his answer. "A person who was insane will never admit it anyway."

Joe did admit declaring that Rose Knellar was "a confounded fool" for turning in Abe's bundle of cash.

"I said my idea it belong to Murt."

With that Joe left the stand.

One family member remained to testify. She had just been released from a month's stay at two different psychiatric institutions. One diagnosed her with "psychosis with psychopathic personality," though having two sons on trial for murder was bound to upset any mother. Carolyn slipped in through a side door as Joe testified, and then Harvey called upon her.

It was late in the afternoon of May 22. She was spared the indignity of standing in the witness box and instead sat in a chair placed on the floor. She was a dozen feet from her sons. The *Post* said she cast "furtive" glances at the boys, while the *Globe* said she smiled at them only once.

In a voice that ranged from "matter of fact" to "trembling" with "cold hatred" at her husband, Carolyn described the birth of her eleven children, the deaths of five, and her thirty-seven years of life with Joe.

"A few weeks after we were married he was actually insane. He struck me continually. He struck and abused the children as he came along, and me, even when I was carrying another child. He did everything he possibly could to abuse us all. He didn't care, even when I had my dead-born baby in my arms."

Twice she obtained a legal separation, but never a final divorce because Joe insisted on custody of the children. "I had seen what he would do to them when I was there. I can imagine what he would do when I was not there."

As she spoke, the reporters swiveled their eyes between Carolyn, Joe, and their notebooks. The "old coot" was taking notes and did not look up.

She detailed Murt's increasingly upsetting behavior. "I saw my boy going insane. If I had only put him away where he would be safer," she said and began to sob. According to the *Globe's* account, Murt turned to a deputy sheriff next to the cage and had him summon Ida Fendel, an assistant to Harvey and friend of Frances Millen. Murt said, "We can't stand this. Don't let her stay there any longer. Don't make her go through anymore of this." If that is correct, Harvey disregarded him.

In testimony that stretched over two days, Carolyn described witnessing her mother's last hours when Carolyn was four months pregnant with Murt, an experience she recalled as half hallucination, half nightmare. She believed that it had traumatized the child in her womb.

"One of her eyes went up, and one went down, and her mouth turned sideways, her whole face, and I sat there paralyzed. I cannot move from the spot." She awoke a few hours later to find her mother dead.

After that, "I woke up night after night. I seemed to see her. I seemed to see crazy people around me. They were pointing at me. They were closing in on me. I could not seem to get away from them. I screeched. I always imagined of them even in the daytime."

Dewing waved away his cross-examination. He stood and faced the witness. "Very sorry, Mrs. Millen, that you have to be here, and I haven't any questions to ask."

Later he obtained her mother's death certificate and compared it with the date on Murt's birth certificate and told jurors it was highly unlikely that Carolyn was even pregnant when her mother died.

Carolyn Millen was followed by seven different psychiatrists. First was Bennett, who returned to put in psychiatric terms the testimony from friends and family.

On cross-examination, however, Dewing managed to demolish much of the imposing chart. While seventeen individuals were labeled insane, Bennett had hospital records for only five. And only three of the seventeen were in the "direct ancestral line." Bennett admitted that Murt could not have inherited a mental illness from the more distant relatives tagged with a red shape. And Bennett's account of his interviews with Murt sounded suspiciously like he was being had, at least some of the time. Murt said the Fitchburg clerk was killed for "laughing uproariously at me, and I let him have it." That supposed reaction from a man suffering a gun-shot left arm was incredulous on its face and was reported by no witnesses, including Abe and the wounded pedestrian. Did Murt hallucinate it? Was Murt goofing on the shrink? Or explaining his rage with a metaphor? He also expressed, in particular, love for the Thompson. "If I don't have a machine gun, my life is lost. I couldn't part with a machine gun. That's music to me, that typewriter." It was language from a B-movie tough guy.

At other times Bennett quoted what seemed to be a genuine insight on Murt's part. "It was the excitement and not the money that took me. It just grew on me. If I had the peace of mind some people have, I wouldn't have gone into it."

But then what to make of this? Bennett testified that Murt felt certain he would somehow be set free, and once free he planned to get an armored car and "go around shooting people in general."

"It seems to me that he has no insight into the situation he is in. He feels that he can get away from the present situation by being found not guilty or by other means."

After Bennett declared that he found Murt insane, three other psychiatrists offered their own analysis of Murt or Irv or both. They were among the out-of-state psychiatrists recruited by Judge Brown, and all agreed, fundamentally, that the brothers were crazy, but sane. Richard J. Farnell, the Rhode Island commissioner of public welfare and the psychiatrist overseeing the state's criminally insane was handsome, charming, and unflustered. Farnell said that by 1933 Murt had "triumphed over his early failures. He was a big shot. He cast aside all rules of society, and entered upon a career of crime. All human feeling left him. He must be a master criminal . . . He even wondered why other criminals didn't shoot to get people out of the way."

Farnell, like the other psychiatrists, said Murt was the leader. "In the wake of this exhilaration, and this eccentric behavior, he swallowed up his brother Irving and Faber." He added that Murt "knew the abstract conditions of right or wrong, but he had formulated his own standards of belief."

Ordinary standards "were not applicable to him." Murt knew that he was committing a crime. He just didn't care.

Forrest C. Tyson, in charge of the Augustine State Hospital in Maine, and Charles H. Dolloff, superintendent of the state hospital in Concord, New Hampshire, had examined Irving. Tyson called him "legally responsible, but not morally responsible. I believe he did not have the restraining power to prevent his doing an act which he knew to be wrong." Dolloff said that Irving was a "borderline or twilight zone case with a drift toward insanity." He refused to say flatly whether Irving appreciated the difference between right and wrong. "To a certain degree, but not to the full extent."

A fourth doctor, Herbert M. Larrabee, a neurologist and psychiatrist from Lowell, described Irv as "subnormal" and "so subservient to the dominant mind of his brother that I believe he was irresponsible."

Larrabee testified on Friday, May 25, seven weeks into the trial.

By now lawyers and reporters who had once arrived in overcoats and felt hats, stepping over the remnants of winter snow, were pulling straw boaters out of the closet. Events elsewhere during the proceeding weeks bore an ill omen for Murt, Irv, and Abe. John Dillinger was ambushed in northern Wisconsin but shot his way out of the trap. The Department of Justice announced a $25,000 reward for the bandit. Another team of agents was closing in on "Pretty Boy" Floyd. And on the morning Carolyn Millen began her second day of testimony, six lawmen in northern Louisiana were waiting with weapons on the side of a tree-lined road. At 9:15 a.m. they fired 130 rounds at a stolen Ford V-8 and killed Bonnie Parker and Clyde Barrow. In Boston the deaths made the front page but, below the Millen-Faber trial coverage.

On May 29, a psychiatrist Harvey had identified only as a mysterious "Dr. Smith" took the stand for the defense. He turned out to be Smith Ely Jelliffe. The famous psychiatrist was sixty-eight and hard of hearing. Few American psychiatrists were more renowned. Jelliffe was a friend of Sigmund Freud and had translated his work from German to English. After his yellow-press fame following the Harry K. Thaw trial, Jelliffe went on to coauthor *Diseases of the Nervous System: A Text Book of Neurology and Psychiatry*. By 1933 the sixth edition had been published. Murt read an earlier edition when he diagnosed himself as a manic-depressive.

Befitting his celebrity, the courtroom was packed when he appeared.

Jelliffe did not disappoint. He proved expert at translating psychiatric jargon into ordinary English and provided a memorable description of the brothers' bloodline: "Nature handed them both a lemon," he declared. Dinneen from the *Globe* wrote that Jelliffe, short, squat, but dignified, had the knack of turning his testimony into a conversation with the jury, one-way though it was. He used a hearing aid, a black device in his ear with a wire that ran into his coat.

Jelliffe also proved capable of eliciting thoughtful responses from both Millen brothers. He quoted Irv's own description of his despair. "I was all mixed up. I was no good. I went to see Dr. Myerson about myself two or three years ago. I gave him five dollars. My father had given it to me. And I was broken down, all worn out, fighting this blinking, this twitching. I was exhausted much of the time. Life is no good. He saw me for about 10 or 15 minutes then. He patted me on the back and gave me good advice, and said that I had to put up with life. And that didn't take me very far."

Sometimes, said Irv, he had "the feeling of being smothered, as if I've been buried alive."

"How did you get into this mess?" Jelliffe asked.

"I guess I'm dumb. It seemed great at the time. I was all excited about it as the others planned it . . . Never again!"

"Well, who planned it?"

"I don't know who did the chief planning, but I was all for Murt."

"What about pistols?"

"I thought with a gun, now I could be a real man and not be ruled, as I was always at school when I was no good. It was a great feeling, getting on top when one was an underdog all his life."

In an era when psychiatric concepts were little used and the genetic code was undiscovered, Jelliffe explained to the jury why so much time was spent on the brothers' ancestry. It was the best, most natural explanation given at the trial.

Standing in the jury box, Jelliffe said that it was "very, very important to know what nature handed to you, what came down from inheritance in your blood. Our noses, ears, eyes, legs, bladders, kidneys, and so forth, including our nervous system, come to us from our ancestors, and if nature gave you a good endowment, as manifested in the family history, why, then you have a better chance to meet with the circumstances which one is called upon to meet in everyday life. With a bad endowment you have got to work harder to adjust to life. Living is not an easy job."

But much of his analysis was based on the tests and observations of other psychiatrists. He spent ninety minutes with Irv, reviewed the records compiled by Harvey, and concluded that the Millen family tree had an incidence of "manic-depressive psychosis" two and a half to three times the average. "The family tree is heavily burdened; if I may use a colloquialism, nature handed them both a lemon."

Jelliffe's grandfatherly image did not preclude brutal candor. Irving, he told the judge, the jury, and Irving himself, "has been a mental defective and a moral imbecile for a number of years." His condition was exacerbated by the violence at home. Jelliffe said that he was legally insane. "He didn't know the difference between right and wrong."

The psychiatrist spent two hours with Murt and was annoyed to find that he sometimes displayed "a very foolish little grin." Nevertheless, "I think I established a good contact with him, and he gave me answers freely and easily."

In his early years Murt "took refuge in books. He took refuge in fairy tales," said Jelliffe. "He liked to read mystery stories, he liked to read to get away from the whole business, try to forget it."

He noted that the family lived in a middle-class area of "fairly capable, well-to-do individuals, and that he didn't live in the slums.

"However, he didn't mix with anybody," Jelliffe said. "He stayed at home and read. He didn't mix. He didn't belong. He didn't enjoy meeting people."

Jelliffe had been introduced to Murt as a "Dr. John Smith" and Murt did not know that he was speaking to the famous man himself. Jelliffe was initially amused. He asked Murt what he thought of the volumes he'd read and was disappointed when Murt recalled no coherent details. "He didn't know the least earthly thing . . . it was just a scramble in his mind. He had no clear, concise ideas about anything that he had read in these books, and he had read them, he said, largely because he had felt badly, that he felt so badly that he was trying to find out what was the matter with him.

"Nobody can get very much from textbooks at that age. In other words, philosophy belongs to a study when somebody is grown up, and knows something about life, rather than when they are 14, 15, 16 years old."

Jelliffe concluded that Murt displayed "delusional thinking." Murt believed "that to everyone he met he became the most important person in the universe." He did worry that people were laughing at him as well as admiring him. Murt cycled in and out of psychotic and manic periods, Jelliffe said, and added he agreed with Bennett that Murt constructed a personal list of dos and don'ts at variance with rules of ordinary society. Murt, said Jelliffe, "has been suffering ever since he was born from his psychopathic inheritance.

"He showed the characteristic splitting between his feeling and his intellect which is spoken of as the schizophrenoid personality or the split personality.

"He had delusional ideas. Yes, he was paranoid," said Jelliffe, and "was suffering from a mental disease and did not know the difference between right and wrong, and was unable to control his acts."

He offered one backhanded compliment. "He had a high intelligence test . . . But that does not mean so very much."

Dewing was outraged, though not surprised.

Throughout the trial he remained amazed that eminent physicians could fail to see, simply put, the forest for the trees. Now Dewing was confronted by a top member of the psychiatric community who was denying the obvious. The question wasn't whether or not Murt had a mental illness; Dewing probably would not have denied that. But how could Jelliffe deny that Murt knew exactly what he was doing, and that it was against the law, when he planned and staged the bank robbery and shot two men?

He put that question to Jelliffe after the psychiatrist insisted that the long list of specific acts Dewing cited—like stealing a Thompson and using it to hold up a bank—was not proof of planning, aforethought, or sanity.

"Do you want to tell this jury that your attention has been called to no known act of his, or failure to act, on his part that indicates to you that on February 2, 1934, he knew the consequences of his act to himself and to others?"

Jelliffe parsed the legalese and offered a disingenuous response.

"Nobody can judge, draw a conclusion from a single act."

"Can you answer that question yes [or] no?" Dewing demanded.

Jelliffe's pleasant demeanor vanished. "Yes, no, and I don't know!"[2]

"And the principal thing is you don't want to. Isn't that so, doctor?"

"No. I say 'no,' and 'I don't know.' That is an adequate answer."

Jelliffe and Dewing simply had different views. To Dewing the acts proved conscious, knowing intent. To Jelliffe the acts themselves were insane.

BRIGGS HAD a different take.

With his van Dyke beard, Briggs seemed the very caricature of a Viennese psychiatrist. But Briggs's American roots were traceable back to 1700, the year his ancestor, John Cabot, settled in Salem, less than a decade after the infamous witchcraft trials. Cabot's descendants became "the Cabots" and with another Massachusetts colonial family, the Lowells, occupied the very peak of the Brahmin pecking order. In Boston it was said, "The Lowells speak only to Cabots and the Cabots speak only to God."

After graduating from Harvard College, he sailed around Cape Horn to Hawaii, where he worked as a physician. Once back in Massachusetts he became a preeminent psychiatrist and eventually an opponent of the death penalty. He had also published a famed exploration of the mind of a murderer, *The Manner of a Man That Kills*.

His reputation approached that of Jelliffe's, so his testimony helped fuel the controversy raging inside the psychiatric community. After the esteemed Jelliffe declared Murt and Irv legally insane, Briggs took the stand and declared the exact opposite. That they were mentally ill was of course true, but Briggs said they were also cognizant that they had committed a crime and were fully aware of the difference between right and wrong. With that declaration he jumped into just the sort of battle of the experts that his Briggs law was intended to forestall. Such a quarrel on the national stage embarrassed the profession. If prominent psychiatrists could examine the same patients, listen to the same trial testimony, and come to such different conclusions, was psychiatry grounded in science or a psychiatrist's opinion? As the Millen-Faber trial wound down, a close associate of Briggs's rose on May 28 at the annual convention of the American Psychiatric Association in New York City to offer a staunch defense of the "Briggs law," insisting that its utter failure to prevent a "battle" and the weeks of contradictory psychiatric testimony at the Millen-Faber trial was an anomaly.

The association's journal later opined that while the law "emerges as still sound and as still the most progressive legislation on legal psychiatric procedure it may well be questioned whether the multitude of psychiatrists who entered the lists for the defense have contributed either to their clients' welfare or to the good name of psychiatry."

Any who limited their reading to the newspaper headlines would have missed that Briggs's conclusion was based on his own extensive research. He interviewed each of the defendants multiple times and sought out family members and even employers for interviews. Few of the other expert witnesses did so, relying largely on interviews with the defendants, a family member or two, and the thick stack of written reports.

Briggs agreed that the Millen family had a "worse than average" history of insanity. "Poor soil," he called it. "The boys never had a chance as far as their home was concerned." Irving had a "mediocre intelligence" hampered by his childhood "in an entirely criminal atmosphere." He was "just on the border" of feeblemindedness.

Asked about Joe Millen, Briggs joked, "I don't want a suit against me. He has so many in court," and said that Joe told him "he had been in court 205 times."

Irving had the mental capacity to determine the difference between right and wrong, despite the domination of his brother, though Briggs conceded, "I think that he didn't very often . . . consider the consequences of his act." But not considering was different from being unable to consider. "The law, of course, does not excuse acts done by reason of low mentality," Judge Brown told the jury. Legally, Irv was sane, even if like his older brother he was a "constitutional psychopath."

Briggs said Murt "explicitly" believed he could "rule those around him." But it was not a symptom of mental illness "if he is able to"—as apparently he had been with Irv and Abe.

"I would say that if he had the idea of ruling everybody and mentally he was capable of doing it, that wasn't a grandiose idea."

Murt's suicidal tendencies were old history, and he found no evidence of depression or mania but did not rule out that Murt had once suffered from manic-depressive insanity, though Briggs had doubts. Once he called Murt a "schizoid." He found no "ideas of persecution."

And he saw some of the same fanciful thinking Jelliffe observed when Murt declared that somehow he would end up alive and out of jail. But Murt also knew that he had broken the law, Briggs said, and so he met the legal definition of sanity.

So did Faber, he added, except for the question of general paresis. Briggs said that if the testimony that Faber had congenital syphilis was correct, he would change his original conclusion and declare Faber insane.

ONE MAY 29 Philip Faber finally told his wife about his youthful indiscretion and the syphilis that he believed resulted. Her reaction is not recorded. When he took the witness stand that day, Philip Faber was not shamed before the public. He was led to the corner of the jury box, where he spoke to the twelve men in a low voice. "I didn't tell my wife up to today," he said. "Today I tell my wife I ought to be in this place. Ought to be in my boy's place in jail instead of him."[3]

But did Abe actually have syphilis? The blood tests conducted by Shattuck said yes, but Dewing argued they were not definitive and claimed Scharton refused to allow yet another round of tests. As the trial entered its final days, Scharton's defense increasingly relied on proving neurosyphilis. Shattuck testified that the pupils of Abe's eyes were unnaturally small and "stiff," or unreactive to light. That was a known, though not definitive, symptom of advanced neurosyphilis. The test could be done anywhere, so Abe was unshackled and escorted to the jury rail, where Shattuck shone a light in his eyes and the jurors peered over his shoulder to see the "pinpoint pupils." Perhaps.

Dewing leaped to his cross-examination. Hadn't Shattuck been forced to resign from the Belchertown school? Scharton objected and the judge excluded the question. But Dewing was only starting.

A month earlier—when the jury was absent—Shattuck had testified that Abe suffered from syphilis but mentioned nothing about neurosyphilis.

"You didn't tell his honor, did you, sir?" Dewing asked.

Shattuck said he would have "if I had been asked."

Dewing cut him off. "No, you didn't tell him that." It was a statement.

"I don't remember."

"But it is a key fact in this case?"

"Yes," said Shattuck.

The prosecutor had one more insinuation.

Earlier that day, May 31, Shattuck had made an unscheduled, early-morning visit to Abe. Dewing posed this question seemingly out of the blue:

"If two drops of a 2% solution of pilocarpine had been dropped into

Faber's eyes this morning, you would expect to find pinpoint pupils, wouldn't you, doctor?"

"Probably."

Pilocarpine is used to treat glaucoma and causes muscles in the eye to contract. Why Dewing chose to ask Shattuck about that particular drug was never revealed. There was no objection from Scharton.

On June 1, a Friday, another witness testified that a dose of morphine could also shrink the pupils, a fact that took on greater significance in the coming days.

But first Abe would testify once again, this time before the jury of twelve men, who had not seen their wives and families since the morning of April 20.

22

Jurors

FOUR PORTABLE BEDS lined the left wall, four were pushed against the right, and four more filled the empty space in the center of the grand jury room. The distance between each bed was measured in inches. Two windows overlooked the main street. One door led to the corridor, where a deputy sheriff was stationed all night, every night, and another opened into a restroom with two sinks and two toilets. After a brief hot spell at the end of May that turned the room sticky and made sleep all but impossible, the temperature dropped back into the 70s, and by the evening of June 1 it was a cool 60 degrees. For seven weeks the second-floor room had been home for the twelve male jurors in the Millen-Faber case. The oldest was fifty-six and the youngest was twenty-eight. All were married, and all but three had children. They were now painfully familiar with each other. They ate every meal together, and whenever they walked down the courthouse's granite steps they moved in a column, two men across and six down, with court officers at each end. Once a week the jurors marched across town to the jail to use its "shower bath."

They had an inside seat at one of the decade's most notorious criminal trials, but theirs was a myopic view; they knew what went on in the courtroom and no more. They read the newspapers in the morning and evening, but any mention of the Millen-Faber trial was scissored out by the deputy sheriffs. That ignorance was particularly unfortunate from the prosecutors' standpoint, as two weeks earlier—after Abe's confession was allowed into evidence—Irv jumped a guard during an exercise period in the corridor outside the cells. He came up from behind and hit the trooper in the jaw and grabbed for the officer's holstered revolver. Irv didn't hit hard enough, and the trooper fought him off until a second officer subdued Irv with "jujitsu," according to a state police report, or a night stick, as the county's guards said. Irv lost his exercise and visiting privileges and was put on a punishment diet.

The newspapers carried front-page stories about Irv's "escape attempt" and called it a dramatic demonstration of his consciousness of guilt. Harvey said that the outburst resulted from Irv's hearing Abe's confession read in open court. It "set off something in his brain. That was why he made the break.

"If he'd been able to get the gun he would have done some shooting, yes. But he didn't," said the defense attorney. One report said that Irv wanted to commit suicide.

On Friday, June 1, the trial became the longest murder trial in state history, surpassing the Saco and Vanzetti case.[1] The date was marked by Abe's second appearance in the witness box, this time with the jury present. Scharton's decision to have Abe testify on his own behalf was an enormous risk. His appearance before Judge Brown four weeks earlier had been rational, and for the most part logical, and certainly not that of a man with any obvious mental illness. Encountered on a street corner, that Abe Faber would appear perfectly normal. And this time Abe would not escape cross-examination. Scharton never publicly explained why he put Abe on the stand. Perhaps Abe had insisted. Perhaps Abe believed he was smarter than his attorney.

Word of Abe's impending testimony leaked out the day before, and the courtroom was packed. Scharton succeeded in throwing Dewing off stride at the start. When Abe took the stand after the lunch break, Scharton asked him only four questions: what his name was, his age, whether he was in jail, and on what charge. Then Scharton turned to Dewing. "You may inquire," he told the surprised prosecutor, who had expected Abe to spend the afternoon answering solicitous queries from his own attorney.

After a long pause he rose from his desk and walked toward the witness box.

"You intend to tell the truth?" he asked.

"I do," said Abe.

At first Dewing covered old ground, though making particular note of neighbor Thomas Larbey's description of Abe's three-wheeled car. "And today a three-wheel car is being experimented with by some of the largest automobile manufacturers, isn't it?" Dewing asked.

"It is," Abe replied.

Abe rested his hands on the witness box railing. His voice was soft. He kept his head down. He did not look at the jurors. Most of his responses were brief. He admitted to the crime in monosyllabic answers to the prosecutor's questions. Dewing took Abe through a recitation of his education at MIT, his ROTC training, the marksmanship commendation awarded him on July 19, 1930, for winning a competitive shooting match against twenty-six fellow ROTC officers. Dewing asked about Abe's undergraduate thesis, a requirement for graduation.

"What was it?"

"Spot welding dural . . ." Abe was about to say "duraluminum," the name of an early aluminum alloy used in aircraft construction. But that was a term the jurors would likely have never heard. So in midsentence he stopped and then continued, "welding aluminum by electricity."[2]

"And will you explain that, Faber, what that is?"

"Well, it is a process where an electrical current is sent through two strips of metal which are close together, and the heat developed welds the two strips of metal." It was a clear, simple explanation of a new technology. Abe wasn't sounding like a crazy man.

"And your postgraduate courses in 1932?" the prosecutor asked.

"Advanced aeronautical construction, advanced airplane stability, and advanced high-speed diesel work," Abe answered.

Then Dewing moved on to the bank robbery.

When did he first plan it? Dewing asked. Abe placed all the responsibility on his former partner, Murt.

"I was doing the listening. He told me what part I was supposed to take and what he wanted me to do," Abe said. "That is all there was to it."

Dewing asked about the scouting trip two days before the robbery, and Abe slipped up.

"You went out with Irving, didn't you?"

"Yes."

"Where did you go?"

"Just drove by the bank."

"Did you go down the different streets?"

"Yes, sir."

"So you would know the route to take?"

"No, sir, Irving was showing me the route."

"Irving was showing you the route that you were going to take—is that right?"

"They were going to take." Abe corrected the prosecutor.

"That you were going to take?" Dewing repeated his question.

"No, sir, I was not to do any driving," Abe said, splitting hairs and sounding like a bright college freshman losing an argument to his professor.

"You were to be in the car," Dewing dryly noted.

Abe admitted that the next evening he was at Murt's Boylston Street apartment to go over the plan one last time.

He tried, and failed, to recant his earlier statement implicating Norma.

"Who also [was] there?" Dewing asked.

"I don't remember," Abe replied. "Irving, I guess, Murt, and I."

Dewing was surprised because he knew the earlier answer, and his voice rose.

"Who else?"

Abe said he didn't recall.

Dewing assumed a look of incredulity. "What is that?!"

Abe kept his head down. "I don't know."

"Who else was there?" Dewing demanded again.

Abe again said he didn't recall.

"Is that your best memory?"

"Yes, sir."

Dewing was now beyond annoyed. His voice swept over the courtroom as he mangled his next question.

"Haven't you told before that there was somebody else there?"

"I might have."

"Well, who else did you say was there?"

"When?" The exchange was veering into farce.

"When you talked this—when Murton Miller talked this matter over with you at the apartment?"

"Well, nobody else."

Dewing's voice again boomed through the courtroom. Scharton interjected, "He can hear you. He is not as deaf as you are."

"Who else did you say was there?" Dewing said as he cranked up his vocal chords.

Abe folded.

"I said Norma was there."

That was the moment Scharton's defense strategy shattered. What better proof of consciousness of guilt was there than lying to protect an accomplice? Not that Abe cared for Norma's fate. The lie was for Murt's sake. Nevertheless, Scharton's gamble had failed. That he had even made it shocked the lawyers who had crowded into the courtroom. Not only had Scharton put Faber before the jury, but he turned him over to Dewing without a direct examination first to tell the jury what he wanted them to think.

Harvey was scornful. His clients had not taken the stand. "An insane man testify on his own behalf?" he said incredulously to Goldberg.

Abe returned to the box Monday morning and did his defense more damage.

"That day Joseph Millen . . . was on the stand," Dewing reminded him of the testimony two weeks earlier, "and made reference to you, calling you a 'sap.' You made some remark when you were in the van going back to the jail, didn't you?"

This Abe recalled.

"'I said, 'I will get even with them,' or something of the sort."

Dewing repeated his answer for emphasis to the jury. "'I will get even with them.' That is all." It seemed that Abe could indeed make a judgment.

The trial broke for the weekend and reconvened on Monday, June 5, to hear a prosecution witness, Earl Holt, the superintendent of the Medfield State Hospital and the second psychiatrist who had prepared the now irrelevant Briggs report.

Holt agreed that Murt's psychological history was rife with evidence of an "abnormal personality." Holt said that he found signs of depression, reclusiveness, suicidal tendencies, and "ideas of persecution and ideas of grandeur.

"Very clearly that man has certain peculiarities of personality which we may comprehend with such terms as a psychopathic personality," Holt said. Nevertheless, being a psychopath did not mean he was insane. Holt had been puzzled during his examination when Murt, again, insisted that he would somehow win the case and get out of jail alive. "It's not quite the same as some other person's appraisal of the same situation," he noted.

Holt called the younger brother "a sub-normal" but not quite "feeble-minded."

Harvey took that opening to push Holt further. It was a dense, confusing, back and forth between lawyer and witness.

Contending that Irv was dominated by the brother he looked up to as a hero, Harvey asked if Irv was "*unable* to differentiate as to his act and the quality of his act."

"Not necessarily *unable*," Holt replied.

"But," Harvey said, "It would be very likely he would be unable to judge, then and there, at that time?"

Holt resisted the insinuation. "I couldn't say that he would be unable." Oh, said Harvey.

"You wouldn't want to say, as a matter of fact, doctor, that the contrary would be true, would you?" Harvey was asking if Irv could indeed judge his act.

No, Holt would not say that. He would not say Irving was legally sane.

"You would not want to say that. So then it is a possibility" that he is not? Harvey asked.

"It is a possibility."

"And it might well be a probability? That is true?"

"It might be a possibility."

"And it might well be a probability?"

"Yes," said Holt, "it might be a probability."

Holt had just agreed that Irv "probably" followed the orders of his older brother without fully comprehending their import.

Holt had encountered the practical conundrum posed by an insanity defense—how to differentiate, in explanation and diagnosis, between "legal insanity" and what some lawyers called "medical insanity" or, as psychiatrists said, "mental illness." By any ordinary measure it was insane to rob a bank and machine-gun two police officers. It was not the act of a well-adjusted person. So the three defendants were shy of normal. But under the law, that did not make them insane. Most of the eminent doctors retained by the defense, and some called into the case by Judge Brown, refused to acknowledge that tension. By their lights anyone who committed such a crime, and particularly one Abe Faber, MIT graduate, was a troubled soul. How could one say that he was not mentally ill? And so, like Shattuck and Bennett, and even Jelliffe, they tied themselves up into knots to avoid acknowledging that any act by the defendants could indicate they knew robbing a bank and killing two cops was wrong.

The last witness, two days later on June 6, was Abe's mother, Rose Faber. The state police detectives had not stopped their investigation with the start of the trial and discovered that an insurance form Rose signed after her sister Lena's death declared it accidental, not suicide. Perhaps there was less insanity in the family than first claimed. Scharton called Rose Faber back to counter the prosecutor. She readily admitted to the signature and explained that it did not affect the payout, as the standard suicide clause in the eighteen-year-old policy had expired after one year.

Rose admitted that she had covered up her sister's act "to conceal from the family that disgrace, so that she may be buried among the others." Under Orthodox Jewish law a suicide could not be buried in a Jewish cemetery, she said.

Was that true?

Dewing was prepared for his cross-examination. "Mrs. Faber, are you familiar with what you call the Talmud Book?" and in butchered Hebrew cited a reference to the compendium of Jewish law dating back to before the fifth century A.D.

"Wait a minute!" Scharton shouted, and pointed to an associate counsel, Myer Goldberg. "I am informed by a learned scholar here that is not part of the Talmud. I don't know much about it myself," he added unnecessarily. Dewing chimed in, "I don't [claim] to be an authority on it."

Rose said she didn't know the Talmud either, but she knew the practice of her synagogue. "That is Orthodox custom."

She stepped down and both sides rested. The testimony was complete.

For the remainder of that day and all of the next, Harvey, Scharton, and Dewing gave closing arguments.

HARVEY HAD NOT WANTED to try both defendants at the same time, and now told the jury so. He firmly believed that fairness required two separate trials, with two independent defense attorneys. This was the first time in Massachusetts history that one lawyer was required to represent two defendants in a murder case, he said.

Harvey also invoked Murt and Irv's religion, the first time he cited it as a potential factor in the case. The defendants' Judaism had been a virtually unspoken subtext since their arrest. Boston in the 1930s and 1940s was considered rife with anti-Semitism.[3] Certainly the Jewish community thought so, and Jews were embarrassed and ashamed that the cop killers came from within their ranks. Yet Murt, Irv, and Abe's religion was rarely mentioned in any of the hundreds of newspaper stories, and then only on the few occasions when the subject arose during court testimony. But Harvey probably didn't want it said he failed to recognize Boston's ethnic tensions.

Harvey noted he had not raised their religion during his defense, and added, "I do it only for the purpose of reminding you that in this country of ours a man's nationality is of no importance, whether he be Jew or Gentile, whether he be English, any extraction that you please, a Negro or a South Sea Islander."

Then Harvey threw Murt under the bus.

"What brought these tragedies about? The answer to that it seems to me is this: there was one fountainhead who thought, and planned, and saw to . . . the execution of those plans, and that, gentlemen, was the diseased mind," and here Harvey must have pointed, "of Murton Millen. You don't really need any doctors to tell you that there must have been something wrong in there, or else these things would not have happened because they don't happen with normal people." Murt remained impassive as his lawyer spoke.

Harvey was arguing not just Murt's insanity, but that he bore primary responsibility for the robbery and murders.

Harvey briefly switched gears. He noted the crowds filling Dedham center day after day and acknowledged the public pressure for vengeance. "You're not responsible for public opinion, and neither am I. If I had been, then I would probably never have taken this case . . . a case of almost unheard-of publicity; nationwide interest is in the case that you have been called on to decide. Public opinion!" And what the public wanted was what Harvey called "Mister Savage." It wanted death.

"You are the ones to stand between that opinion, that high public feeling, and the course of justice and right." Having explained the problem, he then offered a solution, a way to feed the crowd and their own consciences.

Consider the "domination of Murt over Irving," Harvey told the jurors. "Irving, with his low-grade mentality, an imbecile, absolutely dominated by his hero, his older brother, a madman, incapable of being responsible for his acts, follow[ed] him blindly as a dog would follow.

"And remember, gentlemen, most dogs are harmless until someone who owns them calls them out and says 'sic 'em.' And then the dog becomes dangerous. That is a terrible thing to say, Mr. Foreman and gentlemen, but it is absolutely true and the truth must prevail.

"I have done my duty to these boys. I believe in their defense, and now I am passing it along to you. You must do yours, and it is for you to say whether or not it is to be life or death for Murt Millen, the crazy man, the madman, and likewise for Irving Millen, the younger brother, the tool of a mad man's mind."

Harvey was asking the jurors to kill one brother and spare the other.

The plea could not have been made without the permission of the Millen siblings and Murt himself.

A wave of emotion swept the courtroom, and Scharton jumped to take advantage of it. He compared the public clamor for Murt, Irv, and Abe's death to the sort of public clamor he knew as a boy in Virginia. In the heat of the moment he garbled his analogy.

"Down in my home I have seen many times a crowd with bloodhounds howling to have a poor Negro lynched, and then call in the whole white race because they lynched the wrong man; he was innocent. But in the heat of passion reason disappears, the clamor, the public desire for vengeance is to kill. I know it is hard, gentlemen. The community are aroused. They should be aroused. It was a cold, brutal murder. There is no apology for it. There can't be. But, gentlemen, you are not sitting here to satisfy public clamor or attitude."

Scharton urged a different distinction than the one Harvey sought, a distinction between Faber and the Millen brothers. "You could throw them all into one pot. But that would not be fair."

He pointed toward Murt and Abe. "Think of Faber, this man of high intelligence, with the chance to be a genius, sinking to such a point as to become subject to the will of that madman who sits there beside him, so subject to Murton Millen as to lose control of his own mind. This model youth turned into a fiendish murderer under the domination of Murton Millen, the mad killer who shoots men down."

Scharton denounced the prosecution's psychiatric witnesses, saving particular venom for Miner Evans, who served as Dewing's psychiatric adviser. "I was double-crossed by this commercial psychiatrist who would put this unfortunate youth in the electric chair for a fee."

His diatribe, which left him gasping for breath, brought smirks to the faces of the reporters and lawyers in the courtroom. Unbeknownst to the jury, only two days earlier Scharton's own expert psychiatric witness, Ray Shattuck, had been arrested on charges of writing illegal prescriptions for morphine, using his patients' names and filling them himself for his own use. Boston police said that Shattuck admitted using the drug for the past fifteen months. Scharton told reporters the arrest was a "frame-up." Inevitably, speculation was that Shattuck had used his illegal morphine to shrink Abe's pupils.

Not until the next day, Friday, June 8, did Dewing get his chance to speak. He was particularly blunt in dismissing Harvey and Scharton's strategy. "They place their defense on one man that because he is intelligent, he should be called insane, and the other two because they are stupid they should be insane. That is what the defense is offering to you.

"Probably I have stated it a little crudely," he added.

Fifty-eight defense witnesses had been called to testify to the insanity of the Millen brothers, he said. "Neighbors, friends, business associates of the senior Millen; they have brought his schoolteachers to try to impress you with [the] terrible background of these defendants.

"But you find, gentlemen, when you analyze it, there may have been trouble at home, but we find that they stayed at home; even after marriage they stayed, and they benefited from the father who, they tell you, that abused them, who clothed them and educated them and took care of them when they were sick and in the hospital."

Irving was no mindless pet, he said. Irving had a safety deposit box of his own. And he got one-third of the money. Who went to Needham with Abe to case the job but Irving?

Dewing minimized the family's testimony. "Who wouldn't expect the father to come forward in a time like this?" he said of Joe Millen.

For Carolyn, "that was an ordeal," Dewing conceded, but contended, "She did what your mother would do, and mine would do. They would go through hell for the boys. And I commend her for that, gentlemen." But "she exaggerated. She was placed on the witness stand to do her part, and she did it."

Dewing was critical of the defense psychiatrists and expressed particular loathing for Jelliffe, "the itinerant specialist, the one who assisted in that New York travesty, the Harry K. Thaw case, and they brought him over here and put him on the witness stand to do a job on the government."

"Use your common sense," he demanded of the jurors, and offered them a caricature of insanity to judge by. "Did you ever happen, gentlemen, to visit any of these hospitals where insane people are, and see how they act? If you see three people walking from here to Dedham Square together, you will be doing well. They go in different directions," Dewing said, and then offered Murt, Irv, and Abe for comparison. "They knew what they were doing when they went to Needham that morning.

"You have three men here in this case who are claimed to be insane, but they are working together, all of them, and they are carrying out this plan. Why were these men armed? Why did they wear masks? Why did they go there in a high-powered car? Why did they use those human shields when they made their fight? Why did they have a radio in the car?"

A conviction, Dewing said, would allow the jurors to return home—and face the public—with their heads held high.

That brought an objection from Harvey and, moments later, a rebuke from Brown when the judge began his charge.

"We are not at all concerned with public sentiment," he told the jurors. "You cannot try a case of this kind upon the streets, or across the bridge tables, of Norfolk County. This is the only court with authority to declare the truth in this issue. If you have heard the law, and the evidence, and come to the conclusion, and if that evidence is such as it must be, you have nothing but your conscience to answer." Then, no matter the verdict, "you can face your fellows, and say to them, that we do not try this in the streets, or in the kitchens, or over the bridge tables, but in the courtroom only."

As Brown spoke twenty-six state troopers equipped with tear gas and riot guns were assembling in an upstairs chamber. They were rushed to Dedham, in secret, after Daniel Needham's office learned that a lynch mob was ready to administer the death penalty if the jurors voted for insanity.

The vigilantes hoped to strike without interference from local law enforcement officers—who were their friends and neighbors—and so leaked word to what they hoped were sympathetic police. That move backfired, and state officers were dispatched not only to the courthouse but also to the jail.

Automatic weapons were cached nearby, and uniformed and plainclothes officers were scattered throughout the crowd that was already building on Dedham's streets. Soon nearly three thousand people were present, and nearly four hundred pushed their way into the courtroom to hear Brown's charge.

"What we really punish is the wicked mind," said Brown. "We do not find people with no mind at all guilty, because if criminal intent is necessary, then that proof cannot be established . . . Neither do we punish those who do not have the mind and the capacity to formulate criminal intentions."

For Murt, Abe, and Irv that was the nub of the matter. Could they actually claim to be such people?

The judge spoke for three hours and near the end ruefully remarked, "I have been just about three times as long as I thought. We are all anxious to complete this case; I shall be almost as glad as you when you can go to your homes." He explained, almost apologetically, that the painfully long days filled with psychiatric testimony—each witness was examined by three attorneys, Dewing, Scharton, and Harvey—was unavoidable. "We have taken all the time that anyone seemed to think was necessary in order that nothing should be overlooked that could be produced that would be material to this issue.

"Full freedom has been given to the parents to say whatever they please, regardless of the rules of evidence, that they might not go away and ever be able to say that the court would not allow them to say all they wanted to say."

He thanked the jurors' "cheerfulness under discomfit" and suggested the county commissioners spend some money "to make adequate and comfortable provision for juries required to be confined in capital cases."

Then he turned to the foreman and explained the possible verdicts. The defendants could be found guilty, or not guilty by reason of insanity. If guilty, jurors then had to decide whether they had committed first-degree or second-degree murder. First-degree meant the death penalty. At 5:52 p.m. the jurors filed out.

The judge motored to Brookline for dinner at a friend's home. The jurors had their own meal, a choice of steak or lobster with strawberry shortcake for dessert. Deliberations began at 6:30 p.m. Murt, Irv, and Abe ate at the county jail. As dinnertime came and went, the crowd continued to build. Autos were spotted from all the New England states and beyond. Commissioner of Public Safety Needham sent word to the vigilantes that any move to seize the prisoners would be met with "firm resistance" by state police.

No one knew how long the jury would remain out, and the judge had put no limit on how long they could deliberate that evening. Would the jurors want to continue past midnight into Saturday? Weren't they eager to get home?

In the long corridor outside the courtroom, those waiting included Timothy Coughlin, the Needham firefighter wounded by Murt's Thompson. He had survived, but for the rest of his life suffered from his wounds. The widow of Frank Haddock, Helen, was present. Joseph Millen sat on a bench near the entry to the district attorney's office. Carolyn was home in Roxbury. Frances Millen arrived from the jail after speaking with Murt, who reportedly told her, "I'll come out okay. It won't be the chair. Don't forget that."[4]

Around 8:30, the jurors asked to see sixteen exhibits, including Abe's psychiatric records. Rose Faber expressed the hope that they would find him insane, or perhaps guilty of second-degree murder.

Speculation ended a few hours later. Word that the jurors had reached a verdict began circulating shortly before 11:30 p.m. Judge Brown was summoned back to the courthouse. State troopers were ordered to return the men to the cage in the courtroom. Abe stumbled his way in. Murt's expression was described either as a "leer" or as a thin, inscrutable smile. Irv's mouth worked and his lips moved, but he did not speak. Everyone turned when a door opened and the twelve men walked single file to their seats. Each stared straight ahead, and none turned to look toward the center of the courtroom where the defendants sat. The *Herald* described Murt as showing a "cruel twisted smile, which is not a silly grin like his brother's."

In the first row of the spectators' section sat Joe, Idalyn, Frances, and Mary and her husband, Harry. It was just past midnight on the thirty-seventh day of the trial.

The clerk of courts asked the foreman if he had a verdict, and Michael Doherty replied, "We have." The clerk called upon Murt to stand and then turned back to Doherty. "Mr. Foreman, look upon the prisoner. Prisoner, look upon the foreman. What say you, Mr. Foreman? Is the defendant guilty or not guilty?"

"Guilty."

"Guilty of what?" asked the clerk.

"Murder in the first degree."

A shriek rang out from the front row. That came from Mary. Murt's other sisters began to sob.

Irv was next. "Guilty," said the foreman. "Murder in the first degree."

Abe was last, and many in the courtroom thought there might be a surprise. He was an MIT graduate; he had been a good boy. The clerk turned to Doherty for the third time. "Is the defendant Abraham Faber guilty or not guilty?"

"Guilty."

"Guilty of what?"

"Murder in the first degree."

The shrieks in the courtroom grew louder. They were from Abe's mother.

One report said that Abe sat down in shock and had to be pulled back up by Murt, who said, "Keep your head up. Don't let this throw you."

News of the verdict reached some in the crowd via the open windows of the basement press office, where the voice feed from the courtroom was connected to a loudspeaker that boomed out Doherty's pronouncements. Others saw a prearranged signal in an open courtroom window. From the crowd, which had been silent, arose a collective gasp as what amounted to execution was proclaimed. Then the cheering and demands for death began.

As the shouts echoed through the courtroom Scharton demanded a poll of the jurors, and each stood as the clerk asked, one by one, if guilt was his verdict. "It is," each said. Court recessed at 12:25 a.m.

Still handcuffed together, Murt, Irv, and Abe were hurried down the steps and out the back entrance, which opened onto the narrow street where the prison wagon waited with its motor running. The troopers formed a wedge to force a path through the throng. All were inside before the patrol wagon became the target of rocks and empty milk bottles. Voices yelled, "Kill the rats!"[5]

Back in their cells, Murt tore off his suit, tossed it to the guards, and went to sleep. Abe broke down in sobs. Irv tried to comfort him.

Once the prisoners were gone, the crowd quieted and parted to make way for the families of the convicted. Joe Millen walked out of the courthouse alone. His daughters were driven home by their older brother, Harry. Scharton chauffeured Philip and Rose Faber, but only after he persuaded the stunned parents it was time to leave. "Home," Rose Faber sobbed to a sympathetic *Globe* reporter she had come to know during the trial. "I don't know whether I want to go home. I don't know where I want to go. My life, all of it, gone, gone. Go home? That's where I don't want to go. It's too awful. I don't know what to do. I don't know where to go."

The next day Frank Haddock's widow, Helen, stepped onto her front porch and took down the American flag tacked to the wall. It had first draped her husband's casket and then was displayed at his home next to a blue and gold American Legion emblem. "I said they should stand there until his murderers were convicted. But now I shall lay them away. I don't mean to be bitter. I don't mean to stamp tragic memories on the lives of my girls. I can go on now, and face the task he left me of bringing up our children."[6]

23

Lingerie

TO THE RELIEF of the newspaper reporters, whose plum assignment was now an interminable slog, Dewing announced there would be no psychological testimony at Norma's trial and only a dozen or so witnesses. It would be over in a week, or perhaps two.

For Norma even that was too long. The high spirits on display after the New York City arrests had been dissipated by life in a jail cell. She never accepted that she had to stay behind bars while Rose Knellar was released on bail. Norma's lawyer, George Douglas, explained that bail was impossible, as she faced an accessory to murder charge. Did Norma recall that Rose had only been charged with receiving stolen property? At one point Douglas suggested that she turn state's evidence and testify against Abe, but Norma refused, as that would inevitably help the case against her husband. She would not become a "squealer," even though the courtroom strategy, shaped by Douglas and probably with her father's assistance, would depict her as fearful and intimidated by her husband. It was no matter that once Murt was nice and once she was in love.

The press fixation on Norma had never ceased. During Murt's trial every mention of her name in a newspaper report was juxtaposed with a photograph of Norma's formerly well-dressed, carefully made-up self. Even in jail the photographers stalked her. A telephone pole adjacent to a prison wall and offering a clear view of the exercise yard became a favorite of the Boston press, and when police chased photographers from that perch they rented an adjacent second-floor room. From there they delivered blurry photographs of Norma in a prison dress playing ball with other female inmates. The exercise yard was disquieting for another reason, too. In one corner a low window opened onto the "pit" where Murt, Irv, and Abe were held. Sometimes a trooper on guard duty called her over and offered to relay a message to or from her husband. Norma always feared it might be a plan to compromise her. After all, Murt had gotten her into this mess.

She learned of his conviction first from a jail guard but seemed not to fully comprehend its ramifications until her father visited the next day. "Does that mean the electric chair, Dad?" Yes, he told her, according to the *Boston Post*. Murt told his sister Frances that the Millens should do what they could to assist his wife, the newspaper said.

SUMMER WEATHER greeted the start of Norma's trial on Wednesday, June 20. The courtroom was already hot and humid when she arrived to see hundreds of spectators lining the sidewalks. The gawkers were mostly women, housewives towing children, or students home for the summer. In the press room, reporters' friends, mostly girlfriends because the reporters were mostly men, crammed in to follow the testimony via loudspeaker.

From his bench Judge Brown looked out on rows of women in summer dresses, slowly fanning themselves, and felt obliged to declare that the trial was not a public entertainment. Anyone cheering or applauding or booing faced ejection. Dewing opened with a quick summary of the crime, but the crowd had heard or read it all before. They wanted Norma.

She sat at a broad wooden table next to her defense attorney. The prospect of testifying terrified her, and even more so did the prospect of Dewing's cross-examination. The story she was prepared to tell was at odds with the story she knew to be true. Norma was going to tell the story she wanted to be true.

The first day, as she was led through the crowd, up the granite steps, and into the courtroom, her breath came in quick, short gasps.

"All around were newspaper men and artists, staring at me, studying me, drawing pictures of me. Their eyes never left me. They bored into me. Oh, God, why do they make you suffer the torture of being exposed like that during your trial? You cannot hide, you cannot escape."[1]

On the second day Dewing revealed hitherto unseen incriminating evidence. He introduced Norma's mid-February letter to Idalyn asking Murt's youngest sister to clean up the Audubon Road apartment. Norma warned that she and Murt were using an assumed name, "Clifton," and gave her a cover story. "You're our niece if they question you," she wrote. "Watch your step! We all send love. TEAR THE LETTER UP CAREFULLY."

He also disclosed a letter Norma wrote to Messinger, dated January 31, just a few days before the Needham robbery. In it she thanked him for advice on dealing with Murt and their stormy marriage. He warned that her husband had a temper and she should not cross him. She drew a funny caricature of Murt with a tubelike, elongated nose and ended the letter with three postscripts:

"P.S. Can you see Murt as a cunnin' businessman in back of a desk? I can't.

"P.S. Wedding bells may ring soon for Rose and Abel. He'll kill me (poetic license) when he reads this.

"P.S. Please tear up Murt's letter, as it carries evidence."

Another damning paper Dewing waved before the jury was a note in Norma's handwriting that described the division of Murt's "$4,200" share of the robbery cash. In it Norma gives herself "2 G's."

Finally, Stokes testified that on the night of Norma's arrest in New York City (after she had asked Stokes to delay his questions until her father arrived, but before the reverend was present) she admitted she knew that Murt, Irv, and Abe were the robbers and murderers at Fitchburg, Lynn, and Needham.

The crowd absorbed the revelations with gasps of shock, but once Norma took the stand she regained lost sympathy. At every opportunity Douglas referred to her as "the quiet lady-like little girl," which became such a frequent refrain that Judge Brown ordered him to cease. "You might vary your characterization, Mr. Douglas. 'Defendant' is a dignified and proper term."[2] Nevertheless, Douglas's description fit what the spectators saw. Norma looked exceedingly young and not at all like the glamorous young woman who smiled so merrily stepping off the train from New York.

Douglas's plan was to convince the jury, again twelve men, that his client was psychologically a "little girl" taken advantage of by a brute. "The mentality of the defendant . . . is much younger than that of the ordinary girl of 18 or 19," he said. "From the time she began to grow up she has been nothing but a little girl." Rather than a young woman who enjoyed reading the classics and once took the lead in a high school play, as she was described a lifetime ago in February, Norma was a childish creature who preferred nothing more than playing with "doggies and dolls." Douglas ordered her to wear the same dress each day, blue with white polka dots and a large white collar. When her mother brought a new summer dress to the jail, Douglas ordered it sent away.

Norma took the stand in her own defense on Monday, June 25, amid a scene of chaos. More than two thousand spectators, virtually all women, fought for an open seat. "Hundreds of thrill-seeking women . . . clawed and pushed and shoved," the *Boston Post* wrote. One woman was nearly trampled until rescued by troopers, who locked arms against the surge. Other women tried to climb through an open window in the clerk's office. "Inside, the courthouse was as delirious as a midway."

None of this improved Norma's spirit. Norma answered Douglas's questions in a mumble and mostly stared at her feet. One reporter wrote that she resembled a "naughty child brought before a schoolmistress." She denied knowing anything relevant about almost everything that mattered. Nothing about Fitchburg, or Lynn, or Needham. Or the guns. Or where the cash came from. She never suspected, ever, that her husband was a criminal until February 11, when he told her that "gangsters" were threatening the family because of a car battery Irv had repaired. No matter that she was living in the same small apartment with Murt, that Dewing had produced those incriminating letters, or that, as she admitted, she once heard Murt tell his brother to "duck that machine gun" as she walked into a bedroom.

Under Douglas's questioning, Norma said her marriage was unplanned and forced upon her. She said that Margaret Brighton had encouraged the union. "Mother said it was the best thing to do since I had borrowed money from him and could not pay it back. She said it was the best thing to do. Mother also said that I was driving around in Murt's car and it looked bad."

Norma spoke so softly that the court stenographer was forced to halt proceedings and read her answers to the jurors seated merely a few feet away.

Douglas's strategy emphasized her sexual naïveté, and under his questioning Norma testified to their sexual history. She said it was more than two months after their marriage before she and Murt had sexual relations. Their failure at sex "made him angry," she said, "and it made me nervous."

"Did you go to a doctor about it?" Douglas asked.

"Yes. He said I could have an operation, but it would cost $150 and Murt said he couldn't afford it."

"But you finally had relations with your husband?"

"Yes. Murt blamed me for the trouble."

Norma said that the low point came with the soap incident. "One day after Christmas. Murt hadn't been talking to me. He brought me some psychology books to read and told me I was too dumb to live. Then I wanted to go see my mother. He didn't want me to. I told him I would go anyway. He dragged me to the bathroom and put soap in my mouth for talking back to him.

"Then another day, I wanted to drive and he wouldn't let me. He seemed to be getting tired of me. Wouldn't ask what movie I wanted to go to anymore, but took me to the ones he wanted to see. He would glare at me a lot."

And those letters she wrote? The note listing "2 G's" for her was written at Murt's order. She did not even know what "2 G's" meant. Ditto with the other incriminating letters. Murt dictated and she wrote. Why? "I was afraid to disobey him." She denied Stokes's account of their conversation in New York City.

"Murt and Irving were mean to me. I told him I didn't want to go to the apartment [in Washington, D.C.] and he said, 'Start home and you won't get there,' and Irving put his hand in his pocket and I thought they might kill me." While it was true that she was left alone one night when Murt was off on his flying lesson, "I tried to think of some way I could get home, but I only had two dollars."

The next morning, in advance of Dewing's cross-examination, the crowd again swamped the police and court officers. "Throngs of women again battled futilely today with legions of deputy sheriffs and state troopers in a vain attempt to storm the building and see and hear Norma on what they expected to be her last day upon the stand," wrote the *Post*. "The officers were forced to drill a lane through the crowd . . . As Norma was taken inside, the mob closed in behind and rushed the grilled gates." Extra chairs lined the courtroom aisles to accommodate the crowd, and the overflow perched on the interior windowsills.

Dewing was polite but firm. He did not shout. He did confront Norma with each improbable or inaccurate claim that she had made the day before.

Some points were minor. Hadn't she obtained the marriage certificate nearly one month before that "unplanned" wedding?

"Yes, I guess so," she said. "I knew we were going to be married, but we hadn't planned the day."

When Norma said that she did "not 'specially" want to marry Murt, Dewing pulled out a *Boston Record* article published under her signature.

Dewing read slowly: "I knew I would be married, and nothing could stop me. My heart hammered within me." Norma denied writing or authorizing the article.

She admitted writing the note to Idalyn but claimed that it was dictated by Murt, and if she asked a question he told her to mind her own business. She admitted writing the "2 G's" memo but again said that Murt was dictating.

"You know that G's stand for grand, don't you?"

"No."

"You've been to many movies, haven't you? You've heard the expression 'grand' in movies?"

"No."

"Mrs. Millen, did you ask your husband where he got the $4,200?"

"I was too tired to think about it."

"Is that the best answer you can give us?" Dewing wondered. He waved her memo meticulously detailing their fake identity as the "Clifton" couple. It included false hometowns, birthplaces, and parents. Norma again said that she was merely taking Murt's dictation. That she didn't know what it meant and that when she asked he told her to mind her own business. Then she conceded it was an alibi, but "I wasn't going to tell it."

Her voice sank so low that the court stenographer asked her to speak louder. Dewing offered his own advice. "Just imagine you are in dramatics, Mrs. Clifton, and keep your voice up."

She burst into tears.

Dewing called for a recess, and a doctor attended Norma in a chamber at the rear of the courtroom. She washed her face with cold water and returned to the stand as Dewing laid out her wardrobe for the jury's inspection. Piece by piece he held up her clothing seized in New York City or at the Washington apartment and asked how much each item cost and when she purchased it. Didn't she benefit from the Needham bank blood money? When Dewing came upon a brassiere, he blushed in embarrassment and shoved it back into a suitcase. Woman reporters said the clothing was disappointingly ordinary.

Then Dewing brought up the matter of her playing with dolls, as Reverend Brighton had insisted was proof of his daughter's girlish naïveté.

"It is a fact, isn't it, Mrs. Millen, that of all the articles found in the Boston Street apartments and in the apartment in Washington there weren't any dolls?"

She didn't replied.

"Isn't that so?"

"Yes," Norma said.

This time Dewing didn't wait for the court stenographer and repeated her answer himself. "Yes," he said to the jurors.

DELIBERATIONS STARTED Wednesday afternoon after only six days of testimony. Many spectators believed that Norma would be acquitted. Those partisans argued that even if she knew of the crimes, what assistance had she actually provided other than driving the three men back to Dorchester after the Packard was torched? She said she never even saw the flames. And she was so young, and so ashamed.

By evening more than four thousand people lined the streets and sidewalks. Automobiles could not pass. The courtroom was filled, and pitchers of ice water were passed through the crowd. Occasionally spectators dashed out, but they always hurried back to reclaim their seats. Word of a verdict came at midnight. It was read aloud at 12:49 a.m.

Guilty on all three counts of being an accessory after the fact of bank robbery and murder.

Norma almost buckled. An attorney grabbed her arm. She didn't cry. The reverend bowed his head and wept. Norma remained stoic until she returned to her cell. The jail matron gave her a cup of hot milk as she cried.

Margaret Brighton wandered the courthouse buttonholing reporters. "Norma lied. She shouldn't have lied. The truth will always out. She is guilty." An associate of Douglas said that he was genuinely shocked by the verdict. "It was a bitter disappointment."

It was for Murt, too.

In his basement cell he turned over to face the wall and wept.[3]

Norma was sentenced on September 26, 1934, to a year in jail. But first she had an unusual forty-five-minute private conference with Judge Brown. He was unimpressed. "It is her own fault," he said moments later from the bench. "If she had not lied on the witness stand she might not have been convicted." The maximum sentence was twenty-one years, yet there was no sentiment for slamming the cell door on her. She was young. She was beautiful. A minister's daughter led astray—though no one ever said it aloud—by a Jew. Norma's attorney, Douglas, argued for probation. Dewing asked for a fourteen-month sentence, a curiously short term as he took the opportunity to flatly declare that Norma was present at the Fitchburg robbery and murder, a crime for which she never faced indictment or trial. And he said that she was in Lynn the night before that job. Dewing said that she knew her husband was involved in crime but "told nobody."

If she had, "Forbes McLeod and Frank Haddock would be alive today." Norma was entranced by Murt's car, her new clothes, and excitement, Dewing claimed. He blamed her parents for not paying their daughter sufficient attention. Both adult Brightons "cared more for their own comfort than for their children," he declared. Dewing unleashed most of his scorn on the Reverend Brighton for failing to "investigate Murton Millen" after learning of his daughter's impending marriage. And after the crimes the father showed no shame. "This selfsame father, after his daughter had been arrested, posed for pictures with his daughter, aided in the glorification of a daughter that had become mixed up with gangsters."

And, he added, "never once did she offer to assist the Commonwealth. In fact she has taken it upon herself to align herself against society."

Norman Brighton rose to speak on his daughter's behalf and accept Dewing's scolding. "After 16 years of the ministry," he said, "it is not to be wondered at perhaps, that I was too strict, too intolerant, too straight-laced when confronted with the natural desires of youth. I should like to say that when Mr. Dewing scores me as being largely responsible for my daughter's position, when he charges me with being untrue to my trust, I make no effort to escape the blame."

He asked the judge to put Norma on probation, in his custody. "I know how deeply penitent she feels. So severe has been her lesson that Norma, I know, will become a splendid woman. This is a disgrace so deeply engraved upon her consciousness, so written upon her heart, that never again will she offend the law or society."

In the spectator benches Norma's mother, Margaret, gave reporters a running commentary on the proceedings, particularly when Dewing blamed the divorced parents. After each remark she clutched a reporter's arms and said, "Please don't use that!"

Despite his conclusion that Norma had lied on the stand, Judge Brown said he was inclined to go along with probation—almost. The obstacle was Murt. Brown worried that if Norma was released now, "she would have an opportunity to visit her husband . . . and she would be open to further unfortunate exploitation and publicity. Interest in her will cease when interest in her husband ceases." That would not come until Murt was executed. "Out of deference to the interest of the public, and for her own protection, she should stay where she is." She was to be jailed until Murt was dead.

As the weeks and then months dragged on, however, the execution date remained undetermined. Scharton and Harvey filed a lengthy appeal with the state Supreme Judicial Court citing thirty-nine errors, including Judge Brown's refusal to permit separate trials and his order that the prisoners remain handcuffed in court and in view of the jury. The former was particularly prejudicial, as it was widely believed, the defense attorneys argued, that it was impossible for three men committing the same crime to be insane at the same time.[4] The collective trial of Murt, Irv, and Abe made their insanity defense all but moot. Scharton also argued that Dewing, with no evidence, unfairly accused Shattuck of "doping" his client.

The appeals were little more than legal make-work. At some point the state court would rule, and the defense attorneys would ask the U.S. Supreme Court for a review. Would it issue a stay? Unlikely at best.

The end was coming. But first Stokes and Ferrari had another Millen crime to investigate.

24

My Brother

AT 4 A.M. ON JANUARY 10, 1935, a sedan pulled up outside the Dedham jail, and a short, broad-faced man climbed out into the cold. Edward C. Frye looked alert, though not particularly bright. He was weighed down with a rope ladder, a double-barreled sawed-off shotgun, a .38 caliber revolver, and about fifty extra cartridges. He quickly scaled the telephone pole outside the prison wall, threw his rope ladder over the stonework, and somehow managed to scramble down into the prison yard. He scampered over to a low window overlooking the pit and peered inside. Then he drew back and hunkered down in a dark corner.

Frye planned to wait until daylight, when the cells were opened for a guard to collect the privy buckets that substituted for flush toilets. Then he intended to blast open the window with one 16-gauge shotgun charge, threaten the guard with the second, and toss the revolver to Irving. In the cold air just before dawn, Frye heard the cell door bolts click open unexpectedly early. He looked into the window to see Irving, illuminated by a corridor lightbulb, push his bucket into the corridor through his open cell door. An officer stood watching. Irv looked up, somehow spotted Frye, reached into a pocket, and threw a handful of pepper into the guard's eyes. Frye fired one shotgun charge through the window. It hit the lightbulb. The guard remained unscathed. Irv yelled, "Shoot!" and Murt screamed, "Open my cell! Open my cell!"

Instead of firing the second barrel or tossing the .38, Frye panicked and fled. He dropped the shotgun, hid the revolver underneath a thick vine in the yard, and climbed back over the wall. Jail guards descended into the pit and pushed Irving back into his cell.

A woman living adjacent to the jail spotted Frye atop the stonework, and minutes later police arrested him as he walked along a roadway. Frye claimed to be merely poor, unemployed, and making his way to Boston by foot. Then police found the .38 caliber cartridges and a spare shotgun shell. A day later Goldberg and Dinneen realized that Frye was the silent fellow in the car with Irv when they encountered the Millen brother on Lawrence Avenue nearly a year earlier.[1]

Frye was fatherless. He had befriended Irv, and Joe Millen had given him work. "I don't think they deserve what is coming to them," he told police. "I don't believe they could've done these things." His mother and brother lived in a Dorchester tenement and said they hadn't seen Frye for months. Frye told police that Joe Millen hired him to break his sons out of jail, so Joe was dragged out to Dewing's office in Dedham, where Frye retracted the accusation when confronted by Joe.

It was difficult to get an accurate story out of Frye. Asked how he traveled to Dedham, Frye said he took the trolley, which meant that he somehow concealed the shotgun, revolver, and rope ladder during the long ride. Police thought it unlikely.

Frye's escapade prompted Dedham residents to ask that Murt, Irv, and Abe be transferred immediately to the state prison in Charlestown. Under Massachusetts law even convicted murderers remained in local jails until after formal sentencing, and that awaited the high court's decision. It arrived two weeks later, and in a forty-nine-page decision the court said no.

Scharton and Harvey refiled with new claims, but nevertheless the trio made a final appearance before Judge Brown on February 26. The only surprise came when Brown offered each an opportunity to address the court and Irving rose to declare, "I was born with two strikes on me."[2]

Every head in the courtroom snapped around.

"I'm nothing but a nut and I know it; that's why I went to Dr. Myerson a long time ago, because I knew I was a nut and I wanted to be cured, but what did it get me? Two of Dr. Myerson's patients have become bank robbers and murderers. I paid him five dollars and what good did it do me? He sent me out into the world to rob and kill."

The "moral imbecile" with "borderline" subnormal intelligence turned out to have something to say.

"Insanity, sir, is a different proposition from what most people think. You don't have to be going around acting like Napoleon Bonaparte . . . My case isn't much different from Harry K. Thaw's case, but Thaw had lots of money and Thaw got a break. I didn't get a break. I never got a break. As a child coming into this world I didn't have a chance of becoming a decent citizen."

He paused and thought hard about his next point. "I think it is getting pretty low when jurors can't differentiate between Faber and me. He is insane in a different way than I am. He had a chance to make something of himself, but I didn't. I'm not a desperado."

Irv looked directly at the judge. "If your honor, sir, were fully instructed in psychiatry you would see that the doctors told the truth about me. I can't follow the dictates of my own conscience because I have no conscience."

Afterward Irv's attorney declared he was as surprised as anyone else by Irv's eloquence. Wasn't his client, who did indeed have a speech impediment and a twitch and foolish grin, not only dumb but insane? The *Herald* was particularly biting. "Irving Millen . . . painted as almost an imbecile with a brain hardly above that of a loyal dog, stood up and spoke for nearly a half hour."

Abe complained he was betrayed by Ferrari. "He promised to get me out of this. I told him all I knew and a lot more. He said for me to get on the bandwagon and the district attorney would whisper a few words into the judge's ear and I would get a life sentence. He even told me he didn't want the money, that the bankers would get it if I gave it up, and he told me to give it to my people. He did not keep his promise. I believed what he said, but I guess I must've been crazy to believe it."

Murt was angry. He jumped up and spoke so quickly the court stenographer had difficulty recording his words. "We were cheated. We didn't have a chance." He told Brown, "You cheated us. I wish to say to your honor, you cheated us during the trial and before the trial."

The judge had another opinion. He set April 28 as the execution date. "And may God have mercy on your souls," he added, at which Murt—or maybe Irv; reports differed—yelled back, "Don't worry. He will."

Appeals continued. The first week in April, Harvey filed another with the state's high court and argued that the jurors were improperly influenced by a crowd yelling, "Lynch them" and "Burn them" and anti-Semitic slurs as they deliberated. "Not one juror on the panel wanted to go home that night without voting for a first-degree verdict." Dewing said that cries from the mob did not begin in earnest until after the verdict was announced. The court promised a quick decision.

On April 18, a convoy of state and local police escorted the Dedham prison bus to the state prison in Charlestown near the Bunker Hill Monument. Inside, Murt, Irv, and Abe each rode with a ball and chain attached to one leg. The day before, Norma refused Murt's request for a last visit. Murt, who had taken the verdict with a grim sneer, now lost control of himself. He grabbed his cell bars and, in a voice that screamed throughout the cell block, accused the prison guards of abusing him and declared they had no right to remove him from the jail. He became increasingly frantic until, after more than an hour, he collapsed on his cot.

In Boston the trio were locked in the death house, a small brick structure that contained a row of three cells and, in a separate chamber, the electric chair. Scharton and Harvey prepared an appeal to the U.S. Supreme Court and lobbied the governor to approve a delay. On April 22 he did, and the executions were postponed until after May 4 to allow for that appeal.

On April 25 a secret indictment was unsealed charging Harry Millen, Murt and Irv's older brother, and Mary Millen Goodman, the married sister, with plotting the breakout and hiring Frye to spring Irving. Pointedly absent from the allegation, according to the papers, was any claim that Frye was also asked to free Murt. Harry and Mary were arrested at 6 a.m., and by noon they took their turns standing before a judge in Dedham's second-floor courtroom.

The two had been regular visitors to the jail and so knew the layout. They told Irv to ask for extra pepper with his meals and save the excess. Mary, the mother of a four-year-old girl, Gloria, approached Frye. Harry obtained the shotgun in the North End and drove Frye to Dedham early that morning.

The siblings pleaded not guilty and were released on $2,500 bail each. Frye remained in custody and was scheduled for a psychiatric evaluation. The two Millens evinced no emotion in court. Frances Millen was not so blasé when she arrived with an attorney. News reports described her as bombarding officials with questions and asking if Dewing was "trying to embarrass us with these indictments."[3]

The trial date was set for September.

Murt and Irv would miss it.

On Monday, June 3, the U.S. Supreme Court turned down Scharton and Harvey's appeal. Charlestown prison warden Francis J. W. Lanagan announced that the execution would take place within the week. With time short, Scharton hit upon a singularly inventive claim: Faber was already legally dead and so could not be killed again.

His claim was based on an anomaly in Governor James Michael Curley's swearing-in five months earlier. The state constitution required the oath of office to be administered by the state Senate's president. But the Senate was locked in a partisan struggle and had not yet elected its leader, so the secretary of state stepped in to say the words Curley repeated on inauguration day.

Scharton contended that this constitutional sidestep made Curley a "de facto" governor but not the "du jure" governor, and because Curley was "de facto" he had no authority to suspend the April 28 execution date. Legally speaking, the execution had proceeded, so in the eyes of the law Faber was now dead. And if he was dead he couldn't be held in jail. Scharton filed a writ seeking Abe's release.

The issues were "novel," Scharton conceded.[4]

Scharton's claim had a legal life span of one day. The warden announced that the three men would die at midnight the next day, as June 6 became June 7.

KILLING PEOPLE in an electric chair was not as easy as its inventors had hoped it would be. That was graphically demonstrated in 1890 when William Kemmler, a New York fruit peddler who had murdered his girlfriend, was strapped into the chair. It would be the first electrical execution ever. The switch was thrown, and he received fourteen seconds of current. Kemmler was pronounced dead, but the dead man began moving and moaning in pain. It took a few minutes to ramp up for another charge, and then seventy seconds of current made Kemmler's death final, but the entire episode was so disturbing some witnesses called for a return to hanging.

The botch-up was unsurprising, since an electric chair was, given its very purpose, untestable.

Early problems arose because there was no standard design or technique. Each electric chair was built at a local prison, and the electrical circuits were designed by a local electrician with no expertise in the field. Knowledge gleaned from survivors of accidental electrocutions in homes and factories had shown that human beings reacted differently to electric shock, depending on their size, weight, skin texture, and physical composition. Bone, for example, conducts electricity poorly, while watery tissue is more efficient. That may mean that a thin man dies slower than a fat man.

Nevertheless, techniques improved, and by the early twentieth century many states believed that electrocution was more merciful than hanging. Prison officials eventually realized that practice made perfect, which provided a career for Robert G. Elliott, a New York electrical contractor. First hired to repair an electrical fault in a chair, he was later asked to operate it. Elliott became the official executioner in New York, Pennsylvania, Massachusetts, New Jersey, and Vermont. Between 1926 and 1939 he executed 387 people, including Sacco and Vanzetti and Bruno Hauptman, convicted of kidnapping and killing aviator Charles Lindbergh's child, and Murt, Irv, and Abe.

Elliott, married with four children, designed his own electrodes. For the head he cut down a leather football helmet and installed two large natural sponges soaked with water to improve conduction. A second electrode was attached to the left calf.

His own research, followed by on-the-job experience, convinced Elliott that an initial shock of 2,000 volts at 5 to 7 amps "shattered" the nervous system and shut down brain activity before pain could register. The standard became two or three jolts of 2,000 volts at 7 to 12 amps. One or two follow-up jolts would see the job done. Of course, it was impossible to know for sure when life ended, as those who knew were already dead.

In the early twentieth century, researchers believed electricity caused "violent vibrations" in bodily fluids, which destroyed the internal organs and led to death. One scientist who examined the hearts of electrocuted dogs found they had turned into "quivering flesh" and so concluded death was instantaneous. Modern medicine knows that's not true. What the doctor saw was the heart in fibrillation, and while powerful electric shocks do stop the heart and destroy the nervous system, the individual may remain conscious for up to ten seconds. Instantaneous unconsciousness, or painlessness, is unlikely, say neurologists. The best guess, derived from data on survivors of accidental electrocutions, is that in the seconds before unconsciousness, time slows for the condemned as his or her flesh begins to cook. But no one can tell.

"I have often wondered what goes on in the mind of the person about to be hurled into the next world as, trussed and blindfolded, he awaits the bolt of lightning that travels in wires," Elliott wrote in his 1940 book, *Agent of Death.* "Do the events of his wasted life parade before him in rapid succession? Does terror beyond our comprehension seize him? Or does some sort of peace descend upon him easing those last moments? These things we will never know."

IN THE DAYS leading up to the execution, Goldberg's relationship with the Millen family paid off for his newspaper. Behind bars Murt and Irv had taken up drawing, and on June 5 the *Post* ran a front-page sketch by Irv. It was a woman's portrait entitled "To My Dear." The drawing was amateurish, and the identity of Irv's subject remained a mystery. He signed it, "Etching By 'The Great I.'" In the same edition was a remarkably skillful drawing by Murt showing a runner kneeling at the starting blocks.

The *Post*'s story opened with "Murton's last letter," sent to his sister Mary and passed on to the paper. In it Murt enclosed a drawing, from memory, of his niece Gloria. He said that his eyes were bothering him, making it difficult to read or write.

"However I send a few cartoons like so's youse can have or toss them."

He remarked that the three prisoners were moved in and out of the death house as the execution dates shifted. "I suppose we be back there soon and that will be the end of it and glad will I be too. It's too bad you couldn't talk to Norma in your little time in Dedham—a lot goes on I do not hear of—no one tells me anything—nor do I see or hear of no thing—like a vault—or as a desert—you know.

"This is all.

"Yours,

"Murt."

The paper said he apologized to Norma and told her he tried "to get her out of this." An anonymous member of the Millen family was surprised that Murt wrote to anyone at such length. Like every convicted prisoner, Murt complained about his trial. The psychiatrists didn't spend long enough examining him, and why didn't they delve further into the history of his father's family? Irv told a *Post* reporter that Abe was writing a book, but the MIT graduate declined to offer any details, perhaps because he was negotiating the sale of his work to a competitor, the *Boston Daily Record*.

Murt was not indifferent to his responsibility for their current circumstances. "I want to say that I'll take the rap for Abe Faber. I would like to save his life and Brudgie's too," using his brother's family nickname. Legally, the offer was worthless, though perhaps Irv and Abe appreciated the thought. Throughout his conversation with the reporter Murt peppered his remarks with variations of the phrase "Never mind about me."

In those last forty-eight hours Joe Millen was granted an audience with the governor. Curley had been mayor when Joe was a city contractor—and as mayor Curley was accused of accepting bribes from contractors like Joe. Curley told reporters that the two had, indeed, met when he was mayor, so it was only right that he see the man. Two of Curley's own children had died young. Curley told Joe that he could do nothing to save Murt and Irv, though the governor called the prison and arranged for Joe's attorney to visit the brothers and draw up their wills.

"The governor treated me kindly and I have no criticism to make of him and asked him to save the lives of my two boys," Joe told the papers afterward. "No one can blame me for that. I want them to live. I am their father. I do not want to see them die. They are so young."[5]

What Joe did not do, or at least the newspapers never printed it, was offer any apology for what his sons did to four men and their families.

Abe's final statement was in three parts. The first was a letter released to the Boston papers.

"I'm trying to reconcile myself to compulsory death. It may seem strange that having participated in murder, where I left behind the widows and orphaned children, I should not regret to pass out. Yet the instinct to live is tenacious. We cling to it to the very last, and I have clung to it."

He decided that his parents were now worthy of praise, particularly "the courageous soul of my mother who I know and I'm sure left no stone unturned to protect me and to preserve the life to which I am clinging. But the hour of doom approaches now, and I am reconciled to it . . . I can only ask forgiveness for the missteps that I have made.

"I participated in crime. I took my chances. I have failed. Now I have got to be game to the last and a good loser."

The "good loser" concept did not extend to Rose Knellar, whom Abe excoriated in terms so stark some papers struck them out. "She left me like the proverbial rats that leave the sinking ship," Abe wrote. "You failed me in my hour of need."

Back in April, after Rose's testimony, Scharton had released an exchange of letters in which the two pledged their love. Rose wrote, or perhaps it was Scharton, "I'm not even worthy to write to you. I'm not even worthy of seeing a picture of you. But you know, Abe, it wasn't because the district attorney said he would not press the charges against me that I testified and returned the money."

She asked to visit him in jail. "I want you to look at me. To tell me that when all this is over we are going away together and make up for the rest of our lives for all the suffering misunderstanding of the past.

"I blame myself for all that happened, yes, dear, I do, and I am right. It was up to me to stop you from going with that—you know who I mean. I won't even mention his name in this letter." She said her love for him tickled her toes. "So I know the love reaches down to there."

A jail visit between the two never happened, and now Abe wrote, "If she really loved me, I would have expected her to stand by, if not to help at least to give me such sympathetic affection and courage as I might need to bear up in this great hour of my need."

Abe delivered the statement to Scharton, who was allowed into the death house on the night of June 5. Irv asked if he had a moment. Scharton said of course. "Just listen to the song," Irv said and burst into a tune that the lawyer did not recognize but that Irv sang at the top of his lungs. He smiled broadly. Then he said, "Goodbye, Bill."

Outside, Scharton told reporters, "It's still in my ears now, I can't get rid of it."[6]

Scharton then took a chartered flight to Washington to petition the Supreme Court for a stay of execution. Scharton mused that he had represented twenty-three people charged with murder, and while he failed to get them all acquitted, this was the first time a client faced execution.

Norma sent Murt a message though Harvey, but he declined to write it down, knowing that inevitably it would be leaked. It was anyway. Goldberg reported that Norma said, "I'm sorry, Murt. God bless you."

A guard at the Dedham jail reported that he saw her praying around the time of the execution.

Murt left everything to Norma, about $2,000. She later turned it down. Irv left what he had to his father. Faber made no will.

Carolyn Millen, who had not seen her sons since the day of her testimony, never saw them again.

Regulations forbade any contact with the prisoners after they were moved into the death house. Yet the warden waived the rules and allowed Rose Faber to hold Abe's hand. She had been a daily visitor at the prison. Upon leaving for the last time, she collapsed against a brick wall and a reporter helped her into a car. A short while later Joe Millen, Frances, and Idalyn arrived and spent forty-five minutes with the brothers. As they departed, Idalyn screamed out Irv's nickname, "Oh, Brudgie. Don't let them take you. They can't take Brudgie. They mustn't take Brudgie." As she had from the start, Frances retained her composure, shed no tears, and smiled at the reporters as she assisted Idalyn into a car.

On June 6 only Harvey and the prison's Jewish chaplain, Moses L. Sedar, were allowed to visit the men.

Harvey asked for a last-minute psychiatric examination of his clients, which the warden refused, and the brothers declined Harvey's offer to ask Curley to commute their sentences to life imprisonment. All knew that was not going to happen, and the brothers said what they wanted was not a life sentence but a new trial. It was all posturing. They accepted their imminent death, Harvey said. "This talk about their collapsing and their fear of death is all rot."

The *Boston American* ran a detailed drawing of the death house, explaining that each of the three cells inside had a cot, table, chair, and running water. The only light came from a bulb in the corridor that led to the execution chamber. The electric chair, a massive, thronelike seat built of heavy timbers and equipped with belts and straps, was immediately to the right. To the left, behind a screen, was the switch panel. Seats were provided for the witnesses, and behind those seats was a small enclosure with mortuary slabs for the bodies.

The paper also ran a series of illustrations tracing the gang's supposed history, starting with Norma chafing at life on Nonesuch Pond, then meeting Murt, purchasing a fur coat, and living in "a fairyland of bright lights, caviar and champagne," a scene illustrated by a scantily clad dancing girl.[7]

The Millens' last meal was broiled mackerel—either the prison refused them meat or the brothers were keeping kosher—sweet potatoes, ice cream, chocolate-frosted cake, and coffee. Abe refused all solid food but did drink three glasses of milk.

As Harvey departed, he said that Murt's final words to him were "I guess we are all washed up." Irv said, "I'm not afraid to die." It was to be the first time in state history that two brothers were executed on the same night.

Abe said that he "didn't get a break."

From her home, Forbes McLeod's widow spoke briefly to reporters. "I'm glad that the execution is going to take place. They did not show any mercy or any quarter. I don't know why we should feel badly that they got their just punishment." She did have sympathy for Rose and Carolyn. "The experiences their parents are going through are worse than what we went through at the time of the murder and since."

A single long-stem white rose arrived at the prison for Abe. The florist said that he had received an anonymous note asking, "Please send one rose to Abe Faber at states prison." The flower was turned away at the prison gate.[8]

Around 10 p.m. the witnesses began to arrive, including three newspaper reporters, two from the wire services and the third from the *Boston American*, Win Brooks. Outside, a crowd estimated at hundreds of people chanted, "Let 'em burn. Let 'em burn." The witnesses filed directly into the death chamber. They included the prison physician, the state surgeon general, the Boston medical examiner, and a deputy sheriff from Norfolk County.

The chamber was painted yellow and gray. An electric light hung over the electric chair, but otherwise gas jets burned from fixtures on the walls.

Just after midnight the cell doors opened and closed, and Rabbi Sedar read from the Twenty-Third Psalm. "Yea, though I walk through the valley of the shadow of death, I will fear no evil, for thou art with me."

As Rabbi Sedar prayed, Murt stepped out of his cell and shook hands with his brother and Abe. At 12:04 a.m. the door to the execution chamber opened and Murt walked through. His hair was tousled and his face showed several days of stubble. He didn't speak. The guards strapped him into the chair, and Elliott, the executioner, attached electrodes to his head and left leg. A black strap was fastened across his eyes. The switch was thrown. Four separate shocks were administered: the first, 2,000 volts, sufficient to render him unconscious, then 1,600 volts, 1,900 volts, and 800 volts. A moment later the four doctors confirmed his death.

None of the newspaper accounts described the odor of burned flesh and hair that drifted through the room.

Irv was next. He shook hands with Faber, Rabbi Sedar chanted a prayer, and he was strapped into the chair. Irv looked toward the warden and asked if he could make a statement. Lanagan nodded. "I want to say that I salute my brother, Murton."[9]

The switch was pulled at 12:15 a.m. and Irv was pronounced dead at 12:21 a.m.

Faber had no one to shake hands with. He prayed with Rabbi Sedar and wore a yarmulke into the death chamber. He followed the rabbi's lead and in Hebrew recited the Shema, the Jewish declaration of faith. "Hear, O Israel, the Lord our God, the Lord is one."

He was pronounced dead at 12:30 a.m.

JEWISH LAW PRESCRIBES BURIAL within twenty-four hours, but as Friday was a Jewish holiday, and the following day was Saturday, the Sabbath, the funerals were pushed back to Sunday. At dawn a mob, many carrying umbrellas against a torrential rainstorm, was already forming on Lawrence Avenue. Word of the crowd reached the Fabers' home on Blue Hill Avenue and family members made a hurried call to the undertaker asking for Abe's body to be immediately released. At nine o'clock a hearse pulled up to the house, and within minutes it was joined by two automobiles. The three-car procession drove to a Jewish cemetery in West Roxbury, where two dozen mourners conducted a burial service over Abe's grave. They included his parents, four uncles, two cousins, and a relative of Rose Knellar's. She had departed days earlier for an overseas cruise. The traditional plain, pine coffin, prescribed by Jewish law, was enclosed in a mahogany casket, and a prayer was recited as it was lowered into the grave. There was no rabbi present. A crowd of several hundred spectators watched, to the great displeasure of Faber family members, and male relatives attempted to push the curiosity seekers away from the grave. Punches were thrown on both sides.

On Lawrence Avenue, meanwhile, a melee was under way in the Millens' living room.[10]

The brothers' caskets arrived at 9:30 p.m. Jewish law forbids open-casket viewings, so exactly why Murt's and Irv's were carried into the Lawrence Avenue living room and their bodies displayed is unknown. They were clad in suits and lay in pine coffins painted gray. At first only a small group of Millen family members and friends were invited in, but hundreds from the crowd of two thousand, perched in trees around the house and filling the Corinthian-columned front porch, forced their way into the home for a glimpse of the brothers' remains.

Shouting and shoving matches broke out as gawkers pushed their way up to the caskets. Two squads of police were on hand to keep order but found themselves flailing away to little avail. When they finally cleared the house, and after the bodies were returned to the hearses, more than a hundred automobiles filled with specatators followed for the three-mile drive to the Puritan Cemetery in West Roxbury.

A block of graves was owned by a Jewish burial society, which agreed to inter the remains. Chaos was repeated as family members tried to force the crowd away from the graveside. Fistfights broke out between mourners and the morbidly curious. Hundreds stood on the shallow rise above the graves as police and cemetery caretakers fought to open a pathway. Murt's and Irv's caskets were lowered into the ground. The rain pelted down, and the unrelenting storm cut short the graveside services.

NORMA WAS RELEASED on August 21 after eighteen months in jail, which included the time before her trial and the full year's sentence imposed by Judge Brown, minus thirty-six days for good behavior. Her release was front-page news, and a crowd assembled outside the jail. Her father, stepmother, and baby stepsister arrived to take her home at the stroke of midnight but decided to wait until the throng thinned out. By 3:50 a.m. only 150 people remained. With Norma lying in the backseat under a blanket, the reverend's car successfully eluded the waiting reporters and photographers.

It was the beginning of her second chance.

EPILOGUE I

IN 2012 I HAD DINNER with a slim older woman with reddish-brown hair who, as an infant, was present when Norma was released from jail in 1935. She is Norma's half sister, who has asked to remain anonymous.

She was surprised to learn of her father's ambitious courting of the tough Boston reporters, having always considered him to be a very private person. Perhaps that experience with the press was why. He never became a practicing attorney, and for that he faulted the infamy that came with his daughter's trial. He lost his dealership job during the trial but eventually returned to the automobile sales business. After Norma moved away from Natick, a year following her release, Norman Brighton rarely, if ever, saw her again. She did periodically contact him "when she needed something." When Norma's stepsister was in fifth grade, she was surprised one day when her teacher asked how her older sister was faring. At that time she didn't know she had an older sister.

After we left the restaurant, she stopped me as I opened the rear door to her car. Her daughter and son-in-law, who accompanied us to the meal, were out of hearing range. We talked about genes, and family, and our relatives. She wanted me to know about the good Brightons. I said I was sure that there were many. I was with one right now.

We will return to Norma in a moment.

First, we'll tie up some loose ends.

Abe's second and third final statements, published after his death, show that his insanity defense was fraudulent.

In a seven-part series in the *Boston Record*, beginning a week after his execution, and in a lengthy article in the July 4, 1935, edition of *Liberty*, then one of the most popular magazines in America, Abe made it clear that he was fully aware of and fully committed to the crimes. And, like Murt, Abe found that he enjoyed it.

"Was I a killer for greed, lust, thrill? Not at first. If, after once turning wrong, I dreamed of an empire of crime, it was only the expression of education and visions turned the wrong way . . . I might've founded one. It is society's good luck I did not."[1]

The crimes they did commit were "only a beginning. The Millens had larger plans," including the robbery of a U.S. Treasury building in Washington, D.C. "Why not? We had the weapons, I have the technical knowledge, they were indifferent to human life. I was their main tool, to be used at their will.

"I was proud to join my technical skill to the will of Murt Millen. My faith in him was such that I believed he could accomplish anything. I gave him complete loyalty. He gave me more pleasure than any friend I ever had," Abe wrote, and praised Murt for his sense of humor, "a laugh for everything and a good brain, although not as trained as mine."

Abe's concluding boast aside, the devotion, indeed love, he expressed for the man he would follow to the grave can be read as a statement of a sexual as well as a psychological relation. But words change meaning with time. "Gay" was an adjective once used to describe a "merry, lively mood." Was Abe a homosexual? If so, was he active? Was that the root of his attachment to Murt? Was he sexually repressed? That may be likely, given his father's experience.

Abe did not blame Murt for his fate, and he did not blame himself. Much of Abe's *Liberty* article is a screed against "society," which perhaps was a novel scapegoat in the 1930s. Abe blamed popular culture for glamorizing crime and ridiculing law enforcement; and he blamed the Depression, because despite his education he couldn't find a job.

"Society taught me how to work, but not how to play; how to strive, but not how to cooperate; how to hate, but not how to love. And now society has killed me. Well, I didn't ask to be born, I don't ask to die."

Proud and insecure, perpetually unhappy with himself, needing the emotional connection he found only in Murt, Abe waged the human struggle between his good side and bad side. Once he chose he could not go back. In practical terms, Abe's greatest failure was his failure to calculate the odds of beating the law. They are always low.

As for syphilis, if Abe had it he probably caught it from the prostitute. Philip Faber, who believed he had infected his son, lived until the age of ninety-three.

And the others?

In November 1935, Rose Knellar married an Italian American law clerk. The interfaith marriage precipitated a falling out between parents and children on both sides.

Harry and Mary were found guilty of planning the jailbreak and were sentenced to probation. The judge said that he never wanted to see another Millen in Dedham court. Frye got two years in jail.

In 1936 Joe Millen was committed to a mental hospital for ten days of observation after Carolyn and Frances complained that he showed up at their new apartment, stood a ladder against the wall, threw a blanket over his head, and threatened them with bodily harm.[2] Joe passed away in 1941. It appears he was living alone at Lawrence Avenue.

Carolyn never moved back into that home. She, Frances, and Idalyn set up their own household. Carolyn passed away in 1946. She is buried next to Joe, and both lie in graves next to Murt's and Irv's.

On April 8, 1947, Rose Faber was found dead on the sidewalk in front of 148 Blue Hill Avenue. Sometime before dawn she carried a photograph taken at Abe's MIT graduation into her third-floor living room and placed it facedown on a table. Then she jumped out an open window. She was sixty-nine. Her husband was seventy-two years old at the time. "We are only human beings," he told the *Herald* in a front-page story, "and human beings can stand just so much."

Stokes was named commissioner of public safety in 1943, a job he held until 1950. He then served as head of the state's civil defense program for four years. He declined a salary for the latter job. He died at age seventy-four on New Year's Day, 1963. The laudatory obituaries gave prominent mention to the Millen-Faber case.

Ferrari was promoted to head of the state police detective bureau in 1943 and later oversaw security at the Suffolk Downs racetrack. At his retirement he described Faber as "the coolest individual and probably the smartest criminal I ever came in contact with."[3] He died at age eighty-four in 1967.

Dinneen remained at the *Globe* until 1956, when he left to write books and magazine articles. His coverage of another spectacular crime, the 1950 robbery of a Brink's armored truck depot of $1.2 million in cash and $1.5 million in checks and money orders, provided rich material for three books. He authored a biography of James Michael Curley, and his son became managing editor of the *Globe*. Dinneen died in 1964 at age sixty-seven.

His wife, Helen, who took the telephone call from the wife of the neighbor of the battery man, outlived her husband by twenty years.

Goldberg remained at the *Boston Post* until it folded in 1956. Later he set up a public relations consulting firm with his daughter, Chris Courtney, who changed her name to start a modeling career. He died in 1980 at age eighty-two, but not before weathering a minor scandal in 1978 when the *Globe* investigated two no-bid consulting contracts awarded him by Suffolk County district attorney Garrett Byrne.

Goldberg's task was to monitor newspaper, radio, and television coverage of Suffolk County and report to Byrne in daily telephone conversations—which Goldberg recorded, apparently without the prosecutor's knowledge. Goldberg can be heard complaining that no one should ever trust a reporter out for a story.[4]

Psychiatrist Ray Shattuck was convicted and fined $250 on illegal drug charges but was acquitted on appeal.

George Douglas, Norma's attorney, was disbarred and jailed in 1936 after pleading guilty to stealing $10,000 from the estate of a state hospital patient.

Scharton had a run-in with the IRS over back taxes and in 1943 filed for bankruptcy, but before he died in 1947 some three hundred people honored him at a testimonial dinner on his seventy-fifth birthday. The state attorney general and five judges sat at the head table.

Harvey donated his $1,000 fee for defending the Millen brothers to the four women whose husbands Murt killed: Helen Haddock, Mary McLeod, Mary Clark, and Grace Sumner. He also declared that the state needed a systematic method for providing legal help to indigent defendants. He died in 1944 at age sixty-six.

Dewing served as Norfolk County district attorney until 1954, when he was appointed superior court judge. He died in 1981 at age eighty-nine. While he remained renowned for his prosecution of the Millen-Faber case, he achieved a further measure of publicity when district attorney for consulting a "talking horse" while searching for a missing four-year-old boy. The horse tapped out a location, using its hoof, which proved to be correct.

Briggs briefly engaged in a newspaper brawl with Dewing over the execution of Irv. The psychiatrist had come to regret it.

There were many claimants for the reward money. A new commissioner of public safety, with the help of Stokes, Ferrari, and Fleming, prepared a lengthy report for the Governor's Council, which then convened public hearings on how to divvy up the state's $20,000. (The lieutenant governor withdrew the initial $1,000.)

The LeVierge brothers, Alfred and Frank, received $2,500 each. Dinneen and Goldberg, who were nominated for the reward by Chief Bliss in Needham, were voted $2,000 each for convincing Daniel Needham to publish a photograph of the battery. "I think anybody with the facts would say that it was Dinneen's and Goldberg's photographs to which was due the locating of the battery of the Millens," said one council member.

The New York detectives who tracked down Messinger and helped arrest Murt, Norma, and Irv in the hotel lobby divided $4,200, and two Boston police officers, including the officer LeVierge spoke with—who had once ticketed Murt for driving with Louisiana plates—were awarded $1,000 each. The three teenagers from Norwood who found the radio serial number plate received $500 apiece.

Henry DeLoria, who found the burned-out Packard, was given $800, as was his brother, whose role was never mentioned in news reports.

And $500 was given to Ormsby "Bob" Court of the *Boston Daily Record* for getting Murt and Irv to confess in his story of March 1, 1934.

Needham selectmen distributed the town's $1,000 among seven men, including Walter Mills, whom Stokes had retrieve the Packard battery. He received $150.

The state legislature voted Molway and Berrett $2,500 each as compensation for their wrongful arrest and trial. Governor Curley's former campaign manager secretly pocketed $2,000 of the sum, for supposed legal services, but was forced to cough it up when Dinneen wrote about it in his *Harper's* magazine article. The article was the basis for the 1939 film *Let Us Live*, starring Henry Fonda and Maureen O'Sullivan. Fonda is an unjustly accused cabbie; O'Sullivan is his girlfriend. Fonda's performance is mediocre; O'Sullivan's is great.

As for Norma, her second chance worked out, until it didn't.

Within weeks of being released from jail, she sat down with writers from *Detective Fiction Weekly*, which despite its title also published first-person nonfiction accounts of spectacular crimes. The magazine had a large, nationwide circulation, and Norma's ghostwritten story was printed in five parts beginning in November 1935. It opened with a simple declaration: "I am the widow of Murton Millen."

Norma wrote that she had been besieged with offers to tell her story and chose *Detective* because it promised "decent and fair treatment." There was also the matter of finances. "I need the money because it will help me get a new start in life," she wrote.

Norma used the proceeds to attend beautician school in New York City, and while she changed her name in the hope of anonymity, she was nevertheless found out and on at least one occasion posed for press photographers. In the summer of 1936 Norma returned to Boston and renewed an acquaintance with a graduate of the New England Conservatory of Music, Harold H. Clement, who she had met through her brother. Clement played French horn and cornet part time for two local symphony orchestras. They quickly became engaged and within weeks jumped off a New York City–bound bus to be married, at midnight, in the small town of Armonk, New York, on August 16, 1936.[5] She was twenty-one years old; he was twenty-four. Friends had called him "a confirmed bachelor."

Their wedding made the front pages of the Boston papers.

A rough spot came later that year when a Boston newspaper hired Norma to screen applicants for its Christmas charity. Their sad stories depressed her. One day she saw a former woman inmate from the Needham jail waiting in line, and that night Norma swallowed a bottle of pills. But she bounced back.

In March 1939, Norma gave birth to a son, Henry. Shortly afterward, a two-part account of her life after Murt was published by a news syndicate. The first of the ghostwritten articles was published under the headline "A Woman Can Live Down a Dreadful Past!"[6]

Norma said that she had "emerged from a shell" and agreed to be interviewed for the sake of her child, though exactly how the interview helped was left unexplained. But "I'm completely happy," she said. The family was living in a four-story walk-up a few blocks from Central Park. Norma was a stay-at-home mom.

Part II of the account explained why there had been a Part I. The family needed the money. Norma told the writer that her husband, Harold, had lost his job with a radio symphony and resorted to baking apple turnovers in the apartment kitchen and then selling the pastry door-to-door. Norma never finished her beauty school studies, and so could not get the required license.

But she was still cute.

"Being a mother has made me unafraid. It's why I have the courage now to work nights as a hostess in the dime-a-dance place on Broadway while my husband, Harold E. Clement, works days peddling apple turnovers."[7]

Her son was a few months old. Norma found an old gown and refashioned the neckline to show off her décolletage. "I knew I was a good dancer, and I love to dance." When she walked into the dance hall and saw what looked like a cattle auction, Norma said she wanted to turn around and flee. But she thought of Harold and the turnovers.

The manager said her income would depend on her "brains," not her dancing.

A bartender clued her in. "Don't think of these guys who come in here as men. Think of them as pocketbooks, and it's your job to loosen the strings." Using her brains meant "clipping the suckers," and that meant convincing a guy that if he paid enough upfront the night would end with sex. The trick was breaking off the evening before the sex, but after the money.

It was dangerous. More than one girl found that a fellow "they had ducked out on the night before would be lying in wait to beat them up."

"It didn't take me long to learn that the racket was a hazardous one." How long Norma worked at the job, and whether she ever did do more than dance, is unknown.

Eventually Harold joined the NBC Orchestra and then in the early 1950s purchased seven acres of land in Hazlet, New Jersey, where he opened a trailer park. The town was only thirty miles from New York City and undergoing a postwar boom. In 1958 their son, Henry, graduated from high school. His yearbook photograph showed a slight, blond, soft-featured youth with a distant smile. The caption said, "This quiet young man doesn't have much to say." He liked math and enjoyed spaghetti, and his philosophy was to "practice what you preach."

Henry joined the U.S. Army and in 1961 became engaged to a girl from a neighboring town. It did not work out. She later married another man.

By then Norma had stopped giving interviews. In the fall of 1963 she arrived in California, and by January 1964 she was living in a hotel on South Flower Street at the edge of the Los Angeles garment district.

There on January 25, 1964, Norma was found dead. The immediate cause was a heart attack, but the medical examiner noted that a "significant" contributing condition was acute alcoholism.[8] Norma had drunk herself to death.

She was cremated and her remains returned to New Jersey for burial. At some point Norma had sliced four years off her age. Her death certificate reported her birthdate as November 25, 1919, and her age as forty-four, which would have made her fourteen when she married Murt in 1933. Census records give her birth year as 1915. She died at age forty-eight.

Her son, Henry, did not bear up well. In August 1964 he had himself committed to a state mental institution in the New Jersey town of Marlboro. On November 7, 1966, Henry stepped into a shack on the hospital grounds. He was accompanied by another patient, Kathleen Oberman, twenty-eight, who had committed herself to the hospital a month earlier.

Henry killed her.[9] The few records available offer no motive. Her parents were deceased, and while Ms. Oberman was married, she had no children.

Henry was transferred to a New Jersey institution for the criminally insane. He remained there until 1967. In August, he threaded his bed sheets through the bars of his cell window, fashioned a noose, and hung himself.[10]

This, then, was the end to a long arc of misfortune.

EPILOGUE II

SO, DO I? Look like Murt?

The answer to that depends on the decade. In death Murt is frozen at twenty-five, and I am now more than twice that age. When I first met Wayne Urquhart, the Needham police officer, my appearance still bore the remnants of a long-lasting youthfulness. What he saw, I believe, was not someone who looked like Murt so much as someone who looked like a Millen. I was not completely taken aback because my sister, Jonina, had once told me of the resemblance.

After her nighttime conversation with Grandma she found an old newspaper photograph of Murt, and on a break from college told me that we looked alike and then, perhaps thinking twice, said that maybe it was just a family resemblance. I don't recall, or at least don't remember, learning any other details. Jonina recently wrote me this note:

> Regardless of what I may have told you, Grandma told me a lot more. I know for sure she told me they were sentenced to death, because she told me that Mary (and she named her) came to her to ask her to be a character witness; Grandma refused. So, I know for sure I knew there were two brothers. Though I don't have a direct memory, she likely told me about Norma and Abe. When I was a senior in high school, I used the microfiche at the library (while doing a senior history project) to find the story. I don't remember being surprised to find that Abe and Norma were part of the group. Once Grandma told me they were robbers, and had been sentenced to death, I can't imagine she would have held back on the additional parts about the "shikse" and MIT graduate, two types of characters that loom large for Jews. I do remember seeing a photo of them (I think bandaged?) and feeling very queasy! I do believe at that time that I thought it was "just" one robbery and murder.

Looking back, what was more surprising than my sister's announcement that I resembled a bank robber and killer was my reaction. There was none. I had other matters on my mind, as there was some truth to what the psychiatric witnesses said at Murt's trial, though it does not concern schizophrenia or paranoia or any psychopathy (still, one might argue that any reporter needs a touch of personality disorder to do the job). What the psychiatrists had right was a family history of depression.

It landed on me in seventh grade homeroom as I was staring out the window. Multicolored explosions, much like a kaleidoscope, materialized in the space between my brain and my eyes. The shapes did not block my vision, though it felt like a part of what I would now call my consciousness collapsed into the back of my head. I could hear nothing. I did not black out; rather a piece of my mind seemed closed down. Fortunately, my depression was not exacerbated by the sort of violent and chaotic household in which Murt grew up. My parents were strict but loving. The only time my father struck me was at the age of nine or ten when my brother and I started brawling on the street in front of our home.

My mental chaos was ended by the pharmaceutical industry, as I am one of the fortunate who respond well to serotonin-uptake inhibitors. By then I was in my forties. While researching Murt, I did see familiar behaviors, particularly his youthful isolation in books and how he used travel as a psychological escape. After my junior year in high school, I began hitchhiking around the nation. I went to the Woodstock music festival by myself, and during college I hitchhiked out to the West Coast and back, two summers in a row. I traveled for a year after college to Europe and North Africa. The unfamiliar sights and sounds were happily distracting. And, always, I harbored the hope that movement itself would bring me to a place where my interior life was transformed. That was, of course, impossible.

The opportunity to explore Murt's and Abe's minds—or, rather, the minds they disclosed to the psychiatrists—was only one reason for writing this book, and not the primary one. It is, fundamentally what the journalism business calls a "great story." Not as in a "good story," but as in a formidable collection of characters and events that, as Joe Dinneen observed in 1935, could not have been made up.

Some members of the Millen family were not pleased to learn of my plan for a book. Most only asked that their names be omitted, some out of fear that they would be linked to the stigma of Murt's craziness. Perhaps a useful diagnosis of Murt is one I've constructed on my own—sociopathic, nihilistic, manic-depressive. And angry, of course. He knew that his crimes were wrong. He just didn't care.

Other Millen family members wondered why I wanted to admit any sort of connection, to which I shrug. Murt was a long time ago, and there have been no Millen killers since.

I was able to trace one direct descendant from 39 Lawrence Avenue. Early in my research I discovered that Idalyn Millen had, late in life, lived with an elderly companion in a seaside home in Gloucester. It was a rare and beautiful spot, on a narrow isthmus facing a small inlet beyond which was the ocean. The modest, one-story home was painted white, with bright blue shutters. Neighbors told me that when the weather was warm, piano music wafted through open windows and onto the street. Given the musical talents in her family, it was probably Idalyn at the keys. A visit to the county courthouse turned up her last will and testament, which led me to a woman in another state with the name of Gloria. I did not recognize her last name—it sounded very Yankee, so I figured I'd hit a dead end. At that time I knew nothing about Mary Millen's marriage or her child. On Gloria's answering machine I recited my name and added that I was doing research on my family history.

In those days before cell phones I also left my parents' phone number; I was staying at their house while in Boston. I returned home one day to find my mother deeply shaken. She had received a call from a Gloria. The conversation was so disturbing—the woman was so angry—that my mother suggested I not call her back.

I did, of course. Every journalist encounters the angry and unhappy, but Gloria was memorable. She was beyond fury. And I did not even know who she was. She opened our conversation in a normal tone of voice. I explained that I was researching a book about the Millen brothers, as my mother had told her, and had come across her name and address. Did she know the family? Gloria asked if I was writing a novel. No, I said, it would be a nonfiction book. Her voice turned ferocious. "You will kill people," Gloria said. She was almost shrieking. I asked who those people might be, and who she was, only to hear her declaration repeated. She demanded to know how I had located her. I obliged with an account of my reporting.

Then she asked if I had children. I said no, and she said that therefore "you cannot understand what you are doing." She declared I was only in it for the money, which told me two things: she knew nothing about book publishing, and she knew a great story when she heard one.

Needless to say, Gloria declined to cooperate. I understood the basis for her fury only some months later when, buried in a newspaper clipping, I found mention of Murt and Irv's young niece, Gloria, Mary Millen Goodman's child.

The brothers' stain was ineradicable. Urquhart was unsurprised by Gloria's reaction. He observed that Murt, Irv, and Abe brought ruin and pain on the families of innocent men—two of them public servants—and so reaped public opprobrium, and then were slain by the state to the cheers of the crowd. Forbes McLeod and Francis Haddock were dead, too, but they died representing the law. Their survivors and descendants would suffer pain, and anger, forever, but there was the light of pride. Murt and Irv's and Abe's families had only disgrace and shame.

Gloria is now deceased, and as far as I have been able to determine, Joe and Carolyn's children have no other living descendants. Idalyn married a man twenty-eight years her senior, and I believe had no children. Frances was single as of age thirty-nine in 1940. She took a job with the federal Works Project Administration, and in 1941 married another government employee Edward N. Galvin, five years her junior. She died in 1977. Harry married Freda Siegan, the young woman who testified on behalf of Murt and Irv. They passed away in Florida in the early 1990s. Though Abe was an only child, I did locate a descendant on his father's side, a charming woman in Florida who filled in details about the Chelsea branch of the Faber family and told me that the story of Murt, Irv, and Abe would make a fascinating book.

ACKNOWLEDGMENTS

DESPITE THE SINGLE NAME on the title page, this book exists because of the advice, assistance, and friendship of many people.

The list is long, and the only question is where to start.

As in the book, I'll begin with Wayne Urquhart, who shared his knowledge of the case and, most important, his astute observations of police and criminals. He predicted the fate that ultimately befell Norma Brighton Millen Clement. For his advice and friendship I'm grateful.

The long interregnum between the start of my research and the production of this book was due largely to my own limits as a writer, compounded by my disappointingly slow learning curve. Attempts over the years to craft a workable whole out of the many characters and plotlines ended in failure. What changed? I left the ranks of reporters and became an editor, a job that entailed spotting and repairing the flaws in other people's writing. That taught me how to see the failures in my own work. For allowing me that experience and teaching me along the way, thanks to a variety of former editors at the *Philadelphia Inquirer*. They include Eugene Kiely, Tom Stacey, and Ned Warwick, who also gets credit for his conversations on more existential matters, as well as Nancy Cooney and Anne Gordon. Other co-workers to whom I owe much are Chris Satullo, Chris Hepp, Ken Dilanian, Joe Tanfani, Jennifer Linn, Craig McCoy, Dan Biddle, Jeff Gammage, and Kia Gregory. For his early encouragement, I thank John Timpane. Thanks to Steve Seplow, who originally hired me.

I must give a special nod to Marie McCullough, a wonderful reporter and friend in and out of the newsroom. I should also thank those reporters whose work I "danced on," as they used to say in the newspaper biz.

The friendship and camaraderie of the racing sailors on *Rag Trade*, in particular Rich Herrschaft, Bryan Dohmen, Julie Moore, Christopher Horning,

Dave Deptula, Kieth Skowran, Sieren Ernst, and Greg Muennich, who was there for the first sail, provided an entirely different education. A special thanks to everyone who has ever set foot on foredeck.

For reading portions of early drafts, later chapters, and in one or two cases the whole book, and for offering insightful feedback, my thanks go not only to some of those listed earlier but also to Deborah Lichtman, John Paine, Michael DeLeo, Judy Gregory, Joyce Bechtold—an excellent physical therapist who also worked on my painful elbows—and Kevin Foley—a friend, foredeck man, and fellow sailor to whom, along with his wife, Judy, I'm indebted for aid and assistance beyond the ordinary. Also in that latter category are Tessa Gorenstein, Nancy Tarlin, and Azriel Shiloh.

Attorney Tom Ferber was remarkably generous with his time and advice, as was Mark Edmundson with his encouragement.

And for making the book happen, thanks to my agent, John Talbot, and Stephen Hull, my editor at the University Press of New England.

Enormously helpful were many librarians and archivists at a variety of institutions: the Massachusetts Institute of Technology Museum and the Institute Archives and Special Collections; the Northeastern University Archives and Special Collections; the Rauner Library Special Collections at Dartmouth College; the Center for the History of Medicine at the Francis A. Countway Library of Medicine at Harvard Medical School; the Historical and Special Collections Department at the Harvard Law School Library; and the Lynn Public Library.

I also thank the staff of the Motion Picture, Broadcasting and Recorded Sound Division at the Library of Congress, who arranged for my viewing of two 1950s television shows about the investigation and trial. Also very helpful were the staff at the Newspaper Reading Room in the Madison Building.

This would be a much diminished book without the resources and staff at the Boston Public Library's Microtext Department. Its collection of newspapers on microfilm is both outstanding and irreplaceable. Staff members were unfailingly polite and helpful during my many, many visits. I am also grateful to a nephew, Gabriel Schonfeld, who spent many days one summer bent over the microfilm readers.

The retired officers at the Massachusetts State Police Museum and Learning Center in Grafton, Massachusetts, welcomed me and provided my first look at a key document, the report to the Governor's Council apportioning credit and recommending rewards for individuals who helped capture the Millen-Faber gang. And my appreciation to active-duty Trooper Todd Nolan, a very busy state police public information officer, who got up from his desk, walked into a file room, and confirmed that, yes, there still existed a thick stack of records from the investigation. Some months later I received a CD-ROM with more than five hundred pages. There were duplications but also a variety of very helpful unpublished documents, including a detailed memo by Detective Fleming, the Norma Brighton interview transcript, and the account of Dinneen and Goldberg's role in the investigation, which I believe was written by Lawrence Goldberg.

Margaret R. Sullivan, records manager and archivist at the Boston Police Department, was very generous with her knowledge and contact list.

Claude W. Brenner, an MIT undergraduate in the 1940s and an adviser to the MIT Hillel, the Jewish student organization, wrote a lengthy and fascinating email on the Jewish experience at MIT. He studied under some of the very same professors who taught Abe Faber.

The Dedham Historical Society made available its copy of a booklet by a Millen-Faber juror describing each juror and the jury's time in sequestration. At the Norfolk County Courthouse in Dedham, Jenny Foster, the assistant clerk, and staff members Mary Hickey and Debbie Levis dug out a missing volume of the trial transcript, gave me a tour of the courtroom, and showed me the defendants' cage now packed away in the basement.

Much appreciation to Elizabeth Bouvier, head of archives at the Division of Archives and Records Preservation at the Supreme Judicial Court, and her staff for preserving the trial transcript.

Staff members of the Needham Historical Society were exceedingly hospitable, particularly Gloria Polizzotti Greis, the executive director, and archivist Polly Attridge.

James Barnicle, a former police officer and grandson of Frank Haddock, told me stories about Officer Haddock that had been passed down from his grandmother to his mother, Mary, and then to her children. Jeffrey Sadow, also a grandchild of Francis Haddock, collected family information for a Wikipedia entry and gave me permission to use the photograph in this book.

As noted before, my thanks go to Norma's half sister, and her daughter and son-in-law, for their hospitality.

NOTES

CHAPTER 1

1. "3 Seized in Battle in Lobby of Hotel; Shot Is Fired, Guests Flee as One of Two Murder Suspects Fights Policeman for Pistol. Nonchalant Bride Taken; Brothers Are Linked to Raid and Killings in Needham, Mass., Bank on Feb. 2," *New York Times*, February 26, 1934. Also accounts in various Boston newspapers.

2. Joseph Dinneen, "Wanted Woman Quit Her Minister-Father," *Boston Globe*, February 19, 1934.

3. "Record Rush to Nearby Beaches," *Boston Globe*, July 31, 1933.

4. "Throng of 600,000 Visits Greater Boston Beaches," *Boston Globe*, June 12, 1933.

5. Norma Millen, "My Story," Part I, *Detective Fiction Weekly* (November 9, 1935): 34–49. Norma gave a variety of accounts of their meeting and subsequent relationship. The account in this chapter draws primarily on the first of her five ghostwritten *Detective* magazine articles plus interviews Norma, her father, and her mother gave at various times to the *Boston Post, Boston Globe, Boston American*, and other newspapers. It also incorporates testimony at Norma's trial.

CHAPTER 2

1. "Girl Cashier Foils Robbers at Theater," *Boston Globe*, April 3, 1933.

2. "Story of Holdup . . . in Mattapan Is Verified," *Boston Traveler*, March 1, 1934.

3. "Kidnap Theatre Man, Make Him Open Safe," *Boston Globe*, April 3, 1933.

4. "Box Office Boys Get $700 in Cash," *Boston Globe*, April 24, 1933. In various newspaper articles police speculated, anonymously, that the brothers could have been responsible for fifty to a hundred robberies.

5. Smith Ely Jelliffe, *Commonwealth vs. Murton Millen, Irving Millen and Abraham Faber*, Trial transcript [hereafter referred to simply as "Trial transcript"], May 29, 1934, vol. 30.

6. Frances Millen, Trial transcript, May 21, 1934, vol. 24.

7. L. Vernon Briggs, Trial transcript, June 4, 1934, vol. 33.

8. Lawrence Harmon and Hillel Levine, *The Death of an American Jewish Community: A Tragedy of Good Intentions* (Lexington, MA: Plunkett Lake Press, 2012), 32–33.

9. Joe and Carolyn Millen's family history is drawn primarily from court testimony, census documents, and newspaper accounts of the trial and arrest. Their testimony is

in Trial transcript, May 22 and May 23, 1934, vols. 25 and 26. Other family members testified on other dates.

10. Interview with Millen relative.

11. David Pearlstein, Trial transcript, May 15, 1934, vol. 21.

12. Murt's psychological history is drawn from analyses offered at the trial by the many psychiatrists who interviewed one or both brothers and Abe Faber in the Norfolk County Jail. There were seventeen psychiatrists in all, as well as other medical doctors. Defense psychiatric witnesses who examined Murt included Jelliffe, Max Bennett, and Frederic J. Farnell; prosecution psychiatric witnesses included M. H. Evans, Kendall Holt, and Briggs.

CHAPTER 3

1. Thomas Larbey, Trial transcript, May 3, 1934, vol. 13. Also Frank Cheney, *When Boston Rode the El* (*Images of America*) (Charleston, SC: Arcadia, 2012).

2. Rose Faber, Trial transcript, May 2, 1934, vol. 12; May 28, 1934, vol. 29.

3. Gerald H. Gamm, *Urban Exodus: Why the Jews Left Boston and the Catholics Stayed* (Cambridge, MA: Harvard University Press, 2001), 30–49.

4. The U.S. Census in 1920 and 1930 asked respondents if they could read or write in any language.

5. Nat Hentoff, *Boston Boy* (New York: Knopf, 1986). Along with the butcher shop anecdote, Hentoff offered a rich account of growing up Jewish in Boston before World War II (10–11).

6. Theodore H. White, *In Search of History: A Personal Adventure* (New York: Harper & Row, 1978).

7. Christophe Lecuyer, in David Kaiser (ed.), *Becoming MIT: Moments of Decision* (Cambridge, MA: MIT Press, 2010), ch. 3. "Between the early 1910s and the late 1930s . . . the Institute turned itself into a full-fledged research university" (59).

8. "Faber as High Rank Student," *Boston Post*, March 1, 1934.

9. Abraham Faber, "Faber Tells of Early Dreams to Create World of His Own," *Boston American*, June 10, 1935, one of a series of autobiographical articles published posthumously.

10. Debi Unger and Irwin Unger, *The Guggenheims* (HarperCollins e-books, 2009).

11. *Bulletin, Massachusetts Institute of Technology, Catalog Issue*, April 1929, 33.

12. Claude W. Brenner, MIT class of 1947. Brenner studied under many of the same professors as Abraham Faber; he is a former president of the MIT Alumni Association and for many years was a director of the MIT Hillel Foundation. "It was never overtly stated, but it appeared to be common knowledge that MIT had a 5% quota for Jewish students" throughout the 1930s and into the 1940s, he wrote in an email exchange. "But it was in its role in securing post-graduate employment that MIT, despite its apparent quota, stood firm. The general level of anti-Semitism in the larger society at that time made it very difficult for Jews to get jobs in industry. That certainly was true in the aircraft industry, and the situation prevailed for some years after World War II. A friend who entered in 1938 told me that when he came to campus with his father for his admissions interview, the director of admissions asked his father, 'Tell me sir, do you have a job for your son? There are not many jobs for Jews in industry.' Another friend from the class of 1939 told me of his experience at the campus jobs fair in his senior year. A mechanical engineer, he applied for a job at the Cleveland Paper Box Company. The interviewer said to him,

'Steinberg. Is that a Jewish name?' My friend acknowledged that it was. The interviewer then said, 'The Cleveland Paper Box Company does not hire Jews.' My friend reported this encounter to the MIT placement office. The Cleveland Paper Box Company was never again invited to the job fair."

13. Abraham Faber, "Why Did I Die in the Chair?" *Liberty* magazine, July 13, 1935.

14. Various witnesses, Trial transcript, May 16, 1934, vol. 22.

15. "Thrill Quest Led Murton to Auto Racing," *Boston Traveler*, March 5, 1934; "Young Lads Want to Drive at Rockingham," *Boston Globe*, October 8, 1931.

16. Insull was acquitted at his trial.

17. "Roads" (National Council on Economic Education, n.d.), http://www.econedlink.org/lessons/docs_lessons/725_roads1.pdf.

18. "Raid Uncovers Huge Distillery, Abandoned Grove Hall Car Barn Yields 3000 Gallons of Beer and Alcohol-Five Taken," *Boston Globe*, April 17, 1930; "$100,000 Beer Distillery Nets Police Big Haul," *Boston Herald*, April 17, 1930.

CHAPTER 4

1. Joseph Millen, Trial transcript, May 22, 1934, vol. 25. Joe Millen spent much of the day on the witness stand, and most quotations in this book come from his testimony.

2. Seven psychiatrists examined Faber and testified in lengthy court sessions. Some quoted statements made by Faber during their visits at the Norfolk County Jail.

3. Rose Knellar, Trial transcript, April 30, 1934, vol. 10.

4. Jacob Gordon, Trial transcript, May 4, 1934, vol. 14.

5. Myron S. Huckle, Trial transcript, May 3 and 4, 1934, vols. 13 and 14.

6. He did following Abe's arrest, but no trace was ever found.

CHAPTER 5

1. Millen, "My Story," Part I, 11.

2. "Fitchburg Murder Goes to Grand Jury in May," *Boston Globe*, May 28, 1934. No indictment was returned against Norma.

3. "Norma Saw Mother at Tewksbury," *Boston Globe*, March 1, 1934; "Wedding in West Costs Her Child," *Boston Herald*, July 6, 1927; 1920 United States Census, s.v. "Oscar Clinton," Gallatin County, Montana, accessed at Ancestry.com.

4. Accounts of these crucial weeks were provided by Norma in newspaper interviews, in her trial testimony, and afterward in her *Detective Fiction Weekly* articles. Her mother, Margaret, offered her own recollections in newspaper interviews and first-person articles written for two Boston newspapers. Her father, Reverend Norman Brighton, testified at Norma's trial. The account in this chapter is based on those sources.

5. "Fifty-one Cities Plan to Use Radio to Apprehend Criminals," *New York Times*, October 19, 1930.

6. "Police Chiefs See Radio Car Tests," *Boston Globe*, June 5, 1931.

7. Associated Press, October 9, 1934; "EXTRA! $4500 Theater Holdup Is Staged at Worcester," *Boston Globe*, October 9, 1933; "Worcester Four to See Millens," *Boston Globe*, March 3, 1934; Abraham Faber, Interrogation by Massachusetts State Police detective Lieutenant Joseph Ferrari, February 27, 1934, and various newspaper articles.

CHAPTER 6

1. An Iver Johnson .22 caliber revolver was used to kill Robert F. Kennedy.

2. Abraham Faber, "Faber Tells . . . Life Bitter to Him as Fates Prove False," *Boston American*, June 19, 1935. In this article Faber also refers to himself as Murt's "slave."

3. William J. Helmer and Rick Mattix, *The Complete Public Enemy Almanac: New Facts and Features on the People, Places, and Events of the Gangster and Outlaw Era, 1920–1940* (Nashville: Cumberland House, 2006). Also various newspaper accounts.

4. This was probably Abe's first crime. He sometimes exaggerated his criminal activity. He variously claimed to have participated in the Worcester theater robbery and the MIT armory kidnapping, but the victims' accounts make his claims unlikely.

5. "Orders 400 Weeks' Pay to Mrs. Clark," *Boston Globe*, October 9, 1935.

6. Some sources attribute that quote to Abe, but he does not seem to have fired a shot at Clark.

7. Faber, February 27, 1934, confession to Lieutenant Ferrari; various newspaper articles.

8. Dorothy Dunbar Bromley, *Youth and Sex: A Study of 1300 College Students* (New York: Harper & Brothers, 1938).

9. Millen, "My Story," Part I, 17.

CHAPTER 7

1. "Early Mistake of Police Led to Berrett's Arrest," *Boston Traveler*, March 1, 1934. Interview with Daniel Callahan, a private detective and "old time Indian fighter and secret service man" hired by the defense attorneys. Despite the headline, the story is about Molway.

2. "Berrett Tells His Story of Escape from Chair," *Boston Traveler*, February 28, 1934.

3. This account of the crime is drawn from trial testimony in newspaper accounts of the trial in the *Lynn Item*, the *Boston Globe*, and the *Boston Post* and from witness statements in the Massachusetts State Police Archive (hereafter, MSP Archive).

4. Leo Donohue, Paramount Theatre building superintendent, "Murder and Armed Robbery, Paramount Theatre, Lynn," report submitted March 15, 1935, MSP Archive. One slang definition of "monkey" is someone who looks the fool.

5. "Gov Ely Plans to Rid State of Gangsters. Increased State Police Force Indicated Unless Local Departments Are Coordinated to Check Holdups and Murders," *Boston Globe*, January 4, 1934. Also *Boston Post* and *Boston Traveler*.

6. Joseph F. Dinneen, "Murder in Massachusetts," *Harper's* magazine (March 1936): 405.

CHAPTER 8

1. "Armed Robbers Fail to Get Machine Guns. Kidnap National Guard Capt. in Cambridge—Plot Theft from Armory," *Boston Globe*, August 24, 1933. In one account Abe said he was in the car with Murt and Irv, but that contradicts the victims' story that there were only two assailants. Abe likely helped plan the crime, as he was familiar with the armory and its staff.

2. "Stage Holdup at Quincy Armory," *Boston Globe*, August 25, 1933.

3. Details of the robbery are drawn from accounts in the *Boston Globe, Boston Herald, Boston Post*, and Faber's February 27 confession to Lieutenant Ferrari (his second), as well as statements by the two auto show guards found in the MSP Archive.

4. Faber, state police interview, MSP Archive.

5. Associated Press, Fort Smith, AR, January 2, 1932.

6. "Arthur H. Lynch and Radio Noise Suppression Equipment," *Communications* 11, no. 9 (September 1931).

7. "Substitute Woods for Port Orford White-Cedar for Storage Battery Separators," Office of Production Research and Development of the War Production Board, April 1945.

8. Alfred LeVierge and Frank LeVierge, Trial transcript, April 26, 1934, vol. 8.

CHAPTER 9

1. Interview with Wayne Urquhart, Summer 2012. Urquhart is a retired Needham police officer. Soon after joining the force, he discussed the 1934 robbery and McLeod's murder with Charles Stevens, who still operated his family's store in Needham Center. Dinneen also discusses Stevens's recollections in "Murder in Massachusetts."

2. Many sources provide details of the robbery and murders. Very helpful, of course, was the trial testimony of the Needham Trust employees, the witnesses on Great Plain Avenue, the firefighters at Needham Heights, and Needham police chief Arthur Bliss. They are contained in Trial transcript, April 26 and 27, 1934, vols. 8 and 9. Equally important were the detailed newspaper accounts published in late editions on Friday afternoon and on Saturday and Sunday, February 2–4, 1934. The most thorough accounts were in the *Boston Post, Boston Globe, Boston American, Boston Herald*, and *Boston Traveler*. Dinneen also described the robbery in "Murder in Massachusetts." For events inside the bank, this account relies primarily on the trial testimony and, to a lesser extent, on information provided by Faber to Lieutenant Ferrari during Faber's first confession on February 26, 1934. The February 9, 1934, edition of the weekly *Needham Chronicle* also gives a very detailed account, as does the *Needham Times*, February 8, 1934.

3. Marriage license, town of Brattleboro, Vermont, September 4, 1926; 1920 United States Census, s.v. "Martin Edward Gaykan," Suffolk County, MA.

4. Dr. Frederic A. Stanwood, assistant medical examiner, Trial transcript, April 26, 1934, vol. 8.

5. Thanks to Lisa Brems, *Policing Needham: A Story of Suburban Cops* (Orlando, FL: Rivercross, 2004). She found an old Packard and realized its windshield opened upward.

CHAPTER 10

1. "Laying Out Greater Boston Police Net; Heads of 39 City and Town Forces Develop a Proposed Radio and Teletype System," *Boston Globe*, November 10, 1933.

2. Brems, *Policing Needham*, 51–69.

3. Associated Press, Brookline, MA, February 2, 1934; "'Punks' Stole Police Guns, Chiefs Believe," *Boston Globe*, February 2, 1934.

4. "The Tragic Day at Headquarters of Local Police," *Needham Chronicle*, February 9, 1934. The writer greeted McLeod moments before the bank alarm sounded.

5. Arthur Bliss, Trial transcript, April 26, 1934, vol. 8.

6. Copies of the state police bulletins issued February 2, 1934, are in the MSP Archive.

7. Millen, "My Story," Part II (November 16, 1935), 34–36.

8. Letter from a former student recalling the event, Needham Historical Society archives.

9. Dinneen tells the story of the banana and the bullet in "Murder in Massachusetts."

10. Urquhart conversation with Howard Mills in the 1970s.

11. This and other details of the police investigation are drawn from documents in the MSP Archive, the trial transcript, and more than a hundred stories published over the following weeks by the *Globe*, the *Post*, the *Boston American*, the *Herald*, the *Traveler*, the *Boston Daily News*, and the *Boston Transcript*.

12. 1910 United States Census, s.v. "Thomas and Mary Stokes," Middlesex County, MA.

13. "Stokes a Real Detective, Says Partner Ferrari," *Boston Globe*, January 6, 1963.

14. Ibid.

15. Rose Knellar, Trial transcript, April 30, 1934, vol. 10.

16. Millen, "My Story," Part 2, 36.

17. "Hundreds Pay Tribute to Memories of Officers Haddock and McLeod," *Needham Times*, February 8, 1934.

18. Interview with James Barnicle, grandson of Francis Haddock, March 14, 2013.

CHAPTER 11

1. Among the documents obtained from the MSP Archive is a fifteen-page typewritten memo titled "Reporters Goldberg and Dinneen." It details the two reporters' activities during the Millen-Faber investigation. No author's name appears on the document, but the internal evidence indicates it was written by Goldberg, particularly as the author periodically lapses into the first person. In tone and style, the document resembles Goldberg's newspaper stories and is quite unlike the more polished and readable *Harper's* article written by Dinneen. The memo candidly describes the reporters' cooperation with the state police, which included providing detectives with information gathered during their reporting, deliberately omitting from their newspaper stories information the state police asked to be withheld, and refraining from contacting or interviewing Faber during a key point in the investigation. "But for the information these reporters gathered—[and] refrained from publishing at the time—other police officers might have been slain before the activities of the Millens and Faber were halted," Goldberg wrote. Despite that pat on their back, Goldberg repeatedly stated that it was not he and Dinneen, but Stokes and Ferrari, who deserved credit for solving the case. That emphasis suggests that the memo was compiled for the reward hearings held in late 1935.

2. All the major papers covered the consolidation debate. Ely lost the day before Murt, Irv, and Abe were convicted.

3. Joseph William Carlevale, *Leading Americans of Italian Descent in Massachusetts* (Plymouth, MA: Memorial Press, 1946), 322.

4. "Stokes a Real Detective."

5. Herbert A. Kenny, *Newspaper Row: Journalism in the Pre-Television Era* (Chester, CT: Globe Pequot Press, 1987), esp. 5–17, 147–156, 218–229.

6. Louis Martin Lyons, *Newspaper Story: One Hundred Years of the "Boston Globe"*

(Cambridge, MA: Belknap Press of Harvard University Press, 1971), 315. Lyons, along with Dinneen, was assigned full time to the Millen-Faber trial. In February 1934 he covered the Berrett-Molway trial.

7. "Newsman Lawrence Goldberg," Obituary, *Boston Herald American*, December 7, 1980.

8. Obituary, *Malden Evening News*, December 1980.

9. Millen, "My Story," Part II, 39.

10. Ibid.

11. Ibid., 40.

12. Leslie Jones, *Auto and Inside Garage Used by Millen Brothers and Faber after Needham Bank Murder*, photograph, Leslie Jones Collection, Boston Public Library.

13. Packard Service Letter, December 1, 1933.

14. Counted by author from listings in "The Boston Directory," 1933, accessed at Ancestory.com.

CHAPTER 12

1. *Boston Post* and *Boston Globe*, February 27 and 28, 1934.

2. "Papers of Nelson P. Brown, 1853–1945," Bound trial notes, Rauner Library Special Collections, Dartmouth College.

3. Dinneen, "Millens Returning Today with Three Detectives . . . Girl Friend of Messinger Disliked Norma, Calling Her 'High Hat,'" *Boston Globe*, March 5, 1934.

4. Dinneen, "Murder in Massachusetts."

5. MSP Archive.

6. "The Boston Directory," 1933, accessed at Ancestry.com.

7. There is no record of Goldberg ever joining the synagogue, according to a search graciously conducted by Temple archivist Susan Milstein. Nevertheless, he could have attended services.

8. Report to Massachusetts Governor's Council by Paul G. Kirk, Commissioner of Public Safety, November 1935.

CHAPTER 13

1. "Substitute Woods for Port Orford White-Cedar for Storage Battery Separators."

2. Joseph Rothberg, Trial transcript, May 31, 1934, vol. 31.

3. Detective Michael Fleming, "Murder of Forbes A. McLeod," May 19, 1936, MSP Archive. Fleming's lengthy report to the public safety commissioner provides a very useful chronology of what the detectives knew and when they knew it.

4. "Dealers and Service men in Mass–R.I.–N.H," MSP Archive.

5. Joseph L. Ferrari, Trial transcript, May 9, and May 10, 1934, vols. 17 and 16.

6. MSP Archive.

7. Fleming in his 1936 MSP Archive memo writes, "We first learned of the letter when we called at the Needham Police station one night and Lieut. Stokes asked Chief Bliss if there was anything new. He then showed us the letter."

8. "Millens Plotted Death of 3 State Detectives," *Boston Traveler*, March 1, 1934. Also *Boston Herald* and *Boston American*.

CHAPTER 14

1. "Berrett Describes Thrill at Being Alive and Free," *Boston Traveler*, March 1, 1934; "Witness Positively Identifies," *Daily Evening Item* (Lynn, MA), February 15, 1934.

2. "Witness Positively Identifies."

3. "Woman Says Molway Fired Gun at Condon," *Item* (Lynn, MA), February 15, 1934.

4. "Berrett Describes Thrill."

5. MSP Archive.

6. Ibid.

7. Ferrari, Trial transcript, May 9, 1934, vol. 17

8. Fleming, "Murder of Forbes A. McLeod."

9. Saul Messinger, Trial transcript, April 30 and May 1, 1934, vols. 9 and 10.

10. Matthew Murphy, Trial transcript, April 27, 1934, vol. 9.

11. Dinneen, "Murder in Massachusetts."

CHAPTER 15

1. Norma Brighton Millen's trial, evidence introduced by prosecution, June 20, 1934.

2. "Never Had Gun, Berrett Says," *Boston Globe*, February 21, 1934.

3. Jacob Gordon, Trial transcript, June 1, 1934, vol. 32.

4. "Element of Time Fateful for Pair," *Boston Globe*, February 25, 1934.

CHAPTER 16

1. "Man Who Traced Battery Case in Millen Claim," *Boston Globe*, November 22, 1935. It includes reward hearing testimony by New York detective Edmund O'Brien.

2. Fleming, "Murder of Forbes A. McLeod."

3. John F. Stokes, Trial transcript, May 7, 1934, vol. 15.

4. Ibid.

5. The *Globe* and *Post*, as well as the other major papers, extensively covered that winter's weather.

6. Saul Messinger and others, Trial transcript, April 30 and May 1, 1934, vols. 10 and 11.

7. "Hotel Union Plans Walkout Tonight," *New York Times*, January 16, 1934; Restaurant Ware Collectors Network, "Lincoln Hotel, New York."

8. Ferrari, Trial transcript, May 9 and May 10, 1934, vols. 17 and 18.

9. There are various versions of what signal Messinger gave; the handkerchief is most frequently cited.

10. John Fitzsimmons, Trial transcript, May 1, 1934, vol. 11.

11. The *Boston American*, *Boston Globe*, *New York Daily News*, and others all reported different versions of what Norma may have shouted in the hotel lobby.

CHAPTER 17

1. "House Action Ends Death Penalty," *Boston Herald*, April 25, 1963.

2. There is no definitive reference. An MIT graduate and "wealthy Boston architect" was charged with murdering a Florida newspaper executive in 1914 according to

"Architect Who Ran Amuck on Ocean Liner Is on Trial," *State Times Advocate* (Baton Rouge, LA), January 19, 1915. In 1929 an MIT graduate stabbed and killed a woman in Guadalajara, Mexico, was convicted, sentenced to death, and received a temporary reprieve. See "Mexican Slayer Gets Stay," Associated Press, November 24, 1932, Mexico City.

3. James Lardner and Thomas A. Reppetto, *NYPD: A City and Its Police* (New York: Henry Holt, 2001); "New System Ordered in Police Line-Up," *New York Times*, August 1, 1933.

4. Photograph, Leslie Jones Collection, Boston Public Library, www.flickr.com/photos/boston_public_library/collections (accessed February 24, 2014).

5. Transcript of Ferrari's interview, with added comments, found among the papers of Lawrence Goldberg, Howard Gottlieb Archival Research Center, Boston University.

CHAPTER 18

1. Berrett and Molway's sudden reversal of fortune received wide coverage, sharing the front pages with the Millen-Faber arrests but usually given secondary play. The major Boston newspapers gave that trial day-by-day coverage.

2. RKO Keith's, a major Boston movie house on Washington Street, booked the duo and published ads like this in the *Boston Globe*, March 3, 1934: "Snatched from the Chair. In Person. Not Guilty! . . . Freed! . . . By the Millen Confession! See Them in Person. Reliving Those nightmare Hours . . . When Death Loomed Through a Maze of Mistakes."

3. "Sawyer Reiterates Demand Norma Be Tried with a Gang," *Traveler*, March 2, 1934, quoting letter by state representative Roland D. Sawyer.

4. Gene Smiley, "The U.S. Economy in the 1920s," Marquette University, Economic History Association, http://eh.net/encyclopedia/the-u-s-economy-in-the-1920s.

5. Douglas Wilson, dir., *Linotype, The Film*, October 2012. http://www.linotypefilm.com/index.html.

6. Gwenyth L. Jackaway, *Media at War, Radio's Challenge to the Newspapers, 1924–1939* (Westport, CT: Praeger, 1995).

7. Wilson, *Linotype, The Film*.

8. Text from Leslie Jones Collection, Boston Public Library, http://www.flickr.com/photos/boston_public_library/collections (accessed February 24, 2014).

9. The *Boston Post* and *Boston Traveler* reporters paid particular attention to what was on the bookshelves; all the reports of the Brightons' session with the press are remarkably similar.

10. Ormsby "Bob" Court, Jr.'s success at interviewing the Millen brothers in the New York jail may be attributed to his prior experience as a private detective, a job that got him arrested and jailed in 1925 for detecting without a license. He was attempting to entrap a married man into adultery on behalf of his client, apparently the wife, who was seeking a divorce.

11. "Statement of Norma Brighton Millen, Alden St., Natick, taken at Detective Bureau, State House, Boston on March 2, 1934," MSP Archive.

CHAPTER 19

1. Paula Uruburu, *American Eve* (New York: Riverhead Books, 2008), 135–136. "I lost all self-control, I grew dizzy . . . I think it was a matter of too much champagne," Nesbit wrote. Upon waking she was no longer a virgin. "All that I knew was that something terrible had come to me and I screamed."

2. Richard Noll, *American Madness: The Rise and Fall of Dementia Praecox* (Cambridge, MA: Harvard University Press, 2011), 2. This is a wonderfully readable history of what by the mid-twentieth century had been reconceptualized as schizophrenia. Also Emile R. Pinta, *"Paranoia of the Millionaire": Harry K. Thaw's 1907 Insanity Defense* (New York: Nova Science, 2010).

3. Winfred Overholser, "Briggs Law of Massachusetts: A Review and an Appraisal," *Journal of Criminal Law and Criminology* 25, no. 6 (January 1, 1935): 859.

4. March 1, 1934, various newspapers.

5. Edwin Monroe Bacon, "The Book of Boston," 1916, 420.

6. Interview with Faber family member; also "Percy Faber, 91 Chelsea Salvage Yard Owner," *Boston Globe*, January 8, 1989.

7. Judge Nelson P. Brown, Trial transcript, June 8, 1934, vol. 37.

8. All the Boston newspapers provided extensive coverage; as usual, the crowd estimates varied widely.

9. Massachusetts Department of Mental Health, *Annual Report of the Department of Mental Health* (Boston, 1938), http://archive.org/details/annualreportofdep1938mass.

10. Overholser, "Briggs Law of Massachusetts," 879.

11. Ibid., 869.

12. Brown, Trial transcript, May 18, 1934, vol. 23.

13. Various versions of the incident are given in Trial transcript, June 4, 1934, vol. 33, and in newspaper reports. The MSP Archive contains copies of what appears to be Murt's cipher practiced on scraps of paper.

CHAPTER 20

1. "E.R. Dewing . . . Succeeds D.P. Ranney," *Boston Globe*, November 30, 1927. "Edmund Dewing, District Attorney . . . Superior Court Judge," *Boston Globe*, August 24, 1981.

2. Rauner Library Special Collections, Dartmouth College. Dewing's transcript and notice of separation are on file.

3. "Ely May Name Republicans to 2 Posts Today," *Boston Herald*, October 4, 1933.

4. "Two Democrats Named by Dewing on Staff," *Boston Herald*, October 14, 1933.

5. "Her Valentine Strangest Ever . . . Package of Money Turned over to State Police Head," *Boston Globe*, May 1, 1934.

6. William Scharton, Trial transcript, April 30, 1934, vol. 10.

7. "Camera Men Win; Franklin D. Roosevelt Junior Declares Truce, with Smile, as He Leaves Dedham Courthouse," *Boston Post*, May 2, 1934.

8. "The Nobel Prize in Physiology or Medicine 1927." Nobel Media AB 2013, http://www.nobelprize.org/nobel_prizes/medicine/laureates/1927/http://www

.nobelprize.org/nobel_prizes/medicine/laureates/1927/ (accessed February 21, 2014). He later joined the Nazi Party.

9. Nicholas Jabbour, "Syphilis from 1880 to 1920: A Public Health Nightmare and the First Challenge to Medical Ethics," 2000, http://www.uri.edu/artsci/com/swift /HPR319UDD/Syphilis.html.

CHAPTER 21

1. Israel Millen, Trial transcript, May 18, 1934, vol. 23.
2. Jelliffe, Trial Transcript, May 19, 1934, vol. 30.
3. Philip Faber, Trial transcript, May 29, 1934, vol. 30.

CHAPTER 22

1. "Millens Trial Breaks Record," *Boston Globe*, June 1, 1934. The length of the trial was widely commented upon, and the *Boston Post* kept a running tally of the cost to Norfolk County.
2. Abraham Faber. Trial transcript, June 1, 1934, vol. 32.
3. "As a stronghold of Father Coughlin's anti-Semitic Christian Front organization, the city experienced tumultuous interethnic relations, especially among Catholics and Jews living in close proximity to each other in the Dorchester-Roxbury-Mattapan area." Jenny Goldstein, *Transcending Boundaries: Boston's Catholics and Jews, 1929–1965*, Center for Christian-Jewish Learning, www.bc.edu. (accessed October 4, 2012).
4. *Boston Post*, June 7, 1934.
5. "Mob Hurls Bottles at Convicted Trio; 'Kill the Rats' Cry of Surging Throng," *Boston Herald*, June 9, 1934. Also other Boston newspapers.
6. Dorothy G. Wayman, "Needham Folk Agree on Verdict," *Boston Globe*, June 10, 1934.

CHAPTER 23

1. Millen, "My Story," Part 4 (November 30, 1934), 69.
2. An official transcript of Norma Millen's trial could not be located. Quotations in this chapter are taken from versions of the transcript printed in the *Boston Evening Globe*, the *Boston Post*, the *Boston Herald*, and other newspapers, as well as Judge Brown's trial notes.
3. "Jury Declares Norma Guilty; Verdict Surprise to Crowd," *Boston Post*, June 28, 1934. The *Post* said 8,000 people awaited the verdict.
4. Commonwealth vs. Murton Millen & Others, 289 Mass. 411, Massachusetts Supreme Judicial Court.

CHAPTER 24

1. Papers of Lawrence Goldberg, Howard Gottlieb Archival Research Center.
2. No official transcript of the hearing exists. But Irving's comments were extensively

quoted in the *Boston Globe*, the *Boston Herald*, and the *Boston Post* editions of February 27, 1934.

3. "State Links Millens with Jail Plot," *Boston Globe*, April 26, 1935. Also *Boston Post* and other Boston newspapers.

4. "Scharton Makes Last Move Today," *Boston Post*, June 5, 1934, and other Boston newspapers.

5. "Millens Refuse to Ask Clemency—Rather Die in Chair," *Boston Post*, June 5, 1935.

6. Ibid.

7. Ibid.

8. *Boston American*, June 7, 1935.

9. Some accounts omit "I want to say that . . ."

10. "Stage Riot at Millen Home . . . Crowd Forces Way into House during Funeral—Brushes Relatives Aside—Trouble at Cemetery," *Boston Post*, June 10, 1935. Also *Boston Globe*.

EPILOGUE I

1. Faber, "Why Did I Die in the Chair?"

2. "Father of Millens Under Observation," *Boston Globe*, July 21, 1936.

3. "Ferrari, Game, Accepts Bid to Gang Banquet," *Boston Traveler*, February 14, 1947.

4. Goldman recorded dozens of his telephone conversations with the district attorney. Tapes and transcripts are available at the Howard Gottlieb Archival Research Center. Goldberg made this observation as the two discussed the *Globe*'s investigation into Goldberg's contract.

5. Marriage record, Town of North Castle, Armonk, NY, August 16, 1936.

6. Norma Millen Clement, As told to Fred Menagh (King Features, 1939), Part I.

7. Ibid., Part II.

8. Certificate of Death, State of California, Department of Public Health, filed May 1, 1964.

9. "Woman Patient Is Slain; Fellow Inmate Is Arrested," *Asbury Park Press*, November 8, 1966, and State of New Jersey vs. Henry Harold Clement, Indictment No. 179–66, November 7, 1966.

10. "Slayer Commits Suicide," *Evening Times* (Trenton, NJ), July 7, 1967, and "Hazlet Man Found Hanged in Hospital," *Asbury Park Press*, July 8, 1967.

BIBLIOGRAPHY

"Arthur H. Lynch and Radio Noise Suppression Equipment." *Communications* 11, no. 9 (September 1931).

Asher, Robert, Lawrence B. Goodheart, and Alan Rogers. *Murder on Trial: 1620–2002*. Albany: State University of New York Press, 2005.

Baatz, Simon. *For the Thrill of It: Leopold, Loeb, and the Murder That Shocked Chicago*. New York: Harper, 2008.

Bailey, Beth L. *From Front Porch to Back Seat: Courtship in Twentieth-Century America*. Baltimore: Johns Hopkins University Press, 1989.

Battles, Kathleen. *Calling All Cars: Radio Dragnets and the Technology of Policing*. Minneapolis: University of Minnesota Press, 2010.

Bergan, William M. *Old Nantasket*. North Quincy, MA: Christopher, 1969.

Bilstein, Roger E. *Flight Patterns: Trends of Aeronautical Development in the United States, 1918–1929*. Athens: University of Georgia Press, 1983.

Blank, Hanne. *Virgin: The Untouched History*. New York: Bloomsbury USA, 2008.

Brandt, Allan M. *No Magic Bullet: A Social History of Venereal Disease in the United States since 1880*. New York: Oxford University Press, 1987.

Brems, Lisa. *Policing Needham: A Story of Suburban Cops*. Orlando, FL: Rivercross, 2004.

Bromley, Dorothy Dunbar. *Youth and Sex: A Study of 1300 College Students*. New York: Harper & Brothers, 1938.

Burrough, Bryan. *Public Enemies: America's Greatest Crime Wave and the Birth of the FBI, 1933–34*. New York: Penguin Books, 2005.

Carpenter, Laura M. *Virginity Lost: An Intimate Portrait of First Sexual Experiences*. New York: New York University, 2005.

Cheney, Frank. *When Boston Rode the El (Images of America)*. Charleston, SC: Arcadia, 2012.

Clarens, Carlos, and Foster Hirsch. *Crime Movies*. New York: Da Capo Press, 1997.

Coe, Lewis. *Wireless Radio: A Brief History*. Jefferson, NC: McFarland, 1996.

Collins, Paul. *The Murder of the Century: The Gilded Age Crime That Scandalized a City and Sparked the Tabloid Wars*. New York: Crown, 2011.

Committee for the Preservation of Hull's History (Hull, MA). *Hull and Nantasket Beach*. Charleston, SC: Arcadia, 1999.

Commonwealth vs. Murton Millen, Irving Millen and Abraham Faber. Trial transcript, microfilm. Massachusetts Supreme Judicial Court Archives, 1934.

Cox, Jim. *American Radio Networks: A History.* Jefferson, NC: McFarland, 2009.

Dinneen, Joseph, F. "Murder in Massachusetts." *Harper's Magazine,* March 1936.

Fallon, James H. *The Psychopath Inside: A Neuroscientist's Personal Journey into the Dark Side of the Brain.* New York: Current, 2013.

Field, Alexander J. *A Great Leap Forward: 1930s Depression and U.S. Economic Growth.* New Haven, CT: Yale University Press, 2011.

Fitchburg Historical Society (Fitchburg, MA). *Fitchburg.* Charleston, SC: Arcadia, 2005.

Fleming, Michael. "Murder of Forbes A. McLeod." Massachusetts State Police Archive, May 19, 1936.

Foley, Joanne S. *Lynn.* Dover, NH: Arcadia, 1995.

Fried, Albert. *The Rise and Fall of the Jewish Gangster in America.* New York: Columbia University Press, 1993.

Gamm, Gerald H. *Urban Exodus: Why the Jews Left Boston and the Catholics Stayed.* Cambridge, MA: Harvard University Press, 2001.

Goren, Arthur A. *Saints and Sinners: The Underside of American Jewish History.* Brochure Series of the American Jewish Archives. American Jewish Archives, Cincinnati, 1988.

Goren, Arthur A. *The Politics and Public Culture of American Jews.* Bloomington: Indiana University Press, 1999.

Harmon, Lawrence, and Hillel Levine. *The Death of an American Jewish Community: A Tragedy of Good Intentions.* Lexington, MA: Plunkett Lake Press, 2012.

Helmer, William J., and Rick Mattix. *The Complete Public Enemy Almanac: New Facts and Features on the People, Places, and Events of the Gangster and Outlaw Era, 1920–1940.* Nashville: Cumberland House, 2006.

Hentoff, Nat. *Boston Boy.* New York: Knopf, 1986.

History/Mystery, Dedham Tales. https://dedhamtales.wordpress.com/category /historymystery/page/2/.

History Project. *Improper Bostonians: Lesbian and Gay History from the Puritans to Playland.* Boston: Beacon Press, 1999.

Jabbour, Nicholas. "Syphilis from 1880 to 1920: A Public Health Nightmare and the First Challenge to Medical Ethics," 2000. http://www.uri.edu/artsci/com/swift /HPR319UDD/Syphilis.html.

Jackaway, Gwenyth L. *Media at War: Radio's Challenge to the Newspapers, 1924– 1939.* Westport, CT: Praeger, 1995.

Joselit, Jenna Weissman. *Our Gang: Jewish Crime and the New York Jewish Community, 1900–1940.* Bloomington: Indiana University Press, 1983.

Kaiser, David. *Becoming MIT: Moments of Decision.* Harvard, MA: MIT Press, 2010.

Kenny, Herbert A. *Newspaper Row: Journalism in the Pre-Television Era.* Chester, CT: Globe Pequot Press, 1987.

King, Jeffery S. *The Life and Death of Pretty Boy Floyd.* Kent, OH: Kent State University Press, 2013.

Kirchner, L. R. *Robbing Banks: An American History, 1831–1999.* Rockville Center, NY: Sarpedon, 2000.

Kyvig, David E. *Daily Life in the United States, 1920–1940: How Americans Lived through the "Roaring Twenties" and the Great Depression.* Chicago: Ivan R. Dee, 2004.

Lardner, James, and Thomas A. Reppetto. *NYPD: A City and Its Police.* New York: Henry Holt, 2001.

Lindenmeyer, Kriste. *The Greatest Generation Grows up: American Childhood in the 1930s.* Chicago: Ivan R. Dee, 2005.

Lott, George E. "The Press–Radio War of the 1930s." *Journal of Broadcasting* 14, no. 3 (1970): 275–286.

Loughery, John. *The Other Side of Silence: Men's Lives and Gay Identities, a 20th Century History.* New York: Henry Holt, 1999.

Lyons, Louis Martin. *Newspaper Story: One Hundred Years of the "Boston Globe."* Cambridge, MA: Belknap Press of Harvard University Press, 1971.

Massachusetts Department of Mental Health. *Annual Report of the Department of Mental Health.* Boston, 1938.

Massachusetts Institute of Technology. *Technique.* Yearbook of the class of 1931.

Millen, Norma. "My Story." *Detective Fiction Weekly,* November and December, 1935.

Moran, Richard. *Executioner's Current: Thomas Edison, George Westinghouse, and the Invention of the Electric Chair.* New York: Vintage Books, 2007.

Nasaw, David. *The Patriarch: The Remarkable Life and Turbulent Times of Joseph P. Kennedy.* New York: Penguin, 2012.

National Council on Economic Education, "Roads." http://www.econedlink.org /lessons/docs_lessons/725_roads1.pdf.

Needham Historical Society (MA). *Needham.* Dover, NH: Arcadia, 1997.

Noll, Richard. *American Madness: The Rise and Fall of Dementia Praecox.* Cambridge, MA: Harvard University Press, 2011.

Office of Production Research and Development of the War Production. "Substitute Woods for Port Orford White-Cedar for Storage Battery Separators," April 1945.

Okrent, Daniel. *Last Call: The Rise and Fall of Prohibition.* New York: Scribner, 2010.

Overholser, Winfred. "Briggs Law of Massachusetts: A Review and an Appraisal." *Journal of Criminal Law and Criminology* 25, no. 6 (January 1, 1935): 859.

Persson, Sheryl Ann. *Smallpox, Syphilis, and Salvation: Medical Breakthroughs That Changed the World.* Wollombi, NSW: Exisle, 2009.

Pinta, Emil R. *"Paranoia of the Millionaire": Harry K. Thaw's 1907 Insanity Defense.* New York: Nova Science, 2010.

Poli, Joseph. "The Development and Present Trend of Police Radio Communications." *Journal of Criminal Law* 33 (1933).

Potter, Claire Bond. *War on Crime: Bandits, G-Men, and the Politics of Mass Culture.* New Brunswick, NJ: Rutgers University Press, 1997.

Rhodes, Richard. *Why They Kill: The Discoveries of a Maverick Criminologist.* New York: Vintage Books, 2000.

Robinson, Lionel. *Boston's Newspapers.* Boston: Richard Kay Publications for the History of Boston Project, 1974.

Rogers, Alan. *Murder and the Death Penalty in Massachusetts.* Amherst: University of Massachusetts Press, 2008.

Roth, Benjamin, James Ledbetter, and Daniel B. Roth. *The Great Depression: A Diary.* New York: PublicAffairs, 2009.

Samenow, Stanton E. *Inside the Criminal Mind.* New York: Crown, 2004.

Sammarco, Anthony Mitchell. *Dorchester.* Charleston, SC: Arcadia, 2005.

Sammarco, Anthony Mitchell, and Charlie Rosenberg. *Roxbury.* Charleston, SC: Arcadia, 2007.

Sarna, Jonathan D., Ellen Smith, Scott-Martin Kosofsky, and Combined Jewish Philanthropies of Greater Boston. *The Jews of Boston.* New Haven, CT: Yale University Press, 2005.

Shorter, Edward. *A History of Psychiatry: From the Era of the Asylum to the Age of Prozac.* Chichester: John Wiley, 1997.

Solomon, Barbara Miller. *Ancestors and Immigrants: A Changing New England Tradition.* Boston: Northeastern University Press, 1989.

Stack, John F. *International Conflict in an American City: Boston's Irish, Italians, and Jews, 1935–1944.* Westport, CT: Greenwood Press, 1979.

Thernstrom, Stephan. *The Other Bostonians: Poverty and Progress in the American Metropolis, 1880–1970.* Cambridge, MA: Harvard University Press, 1999.

Trout, Charles H. *Boston, the Great Depression, and the New Deal.* New York: Oxford University Press, 1977.

Unger, Debi, and Irwin Unger. *The Guggenheims.* HarperCollins e-books, 2009.

Uruburu, Paula. *American Eve.* New York: Riverhead Books, 2008.

Vieira, Mark A. *Sin in Soft Focus: Pre-Code Hollywood.* New York: Harry N. Abrams, 1999.

Wells, Donna M. *Boston Police Department.* Charleston, SC: Arcadia, 2012.

White, Theodore H. *In Search of History: A Personal Adventure.* New York: Harper & Row, 1978.

Wilson, Douglas, director. *Linotype, The Film.* 2012. www.linotypefilm.com/index.html.

Witte, O. A. *The Automobile Storage Battery: Its Care and Repair—Radio Batteries, Farm Lighting Batteries.* Chicago: American Bureau of Engineering, 1922.

Young, William H. *The 1930s.* American Popular Culture Through History. Greenwood Press, 2002.

INDEX